Christine Manfield is one of Australia's most celebrated chefs – a curious cook, a perfectionist inspired by the culinary melting pot of global flavours, and a writer whose successful, award winning books – *A Personal Guide to India and Bhutan, Dessert Divas, Fire, Spice, Stir, Paramount Cooking* and *Paramount Desserts* have spiced up the lives of keen cooks everywhere.

As one of Australia's leading culinary ambassadors, her professional life as a restaurateur culminated in three award winning restaurants: Paramount in Sydney 1993 to 2000, East@West in London 2003 to 2005 and Universal in Sydney 2007 to 2013. She continues to collaborate with chefs and industry professionals in Australia and overseas.

An inveterate traveller, Christine hosts bespoke culinary adventures to exotic destinations including India, Italy, South America, Bhutan, France and South East Asia. Having eaten her way around India for more than two decades, she is a passionate and erudite guide to the food of this endlessly fascinating land.

www.christinemanfield.com

To Jamshyd Sethna, a kindred spirit whose generosity,
vision, wisdom and passion for his country – 'my country
is yours' – have made this extraordinary journey possible.

Full of adventure and surprise, India's hidden treasures
unfolded before my eyes...

Thank you.

Tasting India

HEIRLOOM & FAMILY RECIPES

Christine Manfield

Photography by
Anson Smart

A JULIE GIBBS BOOK
for

SIMON & SCHUSTER
AUSTRALIA
A CBS COMPANY

CONTENTS

INTRODUCTION

With India, it's difficult to know where to start, how best to capture its essence. But this book is one story of India, my story of India, gathered across many visits. My insights are informed by the connections I've been fortunate enough to make with so many different people. The recipes I've collected along the way reflect the stories of countless mothers, grandmothers, daughters, sons of daughters, brothers, sisters and aunts, as told to me during my travels. So, more importantly, within these pages are their stories. Listening to those stories has been a most nourishing experience, like being enveloped in the generosity of a sari, itself a potent symbol of India.

On each and every visit, I surrender myself to the procession of life before me, as India begins to pulsate through my veins. It is impossible to be indifferent to the world's largest democracy – though it is essential to bring an open mind and a good degree of patience! There is no choice but to jump right in, be brave and grab every exhilarating moment. This is a country where everything happens and anything is possible. Each day is a new adventure, providing another intriguing piece of the puzzle. As soon as I think I have a pretty good handle on it all, something pops up to confound my thinking and make me look at everything anew. But to me, that is just part of the whole Indian experience, the way the place and its people subtly continue to charm, inspire and compel, always daring to challenge. It makes me feel alive.

The art of travel is in allowing yourself to slip your chains. To become,
for a time, someone else.
ALAIN DE BOTTON, *THE ART OF TRAVEL*

India seems to exist in several centuries at the same time, and the tableau of images presented to the curious traveller both bewilders and amuses. Every scene is like a beautiful collision of worlds: a yogi or holy man with a mobile phone pressed to his ear; an iPod sitting in the folded arms of a marigold-festooned deity statue; lucky garlands threaded through the front grilles of the ubiquitous Ambassador taxis; sacred cows ambling their way through the tide of traffic, bullock carts, rickshaws and bicycles, apparently unperturbed by the mayhem around them. There is a saying in India that if you don't believe in God before you experience Indian roads, you will afterwards.

The country is like a living theatre, as daily life in all its forms is played out publicly on the streets and at every street corner. It's a land of paradoxes, contradictions and contrasts, of highs and lows, of beauty and despair,

of joy and sadness, of wealth and poverty – India has it all in unequal measure. India ranks among the world's fastest-growing economies, and in cities across the country, glitzy modern skyscrapers and designer-label shops blend seamlessly with ancient bazaars. Existing cheek-by-jowl with such ostentatious wealth are numbing poverty and sprawling slums. In contrast, the rural landscape remains relatively unchanged, its timeless grace and proud traditions a source of captivation for many travellers.

India is a visual feast and a gastronomic paradise, seducing with its food and contagious hospitality. The states of modern India have distinctive food traditions that reflect their regional and cultural heritage. Food preparation is bound up with spirituality, and demands a thorough understanding to appreciate its nuances. Religion underpins the dietary laws of each sect. To the uninitiated, it's a minefield to navigate and accommodate – but to India's Hindus, Jains, Muslims, Sikhs, Syrian Christians, Catholics, Parsis and Jews, it's second nature, with each respecting the traditions of the others. The country's culinary tapestry is complex, varied and ancient, underpinned by a masterful and enviable use of spice.

The magic of Indian cooking is in the proper use and blending of spices. It is also important to know and understand the spices that are an absolute must with different kinds of food.
RAJMATA GAYATRI DEVI OF JAIPUR

The unique flavours of Indian cuisine are derived from the astute combination of these spices and seasonings with nutritious ingredients such as leafy vegetables, fruits, grains and legumes. Contemporary cooking has its roots firmly planted in Ayurvedic practice, an ancient discipline where food is respected as a most precious resource in the pursuit of life, health and longevity. Ancient texts prescribe herbs and spices for their inherent curative and therapeutic properties: garlic reduces cholesterol and hypertension, while fenugreek stimulates the body's immune system. Pepper is a natural antihistamine, and turmeric is used to cure ulcers and give the skin a healthy glow. Fennel, cloves and cardamom are nature's mouth fresheners, and asafoetida combats flatulence. Spices such as turmeric, cloves and cardamom have antiseptic properties, while others, like ginger, are good for digestion and heartburn.

Cooks incorporate this knowledge into their everyday cooking. Different spices are used for different seasons, in varying quantities. The refined use of spices, aromatics, herbs, pulses and vegetables results in colours as varied as the women's saris and provides each dish with its unique character and flavour. Masalas are made using a wide variety of spices. In addition to the main dishes, the side dishes and condiments like dals, chutneys and pickles contribute to the overall flavour and texture of a meal. India is indeed a food lover's delight.

Traditionally, food remains part of the sanctity of the home, where family forms the fabric of Indian life. Indians rarely eat alone, and hospitality is an honour for any host to bestow on guests, with food a cherished element of the welcome.

No one was ever turned away from our house unfed or unwatered.
The breaking of bread breaks down barriers. Food soothes
and assuages. Romance is continued after breakfast.
Friendships are made over lunch, enmities resolved over dinner.
That is the power of food.
HARDEEP SINGH KOHLI, *INDIAN TAKEAWAY*

The home is the most revered place to eat in India – and, needless to say, everyone thinks that no one cooks as well as their mother. When it comes to food, cooking, looking after family and welcoming visitors into the home, the women hold sway; their gender defines their role in these areas, as it does in so many others. Heirloom recipes are handed down from generation to generation. Wherever you might be, you will hear a grandmother or a mother cautioning how much spice to use, how to do this or that; accomplished cooking becomes as natural as language, as speaking.

In the context of this oral tradition, it is perhaps unsurprising that some of the old family recipes I gathered gave a list of ingredients with no quantities and only the briefest of instructions that assumed a thorough working knowledge of the kitchen, but mostly I've been able to approximate the quantities and method through observation and tasting.

Time-honoured culinary traditions are also upheld by women. As night falls, in numerous households across India, milk is soured, magically turning into curd ready for the next day's cooking, and lentils are soaked overnight in water for the dal that is customary at every meal. And few cooks would entertain the thought of not making their own roti, the everyday flatbread cooked on a tawa griddle pan.

Away from the home, street food is essential, as natural as breathing. It's on the street that food comes to life, as the locals gravitate towards their favourite snacks and tasty morsels. It's vibrant and intoxicating and the flavours resonate; being enveloped by the wafting aromas and full-tilt energy is like shoving your hand into a live socket.

Regional cooking adds another layer to India's vast culinary repertoire, with geography, climate and customs combining to determine what people eat in the various regions. The nuances of Keralan cuisine in the south are set apart from those of Kashmiri cooking in the far north – there is meaning in the complexity or simplicity of every dish.

One of the many reasons I respect and admire Indian food so much is that the history, culture and religion and traditions of each region are expressed perfectly in its food, and in the rituals and traditions that surround it. I learnt early on to use my right hand for eating, and have fine-tuned the art of transporting food to my mouth and savouring it. A common saying that has stuck with me is 'you must make love to your food before you eat it'.

India boasts as many cuisines as it does communities. Food varies from region to region, from village to village, and from cook to cook. The Indian table is an extraordinary feast for the senses – spices are to the taste buds what colour is to the eyes, and the symphony is magical and powerful. It is my ambition to expand on the never-ending culinary journey that I began so many moons ago, to delve further into the gastronomic secrets gleaned from India's people, to attempt to capture more of India's mesmerising energy and mystery, to spend time unfettered by the demands of everyday life, to remain mindful, enticed and connected. Each time I taste those flavours at home, I am transported back, reminded of myriad experiences and enduring memories.

KOLKATA & DARJEELING
Scholars, Tigers & Tea

KOLKATA

As India's cultural capital, with its faded colonial charm and raffish persona, Kolkata is a veritable microcosm of India in an intensely concentrated form. With its beguiling magic and crumbling beauty, it's a city that leaves nobody indifferent, a city living on the edge - intriguing, compelling, chaotic and congested all at once. This is a city that offers its hand in friendship, a place where genuine hospitality welcomes me every time. To experience India at the coal face, with confronting high-voltage energy and streetscapes, this is where your journey should start. As one of India's largest cities with a population estimated at 20 million and growing, it's one of the most crowded cities in the world. Although its name was Indianised from Calcutta in 2001, informally most residents still use the old name.

My first visit to Kolkata coincided with the Durga Puja festival in September, turning the streets into an extravagant Mardi Gras-style carnival with locals celebrating one of the most important festivals of the Hindu calendar, marking the victory of good over evil. In Sanskrit, Durga means 'she who is invincible', and the goddess Durga is an embodiment of Shakti, the divine female force. Locals celebrate the five-day festival by surrendering themselves to all-night shopping and partying. One advantage of being in a country of people with diverse faiths and cultures is being able to experience the delectable foods that are an intrinsic part of all religious festivities. For Durga Puja, the favoured foods are fish, rice and sweets.

It is the food that draws me here. I return time and again to experience its authenticity and come to fully understand Bengali cuisine's well-deserved reputation for subtlety and elegance. Kolkata is at the epicentre of this distinctive cuisine, long influenced by a procession of travellers and people who have settled on Bengal's shores - from the Chinese, Tibetans, Burmese and Arabs to the Europeans. All have left their mark. From the time the East India Company established its first settlement here on India's eastern shores in 1690 until the mid-twentieth century, Kolkata was an important international trading centre and port. It was the capital of British India until the seat of government shifted to Delhi in 1912, and maintains its colonial heritage through its public buildings. Some of the grandest monuments of the British Raj are to be found here, most notably the majestic Victoria Memorial, which faces the Maidan, the city's central expanse of green and one of the largest parks in the world. The Maidan is also home to the august Royal Calcutta Turf Club, one of the many private clubs that are still part of the city's social fabric. Spending a day at the races as I did recently was like nowhere else, full of local colour and infectious enthusiasm. It was certainly a day to remember, one I would recommend to any curious traveller.

Artistic and scholarly endeavours are held in the highest esteem, offering context with which to appreciate and understand the complexities and disparate elements of the densely populated urban sprawl. The city

produces newspapers in 48 languages and boasts over 3000 dialects. The Bengalis consider themselves to be literary scholars, as demonstrated by the presence of several major universities and residences of Nobel Prize winners. The streets around the universities are lined with bookshops, and writers and students meet in coffee shops to discuss and debate politics and share knowledge.

With Santi as our guide on that first visit, we were treated to an intimate and sensitive portrait of his beloved Kolkata. The 74-year-old was proud of his scholarly knowledge and youthful vigour, which he attributed to the copious amounts of coffee he drank each day. The ritual of eating plays an integral role in Bengali life. It is said that 'Bengalis live to eat' and, of all Indians, they seem the most obsessed with food. Every conversation is peppered with talk about food, and an extraordinary amount of time is spent thinking about, discussing, shopping for and eating food. It's an all-consuming passion.

On subsequent visits, my host has been the delightful Husna-Tara Prakash, fourth generation owner of Glenburn Tea Estate in Darjeeling and knowledgeable expert on Kolkata's history and culture. Time spent with her is profoundly rewarding - her anecdotes and insights into what makes India tick are astonishing. She shares my passion for food and together we explore the city's vibrant cultural and culinary landscape. She shows me where to find the best chai, which vendor makes the best moori chat snack or kathi kebab roll, where to experience authentic Bengali home cooking, where to buy the best sweets, and gives me her tips on trusted restaurants. Her crack team of city experts offer a unique collection of private cultural walking tours, their insider knowledge bringing the city to life in the most intimate way, whether it's being indulged with a sunset boat cruise on the Hoogly River or having dinner in a private house with a local art dealer with some of the best authentic Bengali home cooking imaginable. It's easy to get lost in the hedonism that is Kolkata.

BENGALI CUISINE

Bengali food is elegant, richly flavoured and textured. Spicing is more subdued than in other regional cuisines – delicate, even. Lightness of touch is the key, and great stress is placed on how spices are ground and how much water is used to make them into a paste, with the finesse of the paste being paramount. *Panch phoran* is Bengali five-spice mix, and its flavours define the Bengali kitchen. Many dishes are characterised by the astute use of mustard seeds (brown and yellow), tempered in mustard oil with dried chilli and curry leaves; white poppy seeds (*kus kus*) are used in equal measure. Dal and rice are staples and are often combined to make *khichuri*, a basic comfort food that can be stretched to feed many mouths. More affluent Bengalis are staunchly omnivorous - quite a departure from the strict adherence to a vegetarian diet in other Brahmin communities, such as Tamil Nadu to the south. Bengali Brahmins originally justified the

inclusion of fish in their diet by proclaiming it the fruit of the seas and the rivers, and therefore as pure as fruit.

Fish plays an integral role in Bengali cooking, to the extent that fish curry is considered inseparable from the Bengali temperament. The city's coastal position and inland waterways produce abundant supplies, with freshwater fish being more highly sought-after than seawater fish. We are lucky enough to be in Kolkata for the start of the hilsa season. Related to the herring family, these small, silver bony fish are known as *ilish* in local dialect, and their arrival has everyone excited. During their short season, they appear at every meal: we have hilsa for lunch the first day, check it out at the fish market, have it for lunch again the second day and then twice more for dinner.

In the days of colonial rule, the British initiated the tradition of tiffin – little snacks to nibble on – and it has become an essential component of Indian culinary culture. At the same time, the British memsahibs taught and encouraged their house cooks to make cakes and breads, setting the precedent for sweets and desserts. Kolkata is now synonymous with sweets. *Sandesh* is perhaps the most renowned local sweet. Its name is the Bengali word for 'message' and it is held in special regard. Originally produced in the private kitchens of the wealthy, it is now made by *halwai*, professional confectioners, and carries a certain cachet. Everyone is incredibly particular about which flavour they like, where they buy it and who made it. By talking to local friends and contacts, we quickly find the locations of preferred sweet shops and try various examples as we drive around town, stopping to compare and discover our own favourites. We also taste *mishti doi*, the highly revered sweet curd that every Bengali is brought up on. Made from reduced milk combined with caramelised jaggery (palm sugar) and curd, then set in small earthenware cups or vessels, it's rich and luscious.

EATING IN KOLKATA

Kolkata's restaurant scene is rich and varied. There are more Chinese restaurants in Kolkata than there are Indian, which gives some idea of the enormity of the Chinese influence on the city. Many Chinese migrants have settled in Tangra district, midway between the city centre and the airport, so naturally this is where the best Chinese food is found, especially for breakfast.

Dubbed 'the street that never sleeps' by locals, Park Street remains a popular dining district, replete with restaurants, coffee houses and pubs. Sampling one of the stuffed omelettes at Flury's, making a mandatory stop for a kebab roll at Hot Kathi Roll street cart (near the Asiatic Society), and feasting on Bengali specialities at Aheli, I begin to understand why Kolkata is sometimes called the City of Joy. The frenzy of activity around New Market, to the north of Park Street, is palpable. We stop one afternoon at Nizam's for a chicken and egg kathi roll, renowned as one of India's

best street-food snacks. It's a pilgrimage I make each time I visit and the welcome is always warm.

A walk through nearby Dacres Lane reveals another aspect of city life. Popularly referred to as Tiffin *Gali,* the lane has been known for its food offerings since India was a British colony. The place is always bustling with people, sitting together on the narrow benches, enjoying their food. Street vendors compete for attention with high-decibel screams; hawkers and beggars are everywhere; and sadhus (holy men) wander the streets looking otherworldly. The food is inexpensive and it's where poor and low-paid workers come to eat. We try some freshly made *kachoris* (fried pastries filled with green-pea paste), which are utterly delicious, followed by tray coffee – small glasses filled with brewed coffee and dispensed from a tray by a fast-moving coffee wallah. The one thing sold by street vendors that I am wary of and warn against is the sugarcane juice made by hand in rudimentary machines, not using bottled or filtered water.

The daily produce markets play a vital role here, and food shopping is a favoured pastime, especially on a non-work day when it can be done at leisure. Bhayia, a genial host during one of my visits, is keen to share his passion for food. We begin soon after sunrise one morning with a visit to Park Circus market, an early start that will guarantee us the best cut from a freshly slaughtered goat at the halal butcher. Then it's on to the fish hall, lined with rows of fishmongers selling their fresh catch. At every stall, there is a man crouched over a fixed lethal-looking bhoti blade, scaling and slicing fish as it's ordered. Archaic in design, the blade is bow-shaped and razor-sharp, rising primordially from its solid stone or wood base. The potent sharpness of the blade makes me feel slightly squeamish – how more fingers are not lost is beyond me! At the same time, I can't help but marvel at the honed skills of such experienced hands, both here at the markets and again the next day, when the cook at Kewpie's (see page 18) demonstrates his onion-slicing prowess.

Bhaiya chooses his fish, checking the gills and eyes for freshness before passing them to the guy with the bhoti; in a few swift movements, the fish are scaled, gutted and sliced to instructions. He has chosen my favourite fish from this region: bhekti, a firm, white-fleshed freshwater fish that can grow to several kilograms in weight. The fish appears a few hours later at Bhaiya's house, as if by magic, having been marinated with turmeric, chilli and lime, then simmered in a spicy coconut-milk sauce (see page 37). We save the heads to make fish-head dal (see page 33), a prized Bengali delicacy.

At home, Bhaiya oversees the cooking. His cook, Sahana, has been in the household for 20 years or more, since she was 13. She has learnt a few tricks from watching cooking shows on television, and proves a deft hand at vegetable carving. In her tiny kitchen, she produces an amazing procession of dishes that constitute a typical Sunday lunch when the whole family gets together, or when visitors like us arrive in town. We sit down to a banquet lunch of eight courses, complete with *luchi* - the flaky, puffed discs of bread cooked in hot ghee that are wickedly addictive.

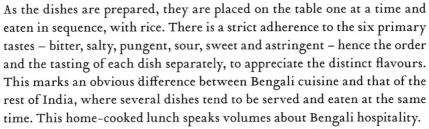

As the dishes are prepared, they are placed on the table one at a time and eaten in sequence, with rice. There is a strict adherence to the six primary tastes – bitter, salty, pungent, sour, sweet and astringent – hence the order and the tasting of each dish separately, to appreciate the distinct flavours. This marks an obvious difference between Bengali cuisine and that of the rest of India, where several dishes tend to be served and eaten at the same time. This home-cooked lunch speaks volumes about Bengali hospitality.

I learn more about the way a Bengali meal is constructed during an afternoon at the home of local cook and food writer Rakhi Purnima Das Gupta. The owner of Kewpie's restaurant, Rakhi is a veritable fount of knowledge when it comes to Bengali cooking. Rakhi's late mother, Minakshie Das Gupta, wrote *Bangla Ranna: The Bengal Cookbook* and compiled *The Calcutta Cookbook*, a treasury of the city's recipes from the pavement to the palace.

Women have a very clear view of their responsibilities towards the prosperity of their family and clan. Food is a moral proposition and certain ideals are expressed in the preparation and consumption of food. The intellectual organization behind the making of pitha reinforces the mother and wife as important contributors to the preservation of the family and clan.
MINAKSHIE DAS GUPTA, *THE CALCUTTA COOKBOOK*

Following in her mother's culinary footsteps, Rakhi has converted part of the ancestral home into a modest restaurant, specialising in the traditional home cooking of Bengal. She also hosts private cooking classes upon request, which is our reason for being here. A tray of glasses filled with ice-cold fresh mango juice and seasoned with ground cumin, black salt and dried chilli arrive as we take our places. It is the perfect thirst quencher before Rakhi guides us through a formidable repertoire of dishes. Once again, I note the importance of the order in which the food is served. Rice is served first, drizzled with warm ghee, and with lime wedges, chopped chilli and salt on the side. *Shukto* follows, then dal and fried vegetable dishes. Fish is up next, beginning with some that are lightly spiced, then on to heavier flavours and textures. Out comes shellfish, before chicken and mutton. Sweet and sour chutneys and crisp pappad wafers act as a finale to the savoury dishes before the meal is completed with a sweet *mishti doi*. Eating like this every day can be a marathon, and such a feast is reserved for special family occasions or when guests pay a visit.

I recently experienced these same Bengali customs and attention to detail at Rajbari Bawali, a magnificently restored former prince's mansion on the outskirts of Kolkata, set amidst a typical rural village. The resident manager and chef Mrinalinee Majumdar is a dynamic, engaging young woman entrusted with the traditions of the house, and the lunch thali she prepared for us revealed a thorough understanding and appreciation of the subtleties of authentic Bengali flavours, dishes handpicked from a traditional Bengali kitchen. Our thali was a composition of *shukto* (vegetables stewed in milk gravy), *aloo bhajia* (grated potato fried in mustard oil), *fool kophi aar shutir dal* (moong dal with peas and cauliflower), *poshto jhinge pyaaj* (ridge gourd cooked in an onion and poppy seed curry), *dhoka dalna* (lentil cakes simmered in a tomato, ginger and cumin gravy), *bhakti paturi* (fish cooked with mustard and coconut in banana leaf over coals), *kosha maansho* (colonial-style mutton curry), a sweet date and mango chutney and baked pappads (lentil wafers). The combination of flavours and textures was inspiring and carefully considered. I have wonderful food memories that will always connect me to that place.

Mrinalinee accompanies us for an early-morning walk along the narrow pathways of the village where bicycles, donkeys and bullock carts replace cars. This is off the beaten track and away from congested roads and humdrum of city life. We chat to women as they do the washing, make chapatis sitting cross legged on the floor, or get their kids ready for school. It's a hive of activity and a flashback in time, a tiny glimpse into the routines and gentle pace of village life, yet only an hour's drive from the city.

Last Rites (Shesh Kaaj)

During mourning, only vegetarian food (with no salt) is eaten, and the bereaved sleep on the floor. Five days after the death, *pindodaan* is performed by the deceased's son or nearest male relative: at a riverside ghat, a holy man makes a dimpled platform from silt taken from the Ganges and balls of rice are placed in its indentations (which have astrological significance) as an offering to the recently departed soul.

The son of the deceased is wrapped in a length of white cloth, which must not be stitched. His shaved head indicates that he is at one with nature in mourning and respecting the soul of his parent, as does not trimming his nails for ten days following the date of death.

After cremation, the ashes are usually immersed immediately, preferably in the Ganges, as it is considered the holiest river.

ON TO DARJEELING

Bound for Glenburn Tea Estate, near the hill-station town of Darjeeling, we fly north to Bagdogra, near the Bangladeshi border, then drive further north still on a road that has long been a trade route between India and Tibet. Tucked away in the far north of West Bengal, Darjeeling and its tea plantations feel like another world – a few hours either way and we would be in Nepal, Bhutan or Tibet.

The four-hour drive to Glenburn takes us through teak and bamboo forests and small riverside villages. We stop for lunch in Teesta Bazaar at a family-run roadside stall, where the matriarch, Janki Chettri, prepares chicken and vegetable *momos* – steamed dumplings cooked in a moktu (a three-tiered vessel similar to a Chinese steamer). Janki smiles wickedly as we dive into a dish of the small round red chillies known as 'bum stingers'. Local trout, pulled from the river below, is smeared with a spicy turmeric paste and grilled. It's perfectly simple and perfectly delicious. While we share her table, Janki offers a taste of her locally famous pickles, made with mustard oil and chilli. She sits opposite me at the table and watches my face intently for a reaction, smiling broadly when I look pleased with everything I am tasting. The flavours are light, frugal even, compared with the rich complexities of our extravagances in Kolkata. However, the food suits the environment; it makes perfect sense. Garlic is used minimally here; instead it's the pungent bite of fresh ginger, mustard seeds and mustard oil that gives the food its distinctive flavour. The choko – known as *isquis* or squash in this part of the world – is a staple and is stir-fried in mustard oil with spinach and a little chilli or turmeric, making the humble vegetable instantly likeable. Tender fiddlehead ferns are also plentiful at the local markets.

A few hair-raising corkscrew bends later, we find ourselves on top of the world at Triveni Lookout, with views across to the peaceful hill station of Kalimpong in one direction and the rugged landscape of Sikkim in the other. This is where the blue waters of the Rangeet River and the green waters of the Teesta River meet, and it is sacred country associated with Shakti, the mother goddess. At one time, before the countryside became so heavily populated, sightings of the Bengal tiger roaming freely in the wild would have been relatively common in these parts.

Finally, we turn off onto an unpaved road that leads down the valley to Glenburn Tea Estate. Nestled below the ridge where Darjeeling perches like a stately princess, against a backdrop of the mighty snow-covered Himalayas, its location is truly breathtaking.

Glenburn is a working tea estate and an idyllic retreat. There are eight suites in the two beautifully restored colonial planter bungalows that offer expansive views of the snow-covered Kanchenjunga mountain range, Darjeeling town on the opposite hilltop, and the surrounding verdant

tea plantations. This is home to some of the finest tea in the world, the champagne of teas; and *chota hazari* (bed tea) is the most indulgent way to taste it – a tray with teapot, cup, saucer and a biscuit is delivered to you in bed as a gentle wakeup call. Beats an alarm clock any day!

Siddharth ('Sid'), our guide for the next few days, is a wise and delightful soul who knows these mountains like the back of his hand, having been raised in Kalimpong. Looking like a rock star and speaking with the fervour of an evangelist, he teaches us more about the Himalayas in a few days than we could learn from books in a lifetime. He has the utmost respect and compassion for his environment, and is eager to share its pleasures and challenges with us. One morning, we set out from our bungalow on the estate and walk for three hours down the side of the mountain to the Glenburn campsite by the Rangeet River. Along the way, we pass through small villages, forests and dense bush. There are views across the river to the neighbouring state of Sikkim, and the emerald terraces of tea plantations surround us. The Glenburn houseboys miraculously appear, descending by jeep with supplies to set up a lovely picnic lunch for us on the riverbank. A slightly shorter walk from the estate in another direction takes us through tea fields down to the River Rung Dung to splash about on its sandy shores and wade in the rock pools while inhaling the pure mountain air.

Woken at 6 a.m. one morning, just as the sun is rising, we see a soft pink sky pierced by the glistening-white peak of Kanchenjunga (Kanchendzonga in the local dialect), the third-highest mountain in the world. The goddess Kanchenjunga has lifted her shroud and is showing her full glory in the gentle morning light, and we immediately understand the power and magnetic pull of these mountains. We sit there on the damp grass, sipping on the estate's first-flush tea, completely mesmerised by such a beautiful vista, just watching for the mere 25 minutes she is there. The heavy monsoonal clouds soon reappear and she is gone. Knowing that some people can wait for weeks and still don't get a glimpse, we feel tremendously privileged.

Kanchenjunga appeared above the parting clouds, as it did only very early in the morning during this season ... The five peaks of Kanchenjunga turned golden with the kind of luminous light that made you feel, if briefly, that truth was apparent. All you needed to do was to reach out and pluck it.
KIRAN DESAI, *THE INHERITANCE OF LOSS*

We drive to Darjeeling to spend time meandering along the Mall and through the bazaar of this former colonial hill station and resort town, to visit the Himalayan Mountain Institute where it's impossible not to be entranced by faded photos of Everest expeditions and equipment used by Tenzing Norgay, Edmund Hillary and the unnamed sherpas who accompanied them. It's spine-chilling and stirring just to be here. At the adjacent Himalayan Zoological Park, we learn of the strong conservationist

spirit that has led to successful breeding programs for endangered snow leopards and red pandas. Elusive in the wild, it's a treat to get close to the Himalayan black bear, Siberian tiger, cloud leopard and Tibetan wolf. Colourful prayer flags floating in the wind indicate the entrance to the nearby Tibetan Refugee Self Help Centre. The centre is built to resemble a small village compound and has workshops, a communal kitchen and living quarters. Many of the older people living here escaped Tibet in the 1950s and '60s when the Chinese army began their invasion and persecution. The atmosphere is inviting, congenial and emotional, and our welcome is endearingly warm – especially from the women in the knitting room, who have tears in their eyes as they speak of their memories, interpreted by Sid.

TEA COUNTRY

The area around Darjeeling is blessed with a climate and topography that are perfect for cultivating tea, and its estates produce some of the finest teas in the world. The mist-shrouded mountains are covered in the distinctive velvety hummocks of tea plantations. While staying at Glenburn, I take the opportunity to treat my taste buds and expand my repertoire. That first visit, it was impossible not to get caught up in the infectious passion of Sanjay, the former estate manager at Glenburn Estate's tea factory. A self-confessed gourmand and a true scholar, he described the subtle nuances of tea using the sort of language normally reserved for fine wines or olive oils. He talked about terroir like a vigneron, explaining that the role of the tea maker is to coax the flavours of the earth from the leaf. He was thoroughly engaging and – as we learnt the difference between the grades of tea, from STGFOP (superfine tippy golden flowery orange pekoe) to GBOP (golden broken orange pekoe) and OF (orange fanning, or dust, often used in teabags) – we were held captive by his charm and knowledge.

On a more recent visit, we discover this passion and enthusiasm has been carried on by Praveez, the estate's current manager and guardian of its traditions. We spend a morning walking through the factory with its enormous airing and drying rooms, watching as women grade and sort tea leaves – a monotonous but painstaking task. We appreciate all the work that has gone into producing such exquisite teas as we are guided through an insightful tea tasting of freshly brewed pots of first and second-flush, monsoon and autumn-flush teas, comparing their flavour notes. Encouraged to use all my senses, I appreciate the differences in aroma, flavour and appearance of tea that has been manufactured in different ways and at different seasons of the year. My favourite is the first flush, picked in spring with its pale amber colour and gentle tannins, and I squirrel a bag to take home with me.

My Bengali sojourns have sparked an intense passion for this intriguing eastern region of the subcontinent. On the streets, in homes and restaurants, I have been extended the most generous hospitality and have tasted flavours I will savour forever. I have come to realise and appreciate that India is not a destination but an experience.

‹Dal-stuffed Pastries

Kachoris

MAKES 18

These fried savoury pastries stuffed with spicy dal are a winner. We first tasted them at one of the food stalls in Kolkata's Dacres Lane, but this popular street snack can also be found in many parts of India. The dal stuffing can be made ahead of time, making the preparation that much faster.

100 g plain flour
100 g wholemeal flour
1 teaspoon salt
3 teaspoons ghee
1 teaspoon finely shredded curry leaves
1 teaspoon nigella seeds
vegetable oil, for deep-frying

DAL STUFFING
100 g urad dal, soaked for 2 hours
2 tablespoons vegetable oil
1 teaspoon cumin seeds
¼ teaspoon ground turmeric
¼ teaspoon asafoetida
2 small green chillies, minced
1 tablespoon minced ginger
50 g peas, blanched and mashed
   to make a rough paste
1 teaspoon salt
½ teaspoon freshly ground black pepper

To make the dal stuffing, drain the dal and blend in a food processor to make a rough paste. Heat the oil in a frying pan and fry the cumin seeds until they pop. Add the turmeric, asafoetida, chilli and ginger, stirring to combine. Add the dal puree to the pan and stir to coat with the spices. Add ½ cup (125 ml) water and cook over a low heat until the water has been absorbed into the dal and the mixture has thickened. Stir through the mashed peas. Add the salt and pepper and allow to cool.

Sift the flours and salt into a bowl, then knead the ghee, curry leaves and nigella seeds into the flour using your hands until the mixture looks like breadcrumbs. Add ½ cup (125 ml) water and continue to work the dough until it is soft and pliable. You may need to add a little extra water. Roll out the dough on a floured surface and knead for another 5 minutes (to stretch the glutens) until it is shiny and smooth. Cover with a clean cloth and leave to rest for 30 minutes at room temperature.

Divide the dough into 18 pieces and roll each one into a ball. Roll each ball out flat so it resembles a pancake about 10 cm in diameter. Place a spoonful of dal stuffing in the centre of each round, then fold the dough over to make a half-moon shape and press the edges together to secure. Flatten slightly with a rolling pin – don't press too hard or the filling will spill out.

Heat the oil in a kadhai or wok to 180°C. To test the temperature of the oil, sprinkle in some flour – if the flour sizzles, it is ready. Fry the pastries a few at a time until golden and crisp (about 2 minutes), then flip over and cook the other side for a minute. Hold the pastries in the oil using a large mesh spoon or spider so they puff up. Drain on paper towel and serve warm with Mint Chutney (see page 76).

Bengali Garam Masala

An essential spice mix used in many Bengali preparations.

2 teaspoons cloves
2 teaspoons seeds from green cardamom pods
2 bay leaves
2 teaspoons ground cinnamon

Grind the cloves, cardamom seeds and bay leaves together to a fine powder, then mix with the cinnamon. Store in an airtight container.

Panch Phoran

Another essential whole spice mix used in myriad dal and vegetable preparations for its warm fragrancy.

2 teaspoons cumin seeds
2 teaspoons brown mustard seeds
2 teaspoons fennel seeds
2 teaspoons fenugreek seeds
2 teaspoons nigella seeds

Combine all the ingredients and store in an airtight container. Grind as required using a mortar and pestle or spice grinder.

Marina's Onion Bhajias

SERVES 6

One balmy summer's night in Kolkata, at friends Sunil and Marina's apartment, Marina prepared these exquisite, feather-light onion bhajias – the perfect accompaniment for pre-dinner drinks. Stir a little shredded mint into yoghurt for a simple dipping sauce.

3 red onions, sliced into rings
1½ teaspoons coriander seeds, cracked using a mortar and pestle
2 small green chillies, finely chopped
½ teaspoon salt
200 g chickpea (gram) flour
vegetable oil, for deep-frying

Combine the onion, coriander seeds, chilli and salt in a bowl. Using your fingers, knead to extract the liquid from the onion. Sprinkle over the flour and add 2 tablespoons water. Continue to knead. If the mixture is too dry, add a little more water, 1 tablespoon at a time. (Marina says it should not look like a batter – more like mayonnaise sticking to shredded cabbage.)

Heat the oil in a kadhai or wok to 180°C. To test the temperature of the oil, sprinkle in some flour – if the flour sizzles, it is ready. Loosely drop tablespoons of batter into the oil. Fry the onion bhajias a few at a time (to maintain the oil temperature and prevent the bhajias going soggy) for 2 minutes until crisp and golden. Drain on paper towel and serve immediately with minted yoghurt (see recipe introduction).

Rice & Dal Soup

Khichuri

SERVES 8

A dish renowned for its nourishing effect, this is traditionally served to invalids, the sick or babies, and on rainy days to anyone in the house. It is also popular during the monsoon season.

250 g rice, washed and drained well
250 g roasted moong dal, washed and thoroughly drained
½ teaspoon ground turmeric
2 teaspoons ground cumin
½ teaspoon chilli powder
½ teaspoon ground coriander
½ teaspoon white sugar
2 teaspoons salt
1 teaspoon Ginger Paste (see page 377)
250 g cauliflower, broken into florets
100 g shelled peas
200 g small potatoes, peeled and quartered
100 g pearl onions, peeled
6 small green chillies, split in half lengthways

SAMBAR
150 g ghee
4 small dried red chillies
4 bay leaves
100 g red onions, finely sliced
2 teaspoons Bengali Garam Masala (see page 25)

Bring 1.5 litres water to a boil in a large saucepan. Add the rice and dal and cook for about 8 minutes until the rice is half-cooked. Mix the dry spices, sugar and salt with the ginger paste and stir into the rice. Simmer for 6 minutes. Add the vegetables and green chillies and simmer until the vegetables are soft. The rice and dal should both be cooked by now.

To make the sambar, heat the ghee in a frying pan and fry the red chillies and bay leaves for a minute until fragrant. Add the onion and fry until golden, then add the garam masala and cook for another 2 minutes.

Stir the sambar into the cooked khichuri. Taste and adjust the seasoning if necessary. Serve hot. For added flavour, hot melted ghee can be poured over the khichuri as it is served.

Star Anise Chicken Kebabs
Kebab Sonargaon
SERVES 6

These kebabs are usually cooked in a tandoor oven, but they work just as effectively if you grill them over hot coals or on a barbecue or grill plate. They are lip-smacking good and full of flavour. Serve with Sonargaon's signature dal (see page 40) – the perfect accompaniment.

   12 chicken thighs
   1 tablespoon Ginger Garlic Paste
      (see page 377)
   2 teaspoons salt
   2 teaspoons lemon juice,
      plus extra to serve
   50 g chickpea (gram) flour
   1 egg
   50 g tomato sauce (ketchup)
   2 teaspoons roasted ground cumin
   2/3 teaspoon ground star anise
   1/2 teaspoon kasoori methi
      (dried fenugreek leaf) powder
   1/2 teaspoon ground ginger
   100 ml cream
   1¼ tablespoons mustard oil
   75 g roasted cashews, coarsely ground

Remove the bones from the chicken thighs, keeping the skin intact. Cut the meat into large (5 cm) cubes. Combine the ginger garlic paste, salt and lemon juice and add the chicken, mixing thoroughly until the meat is coated with the marinade. Leave to marinate for 30 minutes.

Mix the flour with the egg to make a paste, then mix in the remaining ingredients (except the chicken) to make a smooth, thick paste. Add the chicken and mix to coat with the paste. Leave to marinate for 1 hour.

Thread the chicken pieces onto skewers and cook for approximately 6 minutes in a hot tandoor oven (or over hot coals or on a barbecue or char-grill) until meat is tender. Baste regularly with the paste.

When the chicken is cooked, remove it from the skewers and sprinkle with a little extra lemon juice. Serve hot with Mint Chutney (see page 76) and Dal Sonargaon (see page 40).

Charred Eggplant
Baigan Bharta
SERVES 4

This eggplant dish was a regular feature of our meals in Kolkata and Darjeeling. It is best eaten soon after it is made – do not refrigerate it as the cold dulls the flavours. You can stir a little thick plain yoghurt into the eggplant if you wish, to give it a richer, creamier taste.

   2 eggplants (aubergines)
   1 tablespoon finely diced onion
   1 small green chilli, minced
   2 small tomatoes, peeled and finely diced
   2 tablespoons olive or vegetable oil
   2 teaspoons lime juice
   1 tablespoon shredded coriander leaves
   salt and freshly ground black pepper

Cook the whole eggplants over hot coals or a direct flame until they are charred and blistered all over. Remove from the heat. Stand the eggplants in a colander over a bowl until they are cool enough to handle. Remove the charred skin from the eggplants using wet fingers.

Chop the eggplant flesh and stir in the remaining ingredients, adding salt and pepper to taste. Serve at room temperature.

Pumpkin Flowers with Cheese

MAKES 12

Glenburn Tea Estate boasts a wonderful organic vegetable garden that provides much of the produce used for their menus. The flowers from the white pumpkin plant (which is more like marrow than pumpkin) are used for this dish, and when they are not in season, nasturtium flowers are used. Zucchini blossoms are more readily available elsewhere and give much the same result. Fresh mozzarella, goat's feta or cottage cheese can be substituted for the traditional churpi (yak) cheese.

12 small pumpkin or zucchini
    (courgette) flowers
vegetable oil, for deep-frying

CHEESE STUFFING
150 g goat's feta
1 tablespoon chopped chives
½ teaspoon salt
½ teaspoon freshly ground black pepper
2 small green chillies, minced
2 teaspoons Ginger Garlic Paste
    (see page 377)

BATTER
100 g sifted plain flour
50 g chickpea (gram) flour
2 tablespoons cornflour
1 teaspoon salt
½ teaspoon freshly ground black pepper
1 egg yolk
250–275 ml ice-cold soda water

To prepare the cheese stuffing, combine all the ingredients.

Open each flower and gently spoon or pipe the stuffing into the centre. Close the flowers around the stuffing to secure.

For the batter, combine the flours, salt and pepper in bowl.

When you are ready to cook the stuffed flowers, heat the oil in a kadhai or wok to 180°C. To test the temperature of the oil, sprinkle in some flour — if the flour sizzles, it is ready.

Add the egg yolk to the flour mixture and pour in the cold soda water. Mix roughly using a chopstick. The batter should not be smooth —

a lumpy appearance is what you are looking for. Use it immediately.

Dip the stuffed flowers into the batter to lightly coat, then fry a few at a time until golden, turning to cook both sides. Drain on paper towel and serve warm.

Glenburn's Tea-leaf Fritters

SERVES 4

Essentially feathery-light pakoras, these delicious morsels are served with pre-dinner drinks out on the terrace at Glenburn Tea Estate. Betel leaves, Thai sweet leaf or elk leaves can be substituted for the tea leaves, which are picked straight from the bushes outside the door. To use dried tea leaves would be a mistake!

vegetable oil, for deep-frying
24 freshly picked tea leaves
pakora batter (see page 350)

Heat the oil in a kadhai or wok to 180°C. To test the temperature of the oil, sprinkle in some flour — if the flour sizzles, it is ready. Dip the tea leaves into the batter to lightly coat. Fry a few at a time in the hot oil, then drain on paper towel. Serve hot.

Pumpkin Vine Tips Tarkari

SERVES 4

Here, tender leaves from the pumpkin vine
are cooked with spices. This was served for
dinner at Glenburn Tea Estate using produce
straight from their kitchen garden.

3 tablespoons vegetable oil
½ teaspoon ground timur (Sichuan pepper)
½ teaspoon brown mustard seeds
3 dried red chillies, broken into pieces
2 teaspoons Ginger Garlic Paste
   (see page 377)
1 teaspoon ground cumin
1 teaspoon curry powder
500 g pumpkin vine tips, washed, peeled
   and cut into 2 cm pieces
5 mushrooms, sliced
2 red capsicums (peppers), seeded and diced
1 teaspoon salt
1 teaspoon freshly ground black pepper
2 tomatoes, sliced lengthways and seeded

Heat the oil in a large frying pan and fry the timur
and mustard seeds over a medium heat until they
start to splutter. Add the dried chilli and fry for
15 seconds until it colours. Working quickly, stir
through the ginger garlic paste, cumin and curry
powder, frying for a minute or so over a low
heat. Add the pumpkin vine tips, mushroom and
capsicum and stir-fry for 2 minutes.

Add ½ cup (125 ml) water, then cover and cook
for 6–8 minutes until tender. Season with the salt
and pepper.

Add the tomato and stir-fry until the vine tips are
tender and any excess liquid has evaporated. Serve
warm with rice.

Burmese Chicken Noodles

Kawswe

SERVES 8

Kolkata's close ties to its Burmese heritage
are apparent in dishes like kawswe, a coconut
curry noodle soup with comforting qualities.
My friend Jamshyd gave me this favourite
childhood recipe from his mother's notebook
– it is something he eats regularly to this day.

½ teaspoon ground turmeric
½ teaspoon salt
1 × 1.5 kg chicken
1 small onion, roughly chopped
4 cloves garlic, roughly chopped
5 cm piece ginger, roughly chopped
5 long dried red chillies
1 cup (250 ml) vegetable oil
3 tablespoons chickpea (gram) flour
milk from 2 coconuts
soy sauce, fish sauce and chilli oil, to taste
300 g cooked egg noodles

GARNISHES
4 tablespoons fried egg noodles,
   broken into small pieces
5 hard-boiled eggs, sliced
6 limes, cut in half
4 green onions, sliced
soy sauce, fish sauce and chilli
   powder, to taste

Rub the turmeric and salt all over the chicken. Pour
enough water to cover the chicken into a large pan
and bring to a boil. Add the chicken, then reduce the
heat to a simmer and cook for 30 minutes. Remove
the chicken from the pan and transfer to a dish.
Strain the cooking broth and reserve. When the
chicken is cool enough to handle, shred the meat.

Using a mortar and pestle, pound the onion, garlic,
ginger and chillies together. Heat the vegetable oil
in a large saucepan and fry the onion mixture to
make the masala base. Mix the chickpea flour and
coconut milk into the reserved chicken broth, then
pour into the pan and stir to combine. Bring to
a boil, stirring to prevent sticking, then reduce the
heat and simmer for 10 minutes. Add soy sauce,
fish sauce and chilli oil to taste.

To serve, divide the noodles among serving bowls.
Add the shredded chicken and ladle over the hot
broth. Garnish with all the bits.

Vegetables & Bori ›
Shukto
SERVES 8

Our host in Kolkata during an early visit
was Bhaiya, and while staying with him
we were treated to some beautiful home-
style food. Sahana, his cook of many years,
produced an amazing array of dishes from
her tiny kitchen. Shukto is one of Bhaiya's
(and every Bengali's) favourite dishes, and one
about which he waxes lyrical. It is a Bengali
staple, a traditional starter that is usually
served only at lunch, a dish that is served to
me with every visit. Bori are small balls made
from ground and dried urad dal. They can be
purchased ready-made in packets at Indian
grocery stores.

200 ml vegetable oil
2 drumstick vegetables (see page 377), sliced
1 small eggplant (aubergine), cut into batons
2 potatoes, peeled and chopped
1 plantain, peeled and chopped
1 bitter gourd, peeled and chopped
1 white sweet potato, peeled and chopped
3 tablespoons ghee, plus 2 teaspoons extra
4 bay leaves
1 teaspoon cumin seeds
2 teaspoons ground coriander
1 tablespoon Ginger Paste (see page 377)
2 teaspoons salt
1 tablespoon white sugar,
   plus 2 teaspoons extra
4 small green chillies, finely sliced
200 ml milk
2 tablespoons plain flour
2 tablespoons mustard oil
20 bori

Heat the vegetable oil in a large frying pan and fry
the drumstick vegetables until golden. Remove
from the pan and drain on paper towel. Fry each
vegetable separately and drain in the same manner.

When all the vegetables have been fried, add the
ghee to the oil in the pan. Add the bay leaves, cumin
seeds, coriander and ginger paste and cook for
2 minutes. Add the salt, sugar and chilli, stirring to
combine. Pour in 1 cup (250 ml) water and stir, then
add all the fried vegetables and cook for 5 minutes.
Add an extra cup or two of water if necessary so the
mixture doesn't dry out.

Using a stick blender, mix the milk, flour and
2 tablespoons water in a bowl to make a paste.

In a separate frying pan, heat the mustard oil and
fry the bori for 2 minutes until golden. Add the bori
to the vegetables, then stir in the milk paste until
combined. Simmer for 15 minutes.

Stir in the extra ghee and sugar, then take the
pan off the heat and leave to rest for 15 minutes
before serving.

Marrow & Prawns ›
Lao Chingra
SERVES 4

From Bhaiya's kitchen, this is a quick and
easy dish to prepare, full of flavour. You
can substitute zucchini (courgette) for the
marrow, if preferred.

½ teaspoon ground turmeric
½ teaspoon salt
3 tablespoons peeled small uncooked prawns
2 tablespoons vegetable oil
2 bay leaves
1 teaspoon fenugreek seeds
100 g marrow, shredded and boiled
2 teaspoons white sugar
5 small green chillies, minced
½ cup (125 ml) milk
1 tablespoon chopped coriander leaves

Mix the turmeric and salt together and rub into the
prawns. Leave to marinate for 20 minutes. Heat the
oil in a frying pan and fry the marinated prawns
for 3 minutes until golden. Remove the prawns
from the pan and set aside.

Add the bay leaves and fenugreek seeds to the pan
and fry for 1 minute until fragrant. Stir in the
marrow and simmer for a few minutes. Stir in
the sugar and chilli, then cover and simmer for
10 minutes. Add the milk and simmer for another
20 minutes until the liquid has been absorbed.
Add the prawns, tossing to combine, and cook for
5 minutes. Scatter over the fresh coriander to serve.

‹Fish-head Dal

SERVES 6

One of Bengal's signature dishes, this version was prepared for us by Sahana. Always willing to try a different take on a traditional dish, she and Bhaiya would have endless discussions about the various ways in which something can be prepared – it was fascinating to glean a few extra insider tips.

  2 tablespoons vegetable oil
  1 tablespoon mustard oil
  1 bay leaf
  2 teaspoons cumin seeds
  4 tablespoons Onion Paste (see page 379)
  250 g moong dal, washed
  2 teaspoons Ginger Garlic Paste
    (see page 377)
  2 teaspoons ghee
  1 teaspoon ground turmeric
  1 teaspoon chilli powder
  3 teaspoons white sugar
  3 teaspoons garam masala
  1 teaspoon salt, plus extra if needed
  2 tablespoons thick plain yoghurt
  5 small green chillies, finely sliced

SPICED FISH HEADS
  1 teaspoon ground turmeric
  1 teaspoon chilli powder
  1 teaspoon salt
  1 tablespoon vegetable oil
  3 small fish heads (from any white-fleshed
    saltwater fish, such as snapper)

To prepare the spiced fish heads, combine the turmeric, chilli powder and salt with the oil. Add the fish heads and coat well. Heat a frying pan and fry the fish heads over a high heat on both sides until golden. Remove from the pan and set aside.

Heat the oils in a large saucepan. Fry the bay leaf and cumin seeds for 30 seconds, then add the onion paste and cook for 10 minutes until golden.

Meanwhile, dry-fry the moong dal in a separate large saucepan until it is lightly roasted. Pour in 2 litres water and cook for 15 minutes or until soft. Drain the dal, reserving the cooking water.

Add the ginger garlic paste to the saucepan with the onion paste and cook for 2 minutes. Add half the ghee, then stir in turmeric, chilli powder, sugar and 2 tablespoons water. In a bowl, mix 1 teaspoon of the garam masala with the salt and yoghurt, then add to the pan and stir until combined. Add the fish heads and cook for 3 minutes, then stir in the dal and the reserved cooking water. Cover the pan and simmer for 15 minutes.

Add the green chilli and cook for 5 minutes, then add the remaining garam masala and cook for 2 minutes until fragrant. Stir through the remaining ghee. Turn off the heat. Taste and add a little extra salt, if required, before serving.

Stir-fried Squash & Spinach

SERVES 4

We bought this at a Teesta roadside stall, where it was cooked by Janki. She used *isquis* (choko) and served the vegetables with small whole river trout that had been marinated in turmeric, salt, chilli and lime juice before being fried, and a bowl of pickled 'bum-stinger' chillies – it was heaven. You could substitute zucchini (courgettes) for the white squash or choko.

  2 tablespoons vegetable oil
  2 teaspoons minced garlic
  ½ teaspoon chilli powder
  ½ teaspoon ground turmeric
  ½ teaspoon salt
  200 g white squash or choko, sliced
  100 g spinach leaves, washed and
    roughly chopped

Heat the oil in a large frying pan and fry the garlic, spices and salt over a medium heat for 20 seconds. Add the squash or choko and toss to coat with the spices. Fry for 1 minute, then add ⅓ cup (80 ml) water and simmer, uncovered, for 5–6 minutes.

Add the spinach, stirring to combine. Toss over a medium heat until the spinach has wilted and the flavours have combined. Serve warm.

Fish Fry
Bhekti Rongpuri
SERVES 4

We ate this dish, a staple that appears on
many menus across Kolkata, at Bhojohori
Manna restaurant – and it was so delicious
that we polished off the plate in no time.
Crumbed and fried with mustard, ginger,
garlic and lime, the fish was served with
a salad of sliced cucumber and red onion.

> 1 teaspoon smooth mustard
> 1 tablespoon Ginger Garlic Paste
>   (see page 377)
> 2 tablespoons lime juice
> 1 teaspoon salt
> 4 × 100 g haddock (or other firm-fleshed
>   white fish) portions, ideally thick slices
> 35 g fine breadcrumbs
> 2 tablespoons mustard oil

Make a paste with the mustard, ginger garlic paste,
lime juice and salt. Brush the fish with the paste,
then roll the fish in the breadcrumbs until coated.

Heat the oil in a frying pan and fry the fish over a
high heat on one side for 3–4 minutes until golden.
Turn over and fry the other side for 2–3 minutes or
until just cooked (the cooking time will depend on
the thickness of the fish). Drain on paper towel.

Serve the fish with Mango Mustard Pickle
(see page 50) and Puffed Puri Bread (page 38)
or steamed rice.

Fried Tamarind Fish ›
Tatul Ilish Bhaja
SERVES 6

Bhaiya bought hilsa, a local and seasonal
speciality, at the fish market for this dish.
It can be made just as effectively with sea
mullet, bream, freshwater salmon or small
jewfish or mulloway. Choose whole fish, then
ask for it to be gutted, scaled and cut across
the body into 4–5 cm thick slices to make
the cutlets. This preparation can be served
with other dishes at a shared table – it is
equally delicious with Paratha (see page 351)
or steamed rice.

> 2 teaspoons ground turmeric
> 2 teaspoons salt
> 1 teaspoon chilli powder
> 2 teaspoons white sugar
> 1 tablespoon Tamarind Liquid (see page 379)
> 6 × 100 g sea mullet cutlets
> 2½ tablespoons vegetable oil
> 4 dried red chillies

Mix the turmeric, salt, chilli powder and sugar
with enough plain water to make a thick paste.
Add the tamarind liquid and mix. Roll the fish
cutlets in the paste until they are thoroughly coated.

Heat the oil in a frying pan, then add the dried
chillies. Fry the cutlets over a high heat for
3 minutes or until golden on one side, then flip
over and fry the other side for 2 minutes. Serve hot.

‹Whole Fish in Coconut Mustard Sauce
Bhekti Sarson
SERVES 6

In this dish the central bone is removed from the fish, leaving the two fillets attached to the head (you could you ask your fishmonger to do this). Bhaiya bought seer fish at the morning market for this recipe, but you could use kingfish, bonito or mackerel – just be sure the fish isn't too large.

1 × 1.2 kg kingfish, trevally, bonito or
    mulloway, central bone removed
8 small green chillies
2 tablespoons brown mustard seeds
70 g grated fresh coconut
1 teaspoon salt
3 tablespoons mustard oil

FISH MARINADE
½ teaspoon ground turmeric
½ teaspoon chilli powder
½ teaspoon salt
1 tablespoon lime juice

To prepare the fish marinade, mix the ingredients with a little water to make a thick paste. Rub all over the fish, then cover and leave to marinate for 1 hour.

Chop 2 of the green chillies and leave the others whole. Using a stick blender, combine the mustard seeds, coconut, salt, chopped chilli and half the mustard oil with 2 tablespoons water to make a thick paste.

Lay the fish in a wide frying pan and spread the coconut paste over the fish, inside and out. Put 3 of the whole chillies in the centre of the fish between the 2 fillets, then lay the remaining chillies on top of the fish. Pour 1 cup (250 ml) water and the remaining mustard oil over the fish. Cover and cook over a low heat for 12–15 minutes, depending on the thickness of the fish, regularly spooning the sauce over the fish as it cooks. To test if it is cooked, press the flesh just below the head – it should have a slight spring to the touch. Too soft means it is undercooked; firm means it is overcooked.

Serve immediately.

Bengali-style Mashed Potato
Aloo Bhatey
SERVES 4

This is from Minakshie Das Gupta's book *Bangla Ranna: The Bengal Cookbook*. Try it next time you cook a steak – it makes a delicious accompaniment.

500 g potatoes, peeled
2 tablespoons mustard oil
2 green onions, finely sliced
2 small green chillies, minced
1 teaspoon salt

Cook the potatoes in boiling water until tender, then drain. Mash until smooth. Stir through the remaining ingredients and serve.

Puffed Puri Bread ›
Luchi
MAKES 36

Deep-fried puffed bread plays a starring role on the Bengali table. It is irresistible – one is never enough! This recipe comes from Minakshie's *Bangla Ranna* cookbook, where she makes special mention of the temperature of the ghee for deep-frying: it should be heated to smoking point at the start and then the heat should be reduced slightly so the mixture cooks at an even, medium–hot temperature. The puris will not puff up if the ghee is either too hot or not hot enough. I learnt by trial and error.

250 g plain flour
pinch of salt
2 teaspoons melted ghee,
   plus 1 litre for deep-frying

Sift the flour and salt together. Add the melted ghee and sufficient water to bind, then knead into a soft, pliable dough. Knead for 5 minutes – the kneading plays a vital role in getting the 'puff' into the bread. Divide the dough into 36 pieces and roll into balls. Roll out each ball on a floured surface, as evenly as possible, to a thin flat round.

Heat the ghee for deep-frying in a kadhai or large pan to 180°C. To test the temperature, sprinkle in some flour – if it sizzles, it is ready. Deep-fry the luchis one at a time for 1 minute, pressing lightly with a spatula, then flip over and fry the other side until it puffs. Drain on paper towel. Serve warm.

Chicken Dumplings ›
Momos
MAKES 30

These savoury dumplings are related to the well-known Tibetan style of dumpling, and are a typical snack of this mountain region. My first taste of them was at a Teesta cafe, a small roadside place that we stopped at on our drive up to Darjeeling. Often, a basic stock will be made with meat bones and water and the momos will be steamed over this, rather than over water, giving a flavourful perfume to the pastry as it cooks.

675 g plain flour
pinch of salt

FILLING
750 g minced chicken
2 tablespoons finely diced onion
1 teaspoon salt
2 teaspoons minced ginger
2 tablespoons grated carrot (optional)

CHILLI RELISH
1 tomato, charred whole over hot coals
   or a gas flame
6 cloves garlic, chopped
2 teaspoons chilli powder
½ teaspoon salt
1 tablespoon finely chopped green onion tops
2 teaspoons chopped coriander leaves

To make the chilli relish, blend the tomato with the garlic, chilli powder and salt to make a puree. Stir through the green onion tops and coriander leaves. Set aside until ready to serve.

Mix the flour, salt and 2 cups (500 ml) water to form a stiff paste. Roll out thinly on a floured surface. The rolled sheet of dough should be about 70 cm square (enough for 30 momos). Cut out circles of dough using an 8 cm pastry cutter or the rim of a glass or teacup.

To make the filling, combine all the ingredients in a bowl. Place a spoonful of filling in the centre of each pastry round, then fold the pastry over to make a semi-circle and pinch the edges together with a little water to seal. Pleat the edges. Place the prepared momos on a flat plate and cook in a bamboo steamer, covered, for 30 minutes. Serve with the chilli relish.

Braised Lamb ›

Pathar Jhol

SERVES 4

Another fragrant, succulent dish served for lunch at Bhaiya and Arpita's house. I have adjusted the cooking time from how we did it there – the lamb was cooked in a pressure cooker and done after four whistles. Not a commonly used method in modern Western kitchens these days.

4 tablespoons kidney beans
1.5 kg lamb shoulder, diced
300 g grated onion
3 teaspoons Ginger Garlic Paste
  (see page 377)
1 teaspoon chilli powder
1 teaspoon ground turmeric
1 teaspoon ground cumin
1 teaspoon ground coriander
2 bay leaves
4 potatoes, peeled and quartered
500 g curd (drained yoghurt)

SPICE MIX
100 ml mustard oil
2 tablespoons grated fresh coconut
1 teaspoon ghee
4 × 2–3 cm pieces cassia bark
1 teaspoon cloves
1 teaspoon green cardamom pods, cracked
4 small dried red chillies
2 bay leaves
1 teaspoon salt
1 teaspoon white sugar

Soak the kidney beans in cold water for 30 minutes, then drain. Put the lamb in a large bowl and combine with the kidney beans, onion, ginger garlic paste, spices, bay leaves and potato. Mix in the curd and 2 litres water, then leave to marinate for 1 hour.

Transfer the mixture to a heavy-based saucepan or flameproof casserole and cover. Bring to a boil over a medium heat, then reduce the heat to low and simmer gently for 1 hour until the meat is tender.

When the lamb is ready, make the spice mix. Heat the mustard oil in a large frying pan and fry the coconut until golden. Remove the coconut from the pan with a slotted spoon and drain on paper towel.

Add the ghee to the oil in the pan and fry the cassia, cloves, cardamom, chillies and bay leaves until fragrant. Add the lamb mixture and fried coconut, stirring to combine. Simmer for 20 minutes over a medium heat until the sauce has reduced and thickened.

Stir in the salt and sugar, then taste and adjust the seasoning if necessary.

Dal Sonargaon

SERVES 4

A terrific earthy-flavoured dal cooked by chef Sujoy at Sonargaon, the Bengali restaurant at the Taj Bengal Hotel in Kolkata (Sonargaon means 'golden village' in Sanskrit). It makes a perfect accompaniment to their chicken kebabs (see page 27).

400 g black urad lentils
200 g tomato puree
3 teaspoons Ginger Garlic Paste
  (see page 377)
1 teaspoon chilli powder
200 g butter
2 teaspoons salt, plus extra if needed
200 ml cream

Wash the lentils and soak them for 1 hour in cold water. Rinse and drain.

Tip the lentils into a large, heavy-based saucepan and pour in 3 litres water. Bring to a boil and cook for about 2 hours until the lentils are tender. Drain.

Add the tomato puree, ginger garlic paste, chilli powder and 150 g of the butter. Stir over a medium heat until the mixture starts to boil. Add the salt and simmer for about 15 minutes, stirring occasionally, until the mixture thickens.

Stir through the cream and remaining butter. Taste and adjust the seasoning if necessary.

Spicy Roast Chicken
Murgh Mussallam
SERVES 6

Through its use of spices, nuts and style of cooking, the Mughal and Muslim influence on Bengali cuisine is reflected in dishes like this one, which we ate for lunch at 6 Ballygunge Place restaurant in Kolkata.

2½ tablespoons cream
½ teaspoon saffron threads
2 tablespoons roasted cashews, chopped
2 tablespoons blanched almonds, chopped
2 teaspoons pistachios, slivered
2 tablespoons sultanas
2 hard-boiled eggs, cut in half lengthways
1 × 1.5 kg chicken, cleaned
150 g ghee
2 tablespoons Ginger Garlic Paste
    (see page 377)
2 tablespoons Onion Paste (see page 379)
½ teaspoon ground cumin
1 teaspoon ground coriander
½ teaspoon chilli powder
¼ teaspoon ground cardamom
½ teaspoon ground turmeric
2 teaspoons salt
few drops of screwpine (pandan) essence

Put the cream and saffron threads in a small saucepan over a low heat. When the cream starts to simmer, remove from the heat and leave to infuse for 20 minutes.

Mix the nuts and sultanas in a bowl with the hard-boiled egg halves. Stuff the chicken cavity with the nut and egg mix. Truss the chicken with kitchen string and tie to secure. Rub the saffron cream all over the chicken skin to coat.

Heat the ghee in a large saucepan or braising pan (deep enough to hold the chicken) and add the ginger garlic paste and onion paste. Fry over a medium heat for about 5 minutes until they start to colour, stirring constantly to prevent burning. Add the spices and salt and stir to combine. Cook for 2 minutes until the mixture is fragrant and the oil separates.

Add the chicken to the pan and coat the surfaces evenly with the spice mix. Pour in 400 ml water, then cover the pan and reduce the heat to a simmer. Cook over a gentle heat for 40 minutes or until the chicken is cooked, basting the bird every 10 minutes (the steam facilitates the cooking and helps to keep the meat tender). If the water has been totally absorbed before the chicken is cooked, add a little extra water. Test the chicken with a skewer at the thigh joint – the juices should run pale pink.

Turn off the heat and leave to rest for 10 minutes. Lift the chicken from the pan and carve into joints. Stir the screwpine essence through the spice base and spoon over the chicken. Serve with steamed rice.

Kewpie's Tomato Chutney ›
SERVES 8

A delicious fresh relish from Kewpie's, where it is served as an accompaniment to everything.

1 teaspoon mustard oil
2 pinches Panch Phoran (see page 25)
250 g tomatoes, chopped
salt
1 tablespoon thin julienne strips ginger
½ teaspoon chilli powder
1 tablespoon seedless raisins or sultanas,
    soaked in water and drained
3 tablespoons white sugar

Heat the mustard oil in a kadhai or wok. Add the panch phoran and fry over a medium heat until it stops spluttering. Add the tomato and stir to coat with the spices. Mix in 2 teaspoons salt, then cover the pan and simmer for 10 minutes.

Stir in the ginger, chilli powder and raisins or sultanas, then add the sugar and 1 cup (250 ml) water. Simmer for 10 minutes until the tomato is cooked and the chutney has thickened. Season to taste with salt and allow to cool before using.

‹Curried Potatoes
Alur Dom
SERVES 8

Another vegetable dish starring the humble yet versatile potato. Try it with grilled fish – or, for a little carb overload, have it with rich flaky Puffed Puri Bread (see page 38).

4 tablespoons ghee
2 bay leaves
2 cm piece cinnamon stick,
    broken into small pieces
4 green cardamom pods, crushed
4 cloves
3 tomatoes, seeded and diced
1 kg small (chat) potatoes, boiled and peeled
½ teaspoon salt

SPICE MIX
1 tablespoon ground coriander
3 tablespoons ground cumin
1 tablespoon freshly ground black pepper
¼ teaspoon ground turmeric
2 teaspoons salt
2 teaspoons white sugar

To make the spice mix, thoroughly combine all the ingredients. Store in an airtight container and use as required.

Mix 4 tablespoons of the prepared spice mix in a bowl with enough water to make a paste. Heat the ghee in a frying pan over a medium heat and fry the bay leaves, cinnamon, cardamom and cloves for a minute. Add the spice paste and fry for 2 minutes until the mixture is fragrant but not burning. Add the tomato and cook for 20 minutes or until mushy. Pour in 1 cup (250 ml) water and bring to a boil. Add the potatoes and boil for 4 minutes. Reduce the heat to low and cover the pan. Simmer until most of the water has been absorbed.

Season with the salt and serve.

Rakhi's Panch Phoran Prawns
SERVES 4

Another easy-to-cook prawn dish from Kewpie's repertoire.

1 tablespoon Panch Phoran (see page 25)
2 dried red chillies
1 tablespoon mustard oil
300 g peeled uncooked prawns, deveined
2 teaspoons lime juice
½ teaspoon salt

Dry-roast the panch phoran with the chillies. Cool, then grind to a fine powder.

Heat the oil in a frying pan, then add the panch phoran mixture and fry for 30 seconds over a high heat. Add the prawns and toss to coat. Cook over a medium heat for a minute, just until the prawns are cooked. Add the lime juice and salt and toss to combine. Remove from the heat and serve.

Kool Chutney

Kool are Indian plums that are sweet and sour in taste. Small and round with yellowish-red skins, they are sold in the fresh produce markets of Kolkata. I bought some at Park Circus market one morning and asked local friend Papia to show me how to make chutney with them. This is a great condiment to serve with pappads or any type of Indian flatbread. Kool are impossible to find outside India, so in Australia I have made this chutney using the small sugar plums that appear in our markets at the end of summer. I add a little tamarind to the mix to round out the sweetness and to approximate the flavour as best as possible.

2 teaspoons mustard oil
½ teaspoon yellow mustard seeds
½ teaspoon brown mustard seeds
2 small dried red chillies, broken
    into small pieces
500 g kool (small Indian plums)
3 teaspoons salt
500 g jaggery, shaved
1 teaspoon Panch Phoran (see page 25)

Heat the oil in a kadhai or wok over a medium heat and fry the mustard seeds and chilli for 30 seconds. Add the whole plums and salt and stir to combine. Cook over a medium heat for 10 minutes until the plums have softened.

Stir in the jaggery and 150 ml water and cook for 5 minutes. Reduce the heat to low, then cover and simmer for 10 minutes. Remove from the heat and allow to cool, then refrigerate for 1 hour before use.

Sprinkle the panch phoran over the chutney and stir to combine. Serve with crisp pappads.

Spiced Poppy-seed Chicken ›
Murgi Posto
SERVES 4

Adapted from *Bangla Ranna: The Bengal Cookbook*, this recipe works just as well with duck.

4 tablespoons mustard oil
1.5 kg chicken thigh fillets,
    cut into 3 cm chunks
4 small red onions, finely sliced
2 tablespoons Ginger Garlic Paste
    (see page 377)
4 dried red chillies
4 small green chillies, ground to a paste
    with a little water
1 tablespoon lime juice
1 teaspoon white sugar
1 teaspoon salt

POPPY-SEED SPICE MIX
1 teaspoon cumin seeds
2 teaspoons coriander seeds
2 cm piece cinnamon stick
seeds from 4 green cardamom pods
2 teaspoons white poppy seeds
5 cloves
1 teaspoon ground turmeric

To prepare the spice mix, put all the ingredients except the turmeric in a frying pan and dry-roast over a very low heat. Cool, then grind to a fine powder and add the turmeric.

Combine half the spice mix with 1 tablespoon of the mustard oil. Rub the spiced oil into the chicken chunks until they are coated. Cover and leave to marinate for 30 minutes.

Heat the remaining oil in a large kadhai or wok and fry the onion until golden. Add the remaining spice mix, the ginger garlic paste, dried chillies and the green chilli paste, stirring to combine. Cook for 3–4 minutes until softened and fragrant. Add the chicken, stirring to coat with the spices. Fry over a medium heat until the chicken is brown and all the liquid has evaporated. Add 1 cup (250 ml) hot water and bring to a boil, then reduce the heat and simmer for 10 minutes until the chicken is tender and the water has been absorbed.

Add the lime juice, sugar and salt and cook for 2 minutes. Taste and adjust the seasoning if necessary.

Prawns & Water Spinach
Kalmi Saag
SERVES 4

I love the simplicity and pure flavours of this recipe from Rakhi Das Gupta.

  500 g water spinach, chopped
  ½ teaspoon salt, plus extra if needed
  1 tablespoon mustard oil
  250 g peeled small uncooked prawns
  ¼ teaspoon nigella seeds
  ¼ teaspoon ground fennel
  2 cloves garlic, crushed

Put the water spinach in a large, wide pan. Sprinkle with the salt, then cover and steam for 2 minutes until wilted and tender. Drain.

Heat the mustard oil in a kadhai or wok and when it starts to smoke, add the prawns. Reduce the heat and toss the pan to cook the prawns evenly. Almost immediately, add the nigella seeds, fennel and garlic, stirring to combine. Add the steamed water spinach and stir to combine. Cook for a minute, then taste for seasoning and adjust if necessary. Serve immediately.

Steamed Vegetables ›
Bati Chorchori
SERVES 4

This dish came about through thriftiness, with cooks using vegetable stems that would normally be thrown away. When I made it with Rakhi, she used cauliflower, potato, eggplant (aubergine), white radish and peas. Other times, she might use okra, pumpkin or bitter gourd, depending on season and availability. You need to cook the vegetables in a pan that holds them snugly, with a small gap at the top and a tight-fitting lid. Traditionally, a brass bowl or bati is used.

  1 teaspoon ground turmeric
  ½ teaspoon chilli powder
  2 teaspoons mustard powder
  1 teaspoon salt
  4 tablespoons mustard oil
  450 g assorted vegetables, cut into 2 cm dice
  2 tablespoons minced onion
  5 small green chillies, split lengthways

Combine the turmeric, chilli powder, mustard powder, salt and mustard oil in a bowl. Add the vegetables, onion and green chillies, tossing to coat with the spiced oil. Leave to marinate for 30 minutes.

Transfer the vegetables and marinade to a large, heavy-based saucepan or flameproof casserole. Cover and cook over a gentle heat for 20 minutes until the vegetables are tender, stirring regularly to prevent sticking. The vegetables will cook in their own juices.

Remove from the heat and serve with Puffed Puri Bread (see page 38) or steamed rice.

Mustard Prawns
Shorshe Chingri
SERVES 4

Rakhi showed me how to prepare this recipe in her kitchen. The flavours are typical of Kolkata, and go equally well with freshly picked crabmeat.

3 tablespoons mustard oil
1 teaspoon nigella seeds
1 small red onion, finely diced
1 tablespoon Ginger Paste (see page 377)
2 teaspoons caster sugar
1 teaspoon ground turmeric
1 teaspoon chilli powder
16 large uncooked prawns,
   peeled and deveined
4 tablespoons grated fresh coconut
1 small green chilli, finely sliced
2 teaspoons salt
1 tablespoon chopped coriander leaves

MUSTARD PASTE
1 tablespoon yellow mustard seeds
1 tablespoon brown mustard seeds
1 small green chilli, minced
½ teaspoon salt

To make the mustard paste, soak the mustard seeds in 4 tablespoons water for 15 minutes to soften, then drain. Blend the mustard seeds to a paste with the chilli and salt.

Heat the mustard oil in a pan until it starts to smoke, then fry the nigella seeds and mustard paste until the seeds start to pop. Add the onion and cook until it is softened and pink. Add the ginger paste, sugar, turmeric and chilli powder and stir to combine. Cook for 1 minute, then add the prawns and toss to coat.

Pour ½ cup (125 ml) water into the bowl used to mix the mustard paste, then pour it over the prawns. Cook for 2 minutes, then add the coconut and stir to combine. Add the green chilli and salt, tossing to combine.

Taste and adjust the seasoning if necessary. Sprinkle the fresh coriander over to serve.

Mango Mustard Pickle
Aam Kasondi
MAKES 2 x 300 g JARS

This was a discovery I made the first time I visited Kolkata, and it is a great condiment to have on hand in the pantry. Rakhi makes it in her kitchen and sells it in small jars at her restaurant; I took one away with me and devoured it in no time. The recipe comes from her mother's *Bangla Ranna: The Bengal Cookbook*. She specifies coarse sea salt (rock salt), not iodised salt, as iodised salt is not a preservative.

1 kg small green mangoes
250 g coarse rock salt
50 g Ginger Paste (see page 377)
1¼ tablespoons chilli powder
150 g brown mustard seeds, ground
50 g tamarind pulp
salt, to taste
1 cup (250 ml) mustard oil

Peel the mangoes and remove and discard the seeds, then cut the flesh into small, even-sized pieces. Mix the mango with the rock salt and place in a large wooden or porcelain bowl. Leave in the sun for a couple of days until the mango pieces are soft.

Lightly squeeze the mango and drain off the juice that will have accumulated in the bottom of the bowl. Add the ginger paste, chilli powder, mustard seed, tamarind and salt and mix thoroughly. Heat the oil in a large frying pan until it starts to smoke. Add the spiced mango and stir to combine. Cook for 1 minute, then remove from the heat and allow to cool. Pour the kasondi into sterilised glass jars and seal. Store in a cool dark place for at least a month before using.

Bengali Sweet Curd
Mishti Doi
SERVES 8

A Bengali favourite, this is often referred to as the sweet curd of Bengal. The locals insist that no introduction to Kolkata is complete without this taste experience. It is an easy-to-prepare sweetened yoghurt that can be garnished with pomegranate seeds, diced mango or fresh pistachios. The ground cardamom can be replaced with ground nutmeg or mace, if you prefer.

    1 kg thick plain yoghurt
    100 ml full-cream milk
    ¼ teaspoon ground cardamom
    100 g shaved jaggery

Line a large sieve with a double layer of muslin (or a clean Chux or J-Cloth) and stand the strainer over a bowl. Tip the yoghurt into the strainer and cover with a cloth, then refrigerate for 5 hours or overnight. During this time the whey will drip from the yoghurt, leaving a thick curd in the strainer.

Heat the milk with the cardamom in a small saucepan over a medium heat until it starts to simmer. Add the jaggery and stir until it has dissolved. Remove from the heat and allow to cool for 5 minutes.

Whisk the sweetened milk into the yoghurt curd. Spoon the mixture into small serving bowls or glasses. Refrigerate for 2 hours until set, then serve.

Darjeeling Custard
SERVES 4

A cream dessert from Darjeeling that uses refined tea leaves to flavour the custard. It can be eaten with fruit, used to fill a sweet tart shell (as it was served to us), or sandwiched between two sponge-cake discs – perfect to serve with an afternoon cup of tea. I like to use either Monsoon or Autumn Harvest Darjeeling tea leaves when making this silky-smooth dessert.

    400 ml cream
    100 ml full-cream milk
    4 tablespoons Darjeeling tea leaves
    8 egg yolks
    100 g caster sugar
    1 tablespoon lemon juice, strained
    5 g gelatine leaves, softened in cold
       water, squeezed

Gently heat the cream and milk together in a saucepan to simmering point. Stir in the tea leaves, then turn off the heat and leave to steep for 5 minutes. Strain through a fine sieve and discard the tea leaves. Reheat the strained cream to boiling point.

Whisk the egg yolks and sugar in a heatproof bowl for 5 minutes until pale and creamy, then add the lemon juice and stir until combined. Pour the hot cream into the egg mixture and whisk to combine. Cook the cream over a pan of simmering water, stirring, until it is the consistency of thick custard. Whisk the gelatine into the custard and stir until dissolved. Remove from the heat and leave to cool, then refrigerate for 2 hours until cold and thick.

Sanjay's Caramel Bananas

SERVES 4

Sanjay, the former estate manager at Glenburn Tea Estate, shared many food stories with me on my first visit. He kindly gave me the recipe for this dessert as a memento, one of his favourite comfort dishes that is often cooked in the estate's kitchen.

  8 small bananas, peeled and
    cut in half lengthways
  200 g caster sugar
  40 g butter
  2 cm piece ginger, finely sliced
    into matchsticks
  1 teaspoon ground cinnamon
  3 tablespoons dark rum or cognac
  100 ml cream

Roll the bananas in 2 tablespoons of the sugar to lightly coat. Heat the butter in a frying pan and fry the sugar-coated bananas briefly until the sugar caramelises. Turn off the heat.

Heat the remaining sugar in a saucepan with 2 tablespoons water and cook over a high heat until it is a caramel colour. Add the ginger and cinnamon and toss the pan to combine – do not stir as this will cause the caramel to crystallise. Add the rum or cognac and cream and simmer for a few minutes until the sauce is smooth.

Pour the sauce over the bananas in the frying pan and toss gently to coat with the sauce. Serve warm.

Curd-cheese Balls in Rose Syrup ›

Rasagullas

MAKES 8

One of the definitive Bengali sweets and a popular dessert in Kolkata, these are given as gifts for birthdays and wedding anniversaries.

  120 g curd cheese (fresh goat's curd,
    ricotta or quark)
  60 g coarse semolina
  1 teaspoon baking powder
  8 whole blanched almonds
  85 g caster sugar
  1 teaspoon rosewater

Mix the curd cheese with the semolina and baking powder. Knead into a soft dough and roll into 8 small balls. Push an almond into the centre of each ball and close over.

Heat 260 ml water and the sugar in a saucepan and boil for 10 minutes to make a light syrup or until the mixture is pale golden. Pour one-third of the syrup into a heatproof container and add the rosewater. Set aside and allow to cool.

Keep the remaining syrup simmering over a low heat. Gently add the curd balls to the syrup and poach for 15 minutes, turning with a slotted spoon so they cook evenly. They will expand as they cook. Remove the rasagullas from the syrup with a slotted spoon and place in serving dishes. Spoon the cooled rose syrup over the top and serve.

THE INDIAN HIMALAYA

Mountain Villages, Trekking & Temples

The first sight of the Himalayan peaks towering over the plains, range
after purple range, was exhilarating enough. But as the procession of
cars started up those hairpin bends, as the air got cooler, as we saw the
first pines, the first ferns, the first waterfalls and gushing mountain
streams, as we climbed to six, seven, then eight thousand feet above
sea level, as the first mist licked our cars, each one of us, separately
and together, felt that this was our paradise.

MADHUR JAFFREY, *CLIMBING THE MANGO TREES*

The Himalayan mountains are a totally absorbing and mesmerising experience. The almighty presence and power of the youngest of the world's mountain ranges draws you in from every vantage point. Straddling the borders of Pakistan, China and Nepal, the Indian Himalaya is split by state boundaries. In the east, to the north of the Indian state of West Bengal, and sandwiched between Bhutan and Nepal, sits the tiny state of Sikkim. West of Nepal, the state of Uttarakhand holds the Kumaon and Garhwal mountains. The Himalayan range strides on through Himachal Pradesh, which includes the heavily touristed districts of Simla, the Kullu Valley and Manali. North of here lies Ladakh, tucked away in the easternmost corner of Jammu and Kashmir, the fiercely contested jewel of India's northernmost region, which has been repeatedly scarred by political dispute with neighbouring Pakistan.

The Indian Himalaya offers an immense challenge and an unrivalled sense of achievement to those who are adventurous enough to discover its hidden secrets and beauty. The variety of landscapes in the mountains is spectacular, ranging from swathes of lush vegetation teeming with life to bleak, barren and treacherous facades, and dazzling snow-capped peaks and glaciers. The life of northern India comes from the mountains and the water that flows from them, so pilgrimages to the mountains are considered sacred: this is where the ancient sages came to meditate, and it's where monks and holy men still come to find higher understanding and enlightenment. I travel to these remote parts under the assured guidance of my friend Jamshyd Sethna, a visionary whose company Shakti Himalaya combines responsible tourism with a strong sense of community.

SIKKIM

Just north of Darjeeling, sandwiched between Nepal and Bhutan, lies the Indian state of Sikkim. Fed by over a hundred rivers and hot springs, this tiny state bears testament to the generosity of the Himalayas, for it boasts some of the subcontinent's most exotic flora and fauna. Adjoining Tibet to the north, Sikkim is also rich in Buddhist culture; having maintained its independence as a Buddhist kingdom for many centuries, it abounds in ancient monasteries to be explored. Despite its remoteness, Sikkim's location on the primary trade route between Burma, Tibet, Bhutan and

Nepal has always lent it great strategic and economic importance. Unrest in the mid-1970s led to Sikkim becoming a state of India in 1975, but it remains a highly sensitive area today and a special permit is required when entering.

It's about a five-hour drive from Darjeeling to Yangsum, a small village near Rinchenpong in western Sikkim that is the chosen start for our trekking journey. Staying at the three village houses spruced up by Shakti Himalaya, each one showcasing a different Sikkimese community: we walk between each village house, starting at Sandyang Lee then Hee and Radhu Kandu in the Cardamom Hills. Himalayan cuisine combines the traditions of several indigenous cultures, which means that rice, corn, lentils, wheat, vegetables and meat are staples. A basic everyday meal consists of the holy trinity – steamed rice, dal and a vegetable dish – while a typical full-course dinner might include an appetiser, a vegetable or lentil soup, two vegetable or meat curries, an *achar* or chutney, roti (wheat flatbread) and steamed rice or rice pilaf, all washed down with *mahai* (a diluted version of lassi) or beer, and finishing with a simple dessert and tea. Staples like *shafta* (smoked dried beef) are sometimes cooked with spinach or radish, other times with onion, tomato and chilli.

As dawn breaks, the tips of the mountains are bathed in a radiant pink light, and the sound of monks chanting in a nearby monastery drifts through the still air. Watching as eggs are cooked in a banana-leaf cup over hot coals for breakfast reminds me of childhood days as a Girl Guide camping in the bush. Later, at the colourful markets, we feast our eyes on an array of mountain produce: fiddlehead ferns, eggplants, onions, potatoes, choko, squash and marrows, plus tender pumpkin stalks and leaves ready for stir-frying. At a food stall, I taste *chow chow*, a soupy dish of stir-fried noodles and shafta strips spiced with turmeric and dried chilli, cooked with onion, tomato, fresh chilli and salt. The flavours are simple and subtle.

Our days are spent walking through unspoilt villages and serene monasteries against a backdrop of the multiple white peaks of Kanchenjunga, the same mountain we glimpsed from Glenburn Tea Estate near Darjeeling. Following the course of the Rangeet River, far down in the valley below, we are spoilt with panoramic views of the entire valley and the newly constructed Gurung Monastery. In this verdant part of western Sikkim, the lush valleys of the foothills, where thousands of orchid species thrive, are interspersed with forests of towering rhododendrons. Apparently, northern Sikkim is a complete contrast, becoming more barren, dusty and dry as it joins the Tibetan plateau.

UTTARAKHAND – KUMAON VILLAGES

The mountain state of Uttarakhand is broadly divided into two distinct regions. The western half, Garhwal is a pilgrimage destination that contains the ashram town of Rishikesh, from where routes ascend to the mountain temples and the source of the Ganges. To the east is the little-known Kumaon region, which encompasses some of the most stunning mountain scenery anywhere, from the perennially snow-capped summits of the Great Himalaya range in the north to the hill stations of Almora and Nainital in the foothills and Binsar Sanctuary.

The journey to Kumaon cannot be hurried. We catch the early morning train from Delhi, arriving in Kathgodam six or so hours later. The Shakti team pick us up in time for lunch at a local restaurant. We drive for three hours around corkscrew roads leading into the mountains to Jwalbanj, the first village house we stay at, overlooking an expansive valley of virgin forest with no other houses in sight. We sip tea as we sit on the terrace, watching the sun go down over the distant hills. It is a slice of nirvana. The breakfast table is laid with bowls of house-made muesli, fresh fruit, flaky parathas, herb omelettes and pots of steaming tea, all of which we devour while sitting in the pretty garden. On our first visit, our guide Salil led the hikes through herb-filled meadows, past tumbling streams and waterfalls, and through terraced fields tilled by local farmers, who eke out a modest living in this harsh environment. Dotted among the terraced gardens and fenced paddocks are long barns that are built of grey stone and cling low to the ground, providing shelter for people and animals alike. We walked to Chittai temple, which is famous for its statue of Golu Devta, god of justice and peculiar to the Kumaon region – the temple is hung with petitions and bells of all shapes and sizes, brought by grateful devotees. The path continues through forests of cedar and pine, blanketing the foothills and providing a carpet of pine needles under our feet.

As we meander through this bucolic landscape, we notice that, like everywhere, the women seem to be working the fields while the men hang out at the tea shops! The village women's saris are a flash of vivid colour as they go about their daily tasks – just as they have done for centuries. Shy at first, the children soon break into smiles as they run towards us. As night falls, we gather around the fire pit and enjoy a delicious, home-cooked rustic dinner under the stars. It's a lengthy walk to Panchachuli to visit a thriving Women Weavers Cooperative, where more than a thousand women weave pashmina scarves and shawls, a flourishing social enterprise and the ideal place to buy a few shawls and pashminas. I find a purity of spirit in these mountain people that is charming, refreshing and endearing. Their simple way of life and ready smiles stay with me long after we leave.

LETI AND BEYOND

Back on the road, we drive higher up into the mountains for another five hours, passing through Kalmatia, a mountain town nestled in the heart of the Kumaon hills, then through Bageshwar, the last big town on our drive. The higher we go, the more the traffic dissipates, and the road has certainly improved since my first visit. The Nanda Devi range dominates the horizon. Our final destination in the Kumaon is 360° Leti, a luxury lodge perched on a stunning mountain spur close to where Nepal, Tibet and India meet, with expansive views of the Great Himalayan Range. I blink at the sight, trying to comprehend its enormity. A lone eagle soars overhead, its expansive wing span in full view as it surveys the ground for unsuspecting prey. Small birds and butterflies flutter about, we pass women in rainbow-coloured saris carrying enormous bundles of wood on their heads, making it look so effortless.

Here we are, on top of the world, staying in one of the four stunning modern pavilions that meld into the landscape, a true eco-lodge, the elements of which are reflected in the construction materials of local slate and stone. One wall is an expansive glass window that looks straight out onto glistening white mountains and glaciers that seem close enough to touch. Nothing interrupts those spectacular views.

Each morning we indulge in the ritual of bed tea: a tray laid with a pot of tea, cup and saucer and a plate of small biscuits, hot scones or feather-light honey madeleines is brought to our room first thing. It's like a pre-breakfast, a private, cosy extravagance enjoyed while still languishing in bed and waking up slowly. Ardent hikers, on the other hand, will want to make a dawn start to head further up the mountain, through tiny villages full of inquisitive, yet shy faces, in order to reach a vantage point high enough to see across the tops of the range towards the five peaks of Panchachuli, with its perfect pyramid shape. Bhim was our guide on the most recent visit and we opt for more gentle hikes each day, through oak forests passing through streams and up to the Shiva Shrine, perched atop a hill with magnificent views of the Ramganga Valley below, and Heeramani Glacier and Nanda Kot above. Another day, we walk downhill from the campsite to a small plateau in the middle of the valley. We head to Capri village, sit with school kids doing their lessons in the open air and interact with families in the local community – a humbling experience. On our walks we have impromptu picnic lunches in the most divine locations, in a forest clearing with magical views, and sitting on huge rocks in front of a waterfall on the trail beyond Gogina village, not a road in sight.

Back at Leti, the kitchen is the hub of the main living pavilion – rustic and simple in design and perfectly organised. It's astonishing what gets prepared in that room by Yeshi, the chief house cook. Yeshi and I cook together each day, swapping tips and recipes and bonding over life stories that revolve around a love of food. A primitive wood-fired oven sits out in the shed behind the kitchen and works a treat – Yeshi bakes batches of bread, biscuits and cakes every day; he is a magician and emanates the

very heart and soul of the place. Different dishes are served for each meal every day and his fine-tuned sensibility shines in every mouthful, whether it's stuffed paratha or poha for breakfast, kawswe or inventive vegetable salads for lunch, or mild korma curry or biriyani for dinner. The food is the essence of the mountains. The garden produces many of the vegetables and all the herbs that play a starring role in the daily menus. Chickens and goats are killed as required in the nearest village. Yeshi teaches me how to make samosas (see page 66) and Kumaoni curd-based curries, only too happy to share his vast knowledge. Return visits are greeted with open arms and warm cuddles, like a homecoming.

With no electricity, candles and lamps are lit at night, and solar panels supply hot water. The wooden slats in the bathroom floor are laid on top of river stones so the water drains away naturally. A wood-burning slow-combustion stove in each room gets fired up as we have dinner so that when we return to sleep, it is inviting and toasty warm. The canopy of stars in the velvety-black night sky is extraordinary, unlike any I have ever seen. Silent moments are spent lying on yoga mats on dewy grass, wrapped in a rug and gazing upwards, trying to locate familiar constellations.

After several days, having settled very nicely into our mountain digs, cooking up a storm and never wanting to leave, the inevitable day arrives. Down we go, reluctantly retracing our steps and descending the mountain to stay at Kana, another delightful Shakti village house, to break our long road journey back to Kathgodam.

I still marvel at the sheer determination and brilliance of establishing a luxury tourism venture in a place that is so remote. It takes a visionary like Jamshyd to make this happen and for it to deliver on every level and exceed expectation. Therein lies the essence of the journey, a lesson learnt.

LADAKH

We have come to Ladakh – the land of high passes – specifically to gain an insight into Buddhist culture and how it fits into the Indian context. Often referred to as 'Little Tibet', Ladakh shares the geography and culture of Tibet, but its remoteness and political status as part of India meant it was spared the ravages of the Chinese Cultural Revolution. As a result, it is a stronghold of Tibetan Buddhism, and the spirituality everywhere is palpable. Buddhist gompas (monasteries) dominate the landscape, prayer flags flutter in the breeze and prayer wheels are everywhere – even in the centre of the road, where they must be driven around clockwise.

Situated in the far north of the subcontinent, Ladakh shares borders with Pakistan and China, making it a highly sensitive area with a strong military presence. We take the one-hour flight from Delhi to Ladakh's capital, Leh, which sits at an altitude of 3500 metres. I feel as if I have reached the top of the world. Completely remote, magical and surprisingly diverse in its geography, this fascinating corner of the world has drawn rulers, pilgrims, traders and travellers to its captivating heart for centuries.

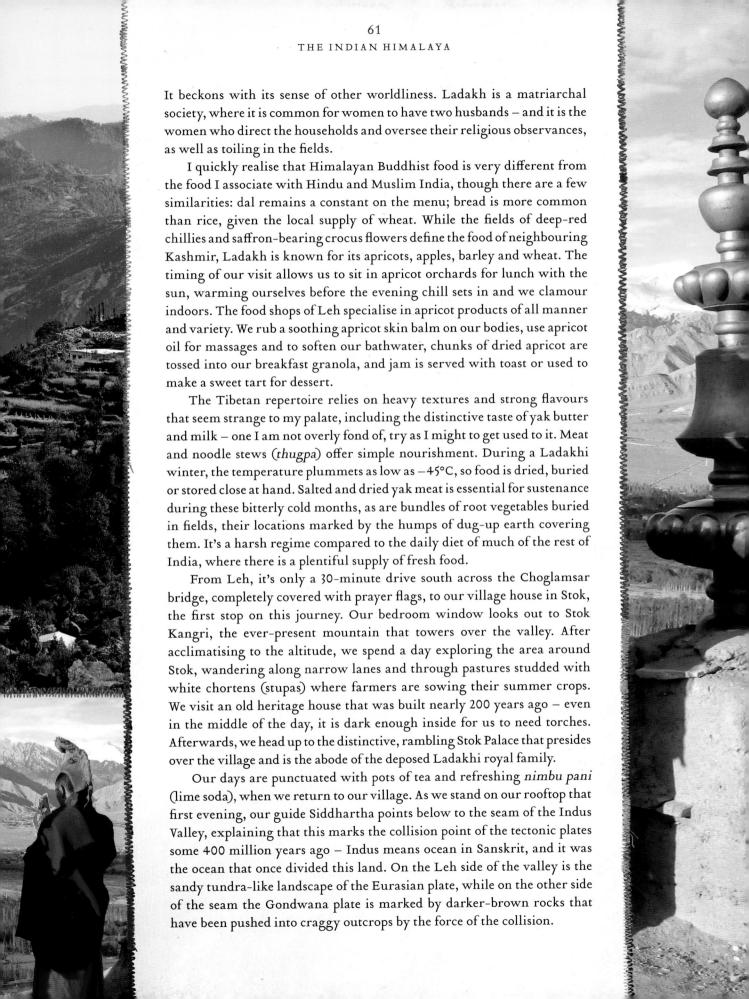

It beckons with its sense of other worldliness. Ladakh is a matriarchal society, where it is common for women to have two husbands – and it is the women who direct the households and oversee their religious observances, as well as toiling in the fields.

I quickly realise that Himalayan Buddhist food is very different from the food I associate with Hindu and Muslim India, though there are a few similarities: dal remains a constant on the menu; bread is more common than rice, given the local supply of wheat. While the fields of deep-red chillies and saffron-bearing crocus flowers define the food of neighbouring Kashmir, Ladakh is known for its apricots, apples, barley and wheat. The timing of our visit allows us to sit in apricot orchards for lunch with the sun, warming ourselves before the evening chill sets in and we clamour indoors. The food shops of Leh specialise in apricot products of all manner and variety. We rub a soothing apricot skin balm on our bodies, use apricot oil for massages and to soften our bathwater, chunks of dried apricot are tossed into our breakfast granola, and jam is served with toast or used to make a sweet tart for dessert.

The Tibetan repertoire relies on heavy textures and strong flavours that seem strange to my palate, including the distinctive taste of yak butter and milk – one I am not overly fond of, try as I might to get used to it. Meat and noodle stews (*thugpa*) offer simple nourishment. During a Ladakhi winter, the temperature plummets as low as −45°C, so food is dried, buried or stored close at hand. Salted and dried yak meat is essential for sustenance during these bitterly cold months, as are bundles of root vegetables buried in fields, their locations marked by the humps of dug-up earth covering them. It's a harsh regime compared to the daily diet of much of the rest of India, where there is a plentiful supply of fresh food.

From Leh, it's only a 30-minute drive south across the Choglamsar bridge, completely covered with prayer flags, to our village house in Stok, the first stop on this journey. Our bedroom window looks out to Stok Kangri, the ever-present mountain that towers over the valley. After acclimatising to the altitude, we spend a day exploring the area around Stok, wandering along narrow lanes and through pastures studded with white chortens (stupas) where farmers are sowing their summer crops. We visit an old heritage house that was built nearly 200 years ago – even in the middle of the day, it is dark enough inside for us to need torches. Afterwards, we head up to the distinctive, rambling Stok Palace that presides over the village and is the abode of the deposed Ladakhi royal family.

Our days are punctuated with pots of tea and refreshing *nimbu pani* (lime soda), when we return to our village. As we stand on our rooftop that first evening, our guide Siddhartha points below to the seam of the Indus Valley, explaining that this marks the collision point of the tectonic plates some 400 million years ago – Indus means ocean in Sanskrit, and it was the ocean that once divided this land. On the Leh side of the valley is the sandy tundra-like landscape of the Eurasian plate, while on the other side of the seam the Gondwana plate is marked by darker-brown rocks that have been pushed into craggy outcrops by the force of the collision.

EAST OF LEH
Monasteries & Lakes

The next day, we rise before dawn to visit Thiksey Monastery, often referred to as Little Potala (after Lhasa's iconic monastery), and witness the start of another day for the 400 monks who call this home. Ranging in age from four to very old, the monks belong to the Geluk order, or Yellow Hat sect, which is associated with the Dalai Lama. As they perform their morning prayer rituals, the playful younger monks jump up to pour butter tea from enormous tin teapots and spoon *tsampa* from large tin buckets. Together, this rich savoury tea and barley meal form the basis of their diet: the barley flour is rolled into balls with the tea, softening its texture and rendering it palatable.

We stop nearby at the ancient capital of Shey for a picnic breakfast by the river, where Shakti's River House now stands. Lounging on cushions set under the apricot trees, we work our way through house-made granola, yoghurt and fruit, boiled eggs and toast, with a pot of Darjeeling tea. Bliss! Suitably fortified, we climb the steep steps to Shey Monastery to see its copper-plated Buddha statue, then head further uphill to the crumbling facade of the semi-derelict palace and across a stretch of sandy desert to a plain crowded with chortens, the only vestiges of this former capital of the Ladakhi kingdom.

Afterwards we drive south along the opposite bank of the Indus River to Hemis Monastery, home to the Drugpa or Red Hat sect and renowned for its festival, which honours Padmasambhava (Guru Rinpoche). Once every 12 years, the monastery's spectacular thangka (a religious artwork mounted on scrolls) depicting Padmasambhava is unfurled in the main courtyard. Other highlights of the festival include a colourful fair held in the grounds, and performances by masked dancers to the sound of cymbals, traditional drums and horns as part of a tantric ritual.

With permits in hand (for this is still a restricted military zone), we devote an entire day to driving to Ladakh's far east, in order to reach the vast Pangong Tso saltwater lake, most of which lies on the Tibetan side of the border. To get there, we drive through the world's third-highest mountain pass, Changla, on a road carved out between massive walls of compacted snow that rise high above us. At an altitude of 5460 metres, the air is thin, making our breathing laboured at times, and movement is hard to sustain. Not that this stops us from briefly skipping about in the snow and throwing snowballs at each other! As the road takes us higher into the mountains, we look down onto an idyllic valley, where the sparsely beautiful Chemrey Monastery clings like a bird's nest to a hill on the opposite side. A patchwork of colours and textures, this valley was once the trade route that linked China with Europe. Along the way, we pass yak herders and nomads, herds of donkeys and wild antelopes, and we stop to

photograph golden-brown marmots as they scamper over rocks. This is also snow leopard territory, but their elusive nature keeps them hidden from our view.

After five hours on the road, the lake appears ahead of us and we set up a picnic lunch on its shores. Saltwater waves lap the shore, where salt crystals have caked (the source of Himalayan salt) and flocks of large white seagulls hover overhead. With cushions laid out on the shingle beach and folding tables set with salads of lettuce, walnuts, beetroot, couscous and pomegranate, baked tomato and onion tarts, our picnic in the sky is our highest picnic point ever, at 4400 metres – a record I don't think is likely to be broken anytime soon. A surreal element to the whole scene comes courtesy of Bollywood. Since the release of Bollywood's biggest blockbuster Three Idiots, which was shot on location at the lake, carloads of Indians flock here daily to stand and have their photos taken in the same spot as their on-screen heroes – the power of Bollywood should never be underestimated!

WEST OF LEH
Buddhist Art & Rafting

Heading west from Leh, it's a 40-minute drive to Nimoo, our base for exploring this part of Ladakh. An entirely different vista awaits us here, eclipsing the last. We overlook the confluence of two mighty rivers, the jade-coloured Indus and the brown Zanskar. The snow-capped mountains are there, but somehow seem more distant. Further west and across the Indus River, amid a patchwork of fields, the unassuming temple complex at Alchi houses some of the most important Ladakhi and Tibetan Buddhist artworks in the world. Representing aspects of enlightenment, the wall murals, friezes, paintings and statues are extraordinarily well preserved, making this one of the most significant collections of sacred art in Asia.

At Nimoo, Yeshi's hand is evident as he trained the cooks in each of the village houses. We are spoilt with fresh and simple flavours perfect for our mountain retreat, the adherence to minimal spicing and reliance on green chilli and ginger for gentle heat soothing the palate. Vegetables dominate, with meat (usually mutton or chicken) used sparingly. One afternoon I join Divyaraj and Tikka, the two resident cooks in the Nimoo house kitchen, and together we prepare a feast of vegetable dishes for dinner, using cauliflower, potatoes, spinach, pumpkin, carrots, oranges, tomatoes, eggplants, coriander and mint bought from the vegetable markets in Leh. The cooks make an intriguing dessert, a bright-red jelly made with rhododendron juice and studded with pomegranate seeds.

A couple of days later, we find ourselves whitewater rafting down the relatively gentle rapids of the Zanskar in a rubber inflatable, with the bare stony cliffs looming high above, forming a deep canyon above our heads. To reach the start of this river journey, we drive around hairpin bends and along narrow, cliff-hanging roads to Chilling, a tiny hamlet tucked

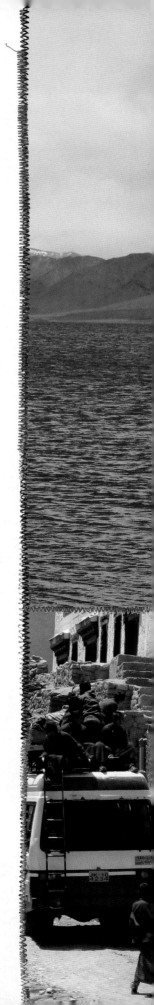

deep within the Zanskar River gorge, and renowned for its traditional silver and copper work. We picnic in one of the grassy fields under willow trees and are invited into a house to watch as an old woman prepares *sque* – little chunks of dough cooked in a large copper pot of boiling stock until softened, then flavoured with strips of yak meat.

Little did I realise when I arrived that my time in Ladakh would turn out to be one of the most beguiling and exhilarating travel experiences of my life. I leave awe-struck by its dramatic landscapes, its high-altitude desert, its dazzling snow-capped mountains and glinting deep-turquoise saltwater lakes. My heart soars with the experience of being in that extraordinary landscape; in the thin, clear, beautiful air.

KASHMIR

This mountain state is divided into the three valleys of Kashmir, Jammu and Ladakh – each separated by the peaks of the Himalayas and culturally distinct. While Ladakh is the epitome of a Buddhist way of life, its food reflected by its extreme climate and remoteness, Kashmir is renowned for its *Wazawan* celebratory feasts, whether they be Kashmiri Muslim or Pandit (Hindu Brahmin), influenced by its rich Persian and Afghan ancestry while Jammu is defined by its *Dogra* Hindu food with its typical north Indian flavours, their staple food consisting of rice, wheat, and pulses. This is what intrigues me and brings me to this part of the world.

The Mughals gave Kashmir the name of Paradise on Earth, a magical wonderland enclosed on all sides by the snow-capped Himalayas. They established Srinagar's many formal pleasure gardens with great love and care, now collectively known as the Mughal Gardens – Pari Mahal, Shalimar and Nishat. They also patronised the development of art and craft among the people of Kashmir, leaving a heritage of exquisite artisanship, while the British legacy left behind the thousands of wooden houseboats on Dal Lake and political disunity.

I have long been smitten with the mysterious allure, compelling beauty, turbulent history, fertile valleys and alpine grasslands of Kashmir. Its food culture is unique and sets it apart from the rest of India. It was once peacefully shared between Muslim and Pandit (Hindu) communities but most Pandits now live in exile since Partition. Both communities have a love of meat and it features prominently in both diets. The details of how they cook and the spices they use for the same dish are different, and it's these subtleties that I am keen to explore. I've come to taste these intriguing regional flavours first hand. It is the depth of winter, snowbound but exhilarating nonetheless, a magical landscape. We huddle around an indoor wood fire for a hearty breakfast. The cook works from a large pot set over a fire pit, in which lamb and its fat has been slowly cooked overnight with rice, herbs, spices and saffron to a thick porridge consistency. This rich and unctuous *harisa* is ladled into small bowls, slathered with hot ghee and served with *chout* – a dense flatbread.

Returning in spring, when the tulip gardens are ablaze with colour and the lakes defrost, gave an entirely different perspective. I think this is the ideal time to visit. Summer weather is glorious but it's peak tourist season. We wander along the path by Jehlum River through the old town to see the crumbling riverfront palaces and early wooden architecture, losing ourselves as we meander through the laneways, seeing the artisans applying tin coating to copper plates in the copper bazaar, watching local bakeries making the morning bread *chout* (like a thick roti) then *chuhworo*, the afternoon bread – small rounds with a hole in the centre, baked with either sesame seeds or *khus khus* (white poppy seeds) on the crust. Exploring bazaars around the beautiful white Hazratbal Mosque, we taste myriad fried snacks like samosa, *pakora* (especially the ones made with lotus stem) and *mutthi* (bread slices fried in ghee or oil). The vendors are selling saffron, fresh morel mushrooms and tiny lotus root, ingredients that define the food of Kashmir.

We escape Srinagar to explore some of the region, driving to the mountains of Gulmarg where there is year-round skiing, gliding past orchards where there is an abundance of crops, including walnuts, apricots, almonds, apples and the prized Kashmiri chillies. In Gulmarg, we are treated to a wazawan feast by chef Manish at Cloves, the restaurant in the Kyber Hotel. Served on a copper tarami (thali) plate, the waiters quickly fill it with *tabakmazz* (sheesh kebabs), *gushtaba* (lamb dumplings in yoghurt gravy), *murgh kanti* (grilled chicken chunks with red onion, sweet peppers and Kashmiri chilli), crispy fried slices of lotus stem tossed in an aromatic spice mix and served with a walnut and radish chutney, *rajhma* (red kidney beans simmered in a tomato cardamom gravy), *haaq saag* (Indian spinach cooked with tempered whole chillies), and a delicate apple and cashew rice pulao.

Taking a shikhara across the lake is an essential experience in Srinagar. One sunrise, we visit the dawn floating markets on Dal Lake. Very little money changes hands but lots of swapping of produce. A boat vendor glides up to us and stops to sell us tea – *kehwa*, a Kashmiri green tea flavoured with saffron, almond and cardamom. We head back to Sukoon, our glamorous houseboat on Dal Lake for breakfast. A sensitively restored floating residence moored in a prime location, it affords the best views across the lake. In summer, we lounge on the rooftop deck and take in the breathtaking vistas of the snow-capped mountains and the unhurried serenity of the lake – sunrise and sunset are equally spectacular.

One evening, we are invited for dinner by the Riyas family. Our host Shakila has prepared the most extravagant feast at her home, Cottage Nigeen, which she has turned into a bed and breakfast to extend the Kashmiri hospitality of which she is so proud. Her chicken kebabs, Rogan Josh and *haaq munji* (spinach and kohlrabi simmered in a light onion broth with fenugreek seeds and garlic) are to die for. We leave with another cherished food memory from the mountains and a deeper appreciation of the diversity of the food cultures right across the Himalaya.

Yeshi's Samosas with Tamarind Chutney

SERVES 8

Yeshi showed me how to make these pastries one afternoon in the kitchen at 360° Leti. This Indian staple made a welcome snack most afternoons.

500 g plain flour
1 teaspoon bicarbonate of soda
½ teaspoon salt
1 teaspoon melted ghee, cooled
½ teaspoon ajwain
vegetable oil, for deep-frying

POTATO STUFFING
2 cups (440 g) mashed potato, cooled
1 teaspoon minced ginger
1 clove garlic, minced
2 small green chillies, minced
1 tablespoon chopped coriander leaves
1 tablespoon roasted peanuts, chopped
1 teaspoon salt
1 tablespoon melted ghee

TAMARIND CHUTNEY
100 ml Tamarind Liquid (see page 379)
2 teaspoons brown sugar
pinch of salt
½ teaspoon chilli powder

To make the tamarind chutney, cook the tamarind liquid and sugar together over a medium heat until reduced and thickened – about 10 minutes. Add the salt and chilli powder, stirring to combine. Taste and adjust the ingredients if necessary so each of the flavours is in balance. Set aside until ready to serve.

Combine the flour, bicarbonate of soda, salt, ghee and ajwain in a large bowl. Pour in 1 cup (250 ml) warm water and knead until the dough comes together. Turn out onto a floured surface and knead for 5 minutes, then return the dough to the bowl, cover with a clean cloth and leave to rest for 1 hour.

To make the potato stuffing, combine all the ingredients in a bowl.

To assemble the samosas, break off 1 tablespoon dough and roll it into a thin, flat, elongated shape on a floured surface. Cut it in half crossways. Rub a little water along the edges, then press together to make a triangular pocket like a cone. Hold it in your hand and fill with potato stuffing until three-quarters full. Wet the top edge, then fold over the flap and press together. Repeat until all the dough

and stuffing have been used. Stand the pastries on a plate in a single layer and refrigerate for 1 hour to become firm.

Heat the oil in a kadhai or wok (or deep saucepan) to 160°C (no hotter, or the pastries will burn). To test the temperature of the oil, sprinkle in some flour – if the flour sizzles, it is ready. Fry the samosas a few at a time for 4–5 minutes until crisp and golden. Remove from the oil with a slotted spoon and drain on paper towel.

Serve hot with tamarind chutney.

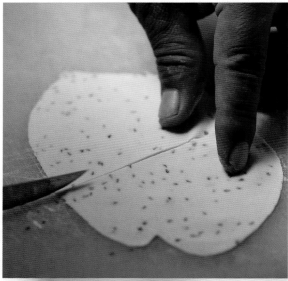

‹ Spicy Scrambled Eggs with Tomato
Akoori
SERVES 4

Just one of the many breakfast egg dishes in Jamshyd's Parsi repertoire and a favourite in the Shakti kitchen, providing perfect fuel for the brisk mountain walks that lay ahead of us each day.

40 g butter
1 small red onion, finely diced
1 teaspoon ground turmeric
3 cloves garlic, minced
3 tomatoes, finely diced
2 small green chillies, minced
1 tablespoon chopped coriander leaves
8 eggs, beaten
salt

Heat a frying pan and melt the butter, then fry the onion until it starts to brown. Add the turmeric and stir to combine, cooking for a few minutes until the onion is brown. Add the garlic and stir, then add the tomato and chilli and stir to combine. Cook until softened, then add the fresh coriander.

Remove from the heat and allow to cool for about 10 minutes so the mixture is not too hot when the egg is added. Return the pan to a low heat and add the egg, stirring gently to scramble. Season with salt, then taste and adjust the seasoning if necessary. Serve immediately.

‹ Breakfast Potato Parathas
SERVES 6

Yeshi, the chef at 360° Leti, is of Tibetan heritage. Born in Assam in north-east India (near the Chinese border), his family now lives in the Tibetan community near Coorg in Karnataka. When 360° Leti is closed for the winter season, he heads across to Ladakh to cook at the Shakti village houses there. We devoured plates of these breads each morning, the mountain air somehow making them even more irresistible, and it was wonderful to see them still on the menu during a recent visit.

250 g wholemeal flour
250 g plain flour
salt
1 cup (220 g) mashed potato, cooled
2 small green chillies, minced
1 tablespoon chopped coriander leaves
2 green onions, finely sliced
vegetable oil, for frying

Put the flours in a bowl with a pinch of salt and add enough warm water to make a dough. The dough needs to be soft, elastic and slightly sticky – this is determined by the amount of water, so it's a 'feel' thing.

Combine the mashed potato, chilli, coriander, green onion and 1 teaspoon salt.

Break off a piece of dough and flatten it on a floured surface using a rolling pin. Spread some potato stuffing across the centre, then fold the dough in half to enclose the stuffing. Roll it out again to make a round, saucer-sized shape. Repeat the process until all the dough has been used, stacking the parathas on top of each other as you go and sprinkling a little flour between so they don't stick.

Heat a tawa or frying pan and sprinkle with a little oil to prevent sticking. Fry each paratha until brown on one side, then flip over and cook the other side until brown. Continue until all the parathas have been cooked, stacking them on top of each other as you go.

Red Rice & Quinoa with Dried Apricots

SERVES 4

The local Himalayan red rice (patni) is a staple mountain food, specific to the Kumaon region and Bhutan in particular, that is often cooked and served with curries or hot meat dishes. It has a nutty, earthy flavour and takes longer to cook than white rice. Quinoa is harvested around the Almora region and is a great source of energy. This dish was another addition to our picnic hamper on one of our daily walks. If quinoa is not available, use pearl barley instead.

> 200 g red quinoa
> 200 g Himalayan red rice, washed and rinsed
> 150 ml olive or vegetable oil
> 1 white onion, sliced
> grated zest and juice of 1 orange
> 1 tablespoon lemon juice
> 1 clove garlic, crushed
> 4 green onions, finely sliced
> 100 g dried apricots, roughly chopped
> 40 g rocket
> salt
> freshly ground black pepper

Fill two saucepans with salted water and bring to a boil. Simmer the quinoa in one saucepan for 15 minutes and the rice in the other pan for 25 minutes.

Meanwhile, heat half the oil in a frying pan and fry the onion for 15 minutes, stirring occasionally, until golden brown. Leave to cool completely.

When cooked, both the rice and the quinoa should be tender but al dente. Drain the grains and spread them out separately on flat trays to cool.

In a large bowl, combine the rice and quinoa with the onion and toss through the remaining oil. Add the remaining ingredients, stirring to combine, then taste and adjust the seasoning if necessary. Serve at room temperature.

Fing Salad ›

SERVES 4

Yeshi prepared this deliciously light salad for us when we arrived at the Stok village house in Ladakh. Its clean fresh flavours and light texture were a perfect welcome and typical of Yeshi's Buddhist food philosophy, showing sensitivity to our needs as we acclimatised to the altitude. The noodles used in the recipe are soybean vermicelli – they look similar to glass noodles but have a softer texture, and are unique to this region. I would substitute either glass noodles or soft wheat-based somen noodles to get a similar texture (cook them beforehand). The green chillies local to the mountains are called sabin: about 4 cm in length and narrow, with a medium heat, they can be found at Indian or Asian grocers.

> 1 tablespoon vegetable oil
> 1 red onion, finely sliced
> 2 green chillies, finely sliced
> 3 small cloves garlic, finely sliced
> 60 g dried soybean vermicelli, soaked in warm water for 30 minutes to soften
> 1 carrot, peeled and finely shredded
> ½ green capsicum (pepper), finely sliced
> 80 g fresh or frozen peas, cooked
> 2 teaspoons light soy sauce
> 2 teaspoons lemon juice

Heat the oil in a frying pan or wok over a medium heat. Add the onion, chilli and garlic and fry gently for 2 minutes until softened. Add the noodles, carrot, capsicum and peas and toss to combine. Simmer for 2 minutes, then season with the soy sauce and lemon juice. Remove from the heat and let stand for 10 minutes. Serve at room temperature.

Potato Patties
Aloo Tikka
SERVES 6

We sampled these fried potato patties from a street vendor in Leh one afternoon. Cooked to order in a kadhai of hot oil, they were the perfect warming snack to eat as the sun began to disappear over the horizon. The potato mixture was made in vast quantities and stored in a large pot, then rolled and portioned by hand before being slipped into the hot oil. An order gave us three patties wrapped in paper with a dollop of mint chutney as a garnish. Total YUM! This Kashmiri garam masala, which is used more extensively in the Muslim cooking of the region, can also be used to season grilled and roasted meats.

vegetable oil, for frying
200 g moong dal, soaked for 30 minutes, then drained
1 small green chilli, minced
2 teaspoons ground turmeric
1 teaspoon Kashmiri chilli powder
3 teaspoons salt
1 teaspoon amchur
1 kg potatoes, peeled, boiled and mashed

KASHMIRI GARAM MASALA
3 teaspoons black cumin seeds
seeds from 2 black cardamom pods
2 teaspoons whole cloves
3 teaspoons black peppercorns
1 stick cinnamon, broken
5 mace blades, broken
1 whole nutmeg

To make the Kashmiri garam masala, dry-roast all the ingredients, except the nutmeg, separately over the lowest flame possible, until fragrant. Cool completely. Combine the roasted spices and blend to a fine powder using a spice grinder. Grate the nutmeg and add to the spice mix. Store in an airtight container and use as required.

Heat 3 tablespoons oil in a frying pan and add the moong dal, chilli, turmeric, chilli powder and 2 teaspoons Kashmiri garam masala. Fry for about 1 minute until fragrant. Add 1 cup (250 ml) water and 1 teaspoon of the salt and cook over a medium heat for about 15 minutes until the dal is soft. Add the amchur and cook for another 2 minutes, making sure the dal has not broken. Add a little more water if the mixture is too dry or the dal is not cooked. Remove from the heat.

Season the mashed potato with the remaining salt and roll into small balls, each made up of about 3 tablespoons potato. Flatten each ball slightly and make a hollow in the centre. Fill with spiced dal, then fold the potato over the filling to completely seal. Flatten again until each patty is 3 cm thick.

Heat enough oil for deep-frying in a kadhai or wok to 180°C. To test the temperature of the oil, sprinkle in some flour – if the flour sizzles, it is ready. Fry the patties in batches for 2–3 minutes until golden on one side, then flip over and fry for another minute until completely golden and cooked through. Drain on paper towel and serve with Mint Chutney (see page 76).

Ladakhi Chicken Soup
Gartok
SERVES 4

Chicken and mutton are the staple meats of the mountains, where they act as support for vegetables rather than being the main feature. Yeshi made this for dinner at the Stok village house in Ladakh. As he was cooking a chicken curry, the carcasses were used to make a stock for this nourishing soup, so nothing was wasted. It did the trick, keeping us warm on the inside as the weather turned cold outside.

600 ml White Chicken Stock (see page 380)
2 tablespoons light soy sauce
¼ teaspoon chilli powder
½ teaspoon freshly ground black pepper
100 g cooked fine egg noodles
1 tablespoon diced green capsicum (pepper)
2 green onions, finely sliced
2 teaspoons chopped coriander leaves

Bring the chicken stock to a boil in a saucepan. Add the soy sauce, chilli powder and pepper, then taste and adjust the seasoning if necessary. Add the noodles and swirl with a fork to heat through, about 1 minute. Stir in the remaining ingredients. Ladle into soup bowls and serve hot with Chapati (see page 85) or Roti (see page 103).

Ladakhi Chicken Curry

SERVES 4

A typical Ladakhi preparation, this simple yet fragrant chicken curry is a recipe from the chefs at Shakti's Stok house in Ladakh.

2 red onions, roughly chopped
8 cloves garlic, roughly chopped
1 tablespoon roughly chopped ginger
2 green chillies, roughly chopped
3 ripe tomatoes, roughly chopped
1 teaspoon chilli powder
2 tablespoons vegetable oil
800 g chicken breast fillet,
   sliced into thin strips
2 teaspoons salt
2 tablespoons chopped coriander leaves

Put the onion, garlic, ginger, chilli, tomato and chilli powder into a food processor and blend until smooth.

Heat the oil in a frying pan and add the chicken. Fry over a medium heat for 1 minute only, then remove from the pan and set aside.

Tip the onion and tomato paste into the same pan and fry over a medium heat for 40 minutes until softened and sauce-like, adding a little water if it appears too dry.

Add the chicken and stir into the sauce until well coated. Cook for 3 minutes, then season with the salt and remove from the heat. Stir through the fresh coriander and serve hot with steamed rice.

Tibetan Chimney Soup

SERVES 6

A simple broth thickened with bread, and augmented with meatballs and mushrooms, this is a typical mountain soup, a nourishing bowl that hits the right spot after a six-hour trek. Traditionally, yak meat would have been used for the meatballs, but I've substituted lamb here.

2 litres White Chicken Stock (see page 380)
2 tablespoons soy sauce
½ teaspoon freshly ground black pepper
6 mogro (black) or shiitake mushrooms, sliced
2 small lotus stems, finely sliced into rounds
1 small green chilli, finely sliced

MEATBALLS
200 g minced lamb
2 teaspoons minced ginger
1 small green chilli, minced
1 teaspoon salt
½ teaspoon freshly ground black pepper
5 slices day-old sourdough bread,
   crusts removed
100 ml milk
vegetable oil, for deep-frying

To make the meatballs, work the lamb, ginger, chilli, salt and pepper together until the mixture is soft and pliable – the texture improves if you slap the meat against the sides of the bowl several times. Tear the bread into small pieces and soak in the milk for 5 minutes until soft. Discard the milk and squeeze any excess moisture from the bread. Rub the softened bread into the lamb mixture until combined (the bread helps to bind it). Roll the mixture into small balls.

Heat the oil in a wok to 180°C. To test the temperature of the oil, sprinkle in some flour – if the flour sizzles, it is ready. Fry the balls a few at a time until golden. Drain on paper towel.

Heat the stock to boiling point, then season with the soy sauce and pepper. Add the meatballs, mushroom, lotus stem and chilli and stir. Simmer for 3–4 minutes, then ladle the soup into bowls.

‹Lamb & Pumpkin Tarkari

SERVES 6

A thick Nepali-style lamb and pumpkin curry, this is a nourishing staple of the Sikkimese village table, where a plate of steamed rice, dal, tarkari and an achar (pickle) is the norm. Tarkari is often made without meat, so this version is a more extravagant offering.

    600 g lamb shoulder, cut into 2 cm cubes
    1 teaspoon freshly ground black pepper
    2 teaspoons salt
    2 teaspoons curry powder
    ½ cup (125 ml) vegetable oil
    2 bay leaves
    2 onions, finely diced
    3 small green chillies, minced
    2 tablespoons Ginger Garlic Paste
        (see page 377)
    1 teaspoon ground turmeric
    1 teaspoon ground cumin
    2 cups (500 ml) White Chicken Stock
        (see page 380) or water
    400 g pumpkin, peeled and
        cut into 2 cm cubes
    6 large mushrooms, quartered
    1 tablespoon ghee
    1 teaspoon brown mustard seeds
    1 tablespoon chopped coriander leaves

Put the lamb in a large bowl and add the pepper, 1 teaspoon salt and 1 teaspoon curry powder. Mix until the lamb is coated with the spices.

Heat half the oil in a large frying pan and fry the lamb over a high heat until brown on all sides (6–8 minutes), then remove from the pan and set aside.

Add the remaining oil to the pan and fry the bay leaves and onion until the onion starts to colour. Return the lamb to the pan and stir. Add the chilli, ginger garlic paste, turmeric, cumin and remaining salt and curry powder. Stir until the lamb is thoroughly coated. Pour in the stock or water and bring to a boil. Reduce the heat and simmer for 40 minutes.

Add the pumpkin and mushrooms and stir to combine. Cook for 25–30 minutes until the lamb and pumpkin are tender. The gravy should thicken and reduce during the cooking. Taste and adjust the seasoning if required.

Heat the ghee in a small frying pan and fry the mustard seeds over a medium heat until they start to pop. Pour them over the lamb.

Serve hot with Roti (see page 103) and steamed rice, garnished with the fresh coriander.

Simple Spicy Greens
Saag

Kale is a leafy green that can be substituted for spinach or silverbeet. It is highly nutritious and a staple vegetable throughout India. This dish can be served simply with steamed rice or a pilaf and raita, as we had for lunch one day when we picnicked on the Rangeet riverbank near Sikkim. Paneer (fresh cheese) or feta can be broken into pieces and stirred through the leaves as they cook, to make saag paneer.

    2½ tablespoons mustard oil
    2 dried red chillies, broken into pieces
    1 teaspoon brown mustard seeds
    2 cloves garlic, finely sliced
    2 small green chillies, chopped
    500 g kale, leaves and stems chopped
        into 3 cm lengths
    1 teaspoon salt

Heat the oil in a large frying pan and fry the dried chillies and mustard seeds over a medium heat until the seeds pop. Add the garlic and green chilli and fry for a minute until softened. Add the kale and toss to combine. Add ½ cup (125 ml) water, then cover and cook for 2 minutes until the kale leaves have wilted and softened. Add a little extra water if it dries out too much before the leaves have softened. Season with the salt and serve warm.

Fresh Cheese with Greens ›
Chaaman Meeth
SERVES 4

While this is traditionally made with paneer (Indian fresh white cheese), you can use firm ricotta instead. The fresh methi leaves can be replaced with mustard greens. This is another Kashmiri favourite from the home kitchen of Almond Villa in Srinagar.

2½ tablespoons vegetable oil
pinch of asafoetida
250 g finely sliced onion
2 teaspoons chopped garlic
250 g tomatoes, chopped
1 teaspoon chilli powder
1 teaspoon ground turmeric
1 teaspoon ground ginger
1 tablespoon ground fennel
400 g Paneer (see page 154) or firm ricotta, cut into cubes
120 g methi (fenugreek) leaves, chopped
1 teaspoon salt
¼ teaspoon ground fenugreek
4 tablespoons chopped coriander leaves

Heat the oil in a saucepan and add the asafoetida, then add the onion and garlic and fry over a medium heat until brown. Add the tomato and cook for a few minutes, then stir in the chilli powder, turmeric, ginger and fennel and cook for 5 minutes. You may need to add a little water to prevent the mixture sticking to the pan.

Add the cheese and methi leaves and cook for 6–8 minutes for the flavours to combine. Season with the salt and fenugreek, then stir through the fresh coriander. Serve with Roti (see page 103) or Chapati (see page 85).

Savoury Dumplings ›
Safalle
MAKES 12

These savoury dumplings are typical of the Ladakhi and Tibetan Buddhist repertoire and are served at Leti and the Shakti village houses.

300 g plain flour
pinch of salt
vegetable oil, for brushing

CHICKEN FILLING
1 tablespoon vegetable oil
½ red onion, finely diced
1 teaspoon minced garlic
300 g chicken thigh fillets, coarsely minced
2 teaspoons light soy sauce
½ teaspoon freshly ground black pepper
2 teaspoons chopped coriander leaves

MINT CHUTNEY
1 bunch mint, stalks removed
2 tomatoes, halved and roasted in a 140°C oven for 20 minutes
pinch of salt
4 cloves garlic, peeled
3 small dried red chillies

Sift the flour and salt into a bowl. Add 1 tablespoon oil and enough water to make a smooth and slightly firm dough – about 1 cup (250 ml). Cover with a cloth and leave to rest for 30 minutes.

To make the chicken filling, heat the oil in a frying pan and add the onion, garlic and chicken. Fry until starting to colour. Add the soy sauce and pepper, then remove from the heat and set aside to cool. Stir through the fresh coriander after it is cool.

To make the mint chutney, blend all the ingredients in a food processor until smooth.

To assemble the dumplings, divide the dough into 12 balls, then roll out each ball to make a disc about 8 cm in diameter. Spoon a small amount of filling into the centre of each disc, brush the edges with water, then fold in half and press the edges together to seal.

Heat a non-stick frying pan and brush lightly with oil. Cook the dumplings a few at a time over a low–medium heat until golden brown on one side (about 5 minutes), then flip over and cook the other side. Keep the cooked dumplings warm in a low oven while you cook the rest.

Serve the dumplings warm with the mint chutney.

‹Stir-fried Mushrooms & Lotus Root
Hadder Nadur
SERVES 4

One of my favourite vegetable dishes from Kashmir prepared for us by chef Deepak on the Sukoon Houseboat, moored on Dal Lake in Srinagar.

200 g fresh lotus root, scraped
    and sliced into thin rounds
2½ tablespoons vegetable oil
2 teaspoons chopped garlic
1 teaspoon asafoetida, dissolved
    in a little water
250 g white onions, finely diced
1 teaspoon ground turmeric
1 teaspoon chilli powder
250 g tomatoes, diced
1¼ tablespoons fennel seeds,
    roasted and ground
1 teaspoon ground ginger
400 g small mushrooms, quartered
1 teaspoon salt
4 tablespoons chopped coriander leaves

Blanch the lotus root in boiling water for 30 seconds, refresh under cold water and drain.

Heat the oil in a large kadhai or wok and fry the garlic and asafoetida over a medium heat until the garlic starts to colour. Add the onion and cook until coloured, then stir through the turmeric and chilli powder. Add the tomato and toss to combine. Cook for 2 minutes, then add the ground fennel and ginger. Toss, then add the mushrooms and lotus root. Toss over heat, adding a little water to moisten. Simmer for 6–8 minutes until the mushrooms have softened. Season with the salt, then taste and adjust the seasoning if necessary.

Stir through the fresh coriander to serve.

Fermented Vegetables
Gundruk
SERVES 4

Because of the limited harvesting conditions that prevail in the Himalayas, vegetables are often preserved during their growing season by dehydrating or fermenting. These fermented vegetables are vital to the Nepali diet, being served as a condiment or side dish. Produced by shredding the leaves of mustard, radish and cauliflower and fermenting them in an earthenware pot for several days (similar to Korean kimchi), then laying them on bamboo mats and drying them in the sun, gundruk is particularly good for pregnant women and anyone with high blood pressure. I first tasted it at Glenburn Tea Estate in Darjeeling and came across it again at other places in the mountains.

2 bunches mustard greens,
    cut into 3 cm lengths
2 tomatoes, quartered
2 tablespoons mustard oil
1 white onion, finely sliced
2 cloves garlic, finely sliced
2 teaspoons minced ginger
2 small red chillies, minced
½ teaspoon ground timur (Sichuan pepper)
1 teaspoon salt
1 teaspoon freshly ground black pepper
1 tablespoon lemon juice

To prepare the mustard greens, slice the leaves and stems into ribbon lengths and pack into a ceramic pot or preserving jar. Seal and leave for 5 days to ferment. Remove the wilted leaves from the jar and squeeze out any moisture. Lay the leaves on a bamboo mat, cover with fine muslin and leave in the sun to dry for 3–5 days.

Remove and discard the seeds from the tomatoes, then cut the tomatoes lengthways into thin strips. Heat the oil in a large frying pan and fry the onion until softened. Add the garlic, ginger and chilli and cook until softened, then add the tomato and cook gently for a couple of minutes. Add the sun-dried leaves and season with the timur, salt and pepper. Cook over a gentle heat, stirring occasionally, until the leaves soften and open out. Add the lemon juice, then taste and adjust the seasoning if necessary. Serve at room temperature.

Pomegranate Raita

SERVES 6

This is my all-time favourite raita. The fresh pomegranate seeds add a great flavour and textural balance. It is served in the mountains when pomegranates are in season, with dal, curry or biryani.

> 280 g thick plain yoghurt
> ½ teaspoon roasted ground cumin
> 1 teaspoon shaved jaggery
> 2 tablespoons pomegranate seeds
> 2 tablespoons grated cucumber
> ½ teaspoon salt

Whisk the yoghurt and mix in the remaining ingredients. Taste and adjust the seasoning if necessary.

Nepalese Tomato Relish

Pyaaj Ko Achar

SERVES 4

This recipe for a Nepalese relish served with steamed rice, roti or *shafta* (salted dried beef strips) was given to me by Siddhartha, a taste memory from his Nepalese childhood.

> 2 tomatoes, quartered
> 4 tablespoons vegetable oil
> 1 white onion, finely sliced
> 4 small green chillies, finely sliced
> ½ teaspoon salt

Remove and discard the seeds from the tomatoes, then cut the tomatoes lengthways into thin strips. Heat the oil in a frying pan and cook the onion until brown, stirring occasionally. Add the tomato, chilli and salt and cook for 10 minutes until softened. Serve warm or at room temperature.

Kashmiri Fish Curry ›

Ranitha Gada

SERVES 4

I was first introduced to Kashmiri cooking by chef Vimal Dhar when he was working in Rajasthan. It prompted a desire to visit the region to further explore the diverse cuisine of this highly contested mountain region. The flavours are deep and complex with an astute use of spice.

> 2 teaspoons chilli powder
> 2 teaspoons ground turmeric
> salt
> 1 kg freshwater fish fillets,
>   cut into 3 cm chunks
> 1 cup (250 ml) mustard oil
> 1 teaspoon ground ginger
> 1 tablespoon ground fennel
> 4 cloves
> pinch of asafoetida
> 1 teaspoon garam masala,
>   plus extra to garnish
> 1 teaspoon cumin seeds
> 4 green cardamom pods, cracked
> 2 cm piece cinnamon stick

Mix the chilli powder, turmeric and 1 teaspoon salt with enough water to make a paste. Toss the fish through the paste to coat.

Heat the oil in a kadhai or wok to 180°C. To test the temperature of the oil, sprinkle in some flour – if the flour sizzles, it is ready. Fry the fish in small batches until crisp and golden. Drain on paper towel. Reserve the oil.

Bring 2 cups (500 ml) water to a boil in a saucepan, add the remaining ingredients and the reserved oil and cook over a medium heat until the gravy thickens and the oil separates. Add the fried fish and simmer for 5 minutes. Sprinkle with a little extra garam masala and season with salt to taste. Allow to cool to room temperature, then serve with steamed rice.

Rich Lamb Curry
Rogan Josh

SERVES 6

Cooked by Shakila at her charming guesthouse Cottage Nigeen on the outskirts of Srinagar, this is a definitive dish of Kashmir. It seems every keen cook in Kashmir has their own version; this one cooks the meat on the bone, which, along with the essential fat, adds a wonderful depth of flavour. Serve with basmati rice flavoured with saffron.

6 lamb chump chops
5 green cardamom pods, cracked
4 black cardamom pods, cracked
12 black peppercorns
3 sticks cinnamon
5 cloves
2 blades mace
1 tablespoon Ginger Garlic Paste
  (see page 377)
2 teaspoons salt
4 tablespoons mustard oil
3 red onions, finely sliced
1 tablespoon Kashmiri chilli powder
2 teaspoons ground coriander
1 tablespoon ground turmeric
2 tablespoons ghee
4 tablespoons blanched almonds
2 tablespoons flaked almonds, lightly roasted

TEMPERING SPICES

8 black peppercorns
2 green cardamom pods, cracked
2 cloves
1 tablespoon fennel seeds

Arrange the lamb chops in a heavy-based saucepan and scatter over the green and black cardamom pods, peppercorns, cinnamon sticks, cloves and mace. Add enough water to just cover the meat, then cover and simmer gently over a medium heat for 15 minutes to soften the lamb.

Stir in the ginger garlic paste and salt and simmer for another 10 minutes. Remove from the heat and skim off any scum from the surface. Transfer the meat to a plate, then strain the cooking juices and reserve for later.

Heat the oil in a frying pan and gently saute the tempering spices for 40 seconds until fragrant and just starting to change colour. Add the onion and fry until brown. Remove from the heat and leave to cool. Blend in a food processor to make a paste, adding enough of the lamb cooking juices to just loosen the mixture.

Mix together the chilli powder, ground coriander, turmeric and 2 tablespoons water to make a paste.

Heat the ghee in a deep frying pan and fry the chilli paste, stirring, until fragrant.

Add the onion paste and 1 cup (250 ml) of the reserved cooking juices and stir to combine. Bring to a boil. Add the lamb chops and another splash of the cooking juices if the mixture is too dry. Reduce the heat to low, cover and simmer gently for 15 minutes until the meat is tender, adding more of the cooking juices as required.

Blend the blanched almonds to a fine powder and stir through the lamb gravy. Continue to simmer for another 2 minutes until the gravy thickens. Add more of the cooking juices if you need to thin it down.

Garnish with the flaked almonds and serve.

‹Shallow-fried Lamb Kebabs with Cinnamon
Shami Kebabs
SERVES 2

For these Kashmiri kebabs, the lamb is pounded for some time into a smooth paste before cooking, so they are velvety-soft. They have also been served to me in Lucknow and Rajasthan, where Muslim communities maintain close ties to Kashmiri traditions.

100 g lamb shoulder, diced
30 g channa dal
2 small green chillies
1 tablespoon Ginger Garlic Paste (see page 377)
1 teaspoon chilli powder
1 teaspoon Kashmiri garam masala (see below)
1 teaspoon ground cinnamon
2 teaspoons chopped mint leaves
1 teaspoon salt
4 tablespoons ghee
1 cup (250 ml) melted ghee
1 teaspoon Chat Masala (see page 376)
1 tablespoon chopped coriander leaves

CORIANDER CHUTNEY
2 tablespoons chopped coriander leaves
1 tablespoon chopped mint leaves
2 teaspoons Ginger Garlic Paste (see page 377)
1 teaspoon ground cumin
½ teaspoon salt

KASHMIRI GARAM MASALA
1 teaspoon black cardamom seeds
½ teaspoon seeds from green cardamom pods
8 cloves
3 cm piece cinnamon stick

To make the coriander chutney, blend all the ingredients with just enough water to make a smooth paste. Set aside until you are ready to serve the kebabs.

To make the Kashmiri garam masala, grind all the ingredients together to make a fine powder.

Pour 1 litre of water into a saucepan and add the lamb, channa dal and green chillies. Bring to a boil, then reduce the heat to medium and cook for 30 minutes until the meat is tender. Strain and allow to cool, then pass the mixture through a mincer or use a knife to finely mince. Add the ginger garlic paste, chilli powder, garam masala, cinnamon, mint and salt, then use your fingers to rub in the 4 tablespoons ghee until the mixture is smooth. Knead and slap the mixture against the sides of the bowl to soften and tenderise it. Roll the mixture into small patties.

Heat the melted ghee in a frying pan, then shallow-fry the kebabs over a high heat until golden brown. Drain on paper towel. Sprinkle with the chat masala and chopped coriander. Serve hot with Paratha (see page 351) and the coriander chutney.

Chapati
MAKES 12

This staple flatbread is served with every meal everywhere across India and is very easy to make, even in the most rudimentary of kitchens.

500 g wholemeal flour
1 teaspoon salt

Mix the flour and salt in bowl, make a well in centre and add 300 ml water. Using your fingers, mix to make a dough, adding a little extra water if it seems too stiff. Roll the dough into a ball, cover with a cloth and leave to rest for 30 minutes.

Divide the dough into 12 pieces and, on a floured surface, roll each piece into a round about 3 mm thick and 12 cm in diameter. Heat a tawa or heavy-based frying pan over a medium heat and cook each chapati until it starts to turn golden brown, then flip over and cook the other side until browned.

Set aside and cover with a cloth to keep warm, stacking the chapatis as they are cooked.

Kumaoni pakora curry

SERVES 4

Made by Yeshi – curd-based curries are typical of the Kumaon region and are served in all the Shakti village houses. Potato, spinach or other vegetables can be substituted for onion in the pakoras.

60 g ghee
3 small dried chillies
½ teaspoon cumin seeds
2 heaped tablespoons chickpea (gram) flour
2 teaspoon Ginger Garlic Paste (see page 377)
280 g thick plain yoghurt, stirred with
   2½ tablespoons water to loosen
½ teaspoon ground turmeric
½ teaspoon chilli powder
½ teaspoon garam masala
1 teaspoon salt, or to taste
2 teaspoon dried methi (fenugreek leaves)

ONION PAKORAS
150 g chickpea (gram) flour
50 g rice flour
1¼ tablespoons vegetable oil, plus extra
   for deep-frying
1 teaspoon chilli powder
½ teaspoon ground turmeric
½ teaspoon garam masala
2 tablespoons chopped coriander leaves
1 teaspoon salt
3 red onions, sliced lengthways

Heat the ghee in a frying pan over a medium heat and briefly fry the dried chillies and cumin seeds until fragrant. Stir in the chickpea flour until smooth, then add the ginger garlic paste and cook for 2 minutes. Add the stirred yoghurt and an extra 2½ tablespoons water and stir for 2 minutes until smooth.

Add ½ cup (125 ml) hot water, then stir in the turmeric, chilli powder, garam masala and salt. Reduce the heat to low and simmer gently for 5 minutes.

To make the pakoras, combine the flours, oil, chilli powder, turmeric, garam masala, fresh coriander and salt in bowl. Stir in enough water (about 150 ml or so) to make a thick batter to coat the onion.

Heat the extra vegetable oil in a kadhai or wok to 180°C. To test the temperature of the oil, sprinkle in some flour – if the flour sizzles, it is ready. Working in small batches, drop onion slices into the batter to coat, shaking off the excess. Drop a few at a time into the hot oil and fry for 2 minutes or until golden and crisp. Drain on paper towel. These can be made ahead and set aside.

When ready to serve, add the pakoras to the hot curry sauce and simmer for 3 minutes – enough to heat them through without making them soggy.

Dry-roast the methi in a dry frying pan over a low heat for 1 minute until fragrant, then rub through a sieve. Sprinkle over the curry and serve.

Jaggery Fudge Cakes
Barfi
MAKES 12

We bought a bag of this favourite Indian sweetmeat in the hill station town of Almora before our long drive up into the mountains, and of course became addicted to its sugary sweetness. I have also come across a recipe for bhang barfi made with hashish, a local speciality offered during festivals – maybe next time!

> 600 ml full-cream milk
> 85 g blanched almonds
> 85 g raw cashews
> 2 tablespoons blanched pistachio slivers
> vegetable oil
> 75 g jaggery, shaved
> ¼ teaspoon ground cardamom
> edible silver leaf (optional)

Heat the milk in a heavy-based saucepan on a simmer mat over a low heat until reduced by just over two-thirds (you need about 120 ml) – this will take about 2 hours. Do not hurry this process; the milk must be reduced slowly and carefully, much the same as making kulfi.

Roast the nuts, then cool and grind finely. Lightly oil a baking tray.

Heat the jaggery and 75 ml water in a saucepan over a medium heat to make a thick syrup, about 10 minutes. Add the sugar syrup to the reduced milk and stir in the nuts. Add the cardamom and continue to stir over a low heat until the mixture comes away from the sides of the pan and is smooth and glossy, about 15–20 minutes. Press the mixture into the baking tray and leave for 3 hours to cool and set.

Turn out the barfi from its tray and cut it into squares. For a special effect, spread edible silver leaf on the top before the barfi is cut into squares.

Almond Halwa
SERVES 4

At Leti, Yeshi likes to serve halwa for dessert – sometimes made with carrot (see page 180), and at other times with nuts, as in this recipe.

> 500 g blanched almonds
> 250 g caster sugar
> 2 cups (500 ml) full-cream milk
> 250 g ghee
> 3 teaspoons green cardamom pods, cracked
> ½ teaspoon saffron threads, soaked
>   in 2 tablespoons hot milk
> 2 teaspoons ground cardamom
> edible silver leaf, to garnish

Blend the almonds until they resemble finely ground crumbs.

Combine the sugar and milk and stir to dissolve the sugar. Set aside.

Heat the ghee in a frying pan and add the cardamom pods and ground almonds. Fry for a few minutes, stirring continuously, until lightly browned. Add the sweet milk and stir to combine. Cook over a medium heat for about 20 minutes until the mixture has thickened and reduced. It should resemble a thick custard.

Strain out the cardamom pods. Add the saffron milk and ground cardamom, stirring to combine. Pour into a serving dish and leave to set (about 2 hours).

Decorate the top with silver leaf and cut into squares to serve.

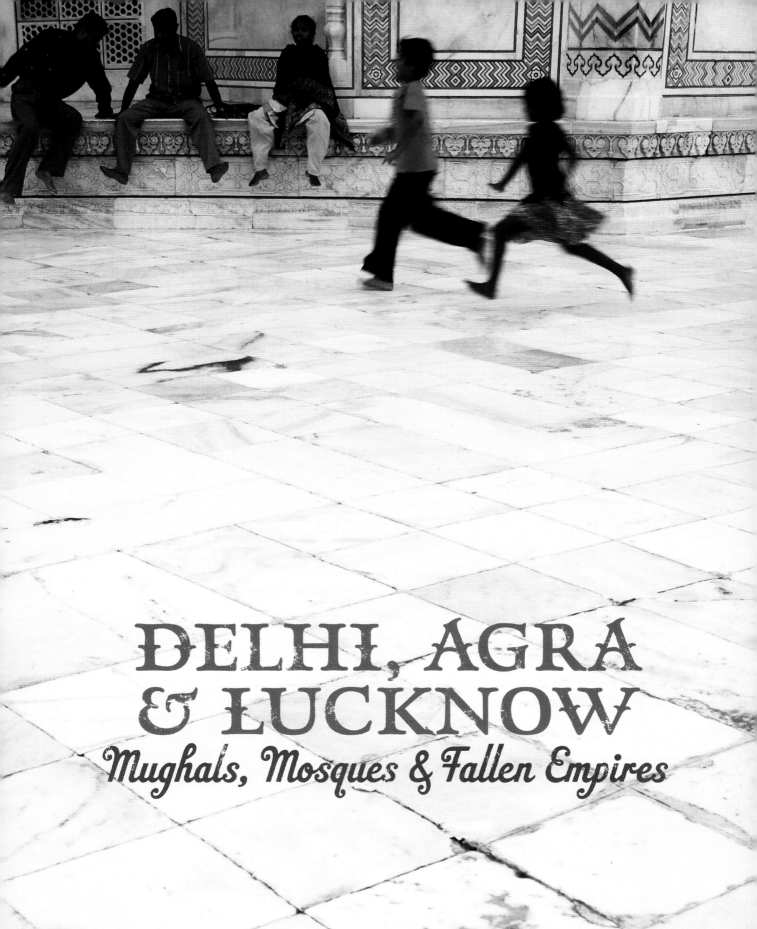

DELHI, AGRA & LUCKNOW
Mughals, Mosques & Fallen Empires

Delhi, the capital of India, is a microcosm of the country: a place of old and new, poverty and wealth, all roads seem to lead here. Scratching the surface of the city's Mughal heritage makes me eager to further explore the legacy of the Mughal empire, particularly its food, so I head to Lucknow, capital of neighbouring Uttar Pradesh and a stronghold of royal cuisine. And of course, no visit to India would be complete without making the pilgrimage to Agra, to stand before the Taj Mahal, the highest expression of Mughal architecture.

DELHI
The Tale of Two Cities

Delhi, the Immortal City and capital of India, is a metropolis of more than 18 million citizens that is characterised by impressive architecture and wide boulevards in the newer colonial city. With its relative sense of space (assuming you stay within the protective inner sanctum of New Delhi), it offers a gentle introduction to India, and has been made even more appealing by the civic works to upgrade the city's transport with an underground metro system. However, Delhi in summer is best avoided due to extreme heat and frequent power cuts caused by a heavily overloaded system – even the locals escape if they possibly can. Walking the streets, it becomes obvious that Old Delhi remains deeply rooted in its Islamic Mughal past, while New Delhi has witnessed an influx of Punjabi immigrants since Partition. The story of Delhi is a tale of two cities. New Delhi, designed by architect Edwin Lutyens early in the twentieth century, is a haven of relative calm. The red-painted road of Rajpath links India Gate to the presidential residence, with expansive gardens on either side. Off to one side is the circular Parliament House, with classic Indian Ambassador cars lined up out the front, while colonial mansions and diplomats' homes create a sense of calm and order. To the north, the concentric circles of Connaught Place form the modern city's commercial hub, with a plethora of shops, the underground market of Palika Bazaar, banks, a couple of groovy bars, bookshops, cinemas – and lots of neon.

Presiding over Old Delhi is the Red Fort, a magnificent and imposing sandstone edifice from the Mughal era that is the city's most significant and famous monument.

The Red Fort is to Delhi what the Colosseum is to Rome or the Acropolis to Athens: it is the single most famous monument in the city. It represents the climax of more than six hundred years of experimentation in palace building by Indo-Islamic architects, and is by far the most substantial monument – and in its day was also by far the most magnificent – that the Moghuls left behind them in Delhi.
WILLIAM DALRYMPLE, *CITY OF DJINNS*

From the Red Fort's grand Lahori Gate, the old city's main thoroughfare of Chandni Chowk runs through the middle of what is effectively one massive bazaar, with maze-like capillaries of laneways that jolt you to the core as you manoeuvre your way through the dense throng of itinerant vendors and road traffic. Women in exquisite colourful saris squat amid the stalls of Asia's biggest wholesale market, threading marigolds onto fine thread for temple offerings. Amid the toil and sweat of backbreaking labour, skinny cows create mayhem as they saunter about at will, protected by their sacred status to all Hindus. Equally skinny and sinewy men pull trolleys laden with fruit, vegetables and all manner of things under a canopy of electrical wires that are strung from one crumbling building to the next.

> *Delhi is a daunting city, constantly changing. One moment your horizon is wide, filled with tree-lined boulevards and colonial architecture. A couple of left turns later you are in the midst of a medieval town, the imposing buildings blocking the moonlit sky. Urban India never sleeps, but Delhi seems to be urban India on espresso.*
>
> HARDEEP SINGH KOHLI, *INDIAN TAKEAWAY*

I always engage a local guide to lead the way, preferably one who shares my passion for food, who is engaging and a fount of knowledge and knows where to find the best food. The easiest starting point for your explorations is at the front of Delhi's main and most impressive mosque, Jama Masjid. The mosque was built by Shah Jahan, the Mughal emperor who built the Taj Mahal, as well as Old Delhi – giving the old city its other name of Shahjahanabad. Entering Paratha Wali Gali ('Alley of Parathas'), we stop at the corner to buy a few hot samosas from a man squatting on the ground over a cauldron of sizzling oil. He deftly takes the piping-hot pastries from the oil, wraps them in paper and sprinkles them with chat masala to make a snack that hits the spot every time. The bloke next to him is similarly occupied, making spinach and vegetable *bhajias*. Along the alley, there are around 25 different types of paratha being cooked to order. I always look out for the busiest shop, the one where the locals hang out. Chai wallahs weave their way through the snaking crowd with seemingly effortless ease, carrying trays of tiny cups or glasses filled with steaming-hot chai to dispense to shopkeepers and workers.

During the winter months when I often visit, I look out for the vendors walking around selling *malaiyo*, a cloud-like ethereal milk concoction with the most delicate texture, a melt in the mouth foam flavoured with saffron, cardamom and pistachio, and only available in the morning before its texture stiffens. A signature dish of Varanasi, it was in the laneways of Old Delhi that I first experienced it. Regardless of where you go, it takes only a nanosecond to realise that Delhi has an extraordinarily rich food culture and culinary traditions.

The cultural hub of Defence Colony and Lodhi Colony is spoilt for choice with restaurants, boutiques and shops. I like to explore Khan

Market, home to some of the city's best fashion designers, homewares, book stores, local and western-style restaurants, something of a playground for the upwardly mobile younger generation. The area's popularity can cause something of a traffic jam on weekends, when it feels like the whole city is out to shop.

THE ULTIMATE KEBAB

Chandni Chowk, although a shadow of its former glory during the Golden Age of Shah Jahan, is home to the city's main spice bazaar and remains the epicentre of the global spice trade. The mounds of spices along the pavement give the air a distinctive aroma as every vendor yells prices to passers-by to grab attention and a sale. An obligatory lunch stop is at Karim's, which is hidden down a lane behind a cluster of Muslim food stalls. You'll have to tangle with the crush of people and rickshaw drivers ferrying families of schoolkids home for lunch through some of the densest pedestrian traffic imaginable, but it's worth it for the authentic charcoal-grilled kebabs and all manner of curries cooked in large handi pots over coals.

By contrast, the Khan Market feels more genteel and middle class, but it soon becomes a regular stop for us when we find some of the most heavenly kebabs at Khan Chacha Kebab Corner, where we are happy to queue for chicken tikka kebab rumali rolls and mutton seekh rumali rolls. Handkerchief-like rumali bread is used to wrap grilled meat, red onion slices and mayonnaise. We can't decide which tastes better: the chicken or the lamb. What the heck – we order another round to decide!

The next stop on our quest for the ultimate kebab is an unlikely-looking spot by the side of a busy road, right near a freeway at Nizamuddin, a few kilometres south of the city centre, close by to the Sufi Temple. Here a couple of makeshift kebab kitchens have been set up, with a handful of rickety plastic chairs on the broad pavement, as they are every night. Our choice is Aap ki Khatir, the place my Delhi friends go to when they want a kebab. By day it is a shop selling tyres for cars and trucks, with tyres piled against the wall to one side, but as the sun goes down, the kitchen comes out. On this grill and these hotplates they cook *the* best lamb kebabs, including kakori kebabs, which are made from tender minced lamb and kidney fat. We order every variety of kebab to try, and the kakori ones are a standout.

Delhi owes its kebab supremacy to the Punjabi Sikhs who have settled in the city. Along with the Muslims, it is they who have established the city's restaurant culture, and they have proven themselves to be enterprising and generous hosts. Their north-west frontier food abounds in kebabs, and so a wide variety is now found everywhere, on street corners and in restaurants.

Just as each ruler left his architectural mark on Delhi, so each has bequeathed to it a culinary legacy.
CHARMAINE O'BRIEN, *FLAVOURS OF DELHI*

Indian Breads

Bread is a staple across the entire country, an everyday necessity as well as a signifier of celebratory and festive occasions. Regardless of where you are in India, bread will always make an appearance at the table in one form or another. The repertoire is expansive and diverse. Most breads are flat and unleavened, and are meant to be eaten warm and freshly cooked. They can be made from wheat, millet, corn, rice, gram (chickpea), semolina, jowar or sorghum flour, depending on the region. Many of the whole grains are ground on a heavy stone slab with a pestle or grinding stone.

Perhaps the most common household bread is the thin, soft chapati, which usually accompanies dal. Slightly richer is roti, which is traditionally cooked on a griddle over hot coals but these days more often than not over a gas flame. It is usually made with wholemeal flour, and is sometimes spiced or stuffed to give it added richness.

Parathas are layered flaky breads enriched with ghee; they are sometimes seasoned with spices or stuffed with potato or herbs. The dough is repeatedly rolled, twirled and flattened, so that when it hits a hot pan or the sides of a hot tandoor oven, it puffs up and becomes flaky in a similar way to puff pastry. It is a most delightfully wicked bread.

Puri is puffed bread, made like a chapati but deep-fried in a kadhai rather than cooked on a griddle. It must be eaten as soon as it is made, because it collapses as it cools. Luchi, a speciality of Bengal, is another deep-fried puffed bread. Its richness comes from being fried in ghee. It is usually eaten at lunch and served with dal, fried fish and meat curries. Bhatura is a spongy fried Punjabi bread with yoghurt added to the dough to give it a light texture and tangy flavour. It makes a perfect accompaniment to gravy- or sauce-based dishes.

Naan was introduced to the Indian repertoire by the Persians when they established their empires in northern India, and has since become one of the most well-known Indian breads in the world. The teardrop-shaped leavened bread is slapped on the walls of a searing-hot tandoor oven. There are many variations to basic naan – it can be flavoured with garlic, herbs, crushed almonds or spices.

Rumali is lacy, fine 'handkerchief' bread made in large soft sheets, the dough stretched over a dome-shaped tawa hotplate. Essential to the Muslim diet, this bread is served with kebabs and grilled meats. Another Muslim bread is kulcha, a leavened bread that is a speciality of Hyderabad. Pressed and shaped by hand, it forms a crust as it bakes in a hot wood-fired oven but remains soft and spongy inside. Just like paratha or naan, kulcha can sometimes be stuffed with onions, spices or paneer.

From the south, there is dosa, made with rice and urad dal that have been soaked overnight to ferment, then ground. Dosas are beautiful, pale-golden pancakes with a crisp surface and spongy soft centre, served as an accompaniment to other foods, such as sambar or dal. The masala dosa, stuffed with spicy potato, has become one of the best-known breakfast foods of India. Idlis are fluffy, light, steamed-rice cakes, while appams are soft pancakes with a lacy appearance, made with toddy (fermented coconut juice) and rice. Pathiri, a bread made from rice flour, sometimes with the addition of coconut, is typical of Kerala and is usually served for breakfast – it's great with a spicy chutney.

A universal favourite, pappads are made with lentil (dal) flour and can be flavoured with black pepper, chilli, cumin or garlic. They are round, wafer-thin discs that are sun-dried and easily stored until you are ready to cook them. Pappads can be either fried in hot oil or roasted over hot coals or – my personal favourite – an open flame. Their texture is crunchy, crisp and delicate, and they are an essential part of the Indian table.

AGRA & THE TAJ MAHAL

Arriving in Agra at dawn, we head straight to the Taj Mahal, just in time to catch the early-morning pink glow that bathes the white marble. A sunset visit later in the day shows it in a different light, and to stay after sunset and see the moonlight dancing on the turrets is mesmerising. Words cannot do justice to the vision in shimmering white marble that is revealed as you walk through the gates.

The Taj Mahal was built by Emperor Shah Jahan as a tribute to the memory of his favourite wife, Mumtaz Mahal, and stands as a supreme expression of romantic love – renowned Bengali poet Rabindranath Tagore memorably described it as 'a tear on the face of eternity'. Given its perfect symmetry and extensive decoration with marble filigree and ancient Su and Sanskrit text, it's no wonder the building took 22 years and tens of thousands of labourers to complete. The vast quantities of marble used in its construction were brought in by elephant from over 300 kilometres away, an extraordinary feat.

Mughlai cooking is the speciality in Agra. At Esphahan restaurant in the Oberoi Amarvilas hotel, the kitchen prepares time-honoured, exquisite Mughlai dishes. It pays to take an appetite. A procession of food arrives at the table – masala chicken, a complex and fragrant lamb dish, and quails cooked in an incredibly spicy, rich gravy – all accompanied by the most delicious baked yoghurt and flavoursome pickles and chutneys. At the breakfast table I love a plate of hot flaky parathas smothered with pineapple-and-watermelon jam, with a masala dosa to follow.

A few kilometres northwest of the Taj Mahal, the dusty red sandstone ramparts of the Red Fort overlook a bend in the Yamuna River. One of my favourite spots within the fort's walls is the white Diwan-i-Am pavilion: I have often thought it would make a spectacular setting for a decadent dinner, with a table stretched along its length. Another favourite spot is the royal pavilions, with their filigreed windows looking across the river to the Taj Mahal – perhaps one of the finest views.

An hour's drive west of Agra, Fatehpur Sikri is definitely worthy of a detour for some historical perspective. The deserted former imperial city was built during the reign of Mughal emperor Akbar before he shifted his capital to Agra. Built in the same dusty-red sandstone as the Red Fort, the buildings remain intact after many centuries and it's surreal to wander around the walled city. After sightseeing, the afternoon is best spent languishing poolside with a cocktail and a few spicy bar snacks to complete your hedonistic experience, emulating the bygone days of those Mughal emperors, whose legacy adds rich layers to the heritage of India.

LUCKNOW

Lucknow, the city of Awadhi nawabs (Muslim nobles), is inextricably linked with fine ingredients and culinary expertise – and I came here in search of edible treasures, to discover the foundations of the rich and complex Mughlai cuisine.

Nurtured by the nawabs, who presided over an era of gracious living, Mughlai cuisine was born when traditional Indian cooking merged with the delectable food of the Persians. The result was a refined cuisine that became the signature of the Mughal empire. Given complete freedom to experiment and create with no economic or time constraints, the royal chefs – *bawarchis* – invented new styles of cooking, testing recipes with new ingredients and flavours. They developed the *dum pukht* or 'slow oven' style of cooking, considered one of the most refined methods in India: long cooking in a sealed pot over a slow fire to enhance delicate aromas, using magical blends of spices. The lid is often sealed onto the pot with a rope of bread dough and when the seal is broken, usually at the table, the aromas are released to captivate the lucky diners.

Back in the glory days, when they weren't eating, the nawabs were building grand palaces, gardens and mosques, and the grandeur remains. The most spectacular edifice is the Bara Imambara, on the banks of the Gomti River. A labyrinth of chambers, rooms and terraces, it's like walking through a maze – but the view from the roof terrace, when you find it, is definitely worth the effort of getting there.

We wander across to the market, stopping along the way to taste street food, including spiced chickpeas served in ingenious takeaway bowls made from dried betel leaves. Street carts everywhere are making biryani in their makeshift kitchens. The market is home to the varq wallahs, makers of the edible gold and silver leaf that is used to embellish many Indian desserts and paan, a local delicacy made by filling leaves of the betel-nut tree with various betel-nut and spice mixtures. Paan is eaten after food as a mouth freshener and digestive. Addictive and gently narcotic, its prolonged use turns the gums and lips a vibrant red colour.

One evening we are invited to have an audience and dinner at the haveli (nobleman's mansion) of one of Lucknow's royal descendants, the Nawab Mir Jafar Abdullah, and his cousin Nawab Masood Abdullah. The ravages of time have taken their toll but the house clings stubbornly to a certain faded elegance, and we are transported back in time as the nawab holds court, flashing his teeth stained red by his daily paan. Afterwards we gather on the rooftop in the cool air as a house-cook squats over a small brazier to cook seekh kebabs – meat that has been pounded until it is silky soft, then moulded around metal skewers. Escorted into the dining room to eat, we sit cross-legged around the edge of a large tablecloth thrown onto the floor. Plates of food are brought in by houseboys and placed on the cloth to form a traditional feast or *dastarkhan*: *dum* (braises), biryani, kebabs and *salan* (gravy dishes) are served with roti bread, an integral part of any Nawabi meal. The flavours are sensational. Like the buildings, the meal smacks of past glories and distant memories of more splendid times.

‹Mughlai Corn & Spinach
Makai Shahzadi
SERVES 4

This nostalgic vegetable dish from the nawabs of Lucknow was made for me by Asish, when he was the chef at Suvarna Mahal Restaurant in Jaipur, whose menu showcases royal Mughlai cooking. The combination of corn and spinach cooked in a fragrant gravy makes a great vegetable addition to a shared table.

500 g spinach leaves
kernels from 1 corn cob
6 baby corn, cut into chunks
10 g butter
1 teaspoon cumin seeds
2 teaspoons minced ginger
2 teaspoons minced garlic
2 tablespoons diced tomato
1 teaspoon kasoori methi
   (dried fenugreek leaf) powder
1 teaspoon salt
1 teaspoon garam masala
2 tablespoons cream

Blanch the spinach leaves in boiling water for 20 seconds, then refresh under cold running water and drain. Squeeze out any excess water. Chop the spinach, then blend to a puree.

Cook the corn kernels and baby corn in boiling water for 1 minute, then drain.

Heat the butter in a frying pan and fry the cumin, ginger and garlic over a medium heat until starting to colour. Add the tomato and corn, stirring to combine. Add the spinach puree and cook over a medium–high heat for a couple of minutes. Stir through the methi powder, salt and garam masala and simmer for a minute. Add the cream and as soon as it starts to simmer, remove from the heat. Taste and adjust the seasoning if necessary.

Serve with hot Naan (see page 101).

Spinach Pakoras
SERVES 4

A favourite snack from the street vendors in Old Delhi – the fried snacks are wrapped in newspaper as soon as they are lifted from their vats of hot oil.

50 g chickpea (gram) flour
1 teaspoon ground turmeric
¼ teaspoon chilli powder
½ teaspoon salt
pinch of bicarbonate of soda
vegetable oil, for deep-frying
100 g small spinach leaves
2 teaspoons Chat Masala (see page 376)

Mix the chickpea flour with the turmeric, chilli powder, salt, bicarbonate of soda and 2 tablespoons water to make a thick batter (it should have the consistency of pancake batter). If it is too thick, add a little extra water; if too thin, add a little extra flour.

Heat the oil in a kadhai or large wok to 180°C. To test the temperature of the oil, sprinkle in some flour – if the flour sizzles, it is ready. Dip the spinach leaves in the batter to coat, then fry for 2 minutes until crisp and golden. Drain on paper towel. Dust with the chat masala to serve.

Stuffed Potatoes with Spiced Tomato Sauce
Dum Aloo Bharwa

SERVES 8

Dum pukht or 'slow oven' cooking, a legacy of the royal nawabs (Muslim noblemen) of Lucknow, is considered one of the most refined methods of cooking in India. Food is steamed in its own juices over a very low flame. This is just one of the dishes I have enjoyed at Dum Pukht, a Mughal restaurant in Delhi that showcases this time-honoured tradition of cooking.

12 small chat (or new) potatoes of even size
vegetable oil, for deep-frying,
    plus 100 ml extra
1 teaspoon fennel seeds
1 teaspoon nigella seeds
2 small onions, finely diced
½ teaspoon ground cardamom
75 g raisins
75 g raw cashews
salt
225 g plain flour
2 tablespoons coriander leaves

SPICED TOMATO SAUCE
1 tablespoon vegetable oil
1 onion, finely diced
2 teaspoons chopped ginger
2 teaspoons chopped garlic
225 g thick plain yoghurt
200 ml tomato puree
2 tablespoons blanched almonds,
    ground to a paste with a little water
1 teaspoon fennel seeds
½ teaspoon ground mace
seeds from 3 green cardamom pods, ground
1 tablespoon coriander seeds, ground
2 teaspoons cumin seeds, ground
5 cloves
½ teaspoon nigella seeds
salt

Peel the potatoes and slice off one end, about a quarter of the way down. Using a melon baller or teaspoon, scoop out the centres, ensuring the potato walls are not punctured or broken. Heat the deep-frying oil to 180°C in a large wok or deep-fryer. To test the temperature of the oil, sprinkle in some flour – if the flour sizzles, it is ready. Deep-fry the potato shells, the cut-out centres and the tops in batches until golden. Drain on paper towel. Mash the centres and tops when they have cooled slightly.

Heat the extra 100 ml oil in a wok or kadhai over a medium heat and fry the fennel and nigella seeds until fragrant. Add the onion and cook for 3–4 minutes until translucent. Add the mashed potato, cardamom, raisins and cashews and stir-fry for 2 minutes, then season to taste with salt. Spoon the stuffing into the fried potato shells.

Preheat the oven to 150°C. To make the dough to seal the pot, mix the flour and ¼ cup (180 ml) water in a bowl to a workable dough. If it is too dry, add a little extra flour; if too wet, add a little extra water.

To make the spiced tomato sauce, heat the oil in a large, deep ovenproof pan. Add the onion and cook over a medium heat until softened and just beginning to colour. Meanwhile, use a mortar and pestle to pound the ginger and garlic with a little water to make a paste. Add the paste to the onion, along with the yoghurt, tomato puree, almond paste and spices. Cook over a medium heat until fragrant (about 10 minutes), then season to taste with salt. Reduce the heat to the absolute minimum and add the stuffed potatoes to the pan in a single layer. Spoon the sauce over to coat.

Roll out the dough on a lightly floured surface and shape into a sausage that is long enough to wrap around the top edge of the pan. Cover the pan with a lid and wrap the dough around the join. Press firmly to seal the pan completely.

Place the pan in the oven and bake for 15 minutes. Remove from the oven, then break the dough seal and discard the dough. Transfer the potatoes to serving plates. Strain the sauce through a sieve and spoon it over the potatoes. Sprinkle with the fresh coriander to serve.

Spinach & Fresh Cheese
Saag Paneer
SERVES 4

This well-recognised vegetarian staple is a great comfort dish throughout India, and is a standard inclusion on most menus. In the north, the addition of cream gives it an added richness (compare it with the recipe from Mumbai on page 355). This recipe was given to me by chef Ritesh in Delhi. Paneer is the Indian equivalent of cottage cheese and is worth seeking out at a reliable local Indian grocer that stocks fresh dairy products.

500 g spinach leaves
100 ml vegetable oil
250 g Paneer (see page 154),
    cut into 2 cm cubes
1 tablespoon ghee
1 tablespoon Ginger Garlic Paste
    (see page 377)
½ teaspoon ground cumin
½ teaspoon chilli powder
1 teaspoon ground coriander
2 tomatoes, diced
2 tablespoons cream
1 teaspoon salt
1 teaspoon garam masala

Blanch the spinach leaves in boiling water for 30 seconds, then drain and roughly chop.

Heat the oil in a frying pan and fry the paneer until golden on all sides. Drain on paper towel.

Wipe out the pan, then heat the ghee and fry the ginger garlic paste until it has softened. Add the cumin, chilli powder and coriander and cook until fragrant. Add the tomato and spinach and cook for a few minutes until any liquid has evaporated. Gently fold in the fried paneer, then simmer for 5 minutes. Stir in the cream and salt, then sprinkle with the garam masala and serve.

Baked Spiced Yoghurt
Tadka Dahi
SERVES 4

From chef Narayan back when he was at the Aman New Delhi, this is easy to prepare and a delicious addition to a dinner feast. The final baking can be done in small ceramic ramekins.

2 teaspoons vegetable oil
2 teaspoons cumin seeds
1 teaspoon ground turmeric
3 teaspoons finely chopped onion
1 teaspoon minced ginger
1 teaspoon minced green chilli
1 tablespoon diced tomato
1 teaspoon chilli powder
2 teaspoons caster sugar
100 g curd (drained yoghurt)
2 teaspoons salt
1 teaspoon chopped coriander leaves
1 teaspoon finely diced long red chilli

Preheat the oven to 160°C.

Heat the oil in an ovenproof frying pan and fry the cumin seeds for 30 seconds over a medium heat. Add the turmeric, onion, ginger and green chilli and fry until starting to brown, then add the tomato and cook for 1 minute. Stir in the chilli powder and sugar. Remove from the heat and add the curd and salt, stirring to combine.

Put the pan in the oven and bake for 3 minutes. Stir through the fresh coriander and red chilli and serve warm with Paratha (see page 351).

Spiced Okra
Bhindi Masala
SERVES 4

Small, tender okra (bhindi) are found right across India, and they are perfect when simply prepared as in this recipe. The versatility and lovely texture of this dish means it can be served with various other vegetable dishes, or with fried fish, spice-baked quail (see page 108) or a rich lamb curry (page 103).

2½ tablespoons vegetable oil
1 teaspoon mustard oil
1 teaspoon brown mustard seeds
12 curry leaves
1 small red onion, finely diced
1 teaspoon ground cumin
1 teaspoon ground coriander
2 teaspoons garam masala
1 teaspoon ground turmeric
500 g small okra, sliced into 1 cm rounds
4 cloves garlic, minced
3 small green chillies, sliced
1 teaspoon salt
1 teaspoon white sugar
1 tablespoon chopped coriander leaves

Heat the oils in a kadhai or wok and fry the mustard seeds over a medium heat until they start to pop. Working quickly, add the curry leaves and fry for about 30 seconds until they are crisp. Add the onion and fry, stirring constantly, until it begins to colour. Add the spices and stir to combine. Cook for a minute until fragrant. Add the okra, garlic and chilli and fry gently for 10 minutes until the okra is soft.

Add the salt and sugar, then taste and adjust the seasoning if necessary. The sauce should be dry and thick, coating the okra. Stir through the fresh coriander to serve.

Naan
MAKES 4

Cooked over hot glowing coals on the inside wall of a tandoor oven, this flatbread is synonymous with India and particularly the food of the north. To approximate the fast cooking time and desired texture of the bread, put a large thick clay tile on the bottom of your oven and turn the heat to its highest setting. If you want a flavoured bread, brush with oil and sprinkle over a few nigella, cumin or sesame seeds before baking. And if you prefer a slightly more dense and chewy texture, use wholemeal flour.

400 g plain flour
1 teaspoon salt
6 g dried yeast
2 tablespoons thick plain yoghurt
1 tablespoon vegetable oil

Sift the flour and salt into a large bowl, then stir in the yeast.

Add 240 ml warm water, the yoghurt and oil and use your hands to work the dough until it comes together. Turn out onto the bench and continue to knead the dough for 5–6 minutes until smooth. Put the dough back into the bowl, cover with a tea towel or cloth and leave to rest for an hour or until the dough has more or less doubled in volume.

Preheat the oven to its highest setting and place a clay tile in it to heat.

Tip the dough out onto the bench and punch down to flatten and expel the air from the dough. Knead for a couple of minutes then divide the dough into four equal pieces. Roll each piece into a ball and, using your fingers, stretch it out and shape it into a thin elongated oval.

Carefully place the stretched dough onto the hot clay tile in the oven and bake for 5 minutes or until the bread puffs up and becomes crisp and golden. (If your clay tile is large enough, you can bake two pieces of bread at a time – just make sure there is enough space between each piece.)

Remove the cooked naan from the oven and repeat the same process with the remaining dough balls. Wrap the cooked naan in tea towel or cloth until all the bread is cooked.

Mughlai Chicken
Murgh Hara Masala
SERVES 4

A luscious chicken masala in true Mughlai tradition, from chef Narayan Rao. He uses mild Kashmiri chilli in this dish for its vibrant colour and gentle flavour – it is readily available in powdered form at Indian grocery stores.

- 1 tablespoon vegetable oil
- 50 g finely sliced white onion
- 2 teaspoons minced ginger
- 2 teaspoons minced garlic
- 2 teaspoons Kashmiri chilli powder
- 225 g chicken fillet, cut into 2 cm cubes
- 100 g thick plain yoghurt, whisked
- 300 ml White Chicken Stock (see page 380)
- 3 teaspoons Mint Chutney (see page 76)
- 50 g finely chopped spinach leaves
- 100 g Spinach Puree (see page 379)
- 2 teaspoons salt
- 20 Fried Curry Leaves (see page 377), slightly crushed
- 1 teaspoon ghee, melted

Heat the oil in a frying pan and fry the onion, ginger, garlic and chilli over a high heat until softened. Add the chicken and toss to combine. Fry for a minute, then add the yoghurt. When the mixture starts to simmer, add the stock. Bring back to simmering point, then stir through the chutney and spinach leaves. Cook for 10 minutes until the chicken is tender.

Add the spinach puree and salt and stir until combined and heated through. Stir in the curry leaves and ghee. Serve hot with steamed rice and Paratha (see page 351).

Slow-cooked Chicken
Dum Ka Murg
SERVES 4

I remember this dish from my first visit to Agra when we were having dinner at Peshawari, and its lingering flavours have stayed with me. It's a typical Mughlai preparation using the dum method of cooking in a sealed pot to retain all the natural juices, moisture and fragrance of the meat. A well-seasoned claypot is ideal when making this dish.

- 2 teaspoons salt
- 1 tablespoon lime juice
- 4 chicken marylands (leg and thigh portions), cut into thigh and leg joints
- 200 g ghee
- 2 white onions, finely sliced
- 2 tablespoons Ginger Garlic Paste (see page 377)
- ½ teaspoon ground cardamom
- 1 teaspoon ground cumin
- 2 small green chillies, finely sliced
- 600 g thick plain yoghurt
- 3 tablespoons shredded coriander leaves

Combine the salt and lime juice, then rub into the chicken.

Heat the ghee in a frying pan and fry the onion over a high heat for 8–10 minutes until it is golden brown and crisp. Remove the onion with a slotted spoon, leaving the ghee in the pan. When it is cool enough to handle, coarsely chop the fried onion.

Combine the ginger garlic paste with the ground spices, green chilli and yoghurt. Stir through the ghee and onion, then add the chicken and mix thoroughly. Transfer to a cast-iron casserole dish and cover with a lid. Seal the lid completely with a rope of dough (made with flour and water; see page 366) or foil.

Cook over a high heat for about 3 minutes until the mixture is boiling, then reduce the heat to low and cook gently for 35 minutes. Remove from the heat and leave to rest for 10 minutes.

Remove the lid and sprinkle with the fresh coriander to serve. The chicken will be meltingly tender. Serve with Paratha (see page 351) or Naan (see page 101).

Dry Lamb Curry
Gosht Kandahari
SERVES 10

The most complex, fragrant and flavoursome lamb curry, this is simply remarkable, and is one of my enduring taste memories from Delhi's Bukhara Restaurant, which showcases the cooking of the north-west frontier. Adding the dhuni, a piece of hot charcoal that imparts an aromatic smoky flavour, is the magic ingredient and a really neat trick. Young goat (kid) is equally delicious cooked in this way, and is the meat generally used in India.

300 g dried pomegranate seeds
200 ml vegetable oil
2 teaspoons ground cumin
1½ tablespoons ground coriander
100 g Kashmiri chilli powder
500 g finely diced onion
50 g minced garlic
30 g long red chillies, finely chopped
2.5 kg suckling lamb leg, cut into 3 cm cubes
3 teaspoons ground fennel
2 tablespoons chopped coriander leaves
3 teaspoons salt
1 small piece charcoal

Blend the pomegranate seeds with a little water to make a thick paste. Heat the oil in a large, heavy-based saucepan and fry the pomegranate paste for a minute over a medium heat, then add the cumin, coriander and chilli powder. Cook until fragrant and the mixture starts to stick to the base of the pan. Add a little water to prevent burning and continue to cook, adding water as you go, until the spices are dark and rich in flavour.

Add the onion, garlic and chilli and stir to coat with the spices. Cook until the onion is translucent. Add the lamb and stir to coat. Fry for 5 minutes until the lamb starts to brown. Add a little water (about 100 ml), then cover the pan and cook over a low heat for 45 minutes, stirring occasionally, until the meat is tender.

Add the ground fennel, fresh coriander and salt. To prepare the dhuni, heat a piece of charcoal over a flame until it is red, then dip the charcoal in a little oil and drop it into the lamb curry. Cover with a lid and allow to sit for 10 minutes so the smoky flavour is absorbed by the lamb. Use tongs to remove and discard the charcoal. Serve with buttery Naan (see page 101).

Roti
MAKES 8

The addition of egg and milk makes roti a little softer and richer than Chapati (see page 85). The dough can also be flavoured with spices, such as fennel or cumin seeds.

250 g wholemeal flour
1 teaspoon salt
1 egg
150 ml milk
2 tablespoons fine semolina
50 g ghee, melted

Mix the flour and salt together in a bowl. Beat the egg and milk in another bowl then add this to the flour and mix with your hands to bring together. Tip the dough out onto the benchtop and knead for a few minutes to make a firm dough, then cover with a cloth and leave to rest for 30 minutes. Divide the dough into eight pieces and roll each into a ball, then cover and leave to rest for another 15 minutes or so.

On a lightly floured bench, roll each dough ball into a 12 cm round about 3 mm thick. Prick with a fork and sprinkle with semolina on both sides.

Heat a tawa or heavy-based frying pan over a medium heat and cook each roti until it starts to colour, about 2 minutes, then flip over and cook other side until golden and crisp.

Brush each roti with ghee while still hot, then stack them and cover with a cloth to keep warm.

Tiny Potatoes with Spices & Coriander

Aloo Dhaniya

SERVES 4

Another one of the thousands of potato preparations in India's expansive tuber repertoire to add to the mix, and a typical Mughlai preparation. The trick is finding or harvesting those tiny new potatoes that are only about 3 cm long.

2 teaspoons cumin seeds
1 teaspoon dried red chillies
1 teaspoon fenugreek seeds
1¾ tablespoons coriander seeds
3 teaspoons fennel seeds
1 teaspoon black peppercorns
200 g tiny new potatoes, peeled
50 g ghee
1 teaspoon salt
2 teaspoons lemon juice
1½ tablespoons chopped coriander leaves

Dry-roast the whole spices, then cool. Grind to a fine powder.

Preheat the grill to hot. Cut the potatoes into halves or quarters, depending on their size. Heat the ghee in an ovenproof frying pan and fry the potato over a medium heat for a few minutes. Add the salt, then cover the pan and cook until the potato is tender. Add the ground spices, tossing to combine, then put the pan under the hot grill and cook until the potato is crisp. Mix in the lemon juice and fresh coriander to serve.

Scallops in Spiced Coconut ›

SERVES 4

Back when Narayan Rao was chef at Aman New Delhi (now the Lodhi Hotel), he served this scrumptious dish for lunch on the poolside terrace one spring day. He cooks with a deft and intuitive hand and understands how to get the most out of spices and aromatics in his cooking. This is a perfect dish to get the taste buds singing.

1½ tablespoons lime juice
1 teaspoon ground turmeric
1 teaspoon salt
16 large sea scallops
1 tablespoon coconut oil
½ teaspoon cumin seeds
1 tablespoon curry leaves
4 red shallots, finely sliced
2 small green chillies, finely sliced
6 cloves garlic, finely sliced
1 cup (250 ml) coconut milk
3 tomatoes, peeled, seeded and finely diced
2 tablespoons chopped coriander leaves
1 tablespoon Fried Curry Leaves
  (see page 377)

Combine the lime juice, turmeric and half the salt. Add the scallops, turning gently to coat with the mixture. Marinate for 15 minutes.

Heat the coconut oil in a frying pan and fry the cumin seeds and curry leaves over a medium heat until the seeds start to splutter. Add the shallot and cook for about 4 minutes until transparent. Add the chilli, garlic and remaining salt and cook for another minute. Pour in the coconut milk and bring to a boil, then reduce the heat and simmer for 3 minutes.

Add the marinated scallops and stir to cover with the sauce. Cook over a gentle heat for 3–4 minutes until the scallops are just cooked. Remove from the heat and stir through the tomato and fresh coriander. Serve immediately, garnished with the fried curry leaves.

‹ Kakori Kebabs

SERVES 4

These kebabs were cooked for us at the home of the Nawab Mir Jafar Abdullah. Invented in the village of the same name for one of Lucknow's early nawabs because he didn't have teeth, this dish features minced meat that is mixed with fat and slapped and tenderised until it is mushy and soft. Kakori kebabs are similar in texture to shami kebabs and are meltingly tender. The enzymes in the green papaya paste act as a tenderising agent for the meat. You will need to order the kidney fat in advance from your butcher. Alternatively, you could substitute lamb or pork fat; the fat is an essential element of the flavour.

500 g boneless mutton, diced
200 g kidney fat
50 g Green Papaya Paste (see page 378)
1¼ tablespoons chickpea (gram) flour
50 g ghee, melted

MARINADE
1 teaspoon Kashmiri chilli powder
¼ teaspoon freshly ground black pepper
⅛ teaspoon ground green cardamom
¼ teaspoon ground black cardamom
⅛ teaspoon ground cloves
⅛ teaspoon ground cinnamon
pinch of ground mace
1¼ tablespoons raw cashews
2 teaspoons blanched almonds
2½ tablespoons diced onion
1½ tablespoons diced red onion
salt
100 g white poppy seeds
2 teaspoons melon seeds
2 teaspoons mawa (khoa) or firm ricotta
1¾ tablespoons chickpea (gram) flour
100 g ghee, melted
¼ teaspoon saffron threads
few drops of rosewater

Mince the mutton, then add the kidney fat and mince together. Repeat seven or eight times, making the meat more tender and pliable each time. Add the green papaya paste and mix well. Set aside for 30 minutes.

To make the marinade, blend all the ingredients to a smooth paste. Stir into the minced meat until thoroughly combined, then cover and refrigerate

for 30 minutes. Mix in the flour and ghee. Refrigerate for at least 1 hour until the mixture is firm.

Preheat a barbecue or char-grill to hot. Oil some metal skewers, then mould the mince onto the skewers using wet hands. Cook the kebabs over hot coals or on the char-grill for 8–10 minutes, turning them every couple of minutes for even cooking. Serve with Mint Chutney (see page 76).

Lamb with Onions

SERVES 4

Another wonderfully fragrant dish cooked in the dum style (like the potatoes on page 98), a taste memory from Karim's, a landmark canteen in Old Delhi. When the seal is broken at the table, the captivating aromas are released.

225 g plain flour
20 g unsalted butter
250 g pearl onions, peeled and blanched
100 ml vegetable oil
1 teaspoon ground turmeric
1 bay leaf
10 cloves
8 green cardamom pods, cracked
8 dried red chillies
3 × 2 cm pieces cinnamon stick
2 onions, finely diced
6 tablespoons Ginger Garlic Paste (see page 377)
250 g tomatoes, peeled, seeded and chopped
1 kg lamb (leg or shoulder), cut into 5 cm cubes
2 teaspoons garam masala
2 teaspoons ground coriander
½ teaspoon ground mace
1 teaspoon ground cumin
¼ teaspoon freshly grated nutmeg
2 teaspoons freshly ground black pepper
1 tablespoon salt
2 tablespoons chopped coriander leaves
2 teaspoons finely shredded ginger

To make the dough to seal the pot, mix the flour and ¾ cup (180 ml) water in a bowl to a workable dough. If it is too dry, add a little extra flour; if too wet, add a little extra water. Roll out the dough on a lightly floured surface into a sausage that is long enough to wrap around the top edge of the pan.

Melt the butter in a large, heavy-based saucepan and fry the pearl onions over a medium heat for a few minutes until golden. Remove from the heat and set aside.

Wipe out the pan, then add the oil. Fry the turmeric, bay leaf, cloves, cardamom, chillies and cinnamon stick over a medium heat for about 30 seconds until fragrant – don't let them burn.

Add the onion and cook until it is translucent. Add the ginger garlic paste and cook until it has softened, then add the tomato. Cook for 5 minutes over a medium heat. Add the lamb and stir to coat. Cook for 10 minutes, stirring occasionally, until the lamb starts to brown. Cover the pan with a tight-fitting lid and wrap the dough around the join. Press firmly to seal the pan completely. Reduce the heat and simmer for 30–40 minutes until the lamb is tender.

Crack the dough apart and remove the lid. Stir in the ground spices and salt. Add the reserved pearl onions, then cover the pot again and cook for 5 minutes for the flavours to infuse. Sprinkle with the fresh coriander and ginger to serve.

Spiced Quail & Saffron Gravy
Bater Masala
SERVES 4

This dish from Esphahan restaurant in Agra's Amarvilas hotel is luscious and spicy, redolent of the decadence of royal Mughlai cooking. Unless you are deft with a small boning knife, I suggest you ask your butcher to tunnel-bone the quails for you.

200 g thick plain yoghurt
2 teaspoons chilli powder
2 teaspoons minced red chilli
1¼ teaspoons garam masala
1 teaspoon ground cumin
3 large (jumbo) farmed quails,
    tunnel-boned
2 teaspoons minced ginger
1 teaspoon black cumin seeds
¼ teaspoon ground fennel
¼ teaspoon ground cubeb pepper
2 cloves, ground
1 teaspoon chopped mint leaves

SAFFRON GRAVY
150 g finely diced white onion
100 g diced tomato
1 tablespoon vegetable oil
2 teaspoons dried red chillies,
    broken into pieces
¼ teaspoon star anise
¼ teaspoon cloves
2 cm piece cinnamon stick
1 teaspoon ground turmeric
½ cup (125 ml) White Chicken Stock
    (see page 380)
3 tablespoons tomato puree
2 teaspoons salt
½ teaspoon garam masala
1 teaspoon saffron threads
100 ml cream

Mix the yoghurt with the chilli powder, red chilli, 1 teaspoon garam masala and the cumin. Rub the mixture into the quails, then cover and leave to marinate for 1 hour.

Preheat the oven to 180°C.

Remove one quail from the marinade. Debone the quail completely and chop the meat finely to resemble a coarse mince. Combine the ginger, cumin seeds, fennel, cubeb pepper, cloves, mint and remaining garam masala with the minced quail meat. Stuff the remaining quails with the spiced mince so they resume their original shape. Sit the quails side by side in a small baking dish and cover with foil. Bake for 25 minutes, then remove the foil and bake for a further 5 minutes until golden.

To make the saffron gravy, blend the onion and tomato to a paste. Heat the oil in a large frying pan and fry the chilli, star anise, cloves, cinnamon stick and turmeric over a medium heat until fragrant. Stir through the onion/tomato paste and simmer for 5 minutes until softened. Add the stock and bring to a boil. Reduce the heat, then stir in the tomato puree and simmer for 20 minutes until the gravy has thickened. Strain the gravy, discarding any solids. Return it to the pan and season with the salt, garam masala, saffron and cream. Bring back to boiling point, then taste and adjust the seasoning if necessary.

Add the cooked quails to the pan, spooning the gravy over, and simmer gently for a few minutes, then serve.

Rosewater-scented Milk with Basil Seeds

Falooda

SERVES 4

Of Persian heritage and introduced to India by the Mughals, this rosewater-scented milk has a silken texture with slippery threads of jelly and tiny black basil seeds. It's a sweet that is typical of the Muslim food of the north, served either as a cooling drink (where the cream is omitted and the milk is poured over crushed ice) or as a dessert.

    2 teaspoons agar agar
    2 tablespoons caster sugar
    few drops of red food colouring
    1 litre full-cream milk
    1 tablespoon icing sugar, sifted
    ½ cup (125 ml) cream, whipped
    2 teaspoons rosewater
    350 ml Sugar Syrup (see page 379)
    30 g basil seeds, soaked in cold water
        for 30 minutes, drained
    1 tablespoon crushed pistachios

Put the agar agar and 1 cup (250 ml) water in a small saucepan and bring to a boil. Stir in the caster sugar and simmer over a low heat for 15 minutes, stirring constantly. Add the red food colouring and stir to combine. Pour into a shallow tray and refrigerate until set. Turn the jelly out of the tray and cut it into thin strips, like short vermicelli.

Whisk the milk and icing sugar together, then fold in the whipped cream until combined.

Combine the rosewater and sugar syrup, then pour into serving glasses or bowls. Mix in some of the falooda jelly threads and softened basil seeds. Spoon the cream over the top and sprinkle with the pistachios to serve.

Cardamom & Pistachio Kulfi

SERVES 4–6

Kulfi is an age-old Indian iced confection, the precursor to Western ice-cream. Eaten as a snack or served as a dessert, it is often garnished with edible silver leaf. It is made without eggs or cream and gets its creamy texture from reduced milk that is flavoured with nuts, spices, saffron or mango. Traditionally, it is set in small conical metal moulds and sealed with a screw-on lid.

    2 litres full-cream milk
    ½ teaspoon ground cardamom
    75 g jaggery, shaved
    1¼ tablespoons chopped pistachios

Put the milk and cardamom in a wide saucepan on a diffuser mat over the lowest heat setting. Cook for about 3 hours, stirring regularly to prevent sticking and a skin from forming, until the milk has reduced to 3 cups (750 ml). It must not boil but should simmer very gently. If you try to speed up the process, the result will not be the same.

Pass the milk through a fine-meshed sieve, discarding the cardamom. Stir the jaggery and pistachios into the hot milk, then blend in a food processor. Allow to cool.

Pour the cooled mixture into kulfi (or similar) moulds and freeze until firm.

Melon-seed Brittle
Kharbooj Beej Chikki
MAKES 24

These little tissue-wrapped sweets were a bedtime offering at the Lodhi Hotel in Delhi, so I asked the kitchen how they are made. Chikki is traditionally made during winter when jaggery and peanuts are in season, but almonds, cashews, pistachios or pine nuts (or a mixture) can be substituted for the peanuts. In Hindi, kharbooj means melon and beej means seeds.

2 teaspoons vegetable oil or melted butter, plus extra for coating the nuts
melon seeds
pistachio slivers
almond slivers
pine nuts
chopped dried fruits
shaved jaggery

Lightly grease a baking tray with the oil or butter.

Measure out a simple two-to-one ratio of nuts, seeds and fruits to jaggery. Put the jaggery in a saucepan with a little water to just wet it, then cook until it reaches 140°C on a candy thermometer and has melted and has a soft ball consistency.

Roast the nuts and mix with a little oil or melted butter to give a gloss, then mix with the jaggery.

Pour the mixture onto the baking tray and flatten using a wooden spoon or, better still, a rolling pin. The mixture should be no more than 1 cm thick, so the amount required depends on the size of the tray you are using. Cut into 3 cm squares while warm, before it cools down and hardens.

Store in an airtight container until ready to use, between layers of baking paper to prevent sticking.

Rose-syrup Dumplings ›
Gulab Jamun
MAKES 20

Gulab jamun is one of the definitive desserts of India, and many sweet shops in Delhi and roadside stalls near markets sell these treats to take away. The dumplings are soaked in an aromatic syrup after being fried, and are best eaten as soon as they are made.

3 tablespoons self-raising flour
1 tablespoon fine semolina
100 g milk powder
½ teaspoon ground cardamom
30 g ground almonds
30 g ground pistachios
½ cup (125 ml) milk, warmed
75 g ghee, melted
vegetable oil, for deep-frying
2 tablespoons pomegranate seeds
2 tablespoons chopped pistachios
1 sheet edible silver leaf

ROSE SYRUP
500 g caster sugar
5 green cardamom pods, cracked
few drops of rosewater

Sift the flour, semolina, milk powder and cardamom into a bowl. Mix in the ground almonds and pistachios. Combine the warm milk and ghee, then pour it onto the flour mixture and gradually incorporate the dry ingredients until a smooth dough forms. Cover the bowl with a cloth or plastic film and leave to rest for 30 minutes.

With wet hands, roll the dough into 20 small balls. Heat the oil to 170°C. To test the temperature of the oil, sprinkle in some flour – if the flour sizzles, it is ready. Deep-fry the balls a few at a time until golden brown (about 3 minutes). Remove from the oil with a slotted spoon and drain on paper towel.

To make the syrup, place the sugar and cardamom in a large saucepan, add 325 ml water and bring to boiling point, stirring occasionally. Simmer for 5 minutes, then add the fried dumplings and simmer for another 10 minutes so they absorb the syrup. Stir in the rosewater.

Stir through the pomegranate seeds and sprinkle over the chopped pistachios. Cut the silver leaf into small pieces and stick to the dumplings. Serve warm.

AMRITSAR & THE PUNJAB
Gurduwaras, Bazaars & Tandoori

Amritsar lies in the heart of the Punjab, the capital of the richest state in India and the holy city of the proud, tenacious Punjabi Sikhs. The state has the most fertile farming land in India, butter and cream are staples in their diet, and richness and extravagance abound.

The bounty of the land is apparent in its food culture – lashings of butter, buttermilk, cream and ghee are the benchmarks of many of its dishes and I was warned to bring a hearty appetite. Take their trademark *dal makhani* for instance – chickpeas cooked in a spicy tomato gravy enriched with butter and cream – wickedly good. As anywhere, the culture and history shapes the food and as the Sikhs scattered after Partition, they took their food culture and portable tandoor ovens with them. Introducing India and the rest of the world to tandoori baked meats and bread, they set up restaurants and dhabas wherever they landed. It was a revelation. There is an addictive quality to the food; it's impossible to pass up on another buttery *kulcha*, *bhatura*, milky *kulfi* or syrupy *jalebi*.

On my first visit, I was fortunate to get some valuable insider tips from local pastry chef Gayatri, whose passion for her food culture emanated with every suggestion. Through her, I was able to dig beneath the surface and taste some terrific food. I also watched Bhangra folk dance performances and visited rural farms and villages to see agricultural production first hand – finding mustard, wheat, corn, rice and tomatoes growing in abundance. I got a real sense of the traditions and daily routines in the country. Everywhere, people offered food as a sign of welcome. We were welcomed into one village house where I helped a woman make chapatis, on a tawa pan over an open fire in her courtyard, as she prepared the other dishes for our lunch using vegetables from her garden. Another time, I explored more of the rural areas, driving north-west from Chandigarh through the Punjab to Amritsar along the famous GT (Grand Trunk) Road. Travelling India's oldest and longest major road we passed expansive wheat farms and small towns and villages, each with its own *gurdwara* (temple). Food stops along the way become an event. This is one of the vital arterial highways linking the east coast to the north-west frontier, and the dhabas and vendors along the way are frequented by truck drivers – which I've learned equates to good food in India. I always ask my drivers to take me to where they eat and I have never been let down once.

THE GOLDEN TEMPLE

Every time I visit, I am immediately drawn to the revered Golden Temple – Sri Harmandir Sahib, a sacred shrine for people of all faiths and the symbol of Sikhism built in the mid-sixteenth century. It is the most visited place in India after the Taj Mahal and the most tangibly spiritual place in the country. Photos just don't do justice to the mesmerising beauty and commanding presence of the temple – it is simply mind-boggling. It stands as a symbol of inclusion, universal brotherhood and equality, essential values for humanity and the future of our civilisations.

I am escorted by my Sikh friend Manjeet, whose towering presence makes him a wonderful bodyguard. We arrive as dawn breaks to sit on the mats in the temple and listen to prayers being chanted, and to catch the golden light in all its mesmerising beauty. Within the temple compound, as in any Sikh temple, apart from the ritual of the chanting of daily prayers, the action centres around the Guru ka Langar, the enormous communal kitchen in the temple run by an equally enormous team of volunteers to produce food for a staggering 100,000 people per day – many more during festival days. One of the beliefs of Sikhism is the premise of equality: every human is treated equally without prejudice to class, caste, religion, social status or gender, with an emphasis on sharing everything with the community. Everyone who visits the temple is welcome to sit on the floor in the dining room and be given a plate of nourishing rice, vegetable dal and chapati. The temple exudes an egalitarian quality, a deep spirituality, openness and welcome to all. This is what underpins the very character of the Punjabi people and it's extraordinary to see.

AMRITSAR

After our early morning visit to the temple, Manjeet steers us to the Basant Ave area for our favourite Punjabi breakfast - steaming hot *kulcha*, a leavened bread stuffed with masala potato and baked on the inside walls of a tandoor oven in the same manner as naan, and slathered with melted ghee. It's finger-licking good. We try the local *chachh*, a lassi made with thin buttermilk and flavoured with black salt and cumin seed. It aids digestion and is a good antidote to the rich food, but is definitely an acquired taste. In contrast, I prefer the richer lassi served at Gian Chand Lassi Wale, an institution of the city, with its thick layer of *malai* (cream) floating on top of the buttermilk. Even more decadent is the *bedhi* lassi – made with *koya* (evaporated milk), jaggery and yoghurt, with a generous amount of cream on top. While we are in Hall Bazaar, we stop for jalebi, made to order at Gurdas Ram Jalebi Wale with semolina rather than flour, rendering their texture fluffy and light, a whisper on the tongue.

We explore the old town along the laneways and atmospheric bazaars that surround the temple, climbing up narrow stairwells along Pappad Warian Bazaar to the rooftops of the pappad workshops, watching thousands of pappadams being handmade and dried on bamboo mats in the sun. In the cramped quarters of the old city behind the seven gates, the lanes too narrow for cars, we discover small dhabas, many without names, munching on chicken pakoras as we go. This is the haunt of local foodies where the street food is best, cooked fresh every hour. Punjabi street food is not as spicy as that in Mumbai, nor as sweet as Delhi, and seasoned mainly with cumin and coriander.

Most locals don't make puri, bhature, paratha or kulcha at home, relying instead on their favourite shop or dhaba to make them. These dhabas do a roaring trade keeping up with demand, adding to the social

atmosphere. A simple lunch of *chole bhatura* (chickpea curry and puffed bread) is more than enough after a full-on dinner the previous night at Crystal Family Restaurant, our table groaning under the array of plates – with *murgh peshawri* (chicken cooked in a black pepper and cardamom masala), *gosht bunda* (lamb curry), *malai kofta jafrani* (vegetable dumplings in a spicy gravy), *dal makhani*, *paneer methi* (cheese and fenugreek leaves) and every bread on the menu.

Ready for a walk, we visit Jallianwala Bagh, a public garden in the city that commemorates the brutal massacre of locals, who were peacefully enjoying an annual religious festival, by the colonial British government at the turn of the twentieth century. The Partition Museum is a recent addition to the cultural heritage of the city. This public museum at the Town Hall aims to collate stories, photographs and documents related to the tragedy and chaos created by the outgoing British government at the time of independence. In the late afternoon, we drive about an hour out of town west to the Wagah Border Gate where the Indian (in their khaki and red uniforms) and Pakistani (in their green and white uniforms) guards on both sides perform the beating of retreat ceremony daily at sunset – it's a total spectacle; their uniforms and movements are so utterly camp.

In the evening the sweet shops along Lawrence Road beckon - *kanha* sweets, delicious *phirni* (saffron rice pudding) and the original *kanpuri aam papad* (a fruit leather made from mango pulp, sugar and then sun-dried) at Ram Lubhaya Ram Di Redi. Kulfi ice-cream gets thrown into the mix. There is so much to taste in this dynamic city and the locals love to feed us. Three words of advice – wear flexible clothing.

Dal Makhani

SERVES 6

Although this dal preparation has its roots in the Punjab region, it has been popularised on menus throughout India and many chefs across the country have their own signature version. Made with black urad lentils, this dal is hearty, enriched with lashings of butter and cream. I like to serve it with kebabs or roasted or barbecued meat.

> 300 g black urad lentils, soaked overnight
> 160 ml tomato puree
> 2 tablespoons Ginger Garlic Paste
>   (see page 377)
> 3 teaspoons salt
> 1 teaspoon Kashmiri chilli powder
> 125 g unsalted butter
> 150 ml cream

Drain the lentils, then rinse with cold water and put in a large saucepan. Pour in 1.5 litres water and bring to a boil. Reduce the heat and cook slowly for about 15 minutes, stirring occasionally, until the lentils have split and are mushy in appearance. Mash until smooth, then add the tomato puree, ginger garlic paste, salt and chilli powder. Cook over a low heat for 1 hour until thick, stirring occasionally.

Stir in the butter and cream and cook for 15 minutes until the dal looks rich and glossy. Taste and adjust the seasoning if necessary. Serve hot.

Pappadams ›

SERVES 6

Pappadams are an essential accompaniment to any Indian meal. After watching them being made on rooftops in Amritsar, I discovered it is both easy and satisfying to make your own. I use a pasta machine to roll out the lengths of dough.

> 125 g white urad dal flour
> 60 g chickpea (gram) flour
> 20 g rice flour
> ½ teaspoon ajwain seeds
> ½ teaspoon brown mustard seeds
> ½ teaspoon fennel seeds
> 10 g salt
> vegetable oil, for deep-frying

Combine the flours, seeds and salt in a food processor and slowly add enough cold water to make a firm dough (like pasta). Turn out the dough onto a clean lightly floured bench and knead until smooth.

Cut the dough into six pieces and flatten each piece with a rolling pin. Roll each strip through a pasta machine (as if you were making pasta) to the second last notch.

Hang the rolled dough sheets over a dowel stick and allow to dry out for 1 hour.

Cut each sheet into 20 cm lengths.

Heat vegetable oil in a kadhai or wok to 160°C. To test the temperature, add a small piece of dough – if it sizzles, the oil is ready. Fry the sheets, a few at a time, until golden and crisp – this should take about 3 minutes.

Remove from the oil with a slotted spoon and drain on paper towel. Allow to cool, then store in an airtight container until ready to serve.

Punjabi Spiced Chickpeas

SERVES 6

Typical of the region, this is a wonderful salad dish to serve with grilled or barbecued meat. I sometimes serve it with roasted chicken that I have rubbed with similar spices to complement the chickpeas. I use dried chickpeas from Indian suppliers; they are smaller and slightly darker than some European varieties.

   2 tablespoons vegetable oil
   12 curry leaves
   2 teaspoons ground cumin
   1 onion, finely diced
   6 cloves garlic, minced
   2 teaspoons minced ginger
   2 small green chillies, sliced
   2 ripe tomatoes, peeled and diced
   100 g thick plain yoghurt
   300 g cooked chickpeas, drained
   1 teaspoon Chat Masala (see page 376)
   2 teaspoons salt
   1 teaspoon lemon juice
   3 tablespoons pomegranate seeds
   2 tablespoons chopped coriander leaves

Heat the oil in a heavy-based frying pan and fry the curry leaves and cumin for 30 seconds over a medium heat until fragrant. Add the onion, garlic, ginger and chilli and gently fry until starting to colour. Stir in the tomato and any juice and bring to simmering point. Add the yoghurt and chickpeas and cook for 4–5 minutes until heated through.

Remove from the heat and stir in the chat masala, salt, lemon juice and pomegranate seeds. Taste and adjust the seasoning if necessary. Sprinkle with the fresh coriander to serve.

Eggplant & Yoghurt Raita
Baingan ka Raita

SERVES 4

Two of my favourite ingredients together in one dish, to accompany other dishes on a shared table or to simply serve with roast chicken or grilled fish.

   1 purple eggplant (aubergine)
   ½ teaspoon ground turmeric
   4 tablespoons vegetable oil
   salt
   300 g thick plain yoghurt, chilled
   1 tablespoon cumin seeds
   1 tablespoon chopped mint leaves

Cut the eggplant in half lengthways and place, cut side down, on a board. Cut crossways into 6 mm thick slices.

Mix together the turmeric, oil and 1 teaspoon salt.

Heat a grill or frying pan. Brush each slice of eggplant with the turmeric oil and fry until golden on both sides. Repeat until all the eggplant slices are cooked, then remove the pan from the heat. You'll be using it later.

Whisk the yoghurt in bowl to loosen, then add ½ teaspoon salt and stir to combine.

Spoon the yoghurt into a serving bowl and arrange the fried eggplant slices on top.

Heat the remaining turmeric oil in the reserved pan and fry the cumin seeds until fragrant. Spoon over the eggplant slices. Gently stir the eggplant into the yoghurt, just a turn or two, and keep chilled until ready to serve. Garnish with the mint to serve.

Creamed Mustard Greens

Sarson ka Saag

SERVES 4

I have fond memories of this simple vegetable dish being cooked for lunch at a rural village house near a farm where mustard was planted. After the seeds are cultivated, the leaves are used in myriad vegetable preparations so nothing is wasted. Mustard leaves are readily available at food shops that sell fresh Asian produce, and at local farmers' markets.

500 g mustard leaves, stems removed
250 g spinach leaves, stems removed
2 large green chillies, chopped
1½ teaspoon salt, or to taste
3 tablespoons mustard oil
1 teaspoon cumin seeds
4 garlic cloves, crushed
1 brown onion, diced
3 tomatoes, chopped
3 teaspoons chilli powder
50 g cornflour
20 g unsalted butter
1 teaspoon garam masala
1 tablespoon lemon juice
1 tablespoon fried garlic slices

Rinse the mustard and spinach leaves under cold water. Drain.

Put the leaves in a large saucepan with the green chilli and salt. Cover and cook over a high heat for 1-2 minutes until the leaves have wilted. Remove and refresh under cold water, then drain in a colander and leave to cool.

When cool, blend the greens in a food processor to make a puree.

Heat the oil in a large frying pan or wok over a medium heat, add the cumin seeds and cook for 30 seconds until they start to crackle. Stir in the crushed garlic and cook for 45 seconds until fragrant but not coloured. Add the onion and cook for 6-7 minutes until softened, then add the tomato and chilli powder. Cook for 15 minutes until the tomato has broken down and any excess liquid has evaporated.

Blend the cornflour with enough cold water to make a paste, then stir into the tomato mix and cook for a few minutes until thickened. Add the mustard leaf puree and stir to combine. Cook over a low heat until heated through, then stir in the butter and season with a little extra salt if needed.

Spoon into a serving bowl. Sprinkle with garam masala and lemon juice, and garnish with fried garlic slices.

Chickpea Curry & Bread
Chole Bhatura
SERVES 4

Chole is chickpeas cooked in a spicy gravy. Bhatura is a heavenly, deep-fried leavened bread, typically served with paneer and spiced chickpeas, a staple of the Punjabi diet. The dish often comes with slices of red onion and pickled vegetables, both of which play an important part in creating a perfect combination of flavours. This is how they cook it at Bharawan da Dhaba in Amritsar, sometimes adding paneer and cooking it in the gravy.

200 g dried chickpeas,
    soaked in cold water overnight
2 teaspoons black tea
    (tied in muslin cloth)
salt
3 tablespoons melted ghee
1 brown onion, finely diced
1 tablespoon Ginger Garlic Paste (see
    page 377)
2 small green chillies, finely sliced
3 tomatoes, chopped and pureed
1 teaspoon ground turmeric
1 teaspoon chilli powder
1 teaspoon amchur
3 tablespoons chopped coriander leaves

MASALA
1 black cardamom pod
1 small bay leaf
1 tablespoon coriander seeds
2 teaspoons cumin seeds
½ teaspoon black peppercorns
1 small dried chilli
2 cloves
2 cm piece cinnamon stick

Rinse the soaked chickpeas. Place in a large saucepan of water, add the muslin bag of tea and 2 teaspoons salt and cook over a medium heat for 45–50 minutes or until soft. Remove the bag of tea and discard.

Drain the chickpeas, reserve the cooking water. Put 3 tablespoons of the cooked chickpeas in a bowl and coarsely mash with back of a spoon.

To make the masala, dry-roast the spices in a non-stick frying pan over a gentle heat for about 90 seconds until fragrant. Allow to cool, then grind to a powder in a spice blender.

Heat the ghee in a large frying pan or khadai and fry the onion until lightly browned, stirring occasionally. Add the ginger garlic paste and green chilli and fry for 1 minute.

Add the tomato puree and 1 teaspoon salt and cook over a medium heat for 5 minutes – during this time the oil will start to separate. Stir occasionally to prevent sticking. Add the masala mix, along with the ground turmeric and chilli powder, and cook for another minute.

Add the whole and mashed chickpeas and 200 ml of the reserved cooking water. Cook until the gravy thickens – add a little extra water if it looks too dry. Remove from the heat and stir in the amchur and chopped coriander leaves. Serve with bhatura bread.

Bhatura Bread
MAKES 10

300 g plain flour
½ teaspoon bicarbonate of soda
1 teaspoon salt
5 tablespoons thick plain yoghurt
1 teaspoon caster sugar
2 teaspoons melted ghee
vegetable oil, for deep-frying

Sift the flour, bicarbonate of soda and salt into a large bowl. Mix the yoghurt with 100 ml warm water and the sugar, then knead into the flour to make a smooth dough. Continue to knead until the mixture stops sticking to the bowl or your fingers. If the dough feels a little dry, add an extra spoonful of warm water. Add the ghee and continue to knead until the ghee is thoroughly mixed in and the dough looks a little shiny or glossy. Cover the bowl with a cloth and leave in a warm place for 3 hours.

Tip the dough onto a lightly floured work surface and divide into 10 pieces. Roll each piece into a ball, then roll each ball into a flat disc about 12 cm in diameter. Lay the discs on a tray as you roll them, separated with a sheet of baking paper. Keep the discs covered as you roll out the remaining balls of dough.

To cook, heat oil in a kadhai or wok to 180°C. To test the temperature of the oil, add a small piece of dough – if it sizzles, the oil is ready. Fry the bread discs, one at a time, until they puff up and become golden, then flip over to fry the other side. Remove from the oil with a slotted spoon and drain on paper towel. Serve hot.

Butter Chicken

SERVES 4

This dish that has come to symbolise Indian cooking across the world and is offered in so many Indian restaurants. It is the Punjabis who have championed this classic dish, one I have tasted in countless places. This version is from Crystal restaurant in Amritsar. The only real trick with this recipe is that the sauce can't be reheated because it's butter based and will split, so be mindful of timing when you prepare it.

560 g curd (drained yoghurt)
2 tablespoons Ginger Garlic Paste
  (see page 377)
2 small green chillies, minced
1 teaspoon Kashmiri chilli powder
½ teaspoon ground coriander
½ teaspoon ground cumin
½ teaspoon garam masala
½ teaspoon ground turmeric
1 teaspoon salt
2 teaspoons lime juice
1 kg chicken thigh fillets,
  cut into 5 cm chunks
100 g ghee
coriander leaves, to garnish

TOMATO BUTTER SAUCE
750 g ripe tomatoes, peeled
  and mashed to a pulp
75 g unsalted butter, diced
  and chilled
1 teaspoon Kashmiri chilli powder
3 teaspoons lime juice
½ teaspoon garam masala
1 teaspoon dried methi (fenugreek)
  leaves, ground to powder
2 teaspoons salt
120 ml cream

Place the curd, ginger garlic paste, green chilli, ground spices, salt and lime juice in a large bowl and stir to combine. Add the chicken and turn to coat well, then cover and refrigerate for 2 hours.

Heat the ghee in a large frying pan over a low heat, add the chicken and the marinade and stir to combine. Cover and simmer gently for 15 minutes or until the chicken is tender, turning it halfway through for even cooking.

To make the sauce, tip the tomato into a large frying pan and cook over a medium heat for 10 minutes until the excess liquid has evaporated and mixture has thickened.

Add the butter and chilli powder and stir until butter has just melted – don't let the butter separate out in the sauce. Season with lime juice, garam masala, ground methi and salt. As soon as it starts to simmer, take the sauce off the heat and pour it over the cooked chicken. Stir through the cream and mix to combine.

Garnish with coriander leaves and serve with steamed rice and Roti (see page 103).

Punjabi Lamb & Spinach
Palak Gosht

SERVES 4

A hearty meat dish that evokes the spirit of the Punjab, we were served this when we visited Ranjit's homestay during autumn for a rooftop lunch. This is the perfect dish for cooler weather and the epitome of good home-style cooking. I sometimes add cooked freekah (whole green wheat) or spelt to the gravy with the spinach puree to add a contrasting texture and extra nourishment from the grains.

2 small green chillies, chopped
1 tablespoon chopped ginger
4 cloves garlic
140 g thick plain yoghurt
8 (800 g) lamb cutlets, trimmed
200 g English spinach leaves
    (or silverbeet), stems removed
3 tablespoons mustard oil
1 bay leaf
1 black cardamom pod
2 cloves
½ teaspoon black peppercorns
3 brown onions, finely diced
1 teaspoon ground coriander
1 teaspoon ground cumin
½ teaspoon ground turmeric
2 tomatoes, chopped
1 tablespoon tomato paste
salt
⅛ teaspoon fresh grated nutmeg
20 g unsalted butter
2 tablespoons chopped coriander leaves

Blend the chopped chillies, ginger and garlic in a food processor to make a paste. Stir the paste into the yoghurt in a bowl. Add the lamb cutlets and turn to coat, then set aside to marinate for 1 hour.

Blanch the spinach in boiling water for 10 seconds. Refresh in iced water, then drain and squeeze out any excess moisture. Place in a food processor and blend to a puree.

Heat the oil in a large frying pan and cook the whole spices until fragrant, about 30 seconds. Add the onion and stir to combine. Fry for 15 minutes over a medium heat, stirring occasionally, until the onion has started to colour.

Stir in the ground spices and cook for a few minutes. Add the lamb and marinade, stirring to combine, and cook for another 10 minutes.

Add the chopped tomato, tomato paste and salt and cook for another 2–3 minutes. Pour in 1 cup (250 ml) hot water and reduce the heat to low, then cover and simmer gently for 10 minutes. Remove the lid and stir through the spinach puree. Check the seasoning and add a little extra salt if required. Simmer for 5 minutes, then remove from the heat.

Stir the nutmeg into the sauce and add the butter and coriander. Pick out the black cardamom pod and bay leaf before serving.

Saffron Rice Pudding ›
Phirni
SERVES 4

This home-style dessert is comfort in a bowl, a wonderful food memory from Amristar when Gayatri cooked us dinner one evening. Please use full-cream milk (preferably unhomogenised jersey milk, and certainly not skim) – anything less diminishes its luscious flavour and texture. I sometimes garnish with a few dried rose petals to give the dessert a more festive look.

150 g short-grain rice, rinsed and soaked
   in cold water for 1 hour
1 litre full-cream milk
100 g caster sugar
½ teaspoon ground cardamom
½ teaspoon saffron threads
few drops rosewater
2 tablespoons pistachios, sliced into
   thin slivers

Drain the rice and process roughly in a food processor to break the grains into a coarse paste. Don't overwork or make it mushy.

Pour the milk into a heavy-based saucepan and bring to the boil. When it starts boiling, stir in the rice paste. Reduce the heat and cook until the mixture has thickened and the rice is soft, about 15 minutes.

Add the sugar and stir for about 3 minutes until it has dissolved, then stir in the cardamom, saffron and rosewater.

Remove the pan from the heat. Spoon the pudding into serving bowls and scatter pistachio slivers over the top.

Amritsari Fried Fish ›
SERVES 6

These are a staple on the menus at Surjit Food Plaza and across the road at Makhan Fish Corner on Lawrence Road in Amritsar. Freshwater fish fillets are marinated in yoghurt and seasoned with ajwain, giving a distinctive fragrance to this snack – the most popular in Amritsar. They are usually made here with either Singhara or Sole but at home I use either freshwater salmon, silver perch or wild barramundi.

750 g freshwater fish fillets,
   skin and bones removed
½ teaspoon ground turmeric
100 ml malt vinegar
250 g curd (drained yoghurt)
150 g chickpea (gram) flour
3 tablespoons Ginger Garlic Paste
   (see page 377)
1 egg, beaten
1 tablespoon lemon juice
2 teaspoons ajwain seeds
2 teaspoons chilli powder
1 teaspoon salt
vegetable oil, for deep-frying
½ teaspoon chat masala

Cut the fish into 3 cm thick slices about 10 cm long.

Lay the fish on a flat tray in a single layer. Mix together the turmeric and vinegar and sprinkle over the fish, then set aside for 15 minutes. Blot the fish dry with paper towel to remove any excess moisture.

In a bowl, combine the curd, flour, ginger garlic paste, egg, lemon juice, ajwain, chilli powder and salt. Add the fish slices and turn gently with your hands to thoroughly coat each piece. Leave to marinate for 20 minutes.

Heat the oil in a wok to 180°C. To test the temperature of the oil, sprinkle in some flour – if the flour sizzles, it is ready. Fry the fish, a few slices at a time, for 5-6 minutes until crisp and golden. Drain on paper towel. Sprinkle with chat masala to serve.

VARANASI
Pilgrims, Ghats &
the Holy River

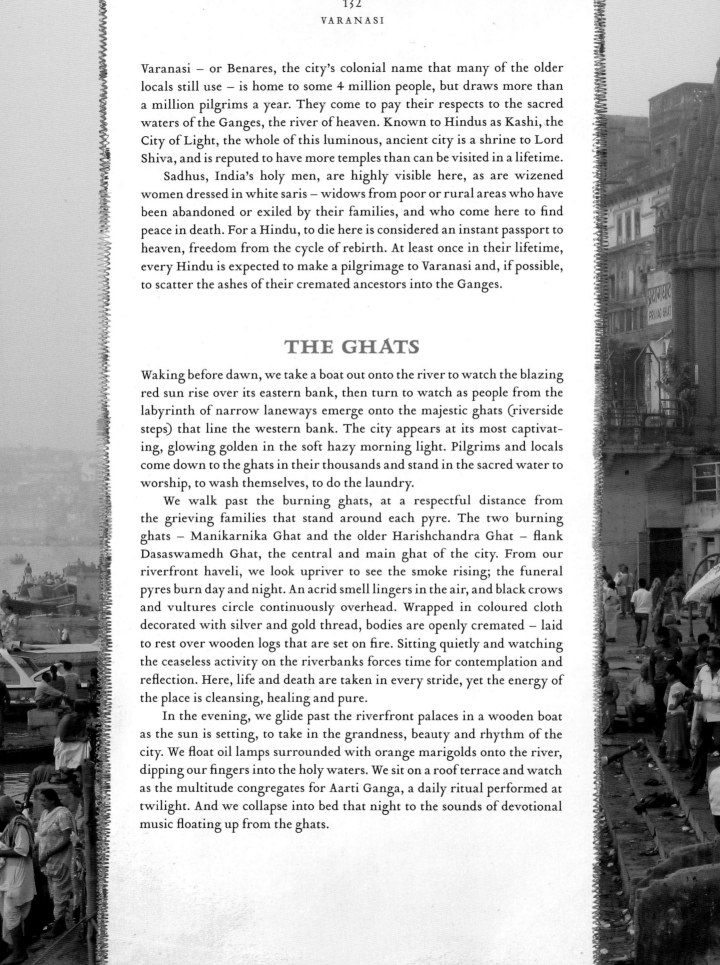

Varanasi – or Benares, the city's colonial name that many of the older locals still use – is home to some 4 million people, but draws more than a million pilgrims a year. They come to pay their respects to the sacred waters of the Ganges, the river of heaven. Known to Hindus as Kashi, the City of Light, the whole of this luminous, ancient city is a shrine to Lord Shiva, and is reputed to have more temples than can be visited in a lifetime.

Sadhus, India's holy men, are highly visible here, as are wizened women dressed in white saris – widows from poor or rural areas who have been abandoned or exiled by their families, and who come here to find peace in death. For a Hindu, to die here is considered an instant passport to heaven, freedom from the cycle of rebirth. At least once in their lifetime, every Hindu is expected to make a pilgrimage to Varanasi and, if possible, to scatter the ashes of their cremated ancestors into the Ganges.

THE GHÁTS

Waking before dawn, we take a boat out onto the river to watch the blazing red sun rise over its eastern bank, then turn to watch as people from the labyrinth of narrow laneways emerge onto the majestic ghats (riverside steps) that line the western bank. The city appears at its most captivating, glowing golden in the soft hazy morning light. Pilgrims and locals come down to the ghats in their thousands and stand in the sacred water to worship, to wash themselves, to do the laundry.

We walk past the burning ghats, at a respectful distance from the grieving families that stand around each pyre. The two burning ghats – Manikarnika Ghat and the older Harishchandra Ghat – flank Dasaswamedh Ghat, the central and main ghat of the city. From our riverfront haveli, we look upriver to see the smoke rising; the funeral pyres burn day and night. An acrid smell lingers in the air, and black crows and vultures circle continuously overhead. Wrapped in coloured cloth decorated with silver and gold thread, bodies are openly cremated – laid to rest over wooden logs that are set on fire. Sitting quietly and watching the ceaseless activity on the riverbanks forces time for contemplation and reflection. Here, life and death are taken in every stride, yet the energy of the place is cleansing, healing and pure.

In the evening, we glide past the riverfront palaces in a wooden boat as the sun is setting, to take in the grandness, beauty and rhythm of the city. We float oil lamps surrounded with orange marigolds onto the river, dipping our fingers into the holy waters. We sit on a roof terrace and watch as the multitude congregates for Aarti Ganga, a daily ritual performed at twilight. And we collapse into bed that night to the sounds of devotional music floating up from the ghats.

FOOD FOR THE GODS

During my first visit, Shashank, the genial owner of the Ganges View Hotel, outlines the three categories of food for Hindus: Satvik Khana, Rajasic and Tamasic. Satvik Khana is a diet based on fruit, vegetables, grains and cereals with turmeric, chilli, mustard and cumin used sparingly; asafoetida is used to enhance flavour, in much the same way as garlic is used in other food traditions (garlic, onions and eggs are all forbidden). Associated with calmness, purity and balance, such pure vegetarian food is considered to promote longevity, intelligence, strength and health. Rajasic embodies activity, passion and restlessness through foods that are salty and highly spiced – such foods are eschewed by those seeking spiritual enlightenment. Tamasic brings sleep, dullness and inertia, with a diet based on meat, ghee-laden and fried foods (that includes most street food) and starchy fast food.

The pure vegetarian food of Varanasi is considered food for the gods, prepared with various herbs that are beneficial for both body and mind – keeping the body healthy and beautiful, and facilitating meditation and purity of thought. As well as being offered to the gods, paan is taken after the evening meal as a digestive and stimulant. The various spices, condiments and mild intoxicants are blended with lime paste and wrapped in a betel leaf to make a small triangular parcel. Shops sell ready-mixed paan masala, but many stay true to the art and buy their chosen condiments to make their own personal paan, or have them made by their favourite paan wallah. Everybody, it seems, vouches for the benefits of paan. I am yet to be convinced.

CITY OF FESTIVALS & STREET FOOD

Our first time in Varanasi coincides with Durga Puja, a nine-day festival devoted to the nine manifestations of Durga, destroyer of evil and protector of humanity. It is like stepping into a giant carnival. The streets come alive in the late afternoon with dancing and drumming, temporary temples sprout everywhere, food vendors ply a busy trade, and spruikers sell balloons, kites and toys on the roadside. At the culmination of the festival, durga idols large and small are transported by truck or on shoulders to the river and immersed in the water amid constant loud drumming and chanting.

Festivals punctuate the city's calendar, particularly during autumn and I plan my visits around them, most recently for Shivrati, the festival in February that gives reverence to Lord Shiva and is a celebration of music, dance, meditations and of course, fireworks. Twenty days after Durga Puja comes Diwali, the festival of light, a fairytale spectacle in Varanasi as the riverfront is lit with thousands of clay lantern candles, with more floating on the water, and sweet shops go into overdrive to meet the demand for *khoa* (concentrated milk) and other sweetmeats. But the biggest event for

Varanasi is the Festival of Ganga, an almighty homage to the holy river, just fifteen days after Diwali.

Food lies at the heart of every festival: it draws people out onto the streets to celebrate, to be swept up by the energy and experience myriad tastes. Along the narrow *gallis* (alleyways) that make up the heart of the old city, street carts are everywhere. At breakfast time, bread pakoras from kadhais of hot oil over coal braziers are consumed as quickly as they can be fried. The poor man's pakoras, they are simply white bread spread with a thin layer of dal paste then coated in a spicy gram-flour batter and deep-fried. Starchy and stodgy, they do the job of filling empty bellies for a few rupees. *Kachoris* are cooked throughout the day, with the filling changing from dal to spiced potato or cauliflower in the evening.

Milk is a signature of Varanasi and we pass many milk markets during our stay, where the pure white liquid is being poured from large steel vats into smaller vessels and carried away on bicycles. The locals have a penchant for milky drinks like lassi, the thirst-quenching yoghurt-based drink that can be sweet or salty, with shopfronts everywhere dispensing creamy lassi in disposable clay cups (*kulhads*). Equally popular are flavoured, brightly coloured sherbets and *thandai*, a cooling drink made with water, sugar, watermelon seeds, almonds, lotus seeds, cardamom, fennel, pepper and rose petals. Some make it with *bhang* (marijuana), to give it an extra kick, a special offering during Shivarati that we experienced on the garden terrace of a private riverfront haveli. A puja blessing by a chanting monk followed later that afternoon at the Nepali Temple. I thought of it as balance and harmony.

On a mission to find one of my favourite street snack of chat – crisp little puri puffs that come with an array of fillings – we venture down Vishwanath Galli, regarded as the most famous laneway in the city for fast food. We jostle for space to watch the vendors as they prepare *papri chat*, *golgappa* (puri puffs), potato chat and spinach pakoras, amid rows of shops selling fruit preserves (*murabbas*) and pickles.

Varanasi is renowned for its pickles, and the local red chilli (*Benarasi lal mircha*) is the brightest red of all the Indian chilli varieties. Due to its plumpness, it can be split lengthways, stuffed with a masala paste and made into a pickle. I buy a jar and tuck it into my bag, so I can savour the memory at home.

Before I leave, I visit the Bharat Mata ('Mother India') temple, inaugurated by Mahatma Gandhi in 1936 as a temple for all to worship at, regardless of religion. For me, it is a personal pilgrimage to honour all those people I have met, spoken to, dined and travelled with in India, a respectful acknowledgement to the spirit of Mother India. The spectacle of the temples, the devotional rituals, the river and its energy, the food – all have left an indelible mark, an emotional connection to this luminous city.

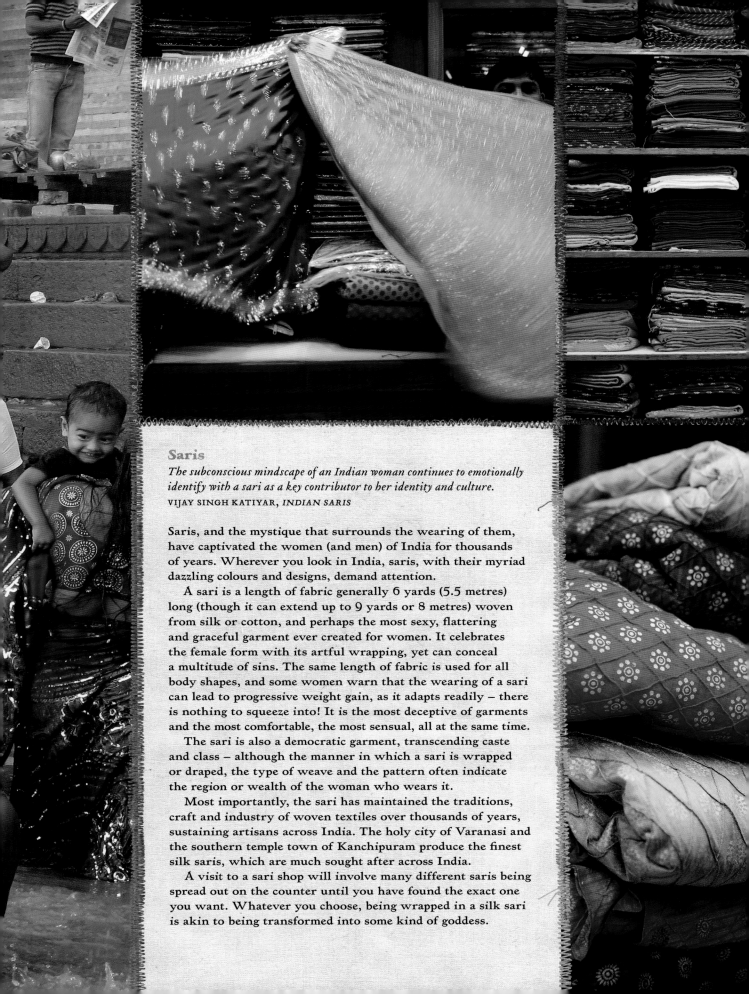

Saris

The subconscious mindscape of an Indian woman continues to emotionally identify with a sari as a key contributor to her identity and culture.
VIJAY SINGH KATIYAR, *INDIAN SARIS*

Saris, and the mystique that surrounds the wearing of them, have captivated the women (and men) of India for thousands of years. Wherever you look in India, saris, with their myriad dazzling colours and designs, demand attention.

A sari is a length of fabric generally 6 yards (5.5 metres) long (though it can extend up to 9 yards or 8 metres) woven from silk or cotton, and perhaps the most sexy, flattering and graceful garment ever created for women. It celebrates the female form with its artful wrapping, yet can conceal a multitude of sins. The same length of fabric is used for all body shapes, and some women warn that the wearing of a sari can lead to progressive weight gain, as it adapts readily – there is nothing to squeeze into! It is the most deceptive of garments and the most comfortable, the most sensual, all at the same time.

The sari is also a democratic garment, transcending caste and class – although the manner in which a sari is wrapped or draped, the type of weave and the pattern often indicate the region or wealth of the woman who wears it.

Most importantly, the sari has maintained the traditions, craft and industry of woven textiles over thousands of years, sustaining artisans across India. The holy city of Varanasi and the southern temple town of Kanchipuram produce the finest silk saris, which are much sought after across India.

A visit to a sari shop will involve many different saris being spread out on the counter until you have found the exact one you want. Whatever you choose, being wrapped in a silk sari is akin to being transformed into some kind of goddess.

Spinach Cooked with Asafoetida
Palak Bhaji
SERVES 4

One of chef Sanjeev's vegetable dishes from the vegetarian thali menu at Nadesar Palace Hotel, this is all about vibrant flavours.

2½ tablespoons mustard oil
2 tablespoons finely diced onion
1 teaspoon minced garlic
3 small red chillies, minced
½ teaspoon asafoetida
½ teaspoon chilli powder
1 teaspoon ground coriander
1 teaspoon ground fenugreek
¼ teaspoon ground turmeric
1 teaspoon ground cumin
500 g spinach leaves, stalks removed
2 teaspoons cream
1 teaspoon salt
½ teaspoon garam masala

Heat the oil in a wok or kadhai over a medium heat and fry the onion, garlic, chilli and asafoetida until softened and starting to colour. Stir in the ground chilli, coriander, fenugreek, turmeric and cumin and continue to fry until the oil separates from the spices in the pan.

Add the spinach leaves, reduce the heat to low and stir until the spinach has wilted, about 2 minutes. Add the cream and season with salt and garam masala. Serve hot.

Eggplant in Mustard Gravy ›
Baigan Saiso
SERVES 6

Annapurna, Shashank's 90-year-old mother and matriarch of the house, still presided over the kitchen at the Ganges View Hotel when I stayed there, her frail yet resilient body perched up on the bench next to the stove as she ministers to the food bubbling away in the kadhais.

1 kg small eggplants (aubergines; ideally the purple egg-shaped Indian ones), each cut into 3 chunks lengthways
1 litre mustard oil
280 g curd (drained yoghurt)
juice of ½ lemon
2 teaspoons salt

MUSTARD-CHILLI PASTE
12 large dried red chillies
4 tablespoons yellow mustard seeds

To make the mustard-chilli paste, soak the dried chillies in warm water for 30 minutes to soften. Grind the mustard seeds using a spice grinder or mortar and pestle. Transfer to a blender, add the drained softened chillies together with ½ cup (125 ml) water and blend to a smooth thick paste.

Soak the eggplant chunks in water for 10 minutes to remove any bitterness, then drain and pat dry with paper towel.

Heat the oil in a kadhai or wok and, when hot, fry the eggplant in batches until softened but not coloured. Drain on paper towel.

Tip all except 2 tablespoons of the oil out of the pan. Add the mustard-chilli paste and fry, stirring constantly, for 10 minutes until fragrant and starting to colour. Stir in the curd, lemon juice and salt and cook for 5 minutes. Return the eggplant to the pan and stir to combine, then cook over a medium heat for another 10–15 minutes. Serve hot.

‹Dal-stuffed Puri Bread
Dal Puri
MAKES 16

This simple bread dough is a staple of the repertoire – it can either be grilled to make chapatis or deep-fried to make puris, here filled with spicy dal.

vegetable oil, for deep-frying

BREAD DOUGH
750 g wholemeal flour

STUFFING
1 tablespoon mustard oil
1 teaspoon cumin seeds
1 large dried red chilli,
   broken into small pieces
½ teaspoon asafoetida
1 teaspoon ground turmeric
2 teaspoons salt
1 cup (200 g) channa dal,
   soaked overnight then drained

To make the bread dough, combine the flour and 400 ml water in a bowl, then tip onto a floured bench and knead the dough for 5 minutes. Set aside in a bowl, covered with a cloth until ready to use.

To prepare the stuffing, heat the oil in a kadhai or wok over a medium heat and fry the cumin seeds and chilli for 1 minute. Stir in the asafoetida, turmeric and salt and fry for another minute or so until fragrant. Stir in the dal and cook for a few minutes, then add just enough water to loosen and continue to cook until soft (about 10 minutes), stirring occasionally. Remove from the heat and leave to cool.

To make the puris, roll the dough into a long cylinder, then cut into 16 pieces and roll into small balls. Roll out the balls of dough on a lightly oiled surface to flatten into rounds about 2 mm thick. Place 1 tablespoon of the stuffing in the centre of each round, pressing it down lightly but taking care not to let it go anywhere near the edges. Fold each round in half and gently start to press from the centre outwards, to flatten the dough without breaking the surface, until the dough returns to a round flat shape. It is essential that the stuffing remain intact inside the dough at all times – a careful, deft hand is required for this.

Heat the vegetable oil in a kadhai or wok to 180°C. To test the temperature of the oil, sprinkle in some flour – if it sizzles, it is ready. Fry the puris, one at a time, pressing lightly with a spatula until they puff up and become golden. Flip over and fry for another 30 seconds, then drain on paper towel. Continue with the remaining puris and serve hot.

Cauliflower & Potato Curry
Dahaiwale Aloo Gobi
SERVES 4

One of the more common vegetable preparations of Varanasi, this version appeared on our dinner thali plate at the Ganges View Hotel.

4 tablespoons mustard oil
200 g cauliflower florets
2 cloves
3 green cardamom pods, cracked
2 teaspoons minced ginger
8 curry leaves
250 g potato, diced and parboiled
1 teaspoon ground turmeric
½ teaspoon ground cinnamon
½ teaspoon chilli powder
1 teaspoon salt
1 teaspoon caster sugar
2 small ripe tomatoes, finely diced
150 g curd (drained yoghurt)
½ teaspoon garam masala
2 teaspoons chopped mint leaves
3 teaspoons chopped coriander leaves

Heat the oil in a large frying pan and fry the cauliflower for 2 minutes until just starting to colour. Remove from the pan with a slotted spoon.

In the same pan, fry the cloves, cardamom, ginger and curry leaves for 30 seconds until fragrant. Add the potato, tossing to coat with the spices. Return the cauliflower to the pan and toss to combine. Stir through the ground spices, salt and sugar. Add 2 cups (500 ml) water and bring to the boil, then reduce the heat to a simmer. Add the tomato and simmer gently for 6–8 minutes until the potato is soft.

Add the curd and simmer gently for another 3 minutes, adding a little extra water if it becomes too dry. Season with garam masala and garnish with mint and coriander.

Saroj's Eggplant & Onion
Baigan Pyaj
SERVES 6

A chance meeting with Ankita on our flight
to Varanasi led us to her family's house in
Sarnath, the place where Buddha gave his first
sermon after attaining enlightenment. Her
parents, Dr Ahbay Jain and his wife Saroj,
are both keen home cooks, and Saroj prepared
this simple eggplant dish as part of a thali
lunch we shared with the family.

4 tablespoons mustard oil
2 small white onions, sliced
2 cloves garlic, sliced
1 small green chilli
½ teaspoon cumin seeds
1 teaspoon ground coriander
½ teaspoon ground turmeric
500 g eggplants (aubergines),
    cut into 3 cm cubes
salt

SAROJ'S GARAM MASALA
1½ teaspoons black peppercorns
1 teaspoon cloves
1½ teaspoons black cardamom seeds
½ teaspoon whole mace blades
1 teaspoon ground green cardamom
3 teaspoons ground cinnamon
1 teaspoon ground ginger

To make the garam masala, grind the whole spices
together until fine and then mix with the ground
spices. Store in an airtight jar.

Heat the oil in a large frying pan and fry the onion
for a few minutes over a medium heat until starting
to soften and colour. Add the garlic and chilli
and fry for another minute or two, until soft and
fragrant. Remove from the pan.

In the same pan, fry the cumin seeds for 15 seconds,
then add the ground coriander and turmeric and
fry for a minute. Return the onion mixture to the
pan and stir to combine. Add the eggplant, together
with just enough water to moisten, and simmer
over a medium heat until the eggplant is soft,
about 15–20 minutes.

Season to taste with salt and 1 teaspoon Saroj's
garam masala.

Potatoes in Curd ›
Aloo Dahi
SERVES 6

Dr Ahbay Jain (who I met in Sarnath) is
a keen cook and this is a favourite from his
repertoire – it makes a delicious salad in hot
weather. He recommends serving it with a
tangy tamarind chutney (see page 210).

½ teaspoon ground cumin
½ teaspoon chilli powder
pinch of ground black salt
½ teaspoon salt
1 teaspoon caster sugar
560 g curd (drained yoghurt)
400 g potatoes, boiled, peeled and
    sliced into rounds
1 tablespoon chopped coriander leaves

In a bowl, mix the cumin, chilli, salts and sugar
with the curd, then stir through the potato slices
until evenly combined. Spoon into a serving bowl
and garnish with chopped coriander.

Puri Puffs with Sweet Tamarind Sauce & Yoghurt

Golgappa

SERVES 4

Golgappa is the North Indian name for the street snack of stuffed crisp puris – in other parts of India they are known as pani puri. Pani refers to the cumin-flavoured water that is added to the crisp puri puffs.

1 tablespoon chopped mint leaves
6 tablespoons thick plain yoghurt

PURI PUFFS
160 g fine semolina
300 g plain flour
vegetable oil, for deep-frying

SWEET TAMARIND SAUCE
1 cup (250 ml) thick tamarind liquid
25 g jaggery, shaved
2 teaspoons roasted ground cumin
1 teaspoon chilli powder
½ teaspoon ground black salt

STUFFING
2 tablespoons vegetable oil
2 tablespoons cooked masoor dal
100 g cooked potato, peeled and diced
1 tablespoon cooked chickpeas
½ teaspoon salt
½ teaspoon chilli powder
2 teaspoons Chat Masala (see page 376)

To make the puris, combine the semolina and flour and add enough water to make a stiff dough. Knead for 5 minutes to soften the glutens. Roll two-thirds of the dough into a long cylinder and cut off twenty 3 cm pieces, then roll each piece into a small ball. Roll out each ball into a round.

Cover the puris with a damp cloth and set aside.

To make the sweet tamarind sauce, bring the tamarind liquid to the boil and simmer for 5 minutes until slightly reduced and thick. Add the jaggery and continue to cook over a medium heat for another 5 minutes. Add the spices and salt, then taste and adjust if necessary. Allow to cool before serving.

To make the stuffing, heat the oil in a large frying pan and fry the dal, potato and chickpeas for 2 minutes, tossing to combine. Season with salt, chilli powder and chat masala.

To cook the puris, heat the oil in a kadhai or wok to 180°C. To test the temperature of the oil, sprinkle in some flour – if it sizzles, it is ready. Deep-fry the puris, a few at a time, pressing lightly with a spatula until they puff up. Flip over and fry for another 30 seconds, then drain on paper towel.

To serve, make a hole in the centre of each puri puff and spoon in a little stuffing. Arrange on plates, swirl the sweet tamarind sauce and yoghurt on top and sprinkle with the chopped mint.

Urad Dal Dumplings in Yoghurt Sauce
Dahi Bhalla

SERVES 6

It's hard to stop at one plate of these delicious dumplings bathed in tangy yoghurt sauce. Traditionally served in little bowls made from dried leaves, they are a festive speciality – we tasted them from a street cart one evening as final celebrations for Durga Puja overtook the city.

1 teaspoon finely shredded ginger
1 long green chilli, finely sliced
½ teaspoon chilli powder
1 tablespoon chopped coriander leaves
4 tablespoons sweet tamarind sauce
   (see page 142)

DUMPLINGS
200 g urad dal, rinsed, then soaked
   for 2 hours
2 teaspoons minced ginger
1 teaspoon ground cumin
2 small green chillies, minced
1 teaspoon salt
vegetable oil, for deep-frying

YOGHURT SAUCE
560 g thick plain yoghurt,
   lightly whipped
½ teaspoon salt
¼ teaspoon ground black salt
1 teaspoon caster sugar
1 teaspoon ground cumin
½ teaspoon freshly ground black pepper

To prepare the dumplings, drain the softened dal and grind to a smooth paste in a blender, adding a little water if necessary. Add the ginger, cumin, chilli and salt and pulse to combine. Remove from blender and roll into small, even-sized balls.

Heat the oil in a kadhai or wok to 180°C. To test the temperature of the oil, sprinkle in some flour – if it sizzles, it is ready. Fry the dumplings, a few at a time, until golden brown. Drain on paper towel. Fill a large bowl with warm water and soak the fried dumplings in the water until soft, about 10 minutes.

Meanwhile, make the yoghurt sauce by mixing all the ingredients together.

Remove the dumplings from the water and squeeze gently to remove any excess liquid. Place the dumplings in the yoghurt sauce and stir to coat, then leave for 15 minutes to allow the flavours to infuse.

Ladle into small serving bowls and garnish with ginger, sliced chilli, chilli powder and coriander. Spoon the sweet tamarind sauce over the top and serve.

Curd Dumplings Soaked in Saffron Milk
Ras Malai
SERVES 4

Sanjeev prepared this special Diwali dessert for us at Nadesar Palace Hotel. If you don't want to start from scratch, just use fresh ready-made cottage cheese or ricotta.

1.25 litres full-cream milk
3 cups (750 ml) cream
2 tablespoons lemon juice
770 g caster sugar
¼ teaspoon ground cardamom
¼ teaspoon saffron threads
1 tablespoon sliced pistachios
1 tablespoon blanched almond flakes

Mix the milk and cream together, then pour 3 cups (750 ml) of the mixture into a saucepan and simmer over low–medium heat until reduced by half. Set aside.

Heat the remaining milk mixture in another saucepan to boiling point. Add the lemon juice and stir to curdle the milk. When thick lumps start to appear, remove from the heat and set aside for 30 minutes.

Pour the curdled liquid through a muslin-lined sieve set over a bowl, so the liquid drains from the curd. Leave to hang overnight, refrigerated.

Place 660 g of the sugar in a saucepan with 3 cups (750 ml) water. Bring to the boil and cook for 5 minutes, stirring occasionally, until the sugar has dissolved to make a syrup.

Tip the curd from the muslin into a bowl. Gently mash with a fork, then, using your hands, roll the curd into 16 small balls. Cook the curd balls in the sugar syrup for 10 minutes.

Bring the reduced milk back to simmering point and add the remaining 110 g sugar. When it starts to boil, reduce the heat to low and add the cardamom and saffron, together with half the pistachios and almonds. Cook for 1 minute, then remove from the heat and leave to cool.

Remove the cooked curd balls from the syrup and drain. Add the balls to the cooled reduced milk, cover and refrigerate for 1 hour.

Garnish with the remaining pistachios and almonds.

Milk Noodles
Dudha Pitthu
SERVES 6–8

Varanasi is renowned for its sweet milk concoctions, and this recipe uses the cream taken from the top of the milk. If you can't find milk that hasn't been homogenised, I suggest you use a mixture of pure cream and full-cream milk to achieve the same result. This dish celebrates the pure unadorned taste of milk and has a similar texture to kheer or rice pudding. Annapurna, matriarch of the Ganges View Hotel, showed me how to make this, while her son Shashank explained that this sweet treat is often made by grandmothers and mothers as a way of expressing their love for their children.

300 g bread dough (see page 139)
3 tablespoons ghee
800 ml full-cream milk
400 ml cream
220 g caster sugar

Using the tips of your fingers, tear off tiny pieces of the dough and roll between your fingers to make elongated balls about the same shape and size as puffed wheat or risoni. Heat the ghee in a frying pan and fry the pitthu (dough pieces) until golden. Remove from the pan and set aside.

Heat the milk and cream in a large saucepan. When it comes to a rolling boil, add the fried pitthu and stir so they don't settle on the bottom of the pan. Reduce the heat and cook for 1 hour over a medium heat so the milk gently bubbles, stirring regularly and reincorporating the milk deposits from the sides of the pan back into the simmering milk.

Add the sugar and stir to dissolve, then taste and add a little extra, if you like – it is sweetened to individual taste. Continue to cook for another 45 minutes or until the milk has reduced and thickened. Serve at room temperature.

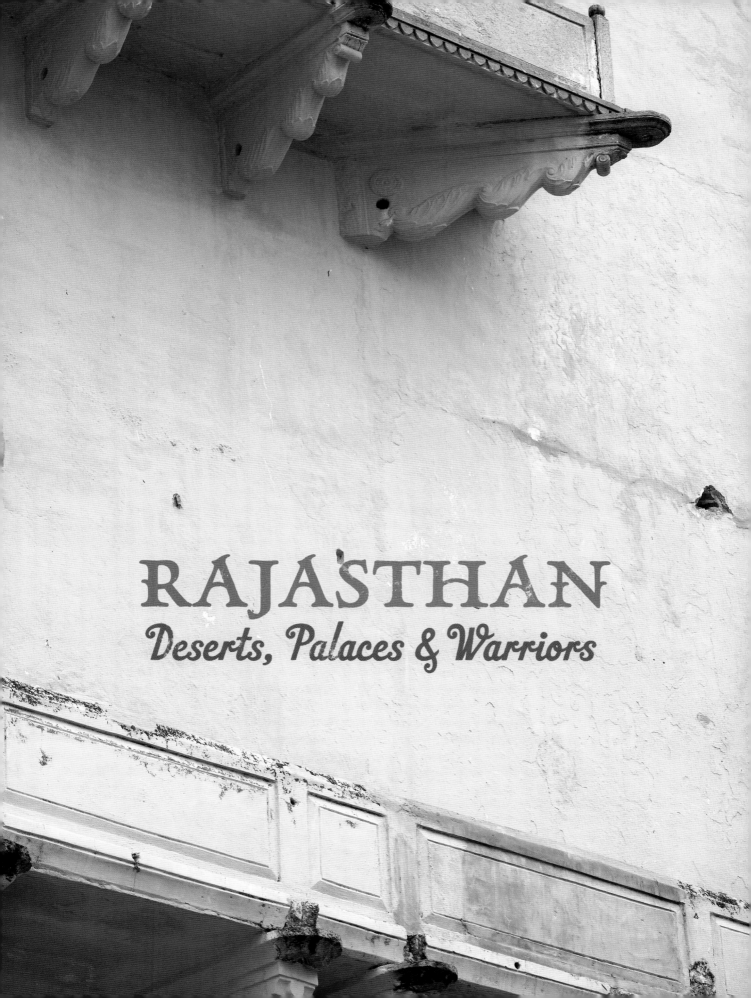

RAJASTHAN
Deserts, Palaces & Warriors

Travelling through the desert state of Rajasthan you discover a region overflowing with an embarrassment of riches. It is perhaps the most dazzling state of all, the 'land of the kings', ablaze with colour everywhere you look – from saris and turbans to forts and palaces to spices and food. Descendants of the seductive kingdom of the mighty Rajput warriors, the Rajasthanis are striking and proud. The men wear their distinctive moustaches and turbans with great pride, while the women are swathed in vividly coloured saris and adorned with dazzling jewellery.

> *Rajasthan was a profoundly conservative state, even by the standards of India. During the Raj, around two-fifths of India's vast landmass remained under the control of its indigenous princely rulers, and a fair proportion of this autonomous territory lay in Rajasthan, where semi-feudal rule had effectively continued up to 1971, when Indira Gandhi finally abolished the maharajas. The absence of any form of British intrusion meant that many surprising aspects of medieval Indian society had remained intact.*
> WILLIAM DALRYMPLE, *NINE LIVES*

The landscape is dotted with Mewari forts dating from the fourteenth century onwards, many of them now converted into luxury accommodation set against the dramatic backdrop of the Aravali mountains, where the Mughals once hunted with maharajas when tigers roamed freely. More recently, luxury trains have offered a new and popular travel experience in Rajasthan. The Royal Rajasthan on Wheels and the Maharaja's Express – both with suites and dining cars – have recreated the grand style of the palaces and the romantic glamour of decadent train travel. Plying between Delhi, Agra, Jaipur and Udaipur, the trains travel at night while guests are sleeping and stop during the day for some on-foot exploration and sightseeing at each stop of the journey. Remember, though, that this is the desert, and summer can be relentless. To avoid the overbearing temperatures and the heat haze, aim to visit during the cooler months between October and March.

Rajasthani food is also prey to the whims of the desert and the paucity of ingredients it yields. Because water is scarce, milk, buttermilk and curd are liberally used to add moisture. Dried lentils, indigenous desert beans, millet, corn and other cereals replace leafy greens, and the dominant spices include mustard seeds, turmeric, fenugreek and coriander.

JAIPUR, JODPHUR & JAISALMER

Known as the gateway to Rajasthan, Jaipur is the largest of the state's fortified cities, the pink hue of the local stone used in its construction reflecting the colour of the desert. Just north of the city is the magnificent Amber Fort, whose lakeside garden in the summer pavilion is planted like a Persian carpet. One of the best times to visit Jaipur is on the eve of the Holi festival (which falls between late February and March), to watch the procession of colourfully decorated elephants trumpet through the streets. The festival culminates in the grand spectacle of an elephant polo match. Another lovely time to visit is late January, when the desert air is still cool and the city plays host to its world-renowned annual literary festival. It's a chance to get up close to some of India's best writers and immerse yourself in the city's culture.

A visit to the shops and markets of the Johri Bazaar is mandatory. Vegetable vendors – on the sides of the streets, in vendor carts and in small shops – display their fresh, colourful and diverse produce invitingly. The shops have narrow frontages and the owners sit out the front on well-worn charpoys, inviting every passer-by in to browse. Wherever you look, business is brisk, and I find it nigh on impossible to leave empty-handed.

For an authentic taste of Jaipur and Rajasthani food, venture into one of the busy dhabas (roadside restaurants) set up under makeshift canopies or overhanging trees, where the locals eat. They rely on fast turnover and, more often than not, are where the best food can be found. Dishes are served from large conical pots called handis and breads are cooked to order over hot coals at a furious pace. At the other end of the culinary spectrum, the late Maharani of Jaipur, Rajmata Gayatri Devi, was a champion of the city's royal cuisine, publishing a collection of heirloom recipes from the palace kitchens. Suvarna Mahal, the restaurant at the Rambagh Palace Hotel, carries on the traditions of the Khansamas, the royal cooks of Rajasthan, and offers a culinary tour of the kingdom with its menu. Likewise, the museums of Jaipur's City Palace showcase the opulence of royal life, and are definitely worth a look to appreciate the richness of the culture.

The second-largest city in Rajasthan, Jodhpur sits at the edge of the Thar desert, which stretches west to Jaisalmer and beyond. Its indigo-blue buildings are at their most beguiling at sunset. The cityscape is dominated by the majestic presence of the Mehrangarh Fort – a powerful reminder that the skills needed to build on such a grand scale go back hundreds of years. Our hotel, a restored haveli within the walled town, has prime position with every room facing the fort. The other impressive building that defines Jodhpur is the majestic Umaid Bhawan Palace, a few kilometres from the centre of town. One of its wings remains the private residence of the Maharaja of Jodhpur, and the rest has been converted into a luxury

hotel, providing a finely tuned sense of space, proportion and opulence.

Further west, on the border with Pakistan, the dramatic desert city of Jaisalmer is one of the oldest kingdoms in Rajasthan. Defined by its medieval and massive twelfth century fort, home to several hundred families within its ramparts, it's one of the rare living forts in India, with palaces, ornate havelis, courtyard houses and a beautifully carved Jain temple. The city's buildings are bathed in a golden hue creating a spectacle as we approach, seemingly appearing out of nowhere, giving a sense of timelessness. We explore the fort, a UNESCO world heritage site rich with hidden treasures, ride out into the desert on camels and stay at Serai luxury camp, giving a whole new meaning to glamping. Under the stars out in the sand dunes, we sit in a circle on small stools around a campfire while being served a thali dinner. The flavours are deliciously authentic and home-style, reflecting the traditions of the Rajputana.

A TASTE OF DESERT LIFE
Tented wilderness camps

On the road between Jaipur and Jodhpur, near the village of Nimaj, the luxury tented camp at Chhatra Sagar takes three weeks to build each year for the season. The tents are set up along the top of a dam wall over-looking a vast reservoir that collects the winter rains: full of water at the start of the season in October (if the rains have been sufficient) and empty by March, the reservoir is the water supply for the property and the surrounding villages and farms. The camp is a blissful hideaway, with uninterrupted vistas over a bird sanctuary and grazing lands for goats, cows and water buffalo.

Chhatra Sagar is the homestead of the genial Singh brothers, Harsh and Nandi, and their cousin Raj. However, it is their wives, Shrinidhi and Vasundhara, who hold sway in the kitchen. Excellent cooks, the women are passionate about regional food, which they prepare in the time-honoured way, yet with a modern sensibility. Both are gracious and generous with their time and knowledge, sharing family culinary secrets with me and cooking sensational food each and every day, never serving the same dish twice. Organic produce is sourced from neighbouring farms, vegetables and pulses feature heavily, textures are fresh and crisp, and flavours are light – exactly the kind of food you crave after hours of road travel.

About an hour's drive south of Jodhpur, in a small village on the edge of the desert, lies Rohet Garh, a charming heritage hotel owned by Siddarth and Rashmi Singh. More recently, they have built from scratch the luxurious Mihir Garh, about 30 minutes further into the desert, resembling a desert palace of yesteryear with spectacular views of the Thar Desert. Both properties offer the enticing options of horse-riding and jeep safaris,

or a few days at their nearby tented wilderness camp. Each morning we travel through the spartan terrain, spotting herds of blackbuck antelopes and getting a glimpse of life in the Thar desert. We stop at different villages and come to appreciate the simplicity of the way of life of the Bishnoi people, who prioritise conservation and live in complete harmony with nature, farming millet, sesame and leafy greens. Their houses, made of dried dung and mud with straw roofs, are pristine and beautifully kept. The shepherds lead a nomadic existence, accompanying their herds of sheep and goats in search of water and feed. We pass many different groups during our travels, and each time we are struck by their dignity and grace.

I spend an afternoon cooking with Rashmi, an accomplished home cook who is faithfully preserving traditional family recipes. She uses recipes inherited from her late mother-in-law, Thakurani Sahiba, who wrote down her recipes in two small cookbooks, *Rohet Garh Cuisine* and *Quick and Easy Rajasthani*, which are now treasured family heirlooms. A purpose-built demonstration kitchen has been added to the house, opening out to a roof terrace, where dinner is served during the cooler months. Sundowners are served in the expansive manicured garden, a delightful and essential daily ritual when we have washed off the day's dust and adventure. For dinner we feast on a thali of sweet-and-sour tomatoes, eggplant cooked with yoghurt, a potato curry, spicy chicken and chutney. Rashmi's cooks (there are eight of them) prepare *churma* for dessert. This is traditionally made with *dal batti*, wholewheat bread dough that is sun-dried and used in myriad dishes in desert food. After the dough is cooked, it is crumbled and cooked again with sugar, ghee and almonds, then pressed into cakes and dressed with edible silver leaf. It's rich and dense – one small piece is more than enough.

AN INTERLUDE
Wedding season in Narlai

We slowly wend our way south to Udaipur, but we're keen to see some of the less-travelled parts of Rajasthan en route. Narlai, midway between Jodhpur and Udaipur, is tucked out of the way in a forgotten corner, seemingly beyond the gaze of most. We have come to stay at Rawla Narlai, where we are greeted with a shower of rose petals as we walk through the massive wooden gates into a beautiful courtyard, its stone walls draped with bougainvillea. Narlai is surrounded by massive granite hills, and in the morning we climb up to see the sunrise guided by Lala, who points out panther caves hidden among the rock formations and stops to pray at Jackali Mahadev, a Shiva temple near the top. As his melodic voice conveys his prayers to the gods, we are afforded views for miles around.

The small town of Narlai boasts more than 100 temples – and we return just after dark to the haunting sound of an orange-robed sadhu (holy man) singing and chanting while playing a stringed instrument called a *tandoora* and clapping *khartals* (castanets). He sits cross-legged

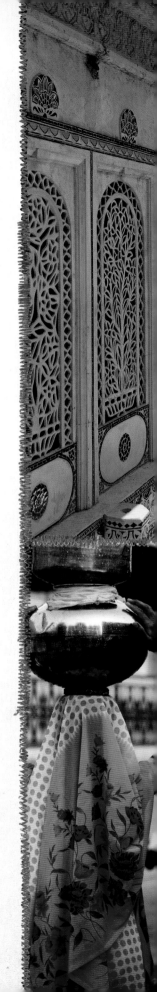

in the lotus position, lit only by a candle, on a low platform overlooking the courtyard garden. He has the most serene face I have ever seen, and we watch and listen to him for an hour, transfixed. It's an extraordinary experience.

The chef at Rawla Narlai, Avinash, is generous and helpful. He cooks with great pride in his region, and his distinctive desert food is a lasting memory. Everything on offer is considered, perfectly executed and done with ease, in keeping with the environment. Breakfast is a perfectly ripe papaya, a paratha stuffed with potato and herbs, yoghurt, mango pickle and a pot of tea. Lunch stays light, with a few vegetable pakoras and lentil patties, both served with mint chutney.

One evening for dinner we are taken by bullock cart through the village streets, which are alive with temple bells and the chatter of curious children. Our destination is an abandoned stepwell, set in an orchard and softly lit by glowing oil lamps that transform the place into a kind of fairyland. The hot food is transported in large metal tiffin carriers and pots. It's hard to imagine a more romantic backdrop. Another dinner is set up on the roof terrace with beautiful lanterns lining the stairway. Stars twinkle in the sky and there is a balmy warmth to the air as we sample Rajasthani desert beans (*ker sangri*) dry-fried in spicy curd with mustard oil, *gatta* curry with gram-flour dumplings, and a local lamb curry called *lal maas*. Later that night, we are awoken by the incessant noise of a wedding procession going up and down the small alleys and streets of the village. The next night is a repeat, and we learn we have arrived in peak wedding season. There is little to do but succumb.

A scenic drive through the countryside, passing herds of goats and nomadic Rabari tribesmen with their distinctive red turbans and small rural villages, brings us to Jawai Leopard Camp. The campsite feels so remote, hidden in a rocky landscape on an expanse of private land that affords the best safari experience in India, with a strong commitment to community and eco-friendly tourism. This is tented luxury beyond compare; I find perfection in every detail. The ethos is to tread lightly and leave no footprint. We feel so privileged to spot leopards on each safari drive from our open-roof jeep. One morning we stop on top one of the huge granite hills to find a lavish picnic breakfast has been set up for us with spectacular views across to the lake. This place is paradise on earth.

UDAIPUR

En route to Udaipur, we stop to visit Kumbhalgarh Fort, built in the fifteenth century, a former Mewari fortress and the second longest wall fortification in the world after China's Great Wall. It is breathtaking in its beauty and we manage to climb to the top through fortified gateways and past shrines to soak in the views from the turret of the Badal Mahal (palace of the clouds).

Udaipur is a city of palaces, lakes, cenotaphs and gardens, all bathed in
an ivory glow from the pale sandstone and white marble of its buildings.
The surrounding country is lush and green with small lakes dotted
around, while imposing hills and mountains provide a dramatic backdrop.
The crowning glory of Udaipur is the Lake Palace Hotel, which appears to
float in the centre of Lake Pichola, its white marble glistening in sunlight
and moonlight. Being ferried across the water in a small flat-bottomed
boat is quite magical, and on a sunset gondola ride around the lake we are
swept away by the spectacular beauty of the city. The more languid pace of
Udaipur from a waterside perspective makes it infinitely more appealing,
but the narrow streets around the bazaar soon jolt us back to the crowded
reality of India.

Devi Garh, an hour's drive to the north-east, offers respite from the
city, and is perhaps the finest of the fort-conversion hotels. Showered with
fragrant rose petals from the roof terrace as we walk through the main
elephant gate, it's a goose-bumps moment. I get the same sensation with
every visit; it never ceases to amaze. With its distinctive, contemporary
white-marble interiors and splashes of colour, the place is a maze of
corridors, courtyards and private rooms we could easily spend a week
exploring, and we realise we could eat in a different place every night
of the week! For a formal dinner, a procession of silver thali dishes
converge onto the table strewn with orange and red rose petals. *Malai
palak* (spinach and corn) and the unctuous Rajasthani *lal maas* (rich lamb
curry) are deeply satisfying, and an indecently rich *churma laddoo*, its ghee
and wheat flour dough sweetened with jaggery and bound with nuts, then
rolled into small balls and coated with silver leaf, finished us off. Yet again,
I am the grateful beneficiary of generous hospitality and the time-
honoured traditions of India, where 'your guest is your god'.

Paneer

MAKES ABOUT 750 g

This fresh curd cheese is a staple in the Indian kitchen, and is used extensively in Rajasthani cooking. Many Western recipes suggest substituting cottage cheese for paneer, but the texture and consistency are not the same. Paneer has a firmer texture and a mild taste that takes on the flavours of the other ingredients with which it is cooked. I prefer to use a firm ricotta in place of paneer if I don't have the time or inclination to make my own. Don't even think of making paneer with anything except full-cream jersey milk — the fat content in the milk is essential for the flavour.

2 litres full-cream milk
1 cup (250 ml) cream
200 ml white vinegar
100 ml lemon juice, strained

Line a sieve with a double layer of muslin and stand it over a bowl.

Pour the milk into a cast-iron or heavy-based saucepan and bring to simmering point. As the milk starts to boil, stir in the cream and then, as it starts to boil again, add the vinegar and lemon juice. Remove from the heat and continue to stir until the milk starts to separate and lumps (curds) start to form. When the milk has cooled slightly and the curds are quite large, gently pour into the strainer. Cover the strainer and bowl with plastic film and refrigerate for 3 hours, to allow the whey to drain through the muslin. At this stage, the curd will be creamy and soft. Rest a weight on top for about 2 hours to press and firm the cheese.

Press the cheese into a rectangular plastic container. Cover and leave at room temperature for another 2 hours, then cut the paneer as desired. It is now ready to use, but will keep for 5 days, covered and sealed in the refrigerator.

Tandoori Prawns
Sarson Jhinga

SERVES 4

One of my favourite tastes on the menu at Neel Kamal in Udaipur's Lake Palace Hotel, this recipe was given to me by Sameer, the charming chef at the time. Although tandoori cooking is relatively new to Rajasthan, having been introduced via Delhi after Independence, it has become very popular in recent times.

12 large uncooked king prawns,
    peeled and deveined
1 teaspoon chilli powder
50 g Ginger Garlic Paste (see page 377)
1 teaspoon salt
1 teaspoon lemon juice
Chat Masala (see page 376), to serve

MARINADE
1½ tablespoons mustard oil
1 teaspoon chilli powder
1½ teaspoons mustard powder
100 g curd (drained yoghurt)
1 teaspoon garam masala
¼ teaspoon ground cardamom
2 teaspoons kasoori methi
    (dried fenugreek leaf) powder
½ teaspoon salt
1 teaspoon Chat Masala (see page 376)

Sprinkle the prawns with the chilli powder. Add the ginger garlic paste, salt and lemon juice and mix well. Set aside for 30 minutes.

To prepare the marinade, combine the mustard oil and chilli powder. Add the remaining ingredients and mix well. Coat the prawns in the marinade and refrigerate for 1 hour.

Thread the prawns onto thin metal skewers and cook in a tandoor (or over hot coals or a barbecue grill) for 5–7 minutes, depending on the size of the prawns, until just cooked. Sprinkle with chat masala and serve.

Baked Cauliflower
Dum Ki Gobi
SERVES 4

One of the delicious vegetable dishes served on the thali plate at Shahpura Bagh, a delightful country retreat south of Jaipur where the home-cooking is outstanding.

400 g cauliflower florets
vegetable oil, for deep-frying
5 mm piece ginger, cut into fine matchsticks
1 tablespoon chopped coriander leaves
2 teaspoons chopped mint leaves

MARINADE
1 egg
2 tablespoons chickpea (gram) flour
½ teaspoon salt
½ teaspoon chilli powder
1 teaspoon ground coriander
1 teaspoon ground turmeric
2 teaspoons Ginger Garlic Paste
    (see page 377)

MASALA
2 tablespoons vegetable oil
75 g finely diced white onion
½ teaspoon fennel seeds
½ teaspoon cumin seeds
1 tablespoon Ginger Garlic Paste
    (see page 377)
125 g chopped tomato
1 tablespoon finely diced green
    capsicum (pepper)
½ teaspoon chilli powder
½ teaspoon ground turmeric
½ teaspoon garam masala
1 teaspoon salt

To make the marinade, beat the egg and mix in the remaining ingredients, stirring until combined. Add enough water to make a thick batter consistency.

Add the cauliflower and stir to coat. Cover and refrigerate for 30 minutes.

Heat the oil in a kadhai or large saucepan to 180°C. To test the temperature of the oil, sprinkle in some flour – if the flour sizzles, it is ready. Fry the cauliflower in small batches for 2–3 minutes until golden. Drain on paper towel.

To make the masala, heat the oil in a kadhai or wok and fry the onion with the fennel and cumin seeds until browned. Add the ginger garlic paste and fry for 2 minutes until fragrant. Add the tomato and cook until it is soft, about 15 minutes. Add the fried cauliflower, capsicum, ground spices and salt, stirring to combine. Cover with a lid and simmer for 5 minutes for the flavours to infuse.

Garnish with the ginger, coriander and mint.

Gram Fritters
Ram Ladoo
SERVES 4

These little fritters made with mixed dal are a memorable street snack I tasted in Jaipur at the Johri Bazaar, served in small disposable bowls made from dried neem leaves.

vegetable oil, for deep-frying
Coriander Chutney (see page 85), to serve
1 tablespoon shredded mint leaves
1 tablespoon shredded white radish

GRAM FRITTERS
400 g channa dal
100 g urad dal
1 teaspoon salt
1 teaspoon freshly ground black pepper
1 tablespoon minced ginger
3 small green chillies, minced
pinch of asafoetida
handful of chopped coriander leaves

To make the fritters, wash both the dals and soak them in separate bowls for 4 hours. Drain and grind the dals separately in a blender with a little water to make a slightly grainy paste. Mix the two dal pastes together with the remaining ingredients, stirring until thoroughly combined.

Heat the oil in a kadhai or wok to 180°C. To test the temperature of the oil, sprinkle in some flour – if the flour sizzles, it is ready. Drop small spoonfuls of batter into the hot oil and fry for about 3 minutes until golden brown, swirling them in the oil with a large mesh spoon so the fritters cook evenly. Drain on paper towel.

To serve, place a small pile of fritters in a bowl and spoon over the chutney. Garnish with the shredded mint and radish.

‹'Lamb Rhapsody'
Laal Maas
SERVES 4–6

When Sameer cooked this classic lamb dish for dinner one evening at Neel Kamal restaurant in Udaipur, it was instantly christened 'Lamb Rhapsody' by my fellow travellers, so the name has stuck – it says it all really! With lingering flavours that just sing on the palate, this is the signature meat dish of Rajasthan, and every household and restaurant has its own version. It tastes even better if you prepare it a few hours ahead and then gently reheat it when ready to serve. Tender young goat (kid) meat can be used instead of lamb, as is done in Rajasthan.

150 ml vegetable oil
1 teaspoon cumin seeds
5 cloves
1 black cardamom pod, cracked
5 green cardamom pods, cracked
¼ teaspoon mace blades
15 small red chillies
250 g red onions, finely sliced
50 g Ginger Garlic Paste (see page 377)
600 g suckling lamb leg meat, diced
1 teaspoon ground turmeric
2 teaspoons chilli powder
2 teaspoons salt
225 g thick plain sheep-milk yoghurt
2 tablespoons chopped coriander leaves

Heat the oil in a heavy-based saucepan. Add the cumin seeds and let them crackle over a medium heat, then add the cloves, cardamom pods, mace and chillies. Fry for a minute until fragrant, then add the onion and fry until it starts to brown, stirring regularly. Add the ginger garlic paste and fry for 5 minutes. Add the lamb and fry over a low heat for 10 minutes until seared and coated with the spiced onion mix. Add the turmeric, chilli powder and salt and fry for 8–10 minutes.

Whisk the yoghurt until smooth, then stir into the lamb. Cook over a medium heat for 10 minutes. Reduce the heat to low and simmer for at least 30 minutes or until the lamb is tender. Sprinkle with the fresh coriander and serve hot with steamed rice or Rice Pilaf (see top right).

Rice Pilaf
Kaisher Pulao
SERVES 6

At Devi Garh one evening, the basmati rice pilaf arrived at the table studded with sultanas and cashews. Quick to make, this dish makes an ideal accompaniment for rich, sauce-based meat dishes.

few saffron threads
2 tablespoons ghee
1 tablespoon raw cashews, chopped
2 tablespoons sultanas
110 g warm cooked basmati rice
2 teaspoons pistachio slivers
½ teaspoon salt

Infuse the saffron in 2 teaspoons hot water for 10 minutes. Heat the ghee in a kadhai or wok and fry the cashews over a medium heat until they are light brown. Add the sultanas and as they become plump, stir in the rice until combined. Stir in the saffron water, pistachios and salt. Serve hot.

Deep-fried Okra
Kurkuri Bhindi
SERVES 6–8

These addictive snacks were served with pre-dinner drinks at Neel Kamal in Udaipur. They are light, crunchy and flavoursome, and a cinch to prepare. Make sure you get very small okra for this – no bigger than your smallest finger (hence their other name, lady's finger).

500 g small okra
1 teaspoon salt
2 teaspoons chilli powder
100 g chickpea (gram) flour
vegetable oil, for deep-frying
1 teaspoon Chat Masala (see page 376)

Wash the okra in cold water and dry immediately. Cut into thin julienne strips. Sprinkle with the salt and chilli powder, then dust with the flour and mix well so the flour sticks.

Heat the oil in a wok to 170°C. To test the temperature of the oil, sprinkle in some flour – if the flour sizzles, it is ready. Deep-fry the okra in small batches until crisp and golden brown. Drain on paper towel. Toss with the chat masala and serve immediately.

Eggplant with Masala Sauce & Spiced Yoghurt
Dahi Baingan
SERVES 4

One of the starring dishes of chef Surendra's dinner thali at Samode Haveli in Jaipur.

½ teaspoon ground turmeric
salt
2 eggplants (aubergines),
  cut into 2 cm thick discs
vegetable oil, for deep-frying
2 teaspoons cumin seeds, roasted and ground
280 g thick plain yoghurt
1 tablespoon shredded coriander leaves

MASALA
2 tablespoons vegetable oil
2 tablespoons finely diced onion
4 tablespoons diced tomato
1 tablespoon Ginger Garlic Paste
  (see page 377)
½ teaspoon chilli powder
1 teaspoon ground cumin
1 teaspoon ground coriander
1 teaspoon ground turmeric
1 teaspoon salt
1 teaspoon kasoori methi
  (dried fenugreek leaf) powder
½ cup (125 ml) tomato puree

Mix the turmeric and 1 teaspoon salt and rub into the eggplant slices. Leave for 20 minutes.

Heat the vegetable oil in a kadhai or wok to 180°C. To test the temperature of the oil, sprinkle in some flour – if the flour sizzles, it is ready. Fry the eggplant slices until golden. Drain on paper towel.

To make the masala, heat the oil and fry the onion until softened, then add the tomato and cook for about 10 minutes until the oil separates. Add the remaining ingredients and cook for 10 minutes or until thick.

Stir half the roasted ground cumin into the yoghurt and season with salt to taste.

Spoon some masala sauce into the base of each serving bowl, then sit an eggplant slice on top and top with some of the spiced yoghurt. Repeat these layers twice. Sprinkle with the remaining roasted ground cumin and the fresh coriander to serve.

Corn Fritters
Bhutteyan Da Kebab
SERVES 8

These were prepared for us by chef Asish at Rambagh Palace Hotel in Jaipur and served with other kebabs on his signature kebab tasting plate. His dinner menu showcases the culinary style of the Rajputana, Avadh, Punjab and Hyderabad palaces. These fritters are a perfect snack to have with a cold drink during the afternoon or before dinner.

300 g plain flour
2 teaspoons baking powder
1 teaspoon salt
1 teaspoon ground cumin
1 teaspoon garam masala
½ teaspoon ground turmeric
1 egg
¾ cup (180 ml) milk
20 g butter, melted
165 g corn kernels
5 green onions, finely sliced
3 tablespoons finely diced green
  capsicum (pepper)
1 small green chilli, minced
3 tablespoons chopped coriander leaves
vegetable oil, for deep-frying

Combine the flour, baking powder, salt and spices in a bowl.

In another bowl, whisk the egg, milk and melted butter, then add this to the flour mixture and stir until smooth. The batter should be quite thick, so if it feels slightly runny, add a little extra flour. Combine the corn kernels, green onion, capsicum, chilli and fresh coriander, then fold into the batter until evenly mixed.

Heat the oil in a kadhai or wok to 180°C. To test the temperature of the oil, sprinkle in some flour – if the flour sizzles, it is ready. Drop a few spoonfuls of corn batter into the hot oil and fry for 3 minutes. Turn over and fry for another minute, then remove with a slotted spoon and drain on paper towel. Continue frying until all the batter has been used.

Serve with Mint Chutney (see page 76) or Tamarind Chutney (see page 210).

Spinach Koftas

SERVES 4

We were served these vegetable balls for lunch at Laxmi Vilas Palace in Bharatpur, on the drive between Agra and Jaipur.

500 g spinach leaves, chopped
2 tablespoons chickpea (gram) flour
½ teaspoon chilli powder
½ teaspoon ground turmeric
1 teaspoon cumin seeds
1 teaspoon salt
1 small onion, finely diced
1 cup (250 ml) vegetable oil

GRAVY
1 teaspoon cumin seeds
2 onions, finely diced
2 tablespoons Ginger Garlic Paste
   (see page 377)
4 tomatoes, chopped
1 teaspoon chilli powder
2 teaspoons ground coriander
1 teaspoon ground turmeric
2 teaspoons salt

Blanch the spinach in boiling water, then drain. Refresh in cold water and drain again, squeezing to remove any excess water. Grind the blanched spinach to make a paste. Add the flour, spices, salt and onion and mix until combined. Roll the mixture into small balls.

Heat the oil in a kadhai or large saucepan to 180°C. To test the temperature of the oil, sprinkle in some flour – if the flour sizzles, it is ready. Fry the koftas a few at a time over a high heat until golden. Drain on paper towel. Reserve the oil.

To make the gravy, add the cumin seeds to the reserved kofta oil and fry over a medium heat for 1 minute. Add the onion and cook until golden, stirring occasionally. Add the ginger garlic paste and stir until combined. Fry for a few minutes, then add the tomato, ground spices and salt. Simmer for about 20 minutes until the tomato softens and breaks down and the sauce becomes a thick gravy. Add 1 cup (250 ml) water and bring to a boil, then add the fried koftas. Simmer for 5 minutes until heated through.

Serve with Chapati (see page 85).

Roasted Lamb Leg
Raan-e-Samode
SERVES 6–8

This extravagant roast was served for dinner at Samode Bagh (about 90 minutes' drive from Jaipur). The meat spit-roasted over hot coals and carved at the table. The heady waft of spices and the magnificent garden setting combined to create a memorable experience.

1 × 1.5 kg suckling lamb leg
2 tablespoons Ginger Garlic Paste
   (see page 377)
2 teaspoons chilli powder
2 teaspoons salt
2 tablespoons Green Papaya Paste
   (see page 378)
100 ml malt vinegar
2½ tablespoons dark rum
1 teaspoon garam masala
¼ teaspoon ground mace
¼ teaspoon ground cardamom
2 red onions, finely sliced into rings
2 red capsicums (peppers), finely sliced
2 tablespoons lemon juice
1 teaspoon salt
½ teaspoon freshly ground black pepper

Prick the lamb all over and cut it at the knee joint. Combine the ginger garlic paste, chilli powder, salt, green papaya paste and vinegar, then massage into the lamb. Cover and set aside for 1 hour.

Mix the rum with the garam masala, mace and cardamom and pour over the lamb. Cover and leave to marinate in the refrigerator overnight.

Preheat the oven to 180°C.

Transfer the lamb to a rack standing in a baking dish and pour over the marinade. Cover with foil and cook for 1½ hours, basting every 15 minutes. Remove the lamb from the dish and allow to rest for 10 minutes.

Bring the pan juices to boiling point and simmer for 10 minutes until thickened. Slice the meat into chunks and arrange on a large serving plate. Spoon the sauce over to moisten. Mix the onion rings and capsicum with the lemon juice, salt and pepper, then arrange on top of the lamb and serve.

Spinach with Fenugreek & Pine Nuts

Palak Chilgoza

SERVES 4

This is a great way of preparing spinach, full of flavour and texture. This recipe was given to me by Sameer, chef at the Neel Kamal in Udaipur, after I had tasted it for dinner. It makes an ideal accompaniment to grilled fish or chicken.

1 kg spinach leaves, roughly chopped
2½ tablespoons vegetable oil
½ teaspoon cumin seeds
10 cloves garlic, chopped
100 g chopped onion
150 g chopped tomato
½ teaspoon ground turmeric
1 teaspoon ground coriander
½ teaspoon chilli powder
1 tablespoon kasoori methi
    (dried fenugreek leaf) powder
50 g pine nuts, roasted
2 teaspoons salt

Wash the spinach and blanch it in boiling water for 1 minute. Drain and plunge into a bowl of iced water for 1 minute, then drain again.

Heat the oil in a frying pan and fry the cumin seeds over a high heat for about 30 seconds until they start to crackle. Add the garlic and onion and cook until golden brown, stirring occasionally. Reduce the heat to medium and add the tomato. Cook for 3 minutes, then add the turmeric, coriander and chilli powder. Cook for 5 minutes, then stir in the kasoori methi and half the pine nuts. Add the spinach and cook for a further 4–5 minutes. Season with the salt.

Transfer to an earthenware bowl, sprinkle with the remaining pine nuts and serve.

Singh's Mutton Dish

SERVES 4

Singh, one of my guides in Jaipur, shared this family recipe with me on our drive to Amber Fort one morning.

1 kg lamb shoulder
200 ml mustard oil
15 cloves
25 black peppercorns
20 green cardamom pods, cracked
5 black cardamom pods, cracked
3 bay leaves
4 white onions, finely sliced
handful of Deep-fried Onion Slices
    (see page 377)

MARINADE
400 g thick plain yoghurt
2 tablespoons Ginger Garlic Paste
    (see page 377)
100 g Onion Paste (see page 379)
1 teaspoon chilli powder
1 teaspoon salt
2 teaspoons ground turmeric

Cut the lamb into thick slices and pound with a mallet (this helps the meat to absorb the marinade).

Combine all the marinade ingredients, then add the lamb and coat thoroughly. Leave to marinate in the fridge for 6 hours, or overnight.

Heat the mustard oil in a large, heavy-based saucepan and fry the whole spices and bay leaves over a medium heat until the seeds start to pop. Stir in the onion and fry until golden. Add the meat and its marinade. Cover and cook over a very low heat for about 1 hour, stirring occasionally, until the liquid has been absorbed. Keep stirring until the meat is tender, adding a little water if it gets too dry and needs more cooking.

Transfer the lamb to a shallow serving dish and scatter over the fried onion to serve.

Spiced Potatoes
Aloo Surwalla
SERVES 4

One of the many vegetable dishes in Rashmi's repertoire at Rohet Garh that she served as part of a lunch spread.

> ½ cup (125 ml) vegetable oil
> 1 teaspoon cumin seeds
> 1 red onion, finely diced
> 3 teaspoons Garlic Paste (see page 377)
> 3 tablespoons tomato puree
> 1 teaspoon chilli powder
> 2 teaspoons coriander seeds,
>   roasted and ground
> ½ teaspoon ground turmeric
> 1 teaspoon salt
> 4 potatoes, parboiled, peeled and quartered
> 1 tablespoon chopped coriander leaves
> 2 small green chillies, minced

Heat the oil in a saucepan and fry the cumin seeds over a medium heat until they start to change colour. Stir in the onion and cook until brown. Add the garlic paste, tomato puree, spices and salt and cook the masala base for 3 minutes until fragrant Add the potato and stir to coat. Cook over a medium heat until the oil separates, then add 2 cups (500 ml) water and cook for 6 minutes or until the potato is soft and the water has evaporated. Add the fresh coriander and chilli and serve.

Ginger Potatoes
Adrak Aloo
SERVES 6–8

This makes a regular appearance on the lunch table at Chhatra Sagar. At home, I often serve it with grilled fish.

> 2 tablespoons vegetable oil
> 1 teaspoon cumin seeds
> 1 small red onion, finely diced
> ½ teaspoon ground turmeric
> 1 teaspoon salt
> 500 g potatoes, peeled and diced
> 280 g curd (drained yoghurt),
>   lightly beaten
> 2 teaspoons minced ginger
> 1 teaspoon cornflour
> 2 teaspoons ghee
> 1 green capsicum (pepper), finely diced
> 1 tablespoon shredded coriander leaves

Heat the oil in a large saucepan and fry the cumin seeds and onion over a medium heat until the onion has softened and is starting to become pink. Add the turmeric and salt, stirring to combine, then add the potato and toss. Add the curd and stir to incorporate. Bring to simmering point, then add the ginger and ½ cup (125 ml) water. Cover and simmer for 15 minutes until the potato is soft. Turn off the heat and leave to cool to room temperature.

Mix the cornflour with a little water to make a thick paste, then stir into the potato mixture.

Heat the ghee in a separate pan and fry the capsicum for 1 minute, then add it to the potato mixture. Garnish with the fresh coriander and serve at room temperature.

Dried Gram-flour Balls in Yoghurt
Boondi Raita

SERVES 6

Serve this as an accompaniment to vegetable dishes and curries, or add it to a thali plate. Boondi are small dried gram flour balls that are available in packets at Indian food stores. They soften when added to yoghurt, soup or sweet syrup, which makes them a versatile pantry staple that is invaluable in a harsh, dry climate.

35 g plain boondi
560 g thick plain yoghurt
½ cup (125 ml) milk
½ teaspoon salt
½ teaspoon freshly ground black pepper
¼ teaspoon chilli powder
½ teaspoon roasted ground cumin
1 tablespoon chopped coriander leaves

Soften the boondi in hot water for 5 minutes, then drain. Whisk the yoghurt and milk until smooth, then season with the salt, pepper and chilli powder. Stir through the softened boondi. Sprinkle the cumin over the top and chill for 1 hour. When ready to serve, garnish with the fresh coriander.

Curd Dumplings with Lentil Curry ›
Daal Bati

SERVES 4

These curd dumplings cooked in a spiced lentil gravy were served for an extravagant roof-terrace dinner at Rawla Narlai, our table surrounded by the most beautiful lanterns.

400 g masoor dal, soaked for 2 hours
2 tablespoons vegetable oil
3 onions, finely diced
1 tablespoon Ginger Garlic Paste
   (see page 377)
2 tomatoes, finely diced
2 teaspoons garam masala
2 teaspoons chilli powder
1 teaspoon ground turmeric
2 small green chillies, split lengthways
2 teaspoons salt
4 tablespoons melted ghee
large handful of coriander leaves, chopped

BATI – CURD DUMPLINGS
800 g wholemeal flour, sifted
1 cup (250 ml) melted ghee
2 tablespoons curd (drained yoghurt)
2 teaspoons salt

Cook the masoor dal in a large saucepan of boiling water until soft, then drain.

Heat the oil in a kadhai or wok and fry the onion over a medium heat until it starts to colour. Add the ginger garlic paste and cook for 2–3 minutes, then add the tomato, stirring to combine. Add the spices, green chilli and salt, then stir in the cooked dal and simmer over a gentle heat for 15 minutes. Set aside until ready to serve.

To make the dumplings, knead all the ingredients together with just enough water to make a soft dough. Roll into small balls about the size of a lime. Rest on a flat plate, covered, for 1 hour. Bake the dough balls over hot coals for about 10 minutes until puffed and golden on the outside and soft and spongy inside.

To serve, reheat the sauce to simmering point. Stir in the ghee and fresh coriander and dip in the hot puffed dumplings.

Sula Lamb
Handi Ka Sula
SERVES 6

A succulent Rajasthani lamb dish that is best served with flaky paratha or naan bread. An Indian handi is a deep vessel with curved sides used for braising. Vimal suggests that sula can be made using any red meat – in the past I have had a venison version that was rich, gamey and delicious. A 'picatta' is the same as a schnitzel or minute steak – the meat is pounded between sheets of plastic film until flattened to about 1.5 cm thick. The recipe also calls for kachri, an ingredient specific to the desert of Rajasthan: it's a type of cucumber that grows wild rather than being a cultivated crop, with a yellow-brown skin and round shape. It can be added to other vegetables, used to make chutney, or dried and powdered to give a tangy avour. Amchur or dried mango powder can be substituted for the kachri, as it offers a similar tart flavour.

800 g lamb shoulder picattas
80 g ghee

MARINADE
80 g Onion Paste (see page 379)
2 teaspoons salt
2 teaspoons Chilli Paste (see page 376)
1½ tablespoons Ginger Garlic Paste
    (see page 377)
3 teaspoons ground kachri or amchur powder
2 teaspoons Green Papaya Paste
    (see page 378)
100 g curd (drained yoghurt)
1½ teaspoons garam masala
1 tablespoon mustard oil

DHUNI (FOR SMOKING)
1 piece hot charcoal
10 cloves
20 g ghee, melted

To make the marinade, put all the ingredients in a glass or ceramic bowl and mix thoroughly. Add the lamb to the marinade and mix to coat. Refrigerate for 1 hour.

Place the lamb in a deep baking dish. Make a well in the centre so the lamb is pushed to the sides of the dish. For the dhuni, put the charcoal and cloves in the centre of the dish and pour over the melted ghee. Cover the baking dish with foil and leave for 30 minutes – this process gives a smoky flavour to the meat. Remove the foil and discard the charcoal and cloves.

Heat the ghee in a large heavy-based frying pan and add the marinated smoked lamb. Cover and cook over a low heat for 45 minutes, stirring occasionally so the lamb does not stick. Serve hot with Indian bread.

Sweet & Sour Tomatoes ›
SERVES 4

This is one of my all-time favourite tomato preparations. From Rashmi at Rohet Garh, it epitomises the food of the desert – simple yet flavoursome. It can be served with other vegetable dishes and makes a great accompaniment to grilled fish or chicken, especially during summer when fresh, light flavours are in demand.

4 tablespoons vegetable oil
1 teaspoon cumin seeds
1 teaspoon brown mustard seeds
4 tomatoes, quartered
½ teaspoon ground turmeric
1 tablespoon ground coriander
1½ teaspoons chilli powder
1 teaspoon salt
2 tablespoons white sugar
2 tablespoons chopped coriander leaves

Heat the oil in a kadhai or wok and fry the cumin and mustard seeds over a medium heat until they splutter. Add the tomato and stir until coated with the seeds, then stir in the ground spices, salt and sugar.

Add 1 cup (250 ml) water, then reduce the heat and simmer for a few minutes – not too long, or the tomato will break down. Sprinkle with the fresh coriander to serve.

‹Crispy Okra &
Pomegranate Salad

SERVES 6

The deluxe Amanbagh hotel resort outside
Jaipur has a fabulous organic vegetable
garden that grows much of the produce the
kitchen needs, essential in these remote parts.
My friend Sally was general manager of the
property for its first four years, and she
always looked forward to the season after the
rains when okra starts growing. This was her
favourite salad – perfect on its own or as part
of a shared table.

30 g chickpea (gram) flour
1 teaspoon chilli powder
1 teaspoon salt
1 teaspoon ground turmeric
1 teaspoon Chat Masala (see page 376)
10 g Ginger Garlic Paste (see page 377)
200 g okra, trimmed and sliced
vegetable oil, for deep-frying

SALAD
180 g cooked chickpeas
250 g pomegranate seeds
    (from about 2 small pomegranates)
50 g coriander leaves
2½ tablespoons lime juice
½ teaspoon salt
½ teaspoon chilli powder
½ teaspoon Chat Masala (see page 376)
1 tablespoon olive or vegetable oil
½ teaspoon freshly ground black pepper

Combine the flour, chilli powder, salt, turmeric,
chat masala and ginger and garlic paste in a bowl,
and add enough water to make a batter. Add the
okra and toss well to coat.

Heat the oil in a wok or large saucepan to 180°C.
To test the temperature of the oil, sprinkle in some
flour – if the flour sizzles, it is ready. Deep-fry the
okra until crispy. Drain on paper towel.

To prepare the salad, mix all the ingredients
together in a bowl. Garnish with the crispy okra
and serve at room temperature.

Pappadam Curry
Rajasthani Papad Methi Ki Sabji

SERVES 4

A staple of the Jain repertoire, this easy-
to-prepare comfort dish typifies the simple
food needed for basic sustenance amidst
the hardship of desert living with the bare
aesthetic of the Jain faith.

50 g fenugreek seeds
1 tablespoon ghee
¼ teaspoon cumin seeds
¼ teaspoon brown mustard seeds
pinch of asafoetida
½ teaspoon chilli powder
1 tablespoon curd (drained yoghurt)
¼ teaspoon ground turmeric
½ teaspoon salt
2–3 medium-sized pappads, broken
    into 2 cm pieces
2 teaspoons chopped coriander leaves

Place the fenugreek seeds in a bowl of hot water and
leave to soak overnight.

Heat the ghee in a frying pan and fry the cumin and
mustard seeds over a medium heat until they start
to splutter. Add the asafoetida, chilli powder and
curd, stirring to combine. Fry until browned, then
add the turmeric and salt, along with 1 cup (250 ml)
water, and bring to simmering point. Add the
pappads and cook for 4–5 minutes until softened.

Drain the fenugreek seeds and add to the pan with
the fresh coriander, stirring to combine. Serve hot
with Chapati (see page 85).

Spiced Eggplant Salad
Baigan Bharta
SERVES 4

Rajasthan is a great place for an eggplant lover to visit – there are myriad preparations like this one on offer wherever you go. I got this recipe from the kitchen at Raas Hotel in Jodphur.

vegetable oil
3 × 250 g eggplants (aubergines)
1 teaspoon cumin seeds
1 small onion, finely diced
1 teaspoon minced garlic
1 teaspoon minced ginger
3 tomatoes, diced
1 teaspoon chopped coriander leaves
2 small green chillies, finely sliced
2 teaspoons lemon juice, or more to taste
1 teaspoon salt
1 teaspoon dried red chilli flakes

Rub a little oil over the eggplants and cook over hot coals or a direct flame, turning a couple of times for even cooking, until the skin has blackened and blistered and the flesh is soft. This should take about 15 minutes. Stand the eggplants in a colander until just cool enough to handle. Peel and discard the blackened skin and mash the flesh.

Heat 2 tablespoons oil in a frying pan and fry the cumin seeds over a medium heat until golden. Add the onion and cook until golden. Add the garlic, ginger and tomato and cook for 5 minutes, then add the mashed eggplant and remove from the heat. Stir through the fresh coriander, green chilli, lemon juice, salt and chilli flakes. Serve at room temperature.

Chicken Cutlets ›
Tawe Ka Murg
SERVES 4

These finger-licking morsels were served at Paantaya Restaurant at Shiv Niwas Hotel in Udaipur, back when chef Vimal was the executive chef. Served with mint chutney and a fresh salad, it makes an ideal lunch choice.

4 chicken breast fillets, cut into thirds
    lengthways (to an even thickness)
vegetable oil, for shallow-frying

MARINADE
40 g small green chillies, finely diced
200 g curd (drained yoghurt)
1 teaspoon ground turmeric
2 tablespoons Ginger Garlic Paste
    (see page 377)
salt, to taste

BATTER
4 eggs
100 g plain flour
1 tablespoon chopped coriander leaves
2 teaspoons chopped mint leaves
¼ teaspoon ground turmeric
salt, to taste

To make the marinade, combine all the ingredients in a bowl. Add the chicken and leave to marinate for 1 hour, refrigerated.

To make the batter, combine all the ingredients in a bowl. Coat the chicken with the batter.

Heat the oil in a large frying pan and fry the chicken over a high heat, presentation side first. Turn over and fry for 8–10 minutes until golden and cooked through. Drain on paper towel and serve hot with Mint Chutney (see page 76).

‹Spiced Goat Curry
Khada Masala Maans
SERVES 4

A gently spiced curry from Chhatra Sagar, this is perfect for a dinner feast with White Dal (see page 177) and a simple rice pilaf.

2 teaspoons coriander seeds
2 teaspoons fennel seeds
1 kg kid or suckling lamb,
    cut into 3 cm cubes
4 tablespoons vegetable oil
280 g curd (drained yoghurt)
5 red chillies
2 teaspoons salt
12 cloves garlic
1 teaspoon Ginger Paste (see page 377)
1 bay leaf
1 black cardamom pod, cracked
3 cm piece cinnamon stick
3 black peppercorns
2 cloves
2 tomatoes, chopped
10 red shallots, peeled
1 tablespoon white poppy seeds
3 teaspoons grated fresh coconut

Tie the coriander and fennel seeds in a piece of muslin and secure with string. Put all the ingredients in a deep, heavy-based saucepan or flameproof casserole and stir to combine. Cover with a tight-fitting lid and seal the edges with a length of bread dough, as in the *dum* cooking style (see page 366). Cook over a medium heat for 1 hour.

Remove from the heat and allow to cool, then break the dough seal and remove the lid. Return the pan to the stove and cook over a medium heat, stirring to crush the shallots, garlic and tomato. Remove the muslin bag of spices and discard. Simmer for about 15 minutes until most of the liquid has been absorbed and the meat is meltingly tender. Serve hot.

Cabbage Salad
SERVES 4

A deliciously light salad from the Chhatra Sagar kitchen that elevates cabbage to a whole new level. Similar to a southern-style *thoren*, this is a perfect summer salad.

3 tablespoons vegetable oil
1 tablespoon mustard seeds
20 curry leaves
1 tablespoon finely shredded ginger
10 savoy cabbage leaves, finely shredded
35 g shredded fresh coconut
2 teaspoons salt
4 tablespoons coriander leaves, chopped

Heat the oil in a frying pan and fry the mustard seeds and curry leaves over a medium heat until the seeds begin to pop. Add the ginger, then stir in the cabbage so it is coated with the spices. Toss over a high heat for about 1 minute until the cabbage wilts, then remove from the heat. Add the coconut, salt and fresh coriander and serve.

Desert-bean Koftas with Onion Curry
Sangria Kismis Ke Kofte
SERVES 6

Sangri, or desert beans, are not found outside Rajasthan; you can substitute thin asparagus or sliced flat Roman beans or snake beans.

100 g sangri
2 cups (500 ml) buttermilk
1 teaspoon salt
¼ teaspoon ground cumin
1 teaspoon garam masala
1 tablespoon chopped green chilli
1 tablespoon chopped ginger
50 g potatoes, boiled and mashed
1 teaspoon chickpea (gram) flour
2 tablespoons chopped coriander leaves
vegetable oil, for deep-frying
1½ teaspoons sultanas, fried in hot oil
    for 1 minute

ONION CURRY
90 g ghee
2 black cardamom pods
2.5 cm piece cinnamon stick
2 green cardamom pods
1 bay leaf
½ teaspoon fennel seeds
1 teaspoon cumin seeds
¼ teaspoon asafoetida
600 g red onions, chopped
1 tablespoon Ginger Garlic Paste
    (see page 377)
1 teaspoon ground turmeric
1 teaspoon chilli powder
1½ teaspoons ground coriander
100 g tomato puree
3 tablespoons curd (drained yoghurt),
    beaten
salt

Bring the sangri and buttermilk to a boil in a saucepan and cook for 2 minutes. In a bowl, combine the salt, cumin, garam masala, green chilli, ginger, potatoes, flour and half the fresh coriander. Add the boiled sangri and buttermilk and mix to combine. Using wet hands, shape the mixture into even walnut-sized balls.

Heat the oil in a kadhai or wok to 180°C. To test the temperature of the oil, sprinkle in some flour – if the flour sizzles, it is ready. Deep-fry the balls until golden, then drain on paper towel.

To make the onion curry, heat the ghee over a medium heat and add the whole spices. Let them crackle, then add the asafoetida and immediately add the onion and fry until golden brown. Add the ginger garlic paste and fry for a few seconds, taking care that it doesn't burn. Mix the ground spices with 4 tablespoons water to make a paste, then stir into the onion mixture. Fry for 5 minutes, sprinkling in a little water, until you see the oil separating from the gravy. Add the tomato puree and curd and bring to a boil. Cook until the oil separates again, then season to taste with salt. Add the koftas and return to the boil.

Serve hot, garnished with the fried sultanas and remaining fresh coriander.

Whole Eggplants with Tomato ›
Sabat Baigan
SERVES 4

This was served for dinner at Neemrana Fort and I have had the same dish at many other homestays throughout Rajasthan. Try to find small round (egg-shaped) eggplants for this dish – they're usually available at Indian food stores that stock fresh produce.

1 cup (250 ml) vegetable oil
2 tablespoons chopped onion
1 tablespoon minced ginger
2 teaspoons minced garlic
2 cups (500 ml) tomato puree
1 teaspoon chilli powder
2 teaspoons ground coriander
½ teaspoon ground turmeric
1 teaspoon salt
8 small round eggplants (aubergines),
    quartered but left intact at stem end
2 tablespoons chopped coriander leaves

Heat the oil in a kadhai or wok and fry the onion over a medium heat until translucent. Add the ginger and garlic and cook until softened and starting to colour. Stir in the tomato puree, coriander, turmeric and salt and bring to simmering point.

Add the eggplants, spooning the sauce over to coat. Cover and simmer for 15 minutes until the eggplants are soft. Stir in the fresh coriander.

‹ Sesame Potatoes
Til Aloo
SERVES 6

Vegetable dishes are the stars of the Chhatra Sagar table, including these delicious potatoes.

2 tablespoons vegetable oil
1 teaspoon fenugreek seeds
8 potatoes, peeled and chopped into
   1 cm chunks
1 teaspoon Ginger Paste (see page 377)
3 tablespoons white sesame seeds,
   roasted and coarsely crushed
1½ tablespoons coriander seeds,
   roasted and ground
salt
squeeze of lemon juice
3 small green chillies, finely sliced

Heat the oil in a large frying pan and fry the fenugreek seeds over a medium heat until brown. Add the potato and toss. Cover and cook over a low heat for 10–12 minutes, tossing occasionally, until the potato is tender. Add the ginger paste, sesame seeds, coriander, salt and lemon juice, stirring to coat the potato. Cook for a minute, then add the chilli. Serve immediately.

‹ Apple & Pomegranate Raita
SERVES 10

This raita is a favourite of Vasundhara's at Chhatra Sagar. In the surrounding countryside, there are often roadside carts piled high with apples in season.

840 g thick plain yoghurt, stirred
1 apple, peeled and finely diced
50 g moong sprouts
2 teaspoons white sugar
1 teaspoon salt
80 g pomegranate seeds
1 teaspoon ground roasted cumin
1 tablespoon chopped mint leaves

Combine the yoghurt, apple, sprouts, sugar and salt in a bowl, then stir through the pomegranate seeds. Sprinkle the cumin and mint over to serve.

‹ Yellow Dal with Spinach
Dal Palak
SERVES 4

This is perfect served with rice and a cabbage salad for a simple, yet complete lunch.

ghee, for cooking
2 teaspoons cumin seeds
1 red onion, finely diced
1 teaspoon minced garlic
1 teaspoon minced green chilli
½ teaspoon ground turmeric
½ teaspoon salt
100 g channa dal
2 tablespoons chopped spinach
½ teaspoon chilli powder

Heat 1 tablespoon ghee in a saucepan and fry half the cumin seeds over a medium heat until they start to crackle. Add the onion and cook until softened and pink, then add the garlic, green chilli, turmeric and salt. Stir to combine, then add the dal and stir until thoroughly coated. Add 1½ cups (375 ml) water and stir, then cover and simmer for 15 minutes until the dal is soft and most of the water has been absorbed without the mixture being dry.

Meanwhile, fry the spinach in a little ghee until wilted. Add to the dal and stir to combine.

Heat 1 tablespoon ghee in a frying pan and fry the remaining cumin seeds and the chilli powder until fragrant. Pour over the spinach dal and serve.

Chicken Methi

SERVES 4

Methi are the fresh, frond-like leaves of the
fenugreek plant and a common vegetable in
Indian cooking, with a distinctive flavour.
This recipe calls for dried methi powder,
which is readily available from Indian
grocers. It is a common green used extensively
in Indian cooking. To grow it yourself,
propagate some fenugreek seeds and plant in
a large pot, then snip the young leaves as you
need them.

150 g thick plain yoghurt
1 teaspoon salt
1 teaspoon freshly ground black pepper
2 small green chillies, minced
4 chicken marylands (leg and thigh portions),
    cut into leg and thigh joints
4 tablespoons vegetable oil
1 teaspoon green cardamom pods, cracked
1 black cardamom pod, cracked
3 cloves
2 cm piece cinnamon stick
3 white onions, finely sliced
2 tablespoons Ginger Garlic Paste
    (see page 377)
1 teaspoon ground turmeric
1 teaspoon ground coriander
1 teaspoon chilli powder
4 tomatoes, chopped
3 teaspoons kasoori methi
    (dried fenugreek leaf) powder
1 tablespoon finely shredded ginger
1 tablespoon shredded mint leaves
2 tablespoons shredded coriander leaves

Mix the yoghurt with the salt, pepper and green
chilli. Rub liberally over the chicken and leave to
marinate for 1 hour.

Heat the oil in a large saucepan and fry the whole
spices over a medium heat until they start to
splutter. Add the onion and fry until starting to
colour. Add the ginger garlic paste and cook for
another 5 minutes. Add the turmeric, ground
coriander and chilli powder and stir to combine.
Cook for another minute, then add the chopped
tomato and simmer for 10 minutes until softened.
Add the chicken and its marinade, stirring to coat
the chicken with the tomato sauce. Reduce the heat
to low and simmer for 20–25 minutes until the
chicken is tender.

Taste and adjust the seasoning if required – a little
salt may be needed to balance the flavours. Stir
through the kasoori methi powder, ginger, mint
and fresh coriander. Serve with Naan (see page 101)
or Paratha (see page 351).

Maize-flour Bread
Makke Ki Roti

MAKES 10

The variety of unleavened roti breads on offer
in Rajasthan is ingenious, making the best
use of what is at hand. This maize bread was
served at Rawla Narlai.

500 g maize flour
1 teaspoon salt
3 tablespoons ghee
large handful of methi (fenugreek) leaves,
    finely chopped
1 teaspoon chilli powder
20 g butter

Sift the flour and salt. Knead 1 tablespoon of the
ghee into the flour with the methi and chilli
powder, adding enough hot water to make a stiff
dough. Divide the dough into 10 pieces, then roll
each piece into a ball. Flatten each ball into a disc
between the palms of your hands.

Melt the remaining ghee and set aside.

Heat a tawa or frying pan over a medium heat,
then put a bread disc into the hot pan and cook it
for about 3 minutes on each side. When it is nearly
done, pour over a little of the melted ghee and fry
both sides until golden. Remove from the pan and
pinch the disc in four or five places on one side.
Smear with butter at the pinched spots. Cook the
remaining discs in the same way. Serve hot.

White Dal
Urad Moga
SERVES 6

This gentle-tasting, desert-style dal makes
a terrific accompaniment to a goat curry
(see page 171), grilled meat or a vegetable thali.

> 200 g white urad dal, soaked
>   for 15 minutes, then rinsed
> 2 teaspoons fennel seeds
> 2 teaspoons coriander seeds
> 1 teaspoon ground cumin
> 2 teaspoons salt
> 3 tablespoons vegetable oil
> 1 bay leaf
> 1 stick cinnamon
> 1 black cardamom pod, cracked
> 2 whole cloves
> 3 black peppercorns
> 3 long dried red chillies
> 200 g Onion Paste (see page 379)
> 1 tablespoon sliced garlic
> 200 g curd (drained yoghurt)
> handful of Deep-fried Onion Slices
>   (see page 377)

Put the urad dal in a large saucepan with 1 litre
water. Add the fennel and coriander seeds, the
cumin and half the salt. Cook over a high heat
for about 15 minutes until tender.

In a separate pan, heat the oil and fry the bay
leaf, whole spices and chillies for 30 seconds over
a medium heat until fragrant, then add the onion
paste and fry until golden. Add the garlic and fry
for another minute, then stir in the curd and the
remaining salt. Stir until it boils, then reduce the
heat and cook until all the liquid has evaporated
and the oil has separated, about 10 minutes.

Add the dal and stir to combine. Stir in half the
fried onion and transfer to a serving plate. Scatter
the remaining fried onion on top to serve.

Dal Mewari
SERVES 6

A lentil preparation of the Udaipur-based
Mewar kingdom, and a favourite of the
royal household. This was cooked for us
at Dera Mandawa Haveli, a charming
homestay in Jaipur

> 250 g urad dal, soaked for 1 hour
> 100 g channa dal, soaked for 1 hour
> 1 teaspoon ground turmeric
> salt
> 2 tablespoons ghee
> 1 teaspoon cumin seeds
> pinch of asafoetida
> 50 g finely sliced onion
> 4 cloves garlic, finely sliced
> 2 teaspoons ground coriander
> 2 teaspoons chopped tomato
> 1 tablespoon chopped coriander leaves
> 2 teaspoons finely shredded ginger

Cook the dals in boiling water with the turmeric
and 1 teaspoon salt until tender, about 15 minutes.
Drain well.

Heat the ghee in a frying pan and fry the cumin
seeds and asafoetida over a medium heat until the
seeds pop, then add the onion and garlic and cook,
stirring regularly, until golden brown. Add the
dal mixture, ground coriander and tomato and
cook for 10 minutes. Season with salt to taste.
Garnish with the fresh coriander and ginger and
serve warm.

Mama's Chicken

SERVES 4

Nothing beats a good roast chook, and this is a family favourite at Rohet Garh. The chicken cooked with yoghurt and spices, a tribute to the former matriarch of the house. Comfort food at its best.

1 × 1.2 kg chicken, cut into chunks
    on the bone
⅔ cup (160 ml) mustard oil
2 teaspoons minced garlic
1 red onion, finely diced
1 tablespoon white vinegar
2 tablespoons chopped coriander leaves
1 teaspoon minced green chilli

MARINADE
2 tablespoons mustard oil
2 tablespoons Ginger Garlic Paste
    (see page 377)
280 g thick plain yoghurt
1 tablespoon chilli powder
1 tablespoon ground coriander
2 teaspoons ground turmeric
2 teaspoons salt

To make the marinade, mix the mustard oil and ginger garlic paste until combined. Massage this mixture into the chicken until it is thoroughly coated. Combine the remaining marinade ingredients, then massage into the chicken. Leave for 30 minutes.

In a large, deep saucepan, heat the mustard oil and add the garlic and onion. Stir over a medium heat until softened, about 5 minutes. Add the chicken and its marinade, then cover and simmer until the chicken is cooked, about 25–30 minutes. Remove the lid and add the vinegar. Cook for a few minutes, then stir through the fresh coriander and chilli. Taste and adjust the seasoning if necessary.

Tomato Chutney

MAKES 2 CUPS (500 ml)

Tomato chutney is one of my favourite Rajasthani chutneys, and this version is from the Chhatra Sagar kitchen. Serve it with dal, steamed rice or bread, or with grilled fish for a perfectly simple lunch.

3 tablespoons vegetable oil
1 teaspoon fennel seeds
½ teaspoon nigella seeds
½ teaspoon brown mustard seeds
10 small cloves garlic, finely sliced
12 roma tomatoes, chopped
1 teaspoon salt
2 teaspoons white sugar
1 teaspoon chilli powder
2 teaspoons Ginger Paste (see page 377)
2 small green chillies, seeded and finely sliced

Heat the oil in a large saucepan and fry the fennel, nigella and mustard seeds over a medium heat until they start to pop. Add the garlic and fry until it has softened, then add the tomato, salt, sugar, chilli powder and ginger paste and stir to combine. Cook over a low heat for 4 minutes until the tomato softens and the oil leaves the sides of the pan. Stir in the green chilli. Remove from the heat and allow to cool a little. Serve warm.

Cheese Kebabs
Paneer Tikka
SERVES 4

When Asish was chef at Suvarna Mahal in Jaipur on one of my early visits, he showed me how to prepare these in his kitchen. They are usually cooked on skewers over hot coals, but you can also bake them on a tray in a conventional oven.

1 teaspoon ground turmeric
200 g Paneer (see page 154),
    cut into 2 cm chunks
2 teaspoons salt
50 g grated cheddar cheese
1 teaspoon chilli powder
2 teaspoons ground cumin
100 ml cream

Bring a saucepan of water to a boil. Add the turmeric, paneer and half the salt and simmer for 5 minutes. Remove the paneer from the water using a slotted spoon.

Combine the cheese, chilli powder, cumin and remaining salt with the cream, then add the paneer and marinate for 30 minutes.

Preheat the oven to 220°C.

Arrange the paneer and its marinade on a baking tray in a single layer. Bake for 10 minutes until golden. Serve with Mango Mustard Pickle (see page 50).

Tamarind Eggplant
SERVES 8 (AS AN ACCOMPANIMENT)

From the kitchen at Chhatra Sagar, Shrinidri showed me how she prepared this vegetable dish the first time I visited, and it has stayed with me ever since. It can be served with other dishes for a shared table or simply served with barbecued fish, quail or chicken.

vegetable oil, for cooking
1.2 kg purple eggplant (aubergine),
    cut in half lengthways,
    then cut into 4 cm chunks
3 small red onions, finely diced
4 small green chillies, minced
3 cloves garlic, sliced
1 tablespoon curry leaves
150 g brown sugar
400 ml tamarind liquid
1 teaspoon ground cumin
2 teaspoons salt
200 g cherry tomatoes, cut in half
    and oven-roasted
5 tomatoes, seeded and diced
1 cup chopped coriander leaves

To cook, heat the oil in a kadhai or wok to 180°C. To test the temperature of the oil, sprinkle in some flour – if the flour sizzles, it is ready. Deep-fry the eggplant chunks a few at a time for 4–5 minutes until golden. Remove with a slotted spoon and drain on paper towel. Repeat until all the eggplant pieces are fried.

Heat 4 tablespoons of the oil in a frying pan and fry the onion, chilli and garlic over a medium heat until beginning to colour. Add the curry leaves and fry for a minute until wilted. Add the sugar, tamarind, cumin and salt and simmer gently for 5 minutes.

Taste and adjust seasoning if necessary – there should be an equal balance of sweet, sour and salty flavours.

Add the eggplant and roasted cherry tomatoes and stir to coat thoroughly. Simmer for 2 minutes. Stir through the diced tomato and coriander leaves and serve warm.

Wholemeal Halwa
Atta Ka Halwa
SERVES 12

A sweet confection from Rawla Narlai, this is a typical dessert of the desert.

440 g white sugar
pinch of ground cardamom
125 g ghee
140 g fine wholemeal flour

Combine the sugar, cardamom and 1 litre water in a saucepan and cook over a high heat until the sugar has dissolved, about 8 minutes. Leave over a low heat.

Heat a large frying pan and add the ghee. Allow to melt, then add the flour and stir to combine. Cook over a medium heat for about 10 minutes, stirring continuously to prevent sticking, until thickened but not sticky. Add the hot sugar syrup and stir to combine and until all lumps are removed. Stir until all the liquid has evaporated and the mixture is firm, about 10 minutes. Pour onto an oiled round tray or plate and press to make a firm layer about 2 cm thick. Cut into 2 cm pieces and serve hot.

Carrot Halwa ›
Gajar Halwa
SERVES 6–8

This popular dessert, made with the tender young red carrots typical of Rajasthan, is one of Rohet Garh's best.

1 kg carrots, grated
1 litre full-cream milk
100 g ghee
250 g white sugar
80 g seedless raisins
50 g flaked almonds
1 teaspoon ground cardamom

Put the carrot and milk in a saucepan and cook over a low heat for about 20 minutes, stirring occasionally, until the carrot is soft and the milk has been absorbed. Add the ghee and increase the heat slightly. Fry until the carrot has started to colour, then stir in the sugar and cook until the mixture becomes dry, about 10 minutes.

Stir through the raisins, almonds and cardamom. Spoon into a serving bowl and serve hot, garnished with a few extra almonds if you like.

Rice & Milk Pudding
Kheer
SERVES 4

A classic Indian dessert and a staple on so many menus, this version comes from the spectacular Jawai Leopard Camp in southern Rajasthan.

1 litre full-cream milk
50 g basmati rice, rinsed
250 g white sugar
½ teaspoon ground cardamom
½ teaspoon saffron threads
10 blanched almonds, chopped
10 pistachios, chopped

Heat the milk to simmering point, then add the rice and stir. Bring to a boil, then reduce the heat and cook until the rice has softened and the milk thickens, about 15 minutes. Stir in the sugar and simmer for 5 minutes. Stir through the cardamom, saffron and half the nuts and cook for a further 2 minutes. Pour into a serving dish and sprinkle the remaining nuts on top.

Apple Rice Pudding
Seb Ki Kheer
SERVES 4

A delicious dessert offered on the menu
at Devi Garh.

1 litre milk
50 g short-grain rice, rinsed
4 tablespoons condensed milk
100 g white sugar
10 seedless raisins
5 pistachios, sliced
4 raw cashews, chopped
1 green apple, peeled and grated
¼ teaspoon ground cardamom

Put the milk and rice in a saucepan and bring to
a boil over a gentle heat. When the mixture starts
to simmer, add the condensed milk and sugar,
stirring to combine. Cook over a low heat until
the rice is tender and the mixture becomes thick,
about 15 minutes. Add the raisins and nuts.

When ready to serve, stir through the apple and
sprinkle with the cardamom. Serve warm.

Nut & Raisin Dessert ›
Churma Laddoo
SERVES 4–6

When Meenakshi was the dessert chef at
Paantya in Udaipur, she served us this typical
Rajasthani dessert for lunch, and afterwards
gave me the recipe. If you don't have silver
leaf, you can roll the balls in a mix of white
sesame seeds and poppy seeds.

250 g coarse wholemeal flour
275 g ghee
100 g icing sugar
1 teaspoon ground cardamom
1 teaspoon blanched almonds, chopped
1 teaspoon pistachios, chopped
1 teaspoon cashews, chopped
1 teaspoon raisins
edible silver leaf, to decorate

Mix the flour and 100 ml water, then add 45 g of
the ghee and knead to make a firm dough. Shape
into discs 7.5 cm in diameter.

Heat 125 g of the remaining ghee in a kadhai or
wok to 180°C. To test the temperature, sprinkle in
some flour – if the flour sizzles, it is ready. Fry the
discs until golden and crisp. Cool, then use a food
processor to grind to a fine powder. Mix with 45 g
of the remaining ghee, the icing sugar, cardamom,
nuts and raisins.

Melt the remaining ghee and stir it into the fruit
and nut mixture until combined. Shape into
balls, then roll in silver leaf and serve at room
temperature in small paper cups.

GUJARAT
Textiles, Milk & Sugar

With my trusty Rajasthani driver Ahbay, we drive four hours from Udaipur in southern Rajasthan along a very decent road across the border to Ahmedabad. The business and cultural capital of the state, it's currently the fastest-growing city in the country with some of the best roads and high literacy rates. As it's a dry state, alcohol is prohibited, which explains the many roadside bars scattered along the highway just before we cross the border, which do a roaring trade. As alcohol is not served anywhere, I was advised that if I did have any, I should discreetly consume it within the confines of my hotel room. It didn't bother me. I was happy to throw a few dry days into the mix, and I was to discover there were many delicious juices and drinks on offer.

This western state has remained one of India's best-kept tourism secrets, with a wealth of history, art and culture. It's home to many treasures and tremendous diversity, and with tourism starting to flourish, the infrastructure has improved. Visitors come to see Gujarat's multitude of ornate distinctive Jain temples and forts, ancient palaces and marine parks, traditional artisans and tribal villages, romantic desert landscapes and wildlife – Sason Gur National Park on the southern tidal shores of the Arabian Sea is the last habitat and the only place on earth to see the Asiatic lion in the wild.

Gujarat is home to some of the best and most inventive vegetarian food in India; it's also the milk capital of India. Its use in the food is pervasive and the lassis, yoghurt and ice creams are to die for, every mouthful so rich and satisfying. Gujaratis love their sugar and the food has a distinctive sweet and sour flavour – many dishes taste sweeter than I experienced in other parts of the country. On every table, there's an array of fruit chutneys to use as condiments and every thali I had included a lump of jaggery on the plate, for added sweetness. Sweet shops are everywhere and rival Bengal in their variety. Those I tasted include *mohanthal*, a fudge made with gram flour, cinnamon and lots of ghee, topped with edible silver leaf and pistachios; *malpuas*, sweet pikelets made with mashed banana, milk and sugar then dipped in sugar syrup for a double dose of sweetness; and the traditional yoghurt-based *shrikhand* that I have had flavoured with saffron or cardamom and often served with chopped nuts and dried fruits. The milk halwa at Farki in Ahmedabad, full of nuts, ghee and sugar, left a lasting impression, while *basundi*, another popular milk-based dessert made with saffron, pistachios and almonds, was so rich that a couple of bites was all I needed to be fully sated.

AHMEDABAD

Gujarati food is predominantly vegetarian, except in the Muslim quarters where the cafes and restaurants are popular with everyone, including Hindus who do not cook meat at home but like to eat it. My local guide Gautam proves to be a knowledgeable food lover and conversations are peppered with food anecdotes and an endless list of what I need to see and

taste. Each time I visit, he takes me on a food reconnaissance of the city. Early one morning, we head towards the elaborately carved Hutheesingh Jain temple in the old town, stopping on the way for the first breakfast snack at a street vendor whose cart is set up under a sprawling tree near the Swaminarayan Temple. We join the locals for a plate of *fafda* – crisp wafers made with chickpea flour served with green chilli, green papaya slices and a thin dal gravy. To the side of the plate sits a sweet jalebi – the ultimate mix of savoury and sweet. We walk on through the heritage quarter, stopping at the chaiwallah for some of the best chai I have had in India (maybe it's the milk!) to another street cart making *kitchu*, a thick porridge of rice flour, green chilli, ginger paste and cumin, topped with red chilli powder, black salt and ghee. Drawing on inner stamina, I spend days exploring the amazing street food, including the vendors at Manak Chowk in the old city and Bhatiyar Gali (the Muslim quarter known for its butcheries and meat restaurants), and around the Law Gardens and other parts of town near Delhi Gate, tasting crunchy samosas, a variety of lassi drinks and *farsan* snacks. The streets come even more alive at night when it seems each district has a plethora of street food vendors and everyone is outdoors being social.

For dinner, we feast on dishes that are definitively Gujarati and vegetarian. At Swati Snacks, there is *pani puri* (puri puffs in spicy peppery water), *dahi sev puri* (with yoghurt), *chola methi dhokla* (a thick fermented chickpea flour and yoghurt batter steamed until pillow soft and cut into squares), paper dosa with coconut chutney and rasam, and *panki chatri* – a savoury rice pancake flavoured with turmeric, spread like a paste onto banana leaves and cooked on a hot tawa pan, served with whole green chillies and mint chutney. A deluxe thali at Agashiye, the rooftop restaurant at M.G. House, has a decadent variety of dishes that are deftly served from copper pots by the waiters, a true celebration of vegetables. The *lilva kachori* – fried lentil balls with tamarind – were a standout, and the smoked eggplant and *kadhi*, a cumin-scented yoghurt gravy, make it impossible to stop eating. *Fulka roti* and the millet and wholewheat *bhakhari* flatbreads are cooked to order and keep arriving from the kitchen, making it unthinkable to say no.

Gujarat is the birthplace of Mahatma Gandhi and his Sabarmati Ashram in Ahmedabad has been sensitively preserved in his honour. Gandhi lived here for 12 years during the struggle for Independence, before he began the Salt March in 1930. The history of colonial India is a savage one and Gandhi's quest for independence through peaceful means and civil disobedience feels very palpable here. I visit in the early morning when it's relatively cool and uncrowded, joining pilgrims who come to pay homage and meditate. It's a lovely riverfront setting, serene and quiet, and the museum has some fascinating photographs and letters written by Gandhi. I have yet to make the pilgrimage to the desert town of Rajkot to see the house where Gandhi was born and to taste the highly prized, freshest milk sweets from the local dairies there.

STITCHING & STEPWELLS

I may have been on a food pilgrimage but it's the vibrant textile industry that brings most people to Gujarat, whether it's to the desert plains of Bhuj or the Great Rann of Kutch in the west bordering Pakistan, a desert saltpan near the Arabian Sea that is home to semi-nomadic tribes and weaving communities with their dazzling array of ornate textiles, glittering embroidery and jewellery – both traditional and contemporary. To honour the tradition of textiles, we visit the small town of Patan, the only place in India where a few remaining families produce the impossibly intricate ikat double weaving. At Patan Patola, owned by the Salvi family, we watch as the looms move slowly back and forth, a length of cloth taking a painstaking 6 months or more to complete. Mrs Salvi prepares a thali lunch in the typical Jain tradition. Sitting in her kitchen we taste the simple vegetarian dishes she has prepared, amongst them a light potato curry, yellow dal and the finest chapatis imaginable.

My wish list included visiting some of the incredible subterranean stepwells I had read about, so on the way, we visit the stepwell in Adalaj on the outskirts of the city, the eleventh century Dada Hari ni Vav Stepwell in Asarwa and Rani ki Vav – the Queen's Stepwell in Patan. These temples are architecturally magnificent, with their elaborate maze-like structures descending seven or so storeys and featuring ornate stone carvings of Hindu religious scenes. They are the oldest and largest in India and simply mind-boggling. While we are on the architecture trail, we also visit the eleventh century sun temple at Modhera, breathtaking in its architectural beauty, with reverence paid to the natural elements and the Vedic gods.

SIDHPUR

Another day, we drive to Sidhpur, a town of once-prosperous tinker merchants and traders, and wander the dusty streets past the intricate wooden havelis of the Bhori Muslim community, followers of Aga Khan. There's a lively market lining one of the main streets, vendors on either side selling fresh produce and household items – the men in their distinctive white caps and the women in colourful burquas.

We are invited for lunch at the haveli (home) of Ibrahim's family, who are the most generous and engaging hosts. We sit on the floor in the customary circle and food is served to us by each member of the family. We start with a small bowl of clear chicken broth, then our plates are filled with a chicken curry simmered in an almond and cashew milk gravy seasoned with cumin and curry leaves, masala potatoes and cauliflower and chapati, hot off the grill. A delicious yet subtly spiced mutton biryani and chicken sheesh kebabs follow, then sweetened tea and melon. What I thought would be a simple lunch turned into a feast; the family were honoured to be able to offer abundance to their guests.

Stepping off the beaten track, I discovered a staggering diversity of flavours and textures, making my visits to Gujarat a festival of eating. It was like discovering the land of milk and honey.

Smoked Eggplant
Vangecha Bharit
SERVES 4

From the kitchens at Agashiye in Ahmedabad, this eggplant dish played a starring role at our dinner table. The eggplants take on a delicious smokiness if they are charred over hot coals rather than a gas flame. Variations of this dish can be found all over India.

500 g eggplants (aubergines)
2 teaspoons salt
1 tablespoon thick Tamarind Liquid
  (see page 379)
1 teaspoon white sugar
1 tablespoon vegetable oil
½ teaspoon brown mustard seeds
2 small green chillies, minced
1 tablespoon ground turmeric
1 onion, finely diced
4 tablespoons chopped coriander leaves

Roast the eggplants over a direct flame until the skin is blackened and blistered, about 15 minutes, turning every few minutes for even cooking. When cool enough to handle, peel off the charred skin. Mash the flesh and stir in the salt, tamarind liquid and sugar until combined.

Heat the oil in a frying pan and fry the mustard seeds, chilli and turmeric over a medium heat for a minute. Add the onion and cook until translucent, then stir in the mashed eggplant. Check the seasoning and adjust if necessary. Remove from the heat and stir through the fresh coriander. Serve warm.

Potato & Pea Samosas
MAKES 16

A staple of street food culture, typical across India and a signature of Ahmedabad, I tasted these perfectly formed crisp pastries at Maharaja Samosa shop.

200 g plain flour
2 teaspoons salt
3 tablespoons vegetable oil,
  plus extra for deep-frying

STUFFING
2 teaspoons vegetable oil
1 teaspoon cumin seeds
1 tablespoon minced ginger
2 small green chillies, minced
250 g potatoes, boiled and diced
2 teaspoons salt
1 teaspoon ground coriander
1 teaspoon Chat Masala (see page 376)
80 g fresh or frozen peas, cooked
1 tablespoon chopped coriander leaves

Combine the flour, salt and oil in a bowl. Add water a little at a time until you have a hard, firm dough. Roll the dough into a ball. Cover with a damp cloth and leave to rest for 30 minutes.

To make the stuffing, heat the oil and fry the cumin seeds over a medium heat for about 30 seconds until they change colour, then add the ginger and chilli and fry for a minute. Add the potato, salt, ground coriander and chat masala, tossing to coat the potato with the spice base. Add the peas and cook for a couple of minutes over a low heat. Stir in the fresh coriander. Remove from the heat and allow to cool.

Divide the dough into 16 equal portions and roll into small balls. On a lightly floured surface, roll out each ball to a 12 cm elliptical length (oblong-shaped). Cut each length in half crossways and wet the edges with a little water. Shape each piece of dough into a cone and fill with stuffing. Press the edges together to seal.

Heat the oil for deep-frying in a kadhai or wok to 180°C. To test the temperature of the oil, sprinkle in some flour – if the flour sizzles, it is ready. Deep-fry the pastries a few at a time for 4–5 minutes until crisp and golden. Drain on paper towel. Serve hot with a tomato or tamarind chutney.

Fried Besan Wafers
Fafda

SERVES 4

I stood and watched as the two guys manning the Shree Govind Farsan street cart in Ahmedabad deftly rolled and fried these dough strips in their vat of hot oil, waiting for my turn to taste this quintessential breakfast snack. It's as easy as making pasta dough and you can use a pasta machine to make it even easier. Best served with whole green chillies, julienne slices of green papaya and a small bowl of yellow dal gravy.

250 g chickpea (gram) flour
½ teaspoon bicarbonate soda
1 teaspoon salt
2 teaspoons ajwain
½ teaspoon asafoetida
¼ teaspoon chilli powder
3 tablespoons vegetable oil,
   plus extra for deep-frying

Mix the flour, bicarbonate of soda, salt and spices in a bowl. Add 2 tablespoons of the oil and ½ cup (125 ml) warm water and knead to form a soft dough. Add the final tablespoon of oil and knead until combined. Cover the bowl with a clean tea towel and leave to rest at room temperature for 30 minutes.

Divide the dough into 16 equal portions and roll each portion into a ball.

Using a rolling pin, roll each ball into a long strip to flatten, then either continue to roll by hand or pass the dough through a pasta machine until the strips are about 3 mm thick.

Heat the oil for deep-frying in a kadhai or wok to 180°C. To test the temperature, sprinkle in some flour – if the flour sizzles, it is ready. Working with just a few at a time, drop the strips into the oil one by one and swirl around to prevent them sticking together. They will naturally curl up as they fry. Cook for 3 minutes or until golden, then remove with a slotted spoon and drain on paper towel. Serve hot with the accompaniments suggested above or with a sweet fruit chutney.

Spiced Lentil Patties ›
Dal Vada

MAKES 18

Each time I visit Ahmedabad, I head to the Anand dal Vada street cart where Anand and his son Suresh do a roaring trade dishing out plates of these mouthwatering crispy snacks.

200 g chana dal
100 g split urad dal
1 small brown onion, finely diced
2 small green chillies, minced
1 tablespoon Ginger Garlic Paste (see page 377)
½ teaspoon Kashmiri chilli powder
1 teaspoon ground cumin
1 teaspoon garam masala
2 tablespoons chopped coriander leaves
2 tablespoons chopped mint leaves
3 tablespoons shredded fresh coconut
2 teaspoon salt
vegetable oil, for deep-frying
½ teaspoon amchur
1 small red onion, finely sliced into rounds
6 small green chillies, split in half lengthwise and fried

Wash both the dals and soak in cold water for 2 hours. Drain and rinse.

Place the soaked dals, onion, green chilli and 3 tablespoons water in a food processor and blend to a thick, coarse paste – add a little extra water if it is too thick.

Transfer the mixture to a deep bowl and add the spices, herbs, coconut and salt. Mix well with your hands to combine thoroughly.

Divide the mixture into 18 equal portions and roll each portion into a round flat patty (vada).

Heat the oil in a kadhai or wok to 180°C. To test the temperature, sprinkle in some flour – if the flour sizzles, it is ready. Fry the vadas, a few at a time, for 4 minutes until golden. Drain on a paper towel, sprinkle with amchur and serve with red onion slices and fried whole green chillies.

‹Steamed Lentil Sponge Cakes
Dhoklas
SERVES 4

Regarded as a signature dish of Gujarat,
my favourite place to eat dhoklas is at Swati
Snacks, where they are feathery light and
cooked to perfection. Fermented gram flour
and yoghurt batter is steamed to a sponge-like
consistency, cut into squares and tempered
with mustard seeds, then topped with fresh
coriander and grated coconut.

300 g chickpea (gram) flour, sifted
280 g thick plain yoghurt, whisked
1 teaspoon salt
1 teaspoon chopped green chilli
1 teaspoon chopped ginger
½ teaspoon ground turmeric
1 tablespoon lemon juice
1 teaspoon bicarbonate of soda
2 tablespoons vegetable oil
1 teaspoon brown mustard seeds
3 tablespoons chopped coriander leaves
35 g shredded fresh coconut

Mix the flour and yoghurt in a bowl, add 200 ml
warm water and whisk until smooth. Stir in the
salt. Cover with clean tea towel and set aside on
a bench for 4 hours to allow the batter to ferment.

Pound the green chilli and ginger together into
a paste, then stir in the turmeric. Add to the
fermented batter.

Grease a 20 cm square non-stick baking tin.

In a small bowl, mix the lemon juice, bicarbonate
of soda and 1 teaspoon oil. Add to the batter and
whisk until combined.

Pour the batter into the greased tin and place it
in a steamer. Cover the steamer with a lid and
steam for 25 minutes or until the cake is just set
in the centre.

Allow to cool for 30 minutes, then cut into 3 cm
squares and arrange on serving plate.

Heat the remaining oil in a small saucepan and fry
mustard seeds until they start to splutter. Remove
from the heat immediately and pour the tempered
oil over the dhoklas.

Garnish with fresh coriander and shredded coconut
to serve.

Savoury Rice Pancakes
Panki Chatni
SERVES 4

An all-time classic from Swati Snacks, this
is the first thing I order from their menu.
Panki is made by cooking a turmeric rice flour
batter between banana leaves. When making
these, it's important to oil the banana leaf
mats well and spread the batter uniformly
to ensure even cooking.

4–6 banana leaves, central spines removed
400 g rice flour
140 g thick plain yoghurt, whisked
1 small green chilli, minced
2 teaspoons Ginger Garlic Paste (see
    page 377)
1 teaspoon salt
¼ teaspoon asafoetida
1 teaspoon cumin seeds, roughly ground
¼ teaspoon ground turmeric
2 teaspoons melted ghee
vegetable oil, for cooking

Rub the banana leaves with a clean wet cloth to
remove any traces of dirt, then cut into eight pieces,
approximately 30 cm x 15 cm.

In a bowl, combine the rice flour, yoghurt and
2 cups (500 ml) warm water and mix thoroughly
to form a thick batter. Add a little extra water if
it is too thick. Cover with clean tea towel and set
aside on a bench for 3–4 hours to allow the batter
to ferment.

Pound the green chilli into the ginger garlic paste
and stir into the batter with the salt, asafoetida,
cumin, turmeric and melted ghee. Add an extra
½ cup (125 ml) water and mix well.

Lay out the banana leaf mats, and brush a little oil
on the shiny side of each leaf. Evenly spread enough
batter over half the length of each leaf to make a
5 mm thick layer. Fold the uncoated leaf over the
batter and press down to secure.

Heat a tawa or non-stick frying pan over a
medium–high heat and brush lightly with oil.
Cook the panki parcels for 2 minutes each side until
brown spots start to appear on the leaves. Test to
make sure the panki layer peels easily off the leaf.

Repeat until all the parcels have been cooked and
serve warm with Mint Chutney (see page 76).

Gujarati Spicy Dal

SERVES 4

A Gujarati thali would not be complete without this dal. I also like to serve it with grilled fish for an easy lunch option.

200 g toor dal
2 tablespoons vegetable oil
1 onion, finely diced
15 g grated fresh coconut
handful of coriander leaves
1 teaspoon cumin seeds
1 teaspoon brown mustard seeds
2 teaspoons white poppy seeds
1 tablespoon curry leaves
1 teaspoon Ginger Garlic Paste (see page 377)
4 small green chillies, minced
1 tomato, finely diced
1 teaspoon ground turmeric
1 teaspoon chilli powder
1 teaspoon ground coriander
½ teaspoon white sugar
2 teaspoons salt

Wash the toor dal in cold water a couple of times, then drain. Put in a saucepan with 2 cups (500 ml) water, then cover and cook until the dal is soft and the water has been absorbed, about 10 minutes. Set aside.

Heat a frying pan and add half the oil. Fry the onion and coconut over a high heat until they start to brown. Transfer to a blender with half the fresh coriander and grind until smooth.

Wipe out the frying pan and heat again. Add the remaining oil and fry the cumin, mustard and poppy seeds over a medium heat until the seeds start to pop. Add the curry leaves, ginger garlic paste and green chilli and stir to combine. Stir in the onion coconut paste and tomato until thoroughly combined. Simmer for a few seconds, then add the turmeric, chilli powder and ground coriander, stirring to combine. Add the toor dal, sugar and salt and mix well. Simmer for 5 minutes.

Serve hot, garnished with the remaining fresh coriander.

Gujarati-style Potato Curry
Batata Raswala
SERVES 4

Raswala is a Gujarati-style gravy and is so easy to prepare. We tried this light potato curry as part of a lunch thali at Swati Snacks. I have also made it with sweet potato.

3 desiree potatoes
2 tablespoons ghee
1 teaspoon mustard seeds
1 teaspoon cumin seeds
¼ teaspoon fennel seeds
2 red onions, diced
3 small dried red chillies, broken into pieces
pinch of asafoetida
1 teaspoon chilli powder
1 teaspoon ground coriander
¼ teaspoon ground turmeric
2 teaspoons salt
1 teaspoon sugar
1 tablespoon lemon juice (or more, to taste)
2 tablespoons chopped coriander leaves

Cook the whole potatoes in boiling water for about 15 minutes until soft. Allow to cool, then peel and roughly chop into cubes.

Heat the ghee in a frying pan, then add the mustard, cumin and fennel seeds and fry over a medium heat until they pop. Add the onion, dried chilli and asafoetida and stir to combine. Add 1½ cups (375 ml) water, the spices, salt and sugar and bring to a boil. Add the potato and lemon juice, then reduce the heat to medium and simmer for 10 minutes. Taste and adjust the seasoning if necessary. Garnish with the fresh coriander and serve hot with Roti (see page 103).

Spiced Cluster Beans with Yoghurt

SERVES 4

This vegetable is a local variety and features in Gujarati thalis. It is hard to replicate, but you can use green beans, snake beans or flat roman beans.

3 tablespoons vegetable oil
1 bay leaf
½ teaspoon cumin seeds
5 dried red chillies, broken into small pieces
pinch of asafoetida
½ teaspoon mustard powder
250 g cluster beans, cut into 3 cm lengths
1 teaspoon salt
3 tablespoons thick plain yoghurt, whisked
1 teaspoon chilli powder
½ teaspoon ground turmeric
1 tablespoon garam masala
½ teaspoon amchur
1 teaspoon ground coriander
½ teaspoon sugar
2–3 pieces dried mango, soaked to soften
2 tablespoons chopped coriander leaves

Heat the oil in a frying pan and fry the bay leaf, cumin seeds, dried chilli, asafoetida and mustard powder over a medium heat until fragrant, stirring continuously. Add the beans and salt and toss the pan to coat with the spices. Add the yoghurt, stirring to combine.

Combine the ground spices and sugar in a bowl with enough water to make a paste. Stir the spice paste into the beans and add the mango. Cook over a gentle heat until the mixture is quite dry, about 8–10 minutes. Garnish with the fresh coriander.

Yoghurt Custard

Shrikhand

SERVES 8

This lovely silky custard, a sweetened yoghurt, is lightly textured, perfect during hot weather and a refreshing finale to a thali. It is served for dessert at Gujarati restaurants. I have tasted one flavoured with lemon instead of saffron that was equally delicious.

1 kg thick plain yoghurt
¼ teaspoon saffron threads
1 tablespoon warm milk
185 g icing sugar
2 teaspoons ground cardamom
1 tablespoon slivered pistachios
1 tablespoon slivered blanched almonds

Place the yoghurt in a muslin-lined sieve set over a bowl in the refrigerator for 24 hours until all the liquid (whey) has drained off.

Heat the saffron in the warm milk for a few minutes. Combine the yoghurt, saffron milk, icing sugar and cardamom in a bowl and churn using a stick blender until combined and smooth. Pass through a sieve, then pour into small serving dishes and refrigerate for a few hours until set.

Garnish with pistachio and almond slivers to serve.

TAMIL NADU
Temples, Vegetables & Silks

Fringed by the Bay of Bengal to the east and the mighty Western Ghats mountain range to the west, the southern state of Tamil Nadu has a deep connection to its Deccan and Dravidian past. It is home to Brahmin Hindus, and some of India's most significant temples dominate its towns. The Tamil way of life is steeped in tradition, but still relevant to modern lifestyles.

> *Other parts of India may be leaping aggressively forward into the*
> *new millennium, but for a visitor at least, rural Tamil Nadu still*
> *seems deceptively innocent and timeless . . . villagers spread their*
> *newly harvested grain on the road to be winnowed and threshed by the*
> *wheels of passing cars . . . bullock carts trundle along red dirt roads . . .*
> *the cattle are strong and white, and their horns are painted blue.*
> WILLIAM DALRYMPLE, *NINE LIVES*

The food of the south is rich, spicy and wet, reliant on fresh curd, buttermilk, lentils, tamarind and an extraordinary array of vegetables – many of which are farmed inland, to take advantage of the more temperate climate around Bangalore in neighbouring Karnataka, and then trucked down to the coast. Every ingredient serves a specific purpose in the diet, whether it be related to health or practical considerations. The various breads (idli, appam, paratha and puri) are considered the stars, with everything else relegated to a supporting role.

CHENNAI

Chennai (formerly Madras) is a city divided into two: the Ville Noire, which is largely untouched by European colonial culture, and the Ville Blanche, whose wide French-style boulevards and whitewashed villas with timber-shuttered windows evoke a sense of another time and place – even the food is an intriguing hybrid of French and Tamil influences – just as they are in Pondicherry, a few hours south along the coast. Although it has grown into a large, bustling city over the years, doubling its population in the last two decades, this southern gateway still offers a relatively gentle introduction to India.

Chennai was the first place I visited in India, when I came to work as a guest chef in 1996 during Diwali, the annual festival of light, with firecrackers being let off in the street at all hours of the day and night and sweet shops doing a roaring trade. It has been fascinating to watch this city expand and grow dramatically with each subsequent visit. As Bollywood fever consumes the country, Tamil-language films are winning huge audiences. The movie-star business is booming, and it's not uncommon for movie stars to later become politicians in these parts – both seem equally revered.

It has become something of a ritual for me to start every visit to Chennai with a tiffin breakfast at Saravana Bhavan, a chain of modest cafeterias that pulse with energy and a steady stream of customers

throughout the day. My plate is filled with miniature *idli* (steamed rice cakes), a heavenly *vadai* (fried lentil patty) and a flat, pancake-like *uttapam* cooked with shredded onion, chilli and carrot. On the side are small bowls of fresh coconut chutney, tomato and onion chutney, and a dark-brown spicy paste. There's also a bowl of *sambar* – a vegetable and lentil stew soured with tamarind or buttermilk – which is eaten with rice and idli and is one of the defining dishes of Tamil Nadu. To follow, there is a small cup of *rasam* (a pepper water that is as versatile as sambar) and a masala dosa. These large, crisp, tissue-thin pancakes are made from rice and lentil batter that is smeared onto a hotplate to cook quickly, so the inside remains steamy and soft. A dollop of mild potato masala is added before the dosa is deftly folded over and put onto the plate.

And when dinner time comes around, I make a beeline for Dakshin Restaurant. Dakshin means 'south', and chef Praveen Anand writes a sensational menu featuring dishes from each of the four southern states: Tamil Nadu, Kerala, Karnataka and Andhra Pradesh. His thorough understanding of India's culinary history is revealed in flavours that are distinct, considered and tantalising. I adore the lightness and purity of *nandu puttu*, freshly picked crabmeat tossed with onion, ginger and green chilli. *Tallale jhalke* turn out to be little lady fish (similar to Australia's red-spot whiting) that have been lightly coated with a spicy chilli and ginger blanket and deep-fried until crisp – utterly delicious with a mild fresh mango chutney. A Karnataka-style prawn masala – *khara sigadi* – consists of tiny prawns simmered in a rich and spicy tomato sauce, excellent with flaky paratha bread. Perfect, lacy *appams* are made by swirling rice batter onto a small hot pan shaped like a deep wok. The batter sets into a vase, and when I pour in my bowl of potato simmered with coconut milk and green chilli (*urlai sadhi*), the spongy appam soaks up the juices. I consume it in an instant. Praveen tells me that appams are served at night as they are light, not cooked in oil and easy to digest. Every meal is finished with sombu – fresh fennel seeds that have been lightly coated with crystallised sugar and act as a natural breath freshener.

The Indian south carries an aura of distinctive identity, culture and mythology . . . the harshness and lushness of nature have created the original culinary moulds, which then evolved through centuries of impact by other races and religions, imported ingredients, and cultural and colonial fusions. But they are bonded with an imperceptible yet defined thread of 'southern-ness' that is further reinforced by an ethos that seems more ancient than what you encounter in other parts of the subcontinent.

CHITRITA BANERJI, *EATING INDIA*

THE TEMPLE TRAIL

Many people visit Chennai to follow the temple trail – a meandering pilgrimage to the temple cities, the pace dictated by agrarian rhythms that have remained unaltered for centuries. An hour's drive south of Chennai, Mamallapuram (Mahabalipuram) is the nearest temple town. Here magnificent temples, dating back to the seventh century, are carved from the surrounding rocky hills. Taking centre stage is the Shore Temple, dominated by its pyramid tower and famed for its bas-relief carved from stone. It is one of the few shore temples that has withstood the ravages of the sea and wind, including the ferocious 2004 tsunami that destroyed so much of the Tamil Nadu coastline. After paying our respects, we head to Fisherman's Cove at Covelong (Kovalam) for a lunch of masala-baked prawns overlooking the empty, windswept beach.

Another temple town is Kanchipuram, some 75 kilometres west of Chennai. Considered one of the holiest temple towns of India, it is an important Hindu pilgrimage centre with several key temples, but is equally famous for its fine silk sari weaving. Before we know it we find ourselves in retail-therapy mode at Shreenivas Silk House, one of the better-known silk emporiums.

We spend the rest of the morning wandering undisturbed through the enormous Ekambareshvara Shiva temple, a fine example of Dravidian architecture that was largely built in the sixteenth century. A food cart by the main internal entrance offers sweet *ponggol* (rice cooked with lentils, molasses, semolina and milk, pictured on page 211) and tamarind rice, dispensed in small disposable bowls made from dried betel leaves. I try one of each out of curiosity, and the tamarind rice proves to be the winner.

Our appetites whetted, we make our way to Kanchi Kudil for lunch. This restored heritage house in Kanchipuram is the ancestral family home of Malavika, who greets us at the front door with her sister-in-law Shael, an American doctor. A delectable lunch is prepared by Vijiya, the house cook, consisting of a dozen or more vegetarian dishes, a chicken curry, curd rice and pickles. Each preparation is spooned onto our banana-leaf plates by waiters who move around the table in procession. In between mouthfuls, I quickly scribble down notes from Vijiya on how to make her potato *poriyal*. Typical of southern cooking and considered an essential element of a thali, poriyals are vegetable-based dry curries that have no sauce, providing balance, texture and freshness to their accompanying dishes. Tiny, sweet bananas, the size of my finger, complete the repast.

A TASTE OF CHETTINAD FOOD

Further south in Tamil Nadu, stretching from the coast inland towards Madurai, lies the Chettinad region, a cluster of 72 towns and villages that is the homeland of the Chettiars. A shrewd, prosperous banking community whose wealth is reflected in their palatial houses, the Chettiars are also the source of one of the spiciest and most aromatic of Indian cuisines.

Intrigued by the nuances of Chettinad cooking, I decide it warrants further investigation, and Karaikudi, a small town in the centre of the region, is a good place to start. There I am fortunate to be able to discuss the intricacies of Chettinad food with Mrs Meenakshi Meyappan, a local authority on gastronomy and architecture. She divides her time between Karaikudi and Chennai, where we meet again on a later visit at her grand beachside home for dinner. I watch her house cooks in the kitchen and ask questions over their shoulders as they work, grabbing a few tips here and there. The wooden shelves are filled with glass jars of various spices that are used liberally as the cooks prepare eggplant masala, dry-fried potatoes that prove to be finger-licking good, a tangy fish curry and the Chettinad speciality of black pepper chicken (colloquially known as 'pepper chicken fry'), all accompanied by a mountain of soft spongy rice-flour pancakes called allam dosa.

From the Chettinad heartland, our eastbound road trip takes us across the Deccan peninsula via Madurai, another important temple city, onto the hill-station towns of the Nilgiris, with a detour along the way to the beautiful hilltop town of Kodaikanal – with its breathtaking views across the mountains and several nearby wildlife sanctuaries. The Nilgiris region is home to expansive tea plantations, where tea pickers working the spongy green slopes are a common sight. The charming and picturesque town of Coonoor, a retreat whose cool air offers refreshing respite from the heat of the plains, is dripping with scenic beauty. And, to add to its charms, there is a tea lounge whose menu includes a long list of locally harvested teas – from the rare silver tips to the blue Nilgiri to spiced tea and milky chai – and yummy snacks, including waffles with local honey. Nearby, the larger and more commercial town of Ooty (short for Ootacamund) was once a snobby British enclave, and its faded oh-so-terribly-Britishness lives on in the names of places, streets and bungalows.

The food in these parts is as diverse as the culture and geography, reflecting religious and regional differences – and we are still in Tamil Nadu! The local cultural and culinary traditions have remained strong and less susceptible to foreign influences, a lesson in restraint and remaining true to indigenous heritage.

Stuffed Savoury Pancakes
Masala Dosai

SERVES 8

These stuffed savoury pancakes, usually served for breakfast, are associated with Tamil Nadu and southern India. This version is from Saravana Bhavan restaurant in Chennai. To make the dosai from scratch, you need to start two days ahead to allow time for soaking and fermenting. Packet mixes for the batter are quite common in Indian cities these days (I have brought some back with me from a few trips) to meet the demands of the time-poor, and they are sometimes available in Indian groceries elsewhere.

½ teaspoon fenugreek seeds
100 g urad dal
200 g medium-grain white rice
1 teaspoon salt
melted ghee, for frying

POTATO STUFFING
400 g potatoes, boiled and peeled
2 tablespoons ghee
1 teaspoon brown mustard seeds
½ teaspoon fenugreek seeds
10 curry leaves
1 white onion, finely diced
2 teaspoons ground turmeric
½ teaspoon chilli powder
1 teaspoon salt
3 small green chillies, finely chopped
3 tablespoons moong dal, cooked

Soak the fenugreek seeds and urad dal in water overnight, covered. In a separate bowl, soak the rice in water overnight, covered. Drain the urad dal and fenugreek seeds and transfer to a food processor. Add 4 tablespoons water and blend to a smooth paste. Transfer to a bowl. Drain the rice. Wipe out the food processor, then add the rice with 4 tablespoons water and blend until smooth. Mix the ground dal and rice together and stir in the salt. Cover the bowl with a clean cloth and leave to stand overnight so the mixture ferments slightly (this gives the dosas their unique flavour).

To make the potato stuffing, mash the potatoes roughly so they retain an uneven texture – they should not be smooth. Heat the ghee in a kadhai or wok and fry the mustard and fenugreek seeds over a medium heat until they start to pop. Add the curry leaves and cook for a few seconds until fragrant, then add the onion and stir to combine. Increase the heat to high and fry until the onion has softened and is starting to colour. Add the turmeric, chilli powder, salt and green chilli and stir to combine. Add the potato and moong dal and toss over heat until the potato is coated with the onion spice mix.

Heat a tawa or shallow non-stick frying pan (a crepe pan works well) over a medium heat and pour a spoonful of batter onto the centre of the pan. Using the back of a ladle, spread the batter in a circular motion to cover the surface. The batter should be very thin (crepe-like). Drizzle a little ghee around the edges of the dosa as it cooks – this will give the dosa its golden colour and crisp texture. When the underside of the dosa is golden, spoon some potato stuffing onto the centre and spread it across slightly. Fold the dosa over, then fold in half again gently without flattening. Transfer to a serving plate and keep warm.

Repeat the process until all the batter has been used. Serve with Coconut Chutney (see page 208).

‹Masala Dal Fritters
Madhurwada
SERVES 4

This recipe was generously given to me by
Praveen Anand, executive chef at Dakshin
Restaurant in Chennai. The crisp fritters
make a perfect accompaniment to your
preferred chutney.

600 g channa dal
1 teaspoon ground cinnamon
200 g grated fresh coconut
1 small onion, finely diced
2 small green chillies, minced
2 teaspoons salt
vegetable oil, for deep-frying

Rinse the channa dal and soak it in cold water
for 1 hour. Drain, then coarsely grind. Add the
cinnamon, coconut, onion, chilli and salt and mix
well. Form into small balls, then press between
two sheets of plastic film to flatten out.

Heat the oil in a kadhai or wok to 180°C. To test
the temperature of the oil, sprinkle in some
flour – if the flour sizzles, it is ready. Fry the
fritters until golden brown and crisp. Drain
on paper towel and serve hot.

Banana Dosai
SERVES 4

These are served at Dakshin Restaurant as
an appetiser with various chutneys – I like
them best with hot ginger chutney. Dakshin's
recipe belongs to the ITC hotel group, so
I can't share it here. Instead, here is one given
to me by a home cook. You make the dosai in
the same way you would pikelets.

4 ripe bananas, mashed
2 tablespoons grated fresh coconut
200 g rice flour
100 g plain flour
2 tablespoons caster sugar
2 tablespoons vegetable oil,
    plus a little extra
½ teaspoon salt
pinch of ground cardamom

Combine the banana, coconut, flours, sugar, oil,
salt and cardamom in a bowl. Make a well in the
centre and pour in 100 ml water. Stir with a spoon
to make a thick batter, adding a little extra water
if the mixture is too thick. It should resemble
a thick pancake batter.

Heat a little extra oil in a frying pan over a medium
heat. Add a spoonful of batter and spread it slightly
so it is about 2 cm thick and a similar size to a drop
scone or pikelet. (If you use a large frying pan,
you can cook three or four at a time.) Cook for
4 minutes until golden on one side, then flip over
and cook the other side for 2–3 minutes. Drain on
paper towel. Repeat the process until all the batter
has been used. Serve hot.

Tomato Rasam

SERVES 4

Typical of the southern states, we were served this dish at Ānalakshmi, a popular vegetarian restaurant in Chennai. Its tangy and peppery broth is lighter than a sambar, it's easy to prepare and makes an ideal digestive. This rasam is often served with Curd Rice (see page 218). It is quite mild and can be made with a little tamarind liquid for an extra kick of flavour and a hint of sourness.

3 tablespoons masoor dal,
    washed and drained
2 teaspoons ghee
1 teaspoon brown mustard seeds
1 teaspoon cumin seeds
1 small red chilli, finely sliced
8 curry leaves
1 teaspoon freshly ground black pepper
½ teaspoon asafoetida
3 small green chillies, minced
1 tablespoon minced ginger
4 ripe tomatoes, finely diced
2 teaspoons salt
1 teaspoon ground turmeric
2 tablespoons chopped coriander leaves

Put the dal in a saucepan with 1 cup (250 ml) water and bring to a boil. Cover and reduce the heat, then simmer for 1½ hours, stirring occasionally, until the dal is soft. Set aside but do not drain.

Heat the ghee in a pan and fry the mustard and cumin seeds, red chilli, curry leaves, pepper and asafoetida over a medium heat until the mustard seeds start to splutter. Add the green chilli, ginger, tomato and 3 cups (750 ml) water. Bring to simmering point, then stir in the salt and turmeric and simmer for 5 minutes. Add the cooked dal and any remaining liquid, plus 1 cup (250 ml) water. Bring to a boil and taste, adjusting the seasoning if necessary.

Stir in the fresh coriander and pour into bowls.

Pineapple Curry ›

SERVES 4

From chef Praveen, this is a sweet, spicy curry that is served with steamed idli. It's a versatile way to cook with pineapple and makes an ideal breakfast dish.

4 small green mangoes
300 g shaved jaggery
salt
pinch of ground turmeric
3 tablespoons diced fresh pineapple

COCONUT MASALA
3 teaspoons vegetable oil
2 teaspoons black sesame seeds
¼ teaspoon fenugreek seeds
pinch of asafoetida
6 small dried red chillies
2 teaspoons urad dal
1 teaspoon channa dal
35 g grated fresh coconut

To make the coconut masala, heat the oil and fry the sesame seeds, fenugreek seeds, asafoetida, dried chillies, urad dal and channa dal over a medium heat until the mixture changes colour. Remove from the heat and cool. Grind with the coconut, adding a little water to make a fine paste. Set aside.

Put the whole mangoes and 3 cups (750 ml) water in a saucepan and bring to a boil. Cook for about 10 minutes, then remove the mangoes, reserving the water, and allow to cool. Remove the skin and seeds from the mangoes, then mix the pulp into the cooking water. Add the jaggery, salt to taste, the turmeric and the coconut masala. Boil for 5 minutes until the gravy has thickened. Stir in the pineapple and remove from the heat.

Fried Lentil Patties with Coconut Chutney
Thair Vadai
SERVES 4

Another street snack that quickly becomes addictive, like a fried savoury donut, these are delicious for breakfast served with coconut chutney.

110 g urad dal
110 g channa dal
2 tablespoons vegetable oil
2 small green chillies, minced
3 red shallots, finely diced
3 tablespoons curry leaves, shredded
1 tablespoon minced ginger
½ teaspoon ground fennel
½ teaspoon garam masala
½ teaspoon ground turmeric
½ teaspoon ground cumin
3 tablespoons grated fresh coconut
3 tablespoons chopped coriander leaves
½ teaspoon salt
2 tablespoons urad dal flour
¼ teaspoon baking powder
vegetable oil, for deep-frying

COCONUT CHUTNEY
1 teaspoon channa dal
1 teaspoon urad dal
150 g grated fresh coconut
2 small green chillies, minced
1 teaspoon sea salt
1 tablespoon vegetable oil
1 teaspoon brown mustard seeds
6 curry leaves
2 teaspoons Tamarind Liquid (see page 379)

To begin the vadai, soak the urad and channa dal in cold water for 5 hours.

To make the coconut chutney, soak the channa and urad dal in cold water for 3 hours, then drain. Blend the coconut, chilli and salt in a food processor to make a fine paste. Heat the oil in a frying pan and fry the mustard seeds and dal over a medium heat until the seeds start to pop and splutter. Add the curry leaves and fry for another minute until the mixture is starting to colour. Stir in the coconut paste and tamarind liquid until combined. Set aside until ready to serve.

Drain the vadai dals, reserving the soaking water. Grind the softened dal with 3 tablespoons of the soaking water, leaving the texture a little coarse.

Heat the oil in a pan and gently fry the chilli, shallot, curry leaves and ginger for a minute until fragrant, then add the spices, coconut, fresh coriander and salt and stir until combined. Add this mixture to the ground dal and combine thoroughly. Using your fingers, mix in the urad flour and baking powder. If the dough feels a little firm, add a splash of water. Shape the dough into walnut-sized balls and flatten each one slightly.

Heat the oil in large wok or saucepan to 180°C. To test the temperature of the oil, sprinkle in some flour – if the flour sizzles, it is ready. Deep-fry a few vadai at a time for 5 minutes until golden and crisp. Flip them over halfway through the cooking time so they brown on both sides. Drain on paper towel and serve with the coconut chutney.

Ginger Chutney
SERVES 10

This is my favourite Indian chutney, pungent and spicy, and Praveen makes the best version. It's the perfect condiment to serve with breads, fried pastries or steamed rice.

30 g chopped ginger
300 ml Tamarind Liquid (see page 379)
1 tablespoon vegetable oil
1 teaspoon urad dal
1 tablespoon curry leaves
¼ teaspoon brown mustard seeds
1 teaspoon chilli powder
pinch of asafoetida

Blend the ginger and tamarind liquid to a fine paste. Heat the oil in a frying pan, add the urad dal, curry leaves and mustard seeds and cook until the mustard seeds crackle. Add the ginger and tamarind paste, stirring to combine. Add the chilli powder and asafoetida and cook for 15 minutes. Allow to cool before serving. Store in an airtight container in the refrigerator and use as required.

Okra Masala
Vendaikkai Masala
SERVES 4

In India, okra is picked young so they have not yet developed that slimy character – use the smallest ones you can find. You could substitute small eggplant (aubergine) for the okra, but you'll need to cut them into chunks and deep-fry or dry roast them before adding them to the mix.

500 g small okra
2½ tablespoons vegetable oil
1 teaspoon sesame oil
1 teaspoon brown mustard seeds
12 fresh curry leaves
1 small red onion, finely diced
1 teaspoon ground cumin
1 teaspoon ground coriander
2 teaspoons garam masala
1 teaspoon ground turmeric
4 cloves garlic, minced
3 small green chillies, sliced
1 teaspoon salt
1 tablespoon chopped coriander leaves

Trim the tops off the okra and cut them in half on the diagonal.

Heat the oils in a kadhai or wok and fry the mustard seeds over a medium heat until they start to pop. Add the curry leaves and fry for about 30 seconds until they are crisp. Add the onion and fry, stirring constantly, until it begins to colour. Stir in the spices and cook for 1 minute until fragrant. Add the okra, garlic and chilli and fry gently for 10 minutes until the okra is soft. Season with the salt, then taste and adjust the seasoning if necessary. The sauce should be quite dry and thick, coating the okra.

Stir through the fresh coriander and serve.

Crab & Ginger Salad
Nandu Puttu
SERVES 4

This deliciously light crab salad, spiked with ginger and pepper, is a speciality of chef Praveen at Dakshin in Chennai, and is one of my favourite Indian salads. At home I use blue swimmer or mud crab, as the inherent sweetness works brilliantly with all the spicy flavours.

1 tablespoon vegetable oil
1 teaspoon brown mustard seeds
½ teaspoon fennel seeds
2 cm piece ginger, cut into thin
    julienne strips
4 cloves garlic, finely sliced
50 g finely sliced onion
2 teaspoons small green chillies, finely sliced
½ teaspoon ground turmeric
1 teaspoon freshly ground black pepper
½ teaspoon garam masala
2 tablespoons curry leaves
150 g freshly picked crabmeat
1 tomato, diced
1 tablespoon lemon juice
1 teaspoon salt

Heat the oil in a frying pan and cook the mustard and fennel seeds over a high heat. When the seeds crackle, add the ginger, garlic and onion. Fry until the onion is translucent. Add the chilli, turmeric, pepper, garam masala and curry leaves and mix well. Working quickly, add the crabmeat and tomato and toss to coat the crab with the masala base. Take care that the mixture is not mashed. Add the lemon juice and salt and toss to combine. Serve immediately.

Tamarind Chutney

SERVES 10

Here is another chutney from Praveen's extensive repertoire. It has typical Tamil flavours.

400 g tamarind pulp
3 tablespoons sesame oil
6–8 small red chillies, chopped
1 teaspoon brown mustard seeds
2 teaspoons urad dal
2 teaspoons channa dal
1 teaspoon cumin seeds
1 tablespoon curry leaves
2 teaspoons salt
1 teaspoon ground turmeric
1 tablespoon chilli powder
30 g jaggery, shaved
¼ teaspoon asafoetida

Wash the tamarind well, then soak it in warm water for 30 minutes. Squeeze out the pulp and strain the liquid. Discard the pulp.

In a heavy-based pan, heat the oil and add the red chilli, mustard seeds, dals and cumin seeds over a medium heat. When the seeds start crackling, add the curry leaves, salt, turmeric and chilli powder and fry until fragrant, making sure the mixture does not burn. Add the tamarind liquid and mix well. Bring to a boil, then reduce the heat to low and cook until reduced by more than half. The mixture should resemble a thick sauce. Add the jaggery and asafoetida, mixing well to avoid lumps. Bring to a boil, then remove from the heat and allow to cool. Serve with steaming-hot plain rice.

Tamarind Rice ›

SERVES 4

This rice is given to pilgrims at Shiva temples. We shared some from the communal pot when we visited the temple at Kanchipuram. This recipe was given to me by our Chennai guide, Geetha.

200 g basmati rice
1 teaspoon salt
2 tablespoons ghee
1 white onion, finely diced
1 teaspoon brown mustard seeds
6 curry leaves
2 small dried red chillies, broken into pieces
½ teaspoon fenugreek seeds
3 tablespoons Tamarind Liquid
   (see page 379)
2 teaspoons tomato puree

Soak the rice in cold water for 20 minutes, then drain and rinse. Bring 2 cups (500 ml) water to a boil in a saucepan. Add the washed rice and the salt, then cover with a lid and reduce the heat to low. Cook the rice for 10 minutes until soft. Drain.

Heat the ghee in a frying pan and fry the onion over a high heat until golden. Add the mustard seeds and fry until they start to pop. Add the curry leaves, chilli and fenugreek seeds and cook for another minute. Stir in the tamarind liquid and tomato puree, then stir through the cooked rice. Taste and adjust the seasoning, adding more salt if required.

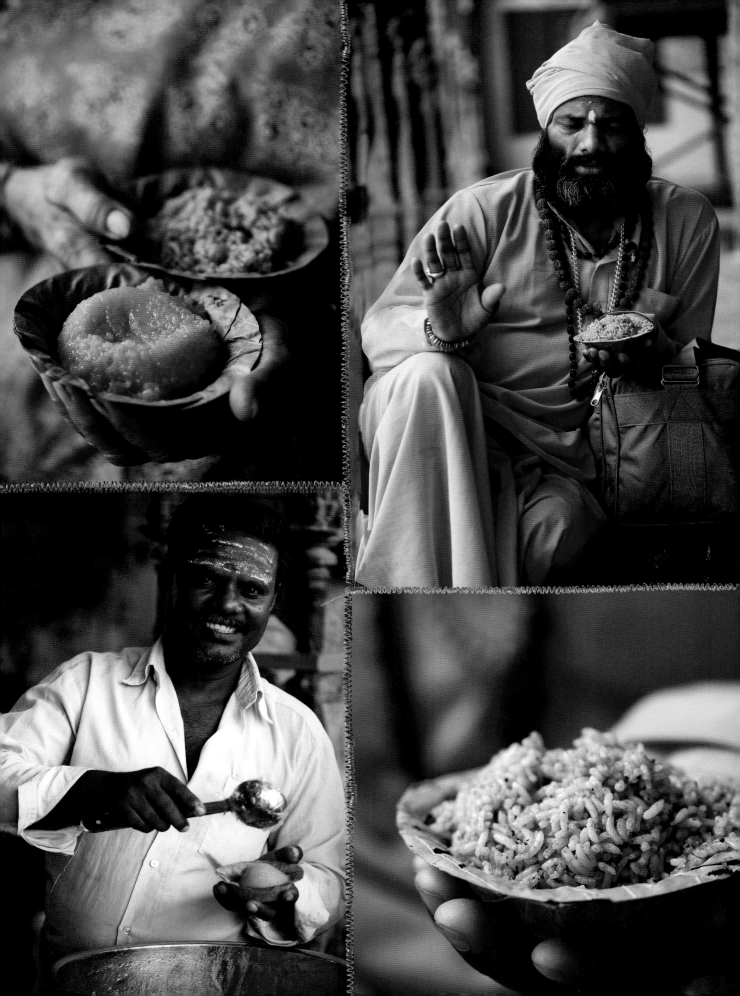

Tamarind Sambar with Snake Beans

SERVES 4

My first taste of sambar was this one, which I had at the Raintree Restaurant in Chennai the first time I visited. It sparked my curiosity about the balance of flavours and textures in a dish that is so representative of the region.

200 g toor dal, soaked for 2 hours,
    then drained
1½ tablespoons ghee
1 teaspoon brown mustard seeds
12 curry leaves
2 small potatoes, diced
6 baby carrots, peeled and
    cut into 1 cm rounds
4 golden shallots, peeled and quartered
12 small okra, trimmed
150 ml Tamarind Liquid (see page 379)
salt
4 tablespoons chopped coriander leaves

SAMBAR SPICE MIX
½ teaspoon brown mustard seeds
1 teaspoon cumin seeds
½ teaspoon coriander seeds
½ teaspoon fenugreek seeds
3 small dried red chillies
½ teaspoon black peppercorns
¼ teaspoon ground cinnamon
pinch of asafoetida
½ teaspoon ground turmeric
2 teaspoons vegetable oil
1 teaspoon channa dal
1 teaspoon toor dal
1 tablespoon grated fresh coconut

To make the sambar spice mix, dry-roast the whole spices over a gentle heat until aromatic. Add the ground spices and toss briefly over the heat. Cool. Heat the oil in a frying pan, then fry the dals over a medium heat until they change colour. Remove the dals from the pan with a slotted spoon and allow to cool. Grind the roasted spices, dal and coconut together in a spice grinder to make a powder. Store in an airtight container and use as required.

Put the toor dal in a heavy-based saucepan with 1 litre water. Cover and bring to a boil, then cook for 1½ hours over a medium heat until the lentils are soft, skimming the surface regularly to remove any scum.

Meanwhile, heat the ghee and fry the mustard seeds and curry leaves over a high heat until the seeds pop. Add the vegetables and fry for 2–3 minutes, then stir in 1 tablespoon of the sambar spice mix. Add the tamarind liquid and bring to a boil, then reduce the heat and simmer, uncovered, for 20 minutes until the vegetables are tender.

Add the cooked toor dal and its water and stir to combine. Simmer for 5–10 minutes until thickened. Season to taste with salt, then add the fresh coriander and serve.

Potato Poriyal

SERVES 4

This poriyal was prepared by Vijiya for our lunch at Kanchi Kudil. It makes an ideal lunch snack, and I sometimes serve it with barbecued lamb or grilled chicken.

400 g potatoes, peeled and cut into small dice
1 tablespoon vegetable oil
2 teaspoons brown mustard seeds
1 onion, finely diced
2 small cloves garlic, minced
1 ripe tomato, diced
200 g green peas, cooked
2 small green chillies, minced
1 tablespoon chopped coriander leaves

Cook the potato in boiling water until soft. Drain. Heat the oil in a frying pan and fry the mustard seeds over a medium heat until they pop. Add the onion, garlic and tomato and cook for 6–8 minutes until softened. Add the potato, peas, chilli and fresh coriander and toss to combine. Serve warm.

Green Bean Poriyal

SERVES 4

Easy to prepare and an ideal lunch or picnic snack, this can also be made with snake beans when they are in season.

4 tablespoons vegetable oil
1 teaspoon brown mustard seeds
1 teaspoon urad dal, washed
10 curry leaves
2 small dried red chillies
½ teaspoon ground turmeric
1 small white onion, finely diced
500 g green beans, sliced into 5 mm rounds
1 teaspoon salt
70 g grated fresh coconut

Heat the oil in a wok or frying pan and fry the mustard seeds, urad dal, curry leaves and chillies over a medium heat until the seeds start to pop. Stir in the turmeric, then add the onion and cook until the onion is soft and beginning to colour. Add the beans and salt and toss over the heat to coat the beans with the spices. Cook for a minute until the beans have softened. Add the coconut and toss to mix, then serve.

Cabbage Poriyal

SERVES 4

This poriyal was served for lunch at Chennai's Analakshmi Restaurant. At home, I like to serve it with grilled fish. On occasion I have used beetroot instead of cabbage in this recipe, and it's delicious.

3 teaspoons vegetable oil
1 teaspoon brown mustard seeds
½ teaspoon cumin seeds
1 teaspoon urad dal, washed and drained
1 teaspoon channa dal, washed and drained
1 tablespoon curry leaves
½ teaspoon asafoetida
1 small red chilli, finely sliced
2 small green chillies, split in half lengthways
400 g white cabbage, finely shredded
4 tablespoons green peas
1 teaspoon salt
3 tablespoons shredded fresh coconut

Heat the oil in a large frying pan and fry the mustard and cumin seeds, urad and channa dals, curry leaves and asafoetida over a medium heat. When the seeds start to pop, add the red and green chilli, cabbage, peas and salt. Toss or stir to combine to make sure the spices are evenly distributed. Add 2–3 tablespoons water, then cover and reduce the heat to low. Cook gently for 5–6 minutes until the vegetables are tender but still have a slight crunch. Stir through the coconut and serve hot.

Grandma's Lamb

SERVES 4

A family favourite from Raka, a travel contact
I met in Chennai who generously shared her
grandmother's recipe with me. Young goat
meat is the norm in India, even though it
is referred to as lamb; you could use either.
This can be served as a snack with pre-dinner
drinks or alongside a simple rice pilaf or
a vegetable poriyal (see page 213).

> 500 g lamb shoulder or leg meat, fat removed
> 1 teaspoon chilli powder
> 1 teaspoon ground turmeric
> ½ teaspoon freshly ground black pepper
> 1 teaspoon white sugar
> 2 teaspoons salt
> 2 tablespoons rice flour
> vegetable oil, for deep-frying

Slice the meat into thin strips, then dry with paper
towel. Mix together the chilli powder, turmeric,
pepper, sugar and salt, then add the rice flour and
mix thoroughly. Rub the spice mix into the lamb
until evenly coated.

Heat the oil in a kadhai or wok to 180°C. To test the
temperature of the oil, sprinkle in some flour –
if the flour sizzles, it is ready. Deep-fry the lamb
strips a few at a time for 2 minutes until crisp and
golden. Drain on paper towel. Serve hot.

Chettinad Fish Curry ›

Fish Kozhambu

SERVES 4

Mrs Meena Meyappan's cooks prepared this
classic Chettinad fish curry for a summer
dinner at her ocean-facing Chennai home.

> 1 white onion, finely diced
> 15 small red shallots, peeled
>   and cut in half
> 10 cloves garlic, peeled
> 100 ml vegetable oil
> ½ teaspoon fennel seeds
> 1 teaspoon fenugreek seeds
> 2 ripe tomatoes, chopped
> ¼ teaspoon ground turmeric
> 1½ tablespoons chilli powder
> 2 tablespoons ground coriander
> 2 tablespoons thick Tamarind Liquid
>   (see page 379)
> 2 teaspoons salt
> 1 kg seer fish, kingfish, bonito
>   or mackerel fillets, skin removed,
>   cut into 3 cm chunks

SPICE MIX
> 1 tablespoon cumin seeds
> 3 teaspoons fennel seeds
> 2 teaspoons white poppy seeds
> 1 teaspoon black peppercorns

To make the spice mix, use a spice grinder to blend
all the ingredients to a fine powder.

Using a mortar and pestle, pound the onion, shallot
and garlic to a paste.

Heat the oil in a wide, heavy-based saucepan or
large wok or kadhai. Fry the fennel and fenugreek
seeds over a medium heat, then add the onion paste
and fry until golden. Add the spice mix and stir to
combine. Cook for about 2 minutes until fragrant.
Add the tomato, turmeric, chilli and coriander and
fry for another 2 minutes. Add 100 ml water, along
with the tamarind liquid and salt. Simmer over
a medium heat until the mixture starts to thicken.

Add the fish and stir until it is well coated. Simmer
for 5 minutes until the fish is just cooked. Remove
from the heat, then check the seasoning and adjust
if necessary.

Drumstick Sambar

SERVES 4

This recipe was given to me by Vijiya, the cook at Kanchi Kudil. Prolific in India, drumstick is a long, green pod-like vegetable shaped like its name. It can be very difficult to find outside India, but snake beans or asparagus can be substituted.

400 g toor dal, soaked for 2 hours
2 drumstick vegetables, stringed and
    chopped into 3 cm lengths
300 g eggplant (aubergine), sliced into batons
1 onion, finely diced
3 cloves garlic, minced
2 tomatoes, diced
200 ml Tamarind Liquid (see page 379)
salt
1 teaspoon chilli powder
1 bay leaf
2 tablespoons chopped coriander leaves
1 tablespoon vegetable oil
1 teaspoon brown mustard seeds
1 tablespoon curry leaves

SAMBAR POWDER
1½ tablespoons small dried red chillies
1½ tablespoons coriander seeds
1 tablespoon cumin seeds
1½ teaspoons fenugreek seeds
1½ teaspoons black peppercorns
2 teaspoons brown mustard seeds
½ teaspoon channa dal
½ teaspoon masoor dal
4 curry leaves
½ teaspoon white poppy seeds
½ teaspoon ground cinnamon
½ teaspoon ground turmeric

To make the sambar powder, dry-roast the whole spices, channa dal and masoor dal separately in a frying pan over a low heat until fragrant. Cool, then blend in a spice grinder with the curry leaves to make a fine powder. Mix in the poppy seeds, cinnamon and turmeric. Store in an airtight container and use as required.

Cook the toor dal in a large saucepan of boiling water for about 6 minutes until soft. Drain. Cook the drumstick and eggplant in boiling water for 3 minutes until softened. Drain. Combine the cooked dal and vegetables with the onion, garlic and tomato in a large saucepan. Add the tamarind liquid, 2 teaspoons salt and the chilli powder, then 3 tablespoons of the sambar powder. Mix and bring to a boil, then add the bay leaf. Simmer for 5 minutes. Season with salt to taste, then stir in the fresh coriander.

Heat the oil in a small frying pan and fry the brown mustard seeds and curry leaves over a high heat until the seeds are spluttering. Spoon over the sambar and serve.

Potatoes with Coconut Milk & Chilli
Urlai Sodhi

SERVES 4

Another delicious vegetable dish from Dakshin Restaurant in Chennai, this is best served with spongy, soft Appam (see page 240).

500 g potatoes, peeled
140 ml sesame oil
1 teaspoon brown mustard seeds
2 tablespoons curry leaves
200 g red shallots, chopped
1 teaspoon turmeric powder
4 long green chillies, split in half lengthways
200 g tomatoes, diced
100 ml coconut milk
1 teaspoon salt
1 tablespoon lime juice

Cut the potatoes into 2.5 cm × 1 cm fingers. Heat the oil in a saucepan, add the mustard seeds and cook over a high heat. When the seeds start to splutter, add the curry leaves, shallot, turmeric, chilli and tomato. Cook for 5–6 minutes over a medium heat, then add the potato, coconut milk and salt. Cook over a low heat for about 10 minutes until the potato is soft, then add the lime juice. Taste and adjust the seasoning, then serve.

Curd Rice

SERVES 4

This rice is served with spicy dishes, dry-fried meats and non-gravy dishes, and is important to the Tamil diet for its cooling and digestive properties – perfect for their hot humid weather. The rice is slightly overcooked, so the grains break and the texture becomes sloppy. Geetha told me that various other ingredients, such as green mango, cashews, grated carrot, sultana grapes and urad dal, can also be added to the rice for extra texture and taste.

200 g basmati rice, washed and drained
1 tablespoon ghee
1 teaspoon brown mustard seeds
2 neem leaves or curry leaves
pinch of asafoetida
1 teaspoon minced ginger
1 small green chilli, minced
280 g curd (drained yoghurt)
2 teaspoons salt

Pour 2 cups (500 ml) water into a large saucepan and bring to a boil. Add the rice, then cover and cook for 15 minutes or until the rice is soft and fluffy and has absorbed all the water.

Heat the ghee in a small frying pan and fry the mustard seeds over a medium heat until they pop, then add the neem or curry leaves and asafoetida. Reduce the heat to low and stir through the ginger and chilli. Cook briefly until fragrant. Stir in the curd and salt and cook for 1 minute until heated through but not boiling.

Mash the rice slightly to break the grains, then stir through the curd mixture until combined. If adding other ingredients, stir them through after the curd. Serve warm or cold.

Black Pepper Chicken Fry ›

SERVES 4

This Chettinad classic was prepared by Mrs Meena Meyappan's house cooks at her Chennai house. Farmed quail can be cooked in a similar way, as I tasted a few years ago at Bangala, her homestay in Karaikudi.

5 cloves garlic, peeled
1 tablespoon minced ginger
2 tablespoons vegetable oil
3 cm piece cinnamon stick
2 green cardamom pods, cracked
2 white onions, finely diced
2 ripe tomatoes, diced
2 teaspoons salt
1 kg chicken thigh fillets

PEPPER MASALA
3 teaspoons fennel seeds
3 teaspoons cumin seeds
3 teaspoons coriander seeds
1 tablespoon black peppercorns
4 small dried red chillies

To make the pepper masala, dry-roast the spices over a gentle heat. Cool, then grind to a fine powder. Store in an airtight container and use as required.

Using a mortar and pestle, pound the garlic and ginger to a smooth paste.

Heat the oil in a wide, heavy-based saucepan and fry the cinnamon and cardamom over a medium heat for 30 seconds until fragrant. Add the onion and stir over a high heat until golden, about 4 minutes. Add half the pepper masala and stir until fragrant. Add the ginger garlic paste and the tomato and fry for a few minutes, then season with the salt and cook, stirring, for another minute or so.

Add the chicken pieces and stir to coat in the aromatics. Fry for 3–4 minutes until the chicken is beginning to colour. Add 1 cup (250 ml) water, then cover the pan with a tight-fitting lid. Reduce the heat and simmer for 20 minutes or until most of the liquid has been absorbed and the chicken is cooked and tender.

Remove from the heat and check the seasoning. Serve with Appam (see page 240) or steamed rice.

Yoghurt

Yoghurt is a staple ingredient in India. Cooling and refreshing, it counteracts spicy food. It also provides balance to the diet, acts as a tenderiser for meat and in marinades, is used to thicken sauces, gravies and curries, and makes delicious drinks such as lassi and majjiga. One hot summer's day I was offered a refreshingly cool drink of plain yoghurt blended with water, sugar, strawberries and a dash of rosewater until it was frothy — poured over ice, it made a perfect thirst-quencher.

And it seems nowhere in India is yoghurt more widely used than in Tamil Nadu, where it is made each day in homes and restaurants, usually set in small reusable earthenware pots. The clay absorbs the water and thickens the yoghurt as it sets, as well as imparting a specific flavour.

To make your own yoghurt, bring 1 litre of full-cream milk to the boil in a heavy-based saucepan, then turn off the heat and leave it to cool until it is just lukewarm. Stir in 2 tablespoons of thick plain yoghurt (preferably probiotic) containing live cultures, transfer to a sterilised container and cover with a cloth (the milk needs to breathe, so don't use a lid). Leave in a warm place overnight, away from any direct airflow. Next day, the yoghurt should be set and thick. If it looks too runny, the milk was probably too hot when you added the yoghurt, and so the cultures died. Start again.

Once it is made, refrigerate the yoghurt. Always remember to save 2 tablespoons of yoghurt from each batch to start the next one.

Eggplant Masala ›

SERVES 4

At Bangala in the Chettinad region, vegetable dishes have a starring role on the table. This one is to die for. I sometimes serve it with steamed fish — too easy!

500 g small round eggplants (aubergines), cut into wedges
1 teaspoon salt
2 tablespoons vegetable oil
1 teaspoon fennel seeds
1 white onion, finely diced
1 ripe tomato, diced
2 tablespoons chopped coriander leaves
1 tablespoon grated fresh coconut

MASALA PASTE
2 small green chillies, chopped
2 small dried red chillies, broken
1 teaspoon cumin seeds
1 teaspoon fennel seeds
½ teaspoon white poppy seeds
4 tablespoons grated fresh coconut
2 cloves garlic
1 teaspoon salt

Sprinkle the eggplant slices with the salt and leave to drain in a colander for 30 minutes. Brush off the salt and wipe off any excess water with paper towel.

To make the masala paste, grind all the ingredients in a blender until smooth.

Heat the oil in a wide, heavy-based saucepan or wok, add the fennel seeds and fry over a medium heat until fragrant. Add the onion and tomato and cook over a medium–high heat until starting to colour. Add the masala paste and cook until the oil rises to the surface. Add the eggplant and toss over the heat to coat with the spice paste. Add 100 ml water and cover the pan, then reduce the heat and simmer for 25 minutes until the eggplant is very soft. Remove from the heat and stir through the fresh coriander. Sprinkle the coconut over the top and serve with steamed rice.

‹Dry-fried Potatoes

SERVES 4

A typical Chettinad potato dish, as served at Mrs Meyappan's homestay, Bangala.

- 1 teaspoon cumin seeds
- 2 cm piece cinnamon stick
- ½ teaspoon urad dal
- 1½ teaspoons fennel seeds
- 3 tablespoons vegetable oil
- ½ teaspoon brown mustard seeds
- ½ teaspoon white poppy seeds
- 1 white onion, finely diced
- 1 kg potatoes, peeled and cut into wedges
- 2 teaspoons salt

Grind the cumin seeds, cinnamon stick, dal and ½ teaspoon of the fennel seeds together to make a fine powder.

Heat the oil in a frying pan and fry the mustard seeds and remaining fennel seeds over a medium heat until they start to pop. Add the onion and stir until golden. Add the ground spices and cook until fragrant, stirring continuously to prevent sticking. Add the potato wedges and toss over heat until they are coated with the spices. Add the salt and 100 ml water, then cover the pan with a tight-fitting lid and simmer over a medium heat for 15–20 minutes or until the potato wedges are soft.

Coconut Rice Pudding with Papaya

SERVES 4

Sweet rice – Kheer – is a common dessert right across South India, and there are myriad versions. It's comfort food at its best, using what's local and in season. You can also serve this with small sweet bananas or mango.

- 125 g short-grain rice
- 2 cups (500 ml) coconut milk
- 200 ml milk
- 50 g caster sugar
- finely grated zest of 1 lime
- 1 teaspoon vanilla extract
- 200 ml cream
- ¼ ripe papaya, cubed
- 2 teaspoons lime juice

Wash the rice under cold running water, then put it in a saucepan with the coconut milk, milk, sugar, lime zest and vanilla. Bring to simmering point over a medium heat, stirring occasionally. Cover and reduce the heat to low. Cook slowly for 1 hour, then remove from the heat and leave to cool.

When the rice is cool, stir in the cream and spoon into serving bowls. Toss the papaya with the lime juice and spoon it on top of the rice to serve.

KERALA
Backwaters, Coconuts & Ayurveda

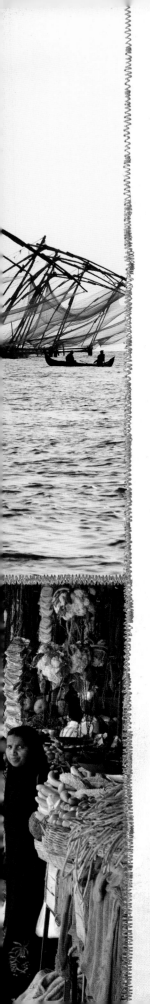

Kerala weaves a pervasive magic and tugs at my heartstrings. There is something so poetically romantic about this southern part of India, with its shimmering emerald landscape and sun-kissed coastline. Its unique, languid charm and heady sensuality make it quite unlike the rest of the country. The people of Kerala voted in the first freely elected communist government in the world, and their state has the highest literacy rate and lowest birth rate in India. With well-maintained houses and services, the region's prosperity is palpable. Time spent here, witnessing such a progressive spirit, restores faith in human nature.

Heaven must be a bit like Kerala, an ancient strip of lush, tropical land that slithers sensuously down the coast of south-western India . . . It has been these spices that have lured traders into Kerala's warm waters since antiquity.
MADHUR JAFFREY, *A TASTE OF INDIA*

Kerala is a diverse state with distinct regions, and each community maintains their traditional religion, architecture, music, arts and food. Hindu, Catholic, Syrian Christian, Jewish and Muslim cultures coexist happily, each embracing their own customs and cuisine. The temples are alive with activity, and being here during any festival is a treat. Everyone congregates to watch the dramatic and colourful rituals with their heady mix of religious zeal and superstition. Food plays a pivotal role.

The fragrance of Kerala is distinctive. It has long traded in black pepper, cardamom, turmeric and ginger with Arab, European and Chinese merchants. Another important cash crop is cashews, which are commonly used in both savoury and sweet preparations. Coconuts and bananas are prolific. The coconut tree is considered a gift from the gods, a tree of wealth, as every part can be turned to profit. Coconuts are used to make coconut cream, milk, oil and vinegar, and then there is the nutrient-rich coconut water. Even the sap from the trunk is tapped into clay pots tied to the tree – the juice ferments to make mildly alcoholic toddy.

KOCHI & A KERALAN FEAST

Kochi (formerly Cochin), on the Kerala coast, is made up of islands and mainland, separated by broad waterways. It is a major port city with a rich, vibrant past and bustling present, and is divided into three parts: Ernakulam is the new town; Fort Kochi is the old town; and the industrial Willingdon Island lies between the two. The streets of the old town are shaded from the heat by canopies of banyan and tamarind trees. As we stroll, we watch fishermen casting enormous, elaborate Chinese-style fishing nets from the shore of Fort Kochi beach. The cantilevered teak contraptions that hold out the nets look like huge preying mantises, and are particularly dramatic silhouetted by the setting sun as it sinks into the Arabian Sea.

Breakfast is hard to beat and impossible to ignore in these parts, so our mornings start on the street opposite the car ferry in Fort Kochi, where vendors do a brisk trade satisfying the hungry hordes. We fill our plates with *idli* (steamed rice cakes) and *vadai* (fried lentil dumplings), but still can't resist trying the *puttu* (rolls of steamed ground rice and coconut) and *idiyappam* (string hoppers) from a street cart on the road behind Mattancherry Palace.

The days become punctuated with new flavours: soft and fluffy red rice; bitter, ribbed, smooth, snake and bottle gourds in salads and curries; lentil and vegetable curries ranging from moist *avial* (vegetables cooked in turmeric water then shredded and mixed with yoghurt, fresh coconut and chilli) and *rasam* (a light pepper broth with lentils, laced with garlic, spices and tamarind) to dry *poriyal* and *thoran*, by way of semi-dry *kootu*. In between times, we snack on wafer-like pappadams flavoured with black sesame and cumin (*achappam*), eaten with chutneys and pickles, and indulge in *payasam* desserts made from coconut milk, rice vermicelli, sultanas and cashews, and scented with cardamom.

Keen to learn how to prepare a Keralan feast for ourselves, we head to visit highly regarded home cook Nimmy Paul at her ocean-front home. With a couple of guest rooms on the upper floor of her lovely bungalow available for a home stay, Nimmy opens her house – and her heart – to small groups who come in search of culinary inspiration. We spend a day in her kitchen, looking out to a beautiful garden planted with soft buffalo grass, curry-leaf shrubs and fragrant with frangipani trees.

Nimmy's food reflects her Syrian Christian heritage. She shows me how to make a few of her favourite recipes, staying close to my shoulder as she offers advice and direction all the way. In the background, her housemaid is busy preparing lunch, which is a feast not to be taken lightly. She shows us the art of making 1-metre chai, pouring the spiced milky tea from pot to cup and back again from a great height to aerate it, and produces a pot-roasted chicken, marinated in whole spices and cooked to a recipe belonging to her grandmother, which is the starring dish of our lunch. It is served with jackfruit *thoran*, snake-bean *poriyal* and steamed Kerala rice (whose grains are shorter and plumper than basmati). We chat well into the afternoon about food, life, travel, people and experiences – a magical time packed with memories.

EXPLORING THE BACKWATERS

South of Kochi, a maze of waterways make up Kerala's renowned backwaters, a magical labyrinth that leads off the massive Lake Vembanad, best explored by boat. We stop in Alappuzha (Alleppey) to meet local historian and conservation activist Rani John, who takes us on a walking tour around the old historic quarter. Along with a group of other women she is helping to document the town's history before it disappears under concrete, and it's evident an injection of money could restore some of its

unique old architecture. We are treated to a delightful outdoor lunch in her garden before we leave and head to Philip Kutty's Farm, a hideaway retreat of eight villas on a small private island in the lake. Reached by paddling across Lake Vembanad in a small wooden vallum (canoe), this homestay is a sanctuary of calm and sustainable practice. Matriarch Aniassa Philip, known to everyone as 'Mummy', and her daughter-in-law Anu cook some of the best food in Kerala, much of it sourced from their organic farm. It's a privilege to watch them cook in well-worn pans: a mellow chicken curry, fish in coconut and pepper gravy (*meen molee*), and stir-fried beans and carrot with mustard seed, curry leaves and chilli. Nourished with distinctive flavours and the tranquillity, it is a hard place to leave, and it's one place that draws me back time and again, to be able to just take a pause from the pressures of everyday life.

We board a *kettuvallam*, a former rice barge converted into a houseboat Traditionally these boats were built of planks sewn together with coir threaded through a 'needle' carved from a palm frond. The seams, caulked with coir plugs soaked in sardine or cashew oil, made the boats waterproof. They were once used to transport heavy cargo such as rice, coconuts and spices from isolated interior villages to the larger coastal towns, while providing accommodation for the boatmen. With the advent of roads, bridges and ferry services, the kettuvallams were gradually phased out – but tourism has given them a new lease of life. Preserving their historic character and style, craftsmen have created a luxurious, self-contained world from which to observe rural life flowing gently by.

We float across the vast expanse of the lake and into the canals, sipping on a refreshing drink of ginger and lime juice blended with fresh mint. Water hyacinths float everywhere and the boats carefully manoeuvre through, so the flowers don't get caught up in the motor. Rice paddies stretch into the distance and small ferries plough back and forth as we glide past communities that live on the water's edge.

Our welcome meal is a typical banana-leaf lunch with small spoonfuls of different dishes arranged around a central mound of steamed Keralan rice, all eaten with the fingers. There's sambar, spooned over the rice because of its runny consistency; crisp banana chips; pumpkin simmered in coconut milk; fish fried with turmeric and chilli, served with fresh lime; a vegetable *thoran*; *avial* made with drumstick vegetable; a cabbage and carrot *pachadi*, seer fish fried with turmeric and ginger paste; pearl spot fish cooked in coconut milk with chilli, ginger and lime; and a couple of other things – all with coconut.

Getting about on the waterways makes for a leisurely pace of life. Ferry boats full of waving schoolkids on their way home for lunch glide past, while women in brightly coloured saris slap their washing against rocks at the water's edge. In the afternoon, labourers head home after a day's hard work, stopping off en route for chai and cake at a waterside stall, and at sunset fishing boats start to appear for their daily catch on the lake. Before we know it, Giresh, our boat cook, is preparing dinner, and more treats magically appear from the tiny kitchen at the back of the boat.

There are tender dry-fried morsels of chicken seasoned with spices, small green chilli and curry leaves; beetroot *pachadi*; local red spinach cooked with cumin and grated coconut; a light yellow dal; and two different okra preparations, one stuffed with rice and shallow-fried, the other chopped and cooked in tangy coconut milk; a prawn curry flavoured with smoked kokum; and a typical sour fish curry. All are superb. But wait, there's more! Bitter gourd peeled and finely sliced, then deep-fried with shallot slices until crisp – and it's delicious, too. I am in love with the languid pace of life, the bucolic landscape and the food, an idyllic moment where time stands still.

SYRIAN CHRISTIAN FOOD

Our journey inland from Alappuzha to Kottayam takes us up into the hills, past gaudy lollipop-coloured houses and rubber plantations, and on to Pala, situated on the banks of the Meenachil River. This large, prosperous town in central Kerala is known for its fine weaving and the making of dhotis (traditional clothing for men). It is also a staunchly Syrian Christian town, with more churches than you can poke a stick at. We have entered the bible belt of Kerala and we arrive at Nazarani Tharavad, with its own church in the front yard no less! We are greeted with a traditional welcome drink of cold, freshly pressed red grape juice and the freshest roasted cashews I have ever tasted. Thressi Kottukapally, who has compiled a book of her household's treasured recipes, and her two sisters-in-law Thressi and Annie, oversee lunch preparations, custodians of family traditions. They fuss over us, telling us of their family history, the plants in the garden, the foods they love to eat and how they are prepared. They are delightful, engaging company.

Lunch is quite a production, a feast usually reserved for weddings or *sradham* (memorial) ceremonies. A huge array of savoury dishes is placed on the table and served to each person on a banana leaf – a thali in true Keralan tradition. The house cooks are led by chief cook Shaji, who has been preparing our arrival meal for three days. There are 26 dishes in total, and that's just lunch! Small quantities of *kallappam*, rice pancakes made with fermented palm toddy and grated coconut, are served with a deliciously mild, sweet-tasting mutton stew. There is bitter gourd and ash gourd, and *motha*, a deep-sea fish from Kerala coastal waters that has been sliced into thin squares then crumbed and fried. It is served with a red onion salsa, the sharpness of the onion softened with coconut vinegar. However, the standout dish of the day is duck roast (*tharavu*): duck legs cooked in a thick masala gravy and browned until crisp. It's unctuous, rich and finger-licking good, and I go back for seconds.

As lunch is finishing, dramatic thunder and lightning flashes erupt and it sheets with rain for the rest of the afternoon. I take shelter in the kitchen, watching Shaji prepare the dishes for our dinner. He works quietly and methodically and his food is full of honest flavours.

The houseboys prepare the dinner table with the best crockery and gold cutlery laid out on a beautifully woven white cloth. The household condiment is a thoroughly addictive ginger chutney, with perfectly balanced flavours of lime, date, spices and some elusive health-giving plants. When I enquire about it, the sisters tell me they source this Ayurvedic pickle from a special shop near Mysore. It is the food of angels.

Dinner starts with a restorative country-style mutton soup (*nadan adu*), a light broth gently spiced with cardamom and pepper and with a few fried shallots floating in it. It's a soup that offers rejuvenation during the steamy monsoon season. A wickedly rich masala-fried pork and chicken coriander curry (*kozhi malliaracha*) follow, with steamed basmati rice as a foil. Two desserts complete the repast: *mottayappam*, an egg-and-coconut crepe filled with a sweet coconut stuffing and rolled up to make a neat little parcel; and a creme caramel that is steamed in a water bath rather than baked, as ovens are generally not a feature of Indian kitchens. A refreshing Nilgiri blue tea completes our feast, then it's time to waddle off to bed to read for a while before falling into a sound sleep.

We drive further into the mountains to Thekkady to spend time exploring the spice plantations, a dense landscape of pepper vines, cloves cardamom, turmeric, nutmeg and allspice trees. The air smells so fragrant and the vibrant, spicy flavours define the food everywhere we eat. We follow a guide one morning, exploring the nature trails in Periyar Reserve, one of India's largest wildlife sanctuaries with an active conservation policy. We take a short boat ride to a small island in the middle of the lake to Lake Palace, a former summer palace of the local king, and sit on the verandah taking in the peaceful ambience. Lunch is a throwback to colonial times with Anglicised Indian staples of chicken cutlets and coleslaw, a simple fish curry and cinnamon apple pie – yet another Kerala perspective.

AYURVEDA

Kerala is a centre for Ayurvedic medicinal practice. Devotees come from around the world to avail themselves of its healing powers and remedies. The ancient science of Ayurveda is not only a system of medicine but a way of life. According to Ayurveda, the body is made up of three doshas: *pitta* (fire), *kapha* (water) and *vata* (air). We are born with one or two dominant doshas and must work to keep all three doshas in harmony, in order to maintain balanced emotions and good physical health.

Indians believe that the knowledge of medicinal plants is older than history itself, gifted hundreds of thousands of years ago to the original inhabitants of India by Brahma, the Divine Creator. Thus, when the sages of Ayurveda sought to heal human suffering they were able to draw on a knowledge that had already been evolving for millennia in the forests of India.

NAVEEN PATNAIK, *THE GARDEN OF LIFE*

At Kalari Kovilakom, a restored nineteenth-century palace in Palakkad (Palghati), 160 kilometres northeast of Kochi, guests commit to a minimum of two weeks and engage in an Ayurvedic program to cleanse the body of toxins. One follows a diet of freshly prepared vegetarian dishes and looks towards balancing the correct fire level with medicinal herbs and spices. As Dr Remya Jayan, head of medicine at Kalari Kovilakom, says: 'The ancient Indian holistic practice of Ayurveda is all about maintaining the digestive fire and trying to achieve a balance in the doshas.' Daily yoga and meditation also play a key role.

Everyone is under the close care of a doctor and has a specially prescribed program and diet. Initial treatment involves taking increasing daily doses of hot liquefied ghee laced with detoxifying medicinal herbs. The ghee is merely the medium for allowing the medicine to penetrate deeply into every channel in the body before returning to the digestive tract, a process aided by daily massages. Once saturated with ghee, the patient is purged before the rejuvenation program. Purging techniques can include induced vomiting, herbal laxatives, enemas, steaming, nasal washouts and even leeches!

Many of the medicines are grown and made right there under Dr Jayan's exacting eye. She takes us to her Ayurvedic kitchen and shows us how the medicated massage oil is prepared in a huge brass bowl set over an open fire. It takes 100 litres of ingredients (including 60 litres of cow's milk, 15 litres of sesame oil and various herbal pastes) to make 15 litres of oil, and it cooks for three days.

Surrounded by gardens and palm trees, the yoga room is beautiful – large and square, open on all sides, with dark wooden floorboards and a high ceiling. A very gentle yet powerful version of Bihar yoga is practised, as energetic poses are counter to Ayurvedic treatments. The daily meditation is an hour of *yoga-nidra*, or deep relaxation and visualisation. One evening there is candlelight meditation, where you stare at a candle flame for 10 minutes and then close your eyes for another 10, quietening any racing thoughts; it induces a very deep sleep.

There's much to help you connect to your childish self – steamed apples for breakfast, childlike yoga poses, warm milk being poured over you, sitting on the ground to play with paints and paper. These combine to peel away the layers, so you have to confront your inner core. The medicine, yoga, meditation and quiet surroundings all cause you to journey inwards.

The final two days of treatment bring all parts of the program together. Njavarakizhi is one of the most important treatments and uses the njavara rice grain that is indigenous to Kerala. The therapist uses calico pouches of the rice grain, heated in medicated buttermilk, to massage the body. The rice powder passes through the fabric to become a nourishing paste, which is then scraped off with a coconut leaf before being washed away. Then you sit in a carved wooden bathtub filled with warm water in which neem leaves float. *Thalapothichi* is a most intriguing practice designed to stimulate the hypothalamus. A cold black gooseberry paste is packed onto your scalp and your head is wrapped in a banana leaf before you sit in

a big chair in front of the pond and garden. The doctor makes an incision in the leaf with a razor blade and then pours in some concentrated medicine. After 45 minutes of sitting still and contemplating the ripples in the pond, a cold mud-pack is applied to your face.

You are sent home from Kalari Kovilakom with a set of rules for maintaining your new, balanced and rejuvenated self. There is much to learn and take home from this special retreat.

MAPPILA CUISINE IN THALASSERY

The early-morning train to Thalassery (Tellicherry), in the north of Kerala, passes through coastal towns and lush countryside alongside temples, churches and brightly decorated ornate mosques on its five-hour journey. On board, we buy super-sweet milk coffee in little cardboard cups and *vadai* with coconut chutney from vendors who wander up and down the carriages announcing their wares.

Thalassery has been the epicentre of the spice trade for centuries, with black pepper from the region being a highly prized commodity. Fish is abundant in these warm waters, and the boats have nets full of sparkling sardines, sea mullet and seer fish. We watch as baskets of mussels collected from the small rocky islands just off shore are unloaded. Later, we take a stroll along Muzhapilangad Beach, a long stretch of beach north of the city. A mix of Muslim and Hindu families come here to relax in the late afternoon sun, their saris, kurtas and scarves floating in the breeze. The beach is so wide that vehicles are allowed to drive along it. Some families set up picnics from the back of their jeeps, teenage girls frolic in the water, boys play ball, and a young woman nearby learns to ride a scooter.

We have come to Thalassery to learn about the distinctive Muslim food of the Mappilas (Moplahs), the origins of which can be traced back to their Arab ancestors. And there is no better place to do this than at Ayesha Manzil, whose owners, Faiza and Moosa, make charming hosts. Faiza learnt her culinary skills from her mother, and is very proud of her Mappila heritage. An exceptional cook, her flavours are defined yet complex and simply sing on the palate.

Our welcome lunch is a table filled with a dozen or so different dishes, served with steamed Keralan rice – a short, fat grain that is perfect for soaking up the gravies and juices of the accompanying dishes. We have cabbage *thoran* that is clean-tasting and refreshing in its simplicity, and fried spiced sea mullet with a salsa of chopped tomato, red onion, chilli powder, salt and lime juice. Okra are simmered in a lightly spiced yoghurt sauce, and drumstick sambar gives a delicious savoury-sour note. I fall upon the mussel dumplings – mussels stuffed with rice and flavoured with coconut and cumin – that reveal Arabic and Chinese heritage. They are

served with eyelash bread. Made from wheat-flour pastry rolled and cut into a square, with the corners folded in so the points meet in the centre. When fried in ghee, it curls to resemble an eyelash. It's wickedly rich.

Faisa offers classes to those interested in the secrets of Mappila cuisine, and each time I visit, we spend an afternoon cooking together in her kitchen. I learn to make tamarind prawns – and a fish biryani with fish bought at the market that is a real labour of love. We spend nearly four hours in the sweltering kitchen being seduced by the heady spices, with sweat dripping from our noses as we stir the pots and watch alchemy transform their contents. Little wonder biryani is such a celebratory dish, reserved for special occasions. When it is finally placed on the table at Ayesha Manzil, it is accompanied by raita, coconut chutney and a delicious date pickle, studded with the tiniest garlic cloves. As the finale, Faiza prepares an English-style custard pudding – queen of desserts – given an Indian makeover with rosewater and cardamom.

The next day we are privileged to see a parade of some of her favourite saris – it is wonderful to see her getting some attention. Her kitchen staff (all men) cook in a separate kitchen out the back while she presides over everything with quiet authority and confidence.

Dinner is another sumptuous affair. We sit out under the stars in the balmy night air, after watching a dramatic sunset over the Arabian Sea, while Faiza presides over the kitchen with a meticulous eye. We start with fried bread that has been stuffed with beef mince and a hard-boiled egg. A divinely wicked dry-fried beef, tender and moist and spicy-hot, decorated with sweet onion rings and fried curry leaves, remains firmly etched in my taste memory bank.

Sitting with Faiza during the afternoons at Ayesha Manzil, in between cooking shifts, she tells us stories about her family, about hanging out with her sisters, her trips within India and overseas as a guest chef to promote Mappila cuisine, and her saris. Faiza's skill at teaching and sharing her recipes with such passion and precision is one of my most enduring memories of Kerala.

Travelling north along the Malabar Coast, we reach the tropical hideaway of Neeleshwar Hermitage, an enchanting beachfront property with palm thatched cottages scattered through its expansive gardens. We succumb to its barefoot elegance with sunset walks along the beach's pristine virgin sands, yoga before breakfast and Ayurvedic massages and treatments that pamper and revive. The catch of the day is brought to the kitchen straight off the fishing boats and given the local treatment. We have black pomfret basted with a fragrant masala paste and grilled, seer fish is simmered in an aromatic molee coconut gravy, and sea *bral* is cooked in coconut milk with ginger, garlic curry leaves, chilli and soured with smoked kokum. Vegetable dishes are equally compelling. The beetroot *thoran* and dry-fried long beans with turmeric, ginger and grated coconut become instant favourites. With a daily changing menu, every bite is delicious, wholesome and nutritious, reminding me of the extraordinary beauty and diversity of Kerala.

‹Buttermilk Lassi

SERVES 1

A nourishing digestive drink that is very easy to prepare – a statement of health in a glass! For a variation, you could replace the curry leaves with a small green chilli and a couple of tablespoons of freshly chopped coriander. Please use authentic buttermilk, not the imitation commercial type – the flavour makes all the difference.

210 g thick plain yoghurt
½ cup (125 ml) buttermilk
1 tablespoon minced ginger
1 tablespoon curry leaves
1 teaspoon salt

Mix all the ingredients with 700 ml water in a blender, then strain. Serve cold.

Banana Kalam

SERVES 4

A houseboat breakfast treat, once again using the Keralan staples of banana and coconut.

1 tablespoon coconut oil
3 red shallots, finely diced
2 teaspoons minced ginger
2 small green chillies, minced
8 small ripe bananas, peeled and sliced
2 tablespoons Turmeric Water (see page 380)
140 g thick plain yoghurt
1 teaspoon salt

COCONUT PASTE
35 g grated fresh coconut
2 red shallots, chopped
2 cloves garlic, chopped
½ teaspoon ground cumin

To make the coconut paste, blend the ingredients to make a paste.

Heat the oil in a frying pan and fry the shallot until softened. Add the ginger and chilli and cook for a few minutes. Add the banana and fry for a minute, then add the turmeric water and coconut paste, stirring to combine thoroughly. Cook for 1 minute, then turn off the heat and stir through the yoghurt and salt to serve.

Banana Coconut Cakes
Pazha Kattey

MAKES 12

These little cakes are a delicious breakfast treat. They can be served with a spicy fruit chutney if desired.

2 large ripe bananas
35 g grated fresh coconut
pinch of ground cardamom
1 tablespoon melted ghee

Steam the bananas in their skin until very soft, then peel and mash. Combine with the coconut and cardamom, then shape into small patties.

Heat a tawa or non-stick frying pan and drizzle in the ghee. Cook the patties until golden on one side, then flip over and cook the other side. The cakes should have a slightly crunchy surface.

‹Ginger Lime Soda

SERVES 4

Giresh, the cook on one of the many houseboats I have been on (who also has his own recipe website: www.boatmanspecials.com), made this cooling drink for us whenever we felt hot and in need of refreshment. It's made in the same manner as a muddled cocktail.

30 g chopped ginger
large handful of mint leaves
3 tablespoons white sugar
2½ tablespoons lime juice
600 ml soda water

Put the ginger and mint in a large glass beaker. Using a wooden pestle or muddling stick, make a paste. Add the sugar and lime juice and blend to combine. Strain through a fine sieve and discard the solids. Add the soda water to the strained juice and stir to combine. Pour over crushed ice to serve.

Beetroot Curry

One of my favourite vegetable curries, the simple spicing of cumin and curry leaf perfectly complements the earthiness of the beetroot. This was served at a Shalimar Spice Garden, a mountain hideaway near Thekkady, amid a spice plantation where curry-leaf trees grew prolifically in the gardens. It's also good with venison and squab, or as an accompaniment to pan-fried mackerel or tuna.

2 tablespoons vegetable oil
1 teaspoon sesame oil
2 tablespoons curry leaves
4 small green chillies, finely sliced
1 teaspoon minced ginger
3 red shallots, finely sliced
1 teaspoon ground cumin
4 beetroot, peeled and cut into matchsticks
2 tablespoons coconut vinegar
2 teaspoons sea salt
2 teaspoons caster sugar
1 cup (250 ml) coconut milk
1 tablespoon Fried Curry Leaves
   (see page 377)

Heat both oils in a frying pan and fry the curry leaves, chilli, ginger and shallot until softened. Stir in the cumin and fry for 20 seconds, then add the beetroot, stirring to coat with the aromatics.

Add the vinegar, salt and sugar and stir-fry until the beetroot has softened, about 2 minutes. Add the coconut milk, cover and cook for 15 minutes until the beetroot is tender and the juices have been absorbed.

Remove from the heat, taste and adjust the seasoning – it may need extra sea salt. Garnish with the fried curry leaves and serve.

Masala Eggs ›
Mutta Kakkathil
SERVES 4

We dubbed this delicious breakfast dish 'sacred eggs'. It was served for breakfast at Ayesha Manzil, in Thalassery, along with a plate of perfectly formed Appam (see page 240). Sitting out on the garden terrace overlooking the Arabian Sea, enjoying the cool breeze before the heat of the day descended, it was idyllic.

4 hard-boiled eggs
2 teaspoons chilli powder
¼ teaspoon ground turmeric
salt
35 g grated fresh coconut
2 tablespoons vegetable oil
250 g onions, finely diced
1 teaspoon Ginger Garlic Paste (see page 377)
3 small green chillies, minced
1 teaspoon ground coriander
¼ teaspoon ground fennel
1 tablespoon chopped curry leaves
1 tablespoon chopped coriander leaves

Shell the eggs, then make slits all over them. Make a paste with ¼ teaspoon of the chilli powder, a pinch of the turmeric, a pinch of salt and a little water. Smear the paste all over the eggs and set them aside.

Blend the coconut with a little water and push through a sieve to extract the thick coconut milk. Discard any solids.

Heat the oil in a frying pan and fry the spiced eggs over a medium heat until they are golden. Remove from the pan and set aside.

In the same pan, fry the onion until softened, then add the ginger garlic paste and green chilli. Cook until the mixture starts to colour, then stir in the ground coriander, fennel, curry leaves, remaining chilli powder and tumeric, and 1 teaspoon salt (or to taste) and cook for a few minutes. Stir in the coconut-milk extract. Simmer the sauce for 10 minutes or until quite thick.

Add the fried eggs, sliced in half lengthwise, spooning the masala sauce over the eggs to coat. Simmer for 5–6 minutes over a low heat. Sprinkle with the fresh coriander to serve.

‹Crisp Lacy Rice Pancakes

Pallappam

SERVES 4

This classic Keralan bread was introduced by the Portuguese from Sri Lanka (formerly Ceylon). It's a typical Syrian Christian food that is still served for family breakfast. This recipe, from Nimmy Paul in Kochi, is versatile: it can be served with a vegetable or meat stew or topped with coconut cream and sugar for dessert.

1 tablespoon fine semolina
150 g rice flour
3 tablespoons coconut toddy
    or ¼ teaspoon dried yeast
1 cup (250 ml) coconut milk
2 tablespoons white sugar
½ teaspoon salt
1 teaspoon sesame oil

Put the semolina and ½ cup (125 ml) water in a saucepan. Cook over a medium heat for about 10 minutes, stirring constantly, until the mixture reaches a porridge consistency. Remove from the heat and cool to room temperature. Add the rice flour, toddy or yeast, coconut milk and sugar and stir thoroughly to make a thick batter. Cover with a cloth and set aside until the mixture doubles in volume. It can be refrigerated if the weather is hot.

When ready to cook, add the salt to the batter. Heat a non-stick frying pan and brush lightly with sesame oil. Ladle a little batter into the centre of the pan and twirl the pan to spread the batter so it forms a fine, lacy layer. Cover and cook over a gentle heat for 2 minutes, being careful not to overheat the pan. Gently remove the pallappam from the pan, being careful not to break it. Set aside, covered with a dry cloth, and continue until all the batter has been used. Stack the pallappams on top of each other as you go.

Mini's Beetroot Pachadi

SERVES 4

My friend Mini Chandran encapsulates the very spirit of Kerala. She is wise, generous, an ardent food lover and the person who has kept me company during my earlier visits to Kochi. Her love for her homeland is totally infectious and I have lost track of the conversations we have had about food. She suggests ash gourd (a round, green gourd with white flesh and a white furry surface on its skin) or green mango as other excellent choices for pachadi. Whenever I make this at home, it's always a huge hit with my friends.

2 tablespoons vegetable oil
3 small green chillies, minced
2 tablespoons curry leaves
2 medium-sized beetroot, peeled and shredded
3 tablespoons grated fresh coconut
1 teaspoon brown mustard seeds
1 teaspoon salt
3 tablespoons thick plain yoghurt

Heat the oil in a frying pan and fry the green chilli and curry leaves over a medium heat for a minute until fragrant (be careful not to burn the leaves).

Add the beetroot and stir until softened. Blend the coconut and mustard seeds to make a paste and add to the beetroot. Cook until the mixture starts to froth and bubble. Season with salt to taste, then turn off the heat and allow to cool for 15 minutes.

Stir through the yoghurt and serve at room temperature.

Appam

MAKES 24

Essential for a true Keralan breakfast, these crisp rice and coconut pancakes are made with a light batter that has been left to ferment overnight. The local rice of Kerala has a shorter grain than basmati and is softer in texture, so it cooks more quickly.

600 g uncooked medium-grain rice
35 g grated fresh coconut
pinch of dried yeast
110 g cooked basmati rice
1 teaspoon salt
1 teaspoon white sugar
½ teaspoon baking powder
vegetable oil, for brushing

Soak the uncooked rice in water for 5 hours – it is best to start this process the day before you intend to cook the appams. Drain, then grind in a blender with the coconut, yeast and cooked rice to form a smooth, thick batter. Add the salt, sugar and baking powder and leave to ferment for 8 hours or overnight at room temperature.

Heat a deep-sided appa chatti pan (a special-shaped vessel) or a wok with a flat base and brush with oil. Ladle some batter into the pan and immediately swirl the pan over a medium heat so the edges become lacy and fine and the batter sets in the middle. Cover the pan and leave for 2 minutes to steam and finish cooking. Tip the appam onto a plate and repeat the process until all the batter has been used.

Serve for breakfast with a wet curry (fish or mutton) or with Masala Eggs (see page 236).

Pineapple Pachadi ›

SERVES 4

Served with Kerala Fried Fish (see page 243) and steamed rice, this was part of an ideal lunch cooked by Sabu during my first houseboat adventure, and more recently by Mummy at Philip Kutty's Farm. I have also used it as a savoury canape, making small (pikelet-sized) Paratha (see page 351) and spooning a little pachadi on top to serve.

½ ripe small sweet pineapple, peeled
1 teaspoon ground turmeric
½ teaspoon chilli powder
2 teaspoons curry leaves
1 small green chilli, minced
½ teaspoon salt
35 g grated fresh coconut
1 teaspoon brown mustard seeds
1 tablespoon coconut oil
2 tablespoons thick plain yoghurt

FOR TEMPERING
1 tablespoon coconut oil
¼ teaspoon brown mustard seeds
2 small dried red chillies, broken into pieces
6 curry leaves

Bring a saucepan of water to a boil. Cut the pineapple into batons and add to the boiling water with the turmeric, chilli powder, curry leaves, green chilli and salt. Cook for a few minutes, then strain.

Grind the coconut and mustard seeds together to make a fine paste. Heat the coconut oil in a frying pan and fry the coconut mustard paste over a high heat for 2 minutes. Add the pineapple mixture and toss to combine, then remove from the heat and stir through the yoghurt.

For the tempering, heat the coconut oil in a small pan and fry the mustard seeds, chilli and curry leaves over a medium heat until they splutter. Spoon the mixture over the pineapple to serve.

‹ Kerala Fried Fish

SERVES 4

On our trip on the Kerala backwaters, one of the boat boys bought pearl spot from a fishing boat that glided past, and Giresh cooked them for lunch with Pineapple Pachadi (see page 240). Simple and delicious.

  4 small freshwater fish, gutted and scaled
  1 tablespoon lime juice
  2 teaspoons salt
  1 teaspoon ground turmeric
  1 teaspoon chilli powder
  1 tablespoon curry leaves, shredded
  2 teaspoons Ginger Garlic Paste
    (see page 377)
  2 tablespoons coconut oil or vegetable oil
  2 sprigs curry leaves, fried
  2 small dried chillies, fried

Score the fish with two or three slashes on each side. Marinate in the lime juice and 1 teaspoon salt for 30 minutes.

Mix the turmeric, chilli powder, curry leaves, ginger garlic paste and remaining salt with just enough water to make a thick paste. Rub the paste liberally over the fish. Heat the oil in a frying pan and cook the fish for 3 minutes on one side, then flip and fry the other side for 2 minutes. Using a slotted spoon, transfer the fish to a serving plate and garnish with fried curry leaves and chillies. Serve with lime wedges and steamed rice.

Keralan Fishy Snacks

Kerala is famous for its short-eats (snacks), available any time of the day at home and from street vendors. The chefs at Neeleshwar served these delectable morsels with our sunset drinks at their beach bar.

Prawns Masala

Small (harbour or school) prawns, coated with masala spice mix, then cooked in a hot pan and served with red onion rings mixed with Fried Curry Leaves (see page 377), diced tomato, green chilli slices, lime juice and salt.

Grilled Squid

Tiny squid, cleaned and split in half lengthways, tossed through chilli powder, salt and lime juice and seared on a hot barbecue.

Masala Fried Fish Fingers

Small fish fillets (silver pomfret) cut into finger-sized strips and coated with spiced flour, then deep-fried until crisp and golden.

Spiced Prawn & Kokum Curry ›
Prawn Vattichathu
SERVES 4

This was prepared for me by chef Amit when he was at Taj Malabar in Kochi; I've also had a version of this at Surya Samudra in Kovalom. Kokum is the dried rind of a sour-tasting fruit that is native to West India. It has a sweet–sour taste and, like tamarind, is used as a souring agent.

½ teaspoon ground turmeric
¼ teaspoon salt
2 teaspoons lime juice
4 large raw king prawns, peeled and deveined but with tails left intact
2 tablespoons coconut oil
1 teaspoon brown mustard seeds
1 teaspoon fenugreek seeds
4 tablespoons diced shallot
1 tablespoon Ginger Garlic Paste (see page 377)
2 tablespoons thick Chilli Paste (see page 376)
200 ml coconut milk
12 curry leaves
2 tomatoes, pureed until smooth
2 tablespoons kokum water (soak a piece of dried kokum in water for 20 minutes)
salt

Combine the turmeric, salt and lime juice, then rub into the prawn tails. Set aside.

Heat the coconut oil in a frying pan and fry the mustard and fenugreek seeds over a medium heat until they splutter. Add the shallot and cook until it starts to colour, then add the ginger garlic paste and cook until brown. Stir in the chilli paste and coconut milk, then reduce the heat and simmer for 10 minutes.

Add the curry leaves and tomato puree and simmer for another few minutes without reducing the sauce. Add the prawns and toss them through the sauce until coated. Simmer for a minute, then add the kokum water and salt to taste. Simmer for 3–4 minutes until the prawns are cooked. Serve with steamed rice.

Fish in Coconut Milk ›
Nimmy's Meen Molee
SERVES 4

Nimmy usually makes this with the ever-popular seer fish, but you can substitute kingfish, jewfish, snapper or blue-eye trevalla. It's gently spiced with hints of ginger, green chilli and garlic, while the tomato provides a mild tartness and the coconut adds a creamy richness. These ingredients are a popular combination in Kerala.

½ teaspoon salt
¼ teaspoon freshly ground white pepper
250 g fish fillet, cut into 4 even slices
10 blanched cashews
vegetable oil, for cooking
10 sultanas
1 tablespoon sunflower oil
1 small red onion, finely sliced
2 small cloves garlic, sliced
1 tablespoon minced ginger
4 small green chillies, finely sliced
1 tablespoon curry leaves
1 cup (250 ml) coconut milk
1 tomato, cut into 4 slices
½ cup (125 ml) coconut cream

Mix the salt and pepper and rub it onto the fish slices. Set aside. Fry the cashews in a little hot vegetable oil over a medium heat until golden, then drain on paper towel. Fry the sultanas in a little more oil until plump, then drain on paper towel. Set the cashews and sultanas aside.

Heat the sunflower oil in a large frying pan and fry the onion, garlic, ginger and chilli for 2 minutes. Add the curry leaves and fry until crisp. Push the onion mixture to the side of the pan. Put the seasoned fish in the centre of the pan and fry for a minute. Turn the fish over, then spoon the onion mixture over the fish to coat. Season with a little extra salt. Pour the coconut milk into the pan and bring to a boil. Reduce the heat and simmer for 2–3 minutes.

Place a tomato slice over each fish slice. Pour in the coconut cream and warm through, taking care that it doesn't boil. Turn off the heat and garnish with the cashews and sultanas. Serve with steamed rice.

‹Coconut Duck Curry
Thengapal Chertha Tharavu
SERVES 4

This beautifully rich duck curry was prepared for me by Sabu, the cook on my first rice-barge trip on the Kerala backwaters, where duck farms are plentiful.

- 1 × 1.5 kg free-range duckling, gutted and cleaned
- 4 tablespoons coconut oil
- 1 tablespoon finely chopped ginger
- 8 cloves garlic, crushed
- 20 small red shallots, peeled and chopped
- 1 tablespoon shredded fresh turmeric
- 4 small green chillies, sliced
- 1 tablespoon ground coriander
- 2 teaspoons freshly ground black pepper
- 1 tablespoon ground turmeric
- 1 × 400 g can peeled tomatoes, roughly chopped
- 400 ml coconut milk
- 8 tiny new potatoes, peeled (or 4 chat potatoes, cut in half)
- 50–60 g raw cashews
- 2 teaspoons ground cumin
- 1 tablespoon sea salt
- 100 ml coconut cream
- 3 tablespoons coriander leaves

Cut the duck in half lengthways, then separate into joints and chop into large pieces, keeping the meat on the bone. Heat the coconut oil in a kadhai or wok and fry the duck pieces over a medium–high heat until browned. Remove from the pan and set aside.

Pour off the excess oil from the pan, leaving about 2 tablespoons, add the ginger and garlic and fry until beginning to colour. Add the shallot and fry until softened, then add the fresh turmeric and chilli and toss. Stir in the ground spices and cook for a minute until aromatic. Add the tomato and its juices and the coconut milk and bring to simmering point. Add the duck and potatoes, then cover and cook over a low heat for 45–50 minutes until the duck and potatoes are cooked.

Meanwhile, soak the cashews in water for 30 minutes to soften. Drain, then blend to a paste and stir into the duck with the cumin. Cook for 5 minutes to thicken the sauce. Season with salt.

When ready to serve, stir through the coconut cream and coriander and remove from the heat – don't allow it to boil. Serve with steamed rice.

Green Peppercorn Quail
SERVES 4

This recipe was prepared for our dinner by young chef Aneesh at 50 Mile Diet, a wonderful 'farm to fork' restaurant in Thekkady. All the produce is organic and sourced from farms within a 50-mile radius, whose names, location and distance from the restaurant are noted on the menu.

- 4 large farmed quail
- 2 red shallots, roughly chopped
- 2 tablespoons green peppercorns
- 2 small green chillies, chopped
- 1 tablespoon chopped ginger
- 2 tablespoons curry leaves
- 1 teaspoon ground turmeric
- 2 teaspoons salt
- 4 tablespoons thick plain yoghurt

Butterfly the quail, split down the backbone and then cut each one in half along the breastbone (or ask your butcher to do this).

Using a mortar and pestle, pound the shallot, peppercorns, chilli, ginger and curry leaves into a coarse paste. Stir in the turmeric and salt.

Place the yoghurt in a bowl and add the spice mix paste, stirring to incorporate. Add the quail pieces, rubbing the marinade into the meat. Set aside to marinate for 25 minutes.

Grill or barbecue the quail, or fry in a heavy-based pan with a splash of oil, until golden and just cooked through – about 3–4 minutes each side. Remove from the heat and serve with a salad of finely sliced raw vegetables.

Char-grilled Rabbit Masala
Kanalil Chutta Muyal Masala
SERVES 4

At Thekaddy's 50 Mile Diet restaurant at the Spice Village Resort, it was inspiring to see locally farmed quail, rabbit and organic pork treated with respect and a passion for flavour.

1 farmed rabbit

MARINADE
1 tablespoon chopped ginger
2 small red chillies, chopped
5 red shallots, chopped
1 tablespoon curry leaves
½ teaspoon ground turmeric
1 teaspoon salt
5 tablespoons thick plain yoghurt

MASALA GRAVY
5 small red chillies, chopped
½ teaspoons ground turmeric
2 tablespoons ground coriander
3 tablespoons coconut oil
3 tablespoons minced ginger
250 g red shallots, finely sliced
2 tablespoons curry leaves
4 ripe tomatoes, pureed
2 teaspoons salt
2 tablespoons coconut milk

Split the rabbit in half and cut each half into six even-sized pieces (or ask your butcher to do this).

To prepare the marinade, puree all the ingredients except the yoghurt in a food processor to make a smooth paste. Add the yoghurt and pulse to combine. Add the rabbit pieces to the marinade and toss to coat. Cover and refrigerate for 5–6 hours. Remove the rabbit from the refrigerator 30 minutes before cooking.

To prepare the masala gravy, blend the chillies, turmeric and coriander in a food processor with just enough water to make a paste. Heat the coconut oil in a frying pan and fry the ginger for 30 seconds. Add the shallot and curry leaves and cook over a medium heat until the shallot is golden brown and the mixture is fragrant, about 5 minutes. Add the chilli paste and stir to combine. Cook for 4–5 minutes over a medium heat, stirring regularly to prevent sticking. Add the tomato puree and salt, then reduce the heat and simmer gently for 5 minutes. Take off the heat and set aside.

Grill or barbecue the rabbit pieces until browned, about 4 minutes each side. Add the grilled rabbit pieces to the masala gravy and simmer gently, stirring occasionally, until the rabbit is tender, about 15–20 minutes. If the gravy reduces too much, add a little extra water.

When ready to eat, stir the coconut milk into the gravy and take off the heat. Serve with steamed rice.

Kingfish Steamed in Banana Leaf ›
SERVES 4

The spice paste used in Mappila cooking is a red masala, whereas the Parsi preparation of Mumbai uses a green masala with the fish cooked in the same manner. At Ayesha Manzil, Faiza sometimes does a vegetarian version of this dish using mashed potato.

2 tablespoons diced onion
3 tablespoons diced tomato
1 tablespoon Ginger Garlic Paste
  (see page 377)
1 tablespoon curry leaves
1 teaspoon chilli powder
1 teaspoon garam masala
½ teaspoon freshly ground black pepper
2 tablespoons lime juice
1 teaspoon salt
4 banana leaves, central rib removed
  and cut into 20 cm squares
vegetable oil, for cooking
4 × 120 g portions seer fish or kingfish,
  mackerel or bonito (ideally thick slices),
  skin removed

In a bowl, combine the onion, tomato, ginger garlic paste, curry leaves, spices, lime juice and salt. Brush each banana leaf with oil, then smear some of this mixture on the centre. Sit a fish portion on top and cover with the remaining mixture. Fold the edges of the leaf over to wrap the fish securely, so that the fish rests on the seam of the leaf.

Heat a frying pan and add a little oil. Lay the fish parcels in the pan in a single layer. Cover, then reduce the heat to low and cook for 6 minutes or until the fish is tender. Transfer to plates and serve.

Beef Fry
Ulathiya Irachi
SERVES 4

A Syrian Christian dish from Shalimar Spice Garden in Thekkady, this twice-cooked beef can be made a day ahead – in fact, the locals told me it tastes even better when it's reheated. You can steam the beef first with the spices rather than using a pressure cooker in the traditional manner (as I saw it being prepared); cooked in this way, the texture of the beef is more succulent. The coconut oil adds to the depth of flavour – make sure you use an organic virgin oil.

½ teaspoon fennel seeds
1 star anise
2 cloves
2 teaspoons chilli powder
1 teaspoon ground turmeric
1 tablespoon ground coriander
1 teaspoon ground cinnamon
6 cloves garlic, minced
1 tablespoon minced ginger
3 small green chillies, minced
4 golden shallots, finely diced
3 teaspoons sea salt
70 g shredded fresh coconut
500 g beef fillet, cut into 2 cm strips
2½ tablespoons coconut oil
1 white onion, finely sliced
2 tablespoons curry leaves

Grind the fennel seeds, star anise and cloves, then mix them with the other ground spices. Place in a wide heatproof bowl and combine with the garlic, ginger, chilli, shallot, salt and coconut. Add the beef and mix to coat thoroughly, then set aside to marinate for 20 minutes.

Place the bowl in a steamer, then cover and steam for 45 minutes. Transfer the beef to a wire rack set over a baking dish. Allow to cool and dry out for 1 hour at room temperature.

Heat the coconut oil in a kadhai or wok and fry the onion over a high heat until it begins to colour, about 5–6 minutes. Add the curry leaves and cook until they begin to crisp up. Add the steamed beef and cook over a medium heat, dry-style, tossing the wok to prevent the beef from sticking or burning. Taste and adjust the seasoning – a little extra salt may be necessary.

Tamarind Prawns ›
Chemmeen Varattiyathu
SERVES 4

My all-time favourite recipe from Faiza at Ayesha Manzil, who faithfully makes it for me each time I visit.

1 teaspoon ground turmeric
1 teaspoon Kashmiri chilli powder
2 teaspoons roasted ground coriander
1 teaspoon salt
500 g raw king prawns, peeled, deveined and butterflied
2 tablespoons sunflower oil
2 tablespoons chopped coriander leaves

TAMARIND SAUCE
2 tablespoons sunflower oil
1 teaspoon brown mustard seeds
1 teaspoon fenugreek seeds
12 curry leaves
6 red shallots, finely diced
2 small green chillies, minced
1 tablespoon Ginger Garlic Paste
   (see page 377)
2 ripe tomatoes, seeded and chopped
1 teaspoon Kashmiri chilli powder
½ teaspoon ground turmeric
1 teaspoon roasted ground coriander
200 ml Tamarind Liquid (see page 379)
1 teaspoon salt

Mix the turmeric, chilli powder, ground coriander and salt with just enough water to make a paste. Stir the prawns into the paste and toss to coat. Set aside for 10 minutes.

Heat the oil in a frying pan and fry the prawns over a high heat for a few minutes until they are just cooked and starting to colour. Remove from the pan and set aside. Reserve the spiced oil.

To make the tamarind sauce, heat the oil over a medium heat in a frying pan and add the mustard seeds. When they start to pop, add the fenugreek seeds and curry leaves and fry for a few seconds, being careful not to burn them. Add the shallot and green chilli and cook for about 10 minutes until softened but not coloured. Stir in the ginger garlic paste and fry for a minute, then add the tomato and the reserved spiced oil. Cook for 5 minutes, then add the ground spices and tamarind liquid.

Simmer the sauce for 5–6 minutes until thickened. Add the prawns and stir to coat, then cook for 2–3 minutes. Stir through the fresh coriander.

Faiza's Fish Biryani

SERVES 6

Known as 'The Labour of Love', this complex recipe makes a feast for six people. Make sure you give yourself a few hours to prepare it for a special occasion. It is mandatory to serve raita, coconut chutney, a tangy pickle and pappadams as accompaniments. In Thalassery seer fish is commonly used, but kingfish, Spanish mackerel, bass grouper, jewfish or large sea mullet all make an ideal substitute.

600 g basmati rice
2 tablespoons ghee
2 small pieces cassia bark
3 green cardamom pods, cracked
3 cloves
1 tablespoon Ginger Garlic Paste
  (see page 377)
2 small green chillies, minced
1 tablespoon chopped coriander leaves
1 tablespoon chopped mint leaves
2 teaspoons salt
¼ teaspoon saffron powder
1 tablespoon rosewater mixed with
  1 tablespoon water

FAIZA'S GARAM MASALA
1 teaspoon ground cumin
1 teaspoon ground caraway
1 teaspoon ground mace
1 teaspoon grated nutmeg
1 teaspoon ground allspice
1 teaspoon ground cinnamon
1 teaspoon ground cardamom
1 teaspoon ground cloves

GARNISH
150 ml sunflower oil
3 tablespoons raw cashews,
  split in half lengthways
2 tablespoons sultanas
3 red onions, finely sliced
1 tablespoon ghee

MASALA FISH
2 small pieces cassia bark
4 green cardamom pods, cracked
4 cloves
1 tablespoon ghee
100 ml sunflower oil
3 red onions, finely sliced
1 kg kingfish fillet, skin removed,
  cut into 12 × 2 cm thick slices
1 tablespoon Ginger Garlic Paste (see
  page 377)
3 small green chillies, minced
1 tablespoon chopped coriander leaves
1 tablespoon chopped mint leaves
2 tomatoes, chopped
3 teaspoons roasted ground coriander
2 teaspoons Kashmiri chilli powder
2 teaspoons ground turmeric
2 teaspoons salt
1½ tablespoons lime juice

To make the garam masala, combine all the ingredients. Store in an airtight jar.

To make the garnish, heat the oil in a frying pan and fry the cashews over a medium heat until golden. Remove from the oil with a slotted spoon and drain on paper towel. In the same oil, fry the sultanas over a medium heat for 30 seconds until they plump up and become golden. Drain on paper towel. In the same oil, fry the onion over a medium heat, stirring constantly, until softened. Stir in the ghee to give extra flavour. Continue to cook until the onion is brown and crisp. Remove from the oil with a slotted spoon. Mix the onion with the cashews, sultanas and ½ teaspoon Faiza's garam masala, tossing with your hands to combine. Set aside until ready to serve.

To prepare the masala fish, grind the cassia, cardamom pods and cloves to a fine powder. Heat the ghee and half the oil in a wide-based frying pan. Fry half the ground spice mix over a medium heat for about 1 minute until fragrant. Add the onion and cook over a low heat for 15 minutes, stirring regularly – it should soften slowly and not colour.

Meanwhile, mix the remaining ground spice mix with just enough water to make a paste. Rub the paste into the fish and leave to marinate for 10 minutes. Heat the remaining oil in a wide ovenproof saucepan and fry the fish in batches, putting in enough fish to cover the base of the pan. Fry for 2 minutes, then flip over and fry for another minute. Remove the fish with a slotted spoon and set aside. Reserve the spiced cooking oil. >

Add the ginger garlic paste, green chilli, coriander and mint to the softened onion and stir to combine. Increase the heat to medium and cook for 2 minutes, then add the tomato and cook until it has softened, about 5 minutes. Stir in the ground coriander, Kashmiri chilli and turmeric, then add 1 cup (250 ml) water and the salt. Cover and leave to simmer for 10 minutes. Add the lime juice and 1 teaspoon Faiza's garam masala and cook for another 15 minutes until the sauce has thickened. Taste and adjust the seasoning if necessary – it may require a little extra salt. Lay the fried fish on top of the masala mix, carefully spooning some mix over so the fish is buried. Turn off the heat and leave until the rice is ready.

Wash the rice thoroughly, then drain. Bring 1.2 litres water to a boil in a saucepan. In a separate large saucepan, heat the ghee and the reserved spiced oil together and fry the cassia, cardamom and cloves for 30 seconds until fragrant. Stir in the ginger garlic paste, green chilli, coriander and mint and cook over a medium heat for 5 minutes. Add the washed rice and the salt and stir until the grains are coated with the aromatics or until the rice starts to jump from the base of the pan. Add the boiling water, stirring to combine. Cover and cook over a low heat for 20 minutes until the rice has absorbed all the water. Check the seasoning. If it needs extra salt, dissolve the salt in a little water then stir it into the rice – this allows for even distribution.

Preheat the oven to 150°C. Combine the saffron with the rosewater mixture.

To assemble the biryani, use a plate to scoop one-third of the cooked rice on top of the masala fish. Level the surface and sprinkle with one-third of the saffron rosewater, then scatter one-third of the garnish over the surface. Repeat this process twice more to give three layers of rice. Cover the pan with a tight-fitting lid and transfer to the oven for 15 minutes to allow the flavours to mingle further.

To serve, scoop the rice onto a large serving plate. Carefully lift the fish and its masala from the bottom of the pot, being careful not to break up the fish. Lay the fish on a separate plate and serve with the rice.

Traditional Duck Roast
Tharavu Roast
SERVES 4

Duck is a staple on the Syrian Christian table, and essential for any festive occasion. We had this peppery-crisp duck for lunch when we visited Rani John at her home in Kuttikanam, en route to Thekkady.

1 tablespoon minced ginger
1½ tablespoons minced garlic
300 g finely diced onion
2 tablespoons freshly ground black pepper
½ teaspoon ground turmeric
1 tablespoon white vinegar
2½ teaspoons salt
1 × 1.2 kg free-range duck, cut into 8 pieces
3 tablespoons vegetable oil

GARNISH
½ cup (125 ml) vegetable oil
250 g finely sliced onion
300 g very finely sliced potato

To prepare the garnish, heat the oil in a large frying pan and fry the onion over a high heat until golden brown and crisp. Remove from the pan with a slotted spoon and drain on paper towel. In the same pan, fry the potato until golden brown. Remove from the pan with a slotted spoon and drain on paper towel. Set the fried onion and potato aside. Reserve the oil and pan for later.

Puree the ginger, garlic and onion in a blender, adding just enough water to make a fine paste. Add the pepper and turmeric and mix until combined. In a bowl, mix the paste with the vinegar and salt. Add the duck pieces and rub to thoroughly coat.

Heat the oil in a heavy-based saucepan, then add the duck and its paste. Cook over a medium heat, covered, until the duck is tender, about 40 minutes. Remove from the heat and lift the duck from its gravy. Heat the reserved oil in the large frying pan and fry the duck pieces over a high heat until golden and crisp, about 3 minutes each side. Remove from the pan and set aside.

Add the gravy to the frying pan and cook over a medium heat until thickened, about 6–8 minutes. Return the fried duck to the pan and cook for a few minutes to coat it with the thick gravy. Transfer the duck and its gravy to a large serving plate and garnish with the fried onion and potato to serve.

Chicken Coriander Curry

Kozhi Malliaracha

SERVES 4

This distinctive Syrian Christian curry was served for dinner at Philip Kutty Farm on the backwaters of Lake Vembanad. It is rich and spicy, and perfect with steamed basmati rice or Crispy Lacy Rice Pancakes (see page 239).

300 g grated fresh coconut
150 ml vegetable oil
250 g red shallots, finely sliced
6 tablespoons ground coriander
1 tablespoon chilli powder
½ teaspoon ground turmeric
1 teaspoon ground fennel
1 × 1 kg chicken, jointed and
    cut into medium-sized pieces
1 teaspoon salt

Whiz the coconut and 300 ml water in a food processor, then strain. Set the thick coconut milk aside. Put the coconut back into the food processor and add 2 cups (500 ml) water. Whiz, then strain. Set aside the thin coconut milk.

Heat the oil in a frying pan or wok and fry the shallot over a high heat until golden and crisp, stirring continuously so it cooks evenly and does not burn. Drain on paper towel and set aside. Reserve the cooking oil.

Mix the spices with just enough water to make a thick paste. Pour the thin coconut milk into a saucepan and add the spice paste, stirring until combined. Add the chicken pieces and salt and bring to simmering point. Cover, then reduce the heat to low and cook for 25 minutes or until the chicken is tender.

Heat the reserved oil in a frying pan. Remove the chicken pieces from the sauce and transfer to the pan. Fry them lightly until browned, then return to the sauce. Stir in the thick coconut milk and bring to a simmer over a low heat – do not let the sauce boil. As soon as the sauce begins to simmer, remove the pan from the heat and stir in half the fried shallots. Sprinkle the remaining fried shallots over the top.

Vegetable Avial ›

SERVES 4

Avial is a traditional Keralan preparation that makes an excellent accompaniment to rice-and-gravy meat or fish dishes. I have eaten countless variations of it across Kerala. Any seasonal vegetable can be used – drumstick, asparagus, eggplant, carrot, snake gourd, potato or yam – as can plantain.

200 g grated fresh coconut
½ teaspoon ground cumin
2 cloves garlic, minced
600 g sliced vegetables,
    cut into 6 cm batons or sticks
2 white onions, finely sliced
6 small green chillies,
    split in half lengthways
2 teaspoons salt
½ teaspoon ground turmeric
½ teaspoon chilli powder
3 tomatoes, sliced
1½ tablespoons coconut oil
2 tablespoons Fried Curry Leaves
    (see page 377)

Combine the coconut, cumin and garlic to make a paste.

Pour 3 cups (750 ml) water into a large saucepan and bring to a boil. Add the vegetable sticks, onion, green chilli, salt, turmeric and chilli powder and cook until the vegetables are soft.

Add the tomato and cook for another 5 minutes until soft. Add the coconut paste and cook for 2 minutes, stirring, then stir through the coconut oil and fried curry leaves. Serve warm.

‹Mashed Salted Mango
Uppu Manga Chalichathu
MAKES 100 g

This easy-to-make pickle was a delicious addition to the Nazarani Tharavad lunch table in Pala. In order to make this you need small green mangoes that have been soaked in a brine solution for a year. Shaji, the house cook, told me that for every kilo of green mangoes, he uses 75 g salt and 200 ml boiling water. He packs the peeled and sliced mangoes into a ceramic jar with the salt, then adds the boiling water. After sealing the jar, he leaves it in the pantry for 12 months before using. Plan well ahead to make this!

100 g salted mangoes (see recipe introduction)
50 g finely sliced red shallots
2 small green chillies, finely sliced
2 tablespoons curry leaves, shredded
2 tablespoons vegetable or coconut oil

Smash the salted mangoes by hand into small rough pieces. Add the shallot, chilli and curry leaves and mix, then stir through the oil to combine.

Carrot Dosas
SERVES 4

These Indian crepes have earthy, sweet and sour flavours. Serve with a vegetable stew or your preferred chutney.

300 g short grain rice
65 g grated carrot
65 g grated potato
salt

Soak the rice in water for 2 hours, then drain. Blend the rice with the carrot, potato and 1½ cups (375 ml) water to make a batter. Cover and leave to stand overnight at room temperature.

Next morning, add salt to taste and stir to combine. Pour a ladle of the batter into a non-stick frying pan and spread it thinly. Cook over a medium heat until the dosa is light golden on one side and small holes appear on the surface. Flip it over and cook the other side until golden. Remove from the pan and set aside.

Continue until all the batter has been used, stacking the dosas on top of each other as they are cooked. Serve warm.

Lemon Rice
SERVES 6

A tangy flavoured rice that partners well with coconut-based curries or a vegetable salad.

1 tablespoon coconut oil
1 teaspoon brown mustard seeds
½ teaspoon cumin seeds
2 teaspoons blanched cashews, coarsely chopped
2 teaspoons channa dal
330 g hot cooked rice
1 teaspoon minced ginger
½ teaspoon ground turmeric
1 teaspoon salt
1 tablespoon chopped coriander leaves
1 teaspoon lemon juice
½ teaspoon asafoetida

Heat the oil in a large frying pan over a medium heat, then add the mustard and cumin seeds. When they start to splutter, add the cashews and channa dal and stir over the heat to roast. When the nuts begin to colour, add the hot rice, ginger, turmeric, salt and fresh coriander. Stir thoroughly to combine.

Sprinkle with the lemon juice and asafoetida to serve.

‹Fried Spiced Fish
SERVES 6

When we arrived at Ayesha Manzil, Faiza served this simple delicious fish for lunch, accompanied by a tomato onion salsa and a gorgeous salad of okra and yoghurt.

1 teaspoon roasted ground coriander
1 teaspoon ground turmeric
½ teaspoon chilli powder
1 teaspoon salt
6 × 150 g whole small mullet or similar small fish, gutted and scaled
2 tablespoons vegetable oil

Mix the spices and salt with a little water to make a paste. Rub the paste onto the fish and leave to marinate for 30 minutes, refrigerated.

Heat the oil in a frying pan. Fry the fish for 4 minutes over a high heat, then turn over and fry the other side for 2–3 minutes or until cooked. Serve immediately.

Mohan's Mutton Curry

SERVES 4

My friend Mohan comes from Kerala but currently lives in Hyderabad. This is a treasured family recipe from his mother, who still lives in Thrissur (Trichur), and its flavours remind me of many beautiful Kerala evenings spent at his parents' house. Serve this rich curry with steamed rice.

coconut oil, for frying
2 onions, sliced
1 tablespoon Ginger Garlic Paste
   (see page 377)
1 tablespoon curry leaves
½ teaspoon ground turmeric
1 tablespoon chilli powder
1 tablespoon ground coriander
1½ cups (375 ml) coconut milk
500 g diced mutton
1 teaspoon mustard seeds
4–5 shallots, sliced

MASALA
35 g grated fresh coconut
4 green cardamom pods
4 cloves
1 teaspoon salt
2–3 red chillies
1 small stick cinnamon
1 teaspoon ground coriander

Heat a little coconut oil in a frying pan, add the masala ingredients and cook until the coconut is golden brown, stirring regularly so it doesn't catch and burn. Using a spice grinder or mortar and pestle, grind this mixture to a paste and set aside.

Heat a little more coconut oil in a saucepan over medium heat and fry the onion and the ginger garlic paste. When the onion is soft, add the curry leaves, turmeric, chilli and coriander and stir well for 4–5 minutes. Add half the coconut milk and, when it comes to a simmer, add the mutton. Turn down the heat and simmer until the meat is almost cooked, about 1½ hours. Add the masala, stir well, then add the rest of the coconut milk and continue cooking until the mutton is tender.

Heat a little coconut oil in the frying pan and fry the mustard seeds until they splutter. Add the shallot and cook until browned and tender, then add to the pan with the curry.

Soothing Lamb Soup ›
Nadan Adu Soup

SERVES 4

A nourishing, rejuvenating country-style lamb or mutton soup, served during the monsoon season and to convalescents. We had it for dinner in Pala one steamy evening while the rain bucketed down outside.

3 tablespoons ghee
200 g finely diced onion
1 tablespoon cornflour
1 teaspoon salt
2 teaspoons freshly ground black pepper
25 g finely sliced red shallots
1 red chilli, finely sliced

SOUP BASE
2 kg suckling lamb leg, chopped
   into small pieces
100 g sliced onion
6 cloves
2 cinnamon sticks
1 teaspoon black peppercorns
1 tablespoon salt

To make the soup base, combine all the ingredients with 3 litres water in a large, heavy-based saucepan. Bring to a boil, then skim the surface. Cook over a medium heat until reduced by a third, about 25 minutes. Remove from the heat. Strain the soup, reserving the lamb but discarding the other solids, and set aside.

Heat 2 tablespoons of the ghee in a large saucepan and fry the onion over a high heat until it is golden brown. Mix the cornflour with a little water to make a paste, then stir it into the onion and cook for a few minutes until browned. Season with the salt and pepper. Add the strained stock and the lamb and bring to a boil. Cook for 5 minutes, then remove from the heat.

Heat the remaining ghee in a frying pan and fry the shallot over a high heat until brown. Stir the shallot and chilli through the soup, then ladle into bowls.

‹Cabbage Thoran

SERVES 4

With minimal cooking required, this versatile thoran can also be made with other vegetables, such as green beans, shredded beetroot or grated carrot. If you make it with spinach or silverbeet, you don't need to add any water during cooking.

1 tablespoon sunflower oil
1 teaspoon brown mustard seeds
12 curry leaves, plus extra to serve
1 white onion, finely diced
3 small green chillies, sliced
250 g white cabbage, shredded
1 teaspoon salt
½ teaspoon ground turmeric
35 g grated fresh coconut

Heat the oil in a frying pan and fry the mustard seeds over a medium heat until they pop. Add the curry leaves, then add the onion and chilli and stir for a couple of minutes. Add the cabbage, then sprinkle over 3 tablespoons water. Stir in the salt and half the turmeric. Cook for 6–8 minutes, stirring occasionally, until the water has been absorbed and the mixture is dry.

Mix the remaining turmeric into the coconut. Stir this into the cabbage until mixed well. Scatter a few extra curry leaves over the top to serve.

Ayurvedic Recipes from Kalari Kovilakom

At this elegant Ayurvedic retreat the food is truly delicious – and there is plenty of it. Each guest has a diet designed especially for them. Chef Narayanan Kutty prepares the food in heavy brass pots according to strict medicinal guidelines. Where possible he uses organic vegetables, herbs and spices from the garden, and ghee made from local organic milk. This being Kerala, coconut and bananas feature in many of the dishes. Lunch is the most substantial meal of the day.

Chef Narayanan says that the healthy qualities and nutritional vitality of the food come first – he does not cook to taste. The food is neither oily nor spicy but is inherently tasty, with light, simple flavours. It is easily digested, and you can literally feel it doing you good. I have included a few recipes for you to try:

Masala Fried Pork
Panni Ularthiyathu
SERVES 4

A favourite for family feasts in the Kottukapally household. This is traditionally cooked in a pressure cooker, a vessel not that common in Western kitchens these days. I have modified the cooking time for a cast-iron casserole-type pan.

500 g pork shoulder, cut into 1 cm dice
1 tablespoon minced ginger
100 g finely diced red onion
2 tablespoons curry leaves
6 tablespoons ground coriander
2 teaspoons chilli powder
¼ teaspoon ground turmeric
1 teaspoon garam masala
1 tablespoon white vinegar
2 teaspoons salt
200 g grated fresh coconut

FOR TEMPERING
4 tablespoons vegetable oil
1 tablespoon brown mustard seeds
100 g finely sliced red onion
2 tablespoons curry leaves

Mix the pork with the ginger, onion, curry leaves, ground spices, vinegar, salt, coconut and 100 ml water until thoroughly combined. Transfer to a cast-iron casserole, cover and cook over a low–medium heat for 1 hour until the meat is tender.

For the tempering, heat the oil in a large frying pan and fry the mustard seeds over a medium heat until they start to pop. Add the onion and curry leaves and cook until the onion is browned. Add the cooked pork mixture to the pan and fry to a deep-brown colour, stirring occasionally. Serve with Lemon Rice (see page 259).

Okra Pachadi
SERVES 4

This was one of the vegetable dishes Chef Amit of the Rice Boat restaurant at the Taj Malabar in Kochi made for our dinner one night.

4 tablespoons coconut oil
3 tablespoons diced red shallot
2 teaspoons Ginger Garlic Paste (see page 377)
12 small okra, sliced into rounds
3 tablespoons curd (drained yoghurt)
1 teaspoon salt
½ teaspoon ground turmeric
1 teaspoon brown mustard seeds
2 small dried red chillies, broken into small pieces
12 curry leaves

Heat 3 tablespoons of the coconut oil in a frying pan and fry the shallot over a high heat until it is translucent. Add the ginger garlic paste and stir until softened. Add the okra and cook until it has softened, about 2–3 minutes. Whisk the curd with the salt and turmeric and stir into the okra. As soon as the mixture is combined, turn off the heat to prevent it from curdling.

Heat the remaining coconut oil in a small pan and fry the mustard seeds, chilli and curry leaves over a high heat until the seeds start to splutter. Spoon over the pachadi and serve.

Moong Sprout & Spinach Salad

SERVES 4

This light salad is simple to prepare and easy to digest. You can feel yourself getting healthier with every mouthful.

    leaves from 1 bunch spinach, washed
    50 g moong sprouts, soaked
       in warm water for 2 hours
    35 g grated fresh coconut
    salt, to taste
    1 tablespoon lime juice

Blanch the spinach leaves in a saucepan of boiling water for a minute. Drain and rinse quickly under cold water, then coarsely shred the leaves. Mix with the remaining ingredients and serve.

Coconut Rice

SERVES 8

An Ayurvedic staple that is good for losing weight, lowering cholesterol and reducing fluid retention.

    400 g basmati rice
    2 teaspoons coconut oil
    35 g grated fresh coconut
    salt

Bring 2 litres water to a boil in a large saucepan. Add the rice and cook until soft, about 15 minutes. Drain well.

Heat the oil in a frying pan and fry the coconut over a medium heat until it turns golden. Stir the coconut through the rice and season with salt to taste. Serve hot.

Papaya Thoran

SERVES 4

A thoran is a dry vegetable preparation served as a salad. This one is restorative and nutritious, with clean, light flavours. Green mango can be used instead of green papaya when it is in season during summer. It doesn't suit ripe fruit.

    1 teaspoon coconut oil
    1 teaspoon brown mustard seeds
    1 teaspoon urad dal
    250 g finely shredded green papaya
    ½ teaspoon ground turmeric
    1 teaspoon salt
    70 g grated fresh coconut
    1 small clove garlic, finely sliced
    2 tablespoons curry leaves
    pinch of ground cumin

Heat the oil in a frying pan and fry the mustard seeds over a medium heat until they splutter. Add the urad dal and cook until roasted, about 1 minute. Add the papaya, turmeric and salt, then sprinkle with 1 tablespoon water. Cook until the papaya softens, then add the coconut, garlic, curry leaves and cumin, tossing to combine. Stir for a few minutes over a low heat to allow the flavours to infuse. Serve warm or at room temperature.

Coconut Souffle with Pineapple & Candied Cashews

SERVES 6

This has to be the most delicious dessert in Kerala, cooked by Anu at Philip Kutty's Farm on Lake Vembanad. More like a rich cream than a souffle, its flavours are tropical and sweet and the texture is velvety smooth.

½ pineapple, cut into 1 cm dice
60 g caster sugar
400 ml condensed milk
400 ml coconut milk
few drops vanilla extract
5 teaspoons lime juice, strained
1 × 7 g sachet gelatine powder
1 large egg white, whisked to firm peaks
2 tablespoons brown sugar
75 g salted roasted cashews,
    roughly chopped
½ pineapple, extra, cut into chunks

Place the diced pineapple and caster sugar in a frying pan and cook over a medium heat, stirring, until the sugar has dissolved and is beginning to caramelise, and the pineapple is soft. Spoon into the base of a 15 cm square glass dish (or six individual ramekins), smoothing the surface. Allow to cool.

In a large heatproof bowl, whisk the condensed milk, coconut milk, vanilla and 1 tablespoon of the lime juice until smooth and thoroughly combined. Place the gelatine powder and 3 tablespoons water in a small saucepan over a medium heat and stir until the gelatine has dissolved completely. Pour this over the milk mixture and stir to combine. Gently fold in the whisked egg white, then spoon the mixture over the pineapple, again smoothing the surface. Cover and refrigerate until set, about 3 hours or overnight.

When the coconut soufflé has set, place the brown sugar and remaining lime juice in a small saucepan and cook over a medium heat until the sugar has melted. Add the chopped cashews and stir to coat with the sugar. Pour onto a tray and leave to cool and harden.

Cut the coconut souffle into six rectangular portions and transfer to serving plates with a spatula. Sprinkle with the candied cashews and serve with chunks of ripe sweet pineapple.

Steamed Rice Pudding ›
Kinnathappam

SERVES 12

A dessert and childhood favourite from Nimmy Paul's grandmother, this is quite light. Any leftovers can be served as a cold snack.

150 g rice flour
1 tablespoon ghee
1.25 litres thick coconut milk
½ teaspoon salt

Combine all the ingredients to form a thick porridge consistency. Pour into a saucepan and cook over a very low heat, stirring continuously to prevent any lumps forming. Stir in one direction and be sure to scrape the edges of the pan. It is important that the mixture cooks very slowly to prevent it from colouring.

Pour the cooked mixture into a tray so that it is about 5 cm thick. Smooth the surface, then place in a steamer tray. Cover and steam over simmering water for 10 minutes. Remove and allow to cool for 10 minutes.

Turn out the pudding onto a flat surface and cut into wedges. Serve as is, or with seasonal fruit such as mango, pineapple or peach.

Coconut-stuffed Rice Pancakes in Banana Leaf
Ela Ada
SERVES 4

Another sweet coconut preparation served for lunch at the Fort House in Fort Kochi – the flavours and textures are just dreamy.

150 g rice flour
¼ teaspoon salt
banana leaf, cut into 4 × 10 cm rounds
   (use a pastry cutter)

COCONUT FILLING
250 g jaggery, shaved
250 g grated fresh coconut
¼ teaspoon ground cardamom

To make the coconut filling, boil the jaggery and 2½ tablespoons water in a saucepan until smooth, about 2 minutes. Stir in the coconut and cardamom and cook for 4–5 minutes until dry. Allow to cool.

Mix together the rice flour and salt, then pour 175 ml boiling water over. Knead well to make a soft dough. While the dough is still warm, divide it into four equal portions and roll each one into a ball (if the dough is allowed to cool, it will lose its softness and pliability).

Brush the banana-leaf rounds with a little water. Place a piece of the rice dough in the centre of each leaf. Using wet fingers, spread the dough thinly across the leaf. Spoon some coconut filling into the centre, then fold the leaf over to form a half-moon shape and press the edges together to seal.

Heat a char-grill or frying pan and cook the banana-leaf packages on both sides until browned. Alternatively, cook in a claypot over a medium flame, sprinkling with water occasionally so the banana leaves do not burn too much.

Unwrap the banana leaves to serve.

Egg & Coconut Pancakes ›
Mottayappam

These delicious morsels are a real treat and similar to Arabella (a classic Goan dessert). The crepe-like pancakes are a breeze to make and I find it hard to say no to a third serve!

1 egg
100 g plain flour
1 tablespoon white sugar
¼ teaspoon salt
vegetable oil, for brushing

COCONUT FILLING
100 g white sugar
200 g grated fresh coconut
¼ teaspoon ground cardamom

To make the coconut filling, boil the sugar and 3 tablespoons water together for a few minutes to make a thick syrup. Add the coconut and cook until the mixture has absorbed three-quarters of the liquid and is slightly sticky to touch. Stir through the cardamom.

In a blender or bowl, whisk the egg, then mix in the flour. Add 275 ml water and mix until smooth, then add the sugar and salt. Heat a frying pan and brush lightly with a little oil. Pour in enough batter to coat the base of the pan, then cover and cook over a high heat for 3 minutes. Remove the lid and cook for another minute. Spoon some coconut filling lengthways on one side of the pancake, then roll it over and remove from the pan. Transfer to a plate and keep warm.

Continue until all the batter and filling have been used. Serve warm.

KARNATAKA

Sandalwood, Coffee & Market Gardens

Here I am ... watching the beautiful golden light of Karnataka in the morning. There is a curious thing about the light in India. For some reason film never seems able to capture the sun's resplendent haze as dawn breaks beautifully over the subcontinent. Beautifully lit coconut groves, shimmering with texture and contrast to the naked eye become just a bunch of coconut trees when committed to film. Or perhaps I am viewing India through my own personal rose-tinted filter?

HARDEEP SINGH KOHLI, *INDIAN TAKEAWAY*

The southern state of Karnataka has a common heritage with Tamil Nadu and shares its food traditions, with equal attention and diligence paid to vegetarian dishes, rice a constant at the table and fish from the coastal waters of Mangalore a firm favourite. Its capital, Bangalore (Bengaluru), boasts a welcoming hill-station temperate climate and a hybrid personality of colonial past and techno-modern future. Once known as the Garden City, a headlong rush to modernity coupled with massive investment in scientific research, telecommunications and information technology means that Bangalore is now India's Silicon Valley, and is among its fastest-growing cities. Appropriately enough, we are welcomed by text message: as we disembark from our flight, a message flickers across the screen of my phone: 'Spice Telecom welcomes you to Karnataka. Enjoy roaming with Spice and have a pleasant stay.' As someone enamoured with spices, such a greeting makes me feel as if I was meant to be here, in this land of spice!

BANGALORE
Discovering the food of Karnataka

My introduction to Karnataka's cuisine on my first visit was a morning tea with local cookbook author Ranee Kuttaiah at her home, an eccentric character who prepared vermicelli with shredded coconut spiced with red shallot, mustard seeds, curry leaves and green chilli; and white urad dal seasoned with tempered mustard seeds and salt and flavoured with melted ghee. A small slice of a sweet saffron semolina pudding completed the spread as she regaled me with her favourite food stories.

Eager to explore the city, we head to Russell Market, one of the city's longest-established produce markets. The vegetables and fruit are lovingly polished and arranged in perfect pyramids. There are glossy eggplants, small red tomatoes, dark purple onions, huge mounds of pomegranates, new-season mangoes and chillies in shades of yellow, green and red. The variety of leaves is staggering and includes *gongura* (a bitter-tasting green leaf similar to sorrel that's used for making a pickle), massive stacks of betel leaves and fragrant curry leaves, and bunches of mint and coriander. I make a point of returning to this bustling colourful market every time I visit.

Local friend Cherian takes us to the Windsor Pub for lunch, an unpretentious place full of locals with the ambience of a friend's lounge

room. There is beer on tap and a soundtrack of laid-back jazz, but it is the food that really surprises. While some of the dishes are predictable pub food, others are standouts; one of my defining food moments is the curry-leaf chicken. No sooner have I polished it off than our genial host Sathish Thomas is there to share the recipe with me (see page 280). We also taste a Coorgi pork curry served with soft and pillow-like steamed *sanna* (rice) cakes. All in all, it is a timely reminder of an important lesson: trust the locals to show you the secrets of a city. On another visit, I meet Joe, a food connoisseur and avid city historian who steers me in the direction of some of the city's most authentic street food. We grab an early lunch at the popular Halli Mane Rural Restaurant, sitting by the open kitchen watching their frenetic activity, ordering a plate of *vada* (fried lentil dumplings) and *chow chow bhath*, a specialty of Karnataka that brings two classic semolina preparations together – one spicy and one sweet – *khara abd kesari*.

I make it a ritual to have breakfast every visit at the Mavalli Tiffin Room, just before the main gate to Lalbagh Botanical Gardens. A typical working-class canteen spread across several rooms, it's like stepping back in time and an essential experience. Constantly packed with locals, the rooms have an old-world well-worn charm with the menu posted on an old blackboard on the wall. We join the row of men sipping their tea and share a masala dosa and steamed rice idlis with sambhar and fresh coconut chutney. The city boasts a diverse restaurant scene as its population has rapidly expanded to meet the demands of the workers who have flocked to this city for business – from other parts of India and abroad.

A casual dinner at Nagarjuna, chock-full of students and family groups, offers authentic cooking of the region. The look of the restaurant is 1960s-style diner, and the menu claims that the place is 'the spicy trendsetter in good eating'. The waiters fill our metal plates with everything on offer, including the 'chicken 65' made with a signature spice blend, a house speciality. The spices include ground chilli, fennel, turmeric, black pepper, cumin, nutmeg, cinnamon and white poppy seeds, and the spice mix is stirred into a little water to make a paste, then rubbed into the chicken before it is dipped in a light batter of flour and egg and deep-fried. We are not disappointed. It's a fiery plate of fried chicken with copious amounts of red chilli that makes the homogenous commercial brands of fried chicken taste like blotting paper. The prawn sholay kebabs go down a treat, too. I opt for all the chutneys – gunpowder, green-leaf and mango – and fried dried chillies to stir through my rice.

Dinner at Karavelli proves to be a benchmark experience and one I repeat each time I am there. The menu is a showcase of seafood from the south-west coast, with chef Naren creating culinary magic from years of collecting authentic, well-researched household recipes with a commitment to provenance. We feast on tiger prawns roasted with ginger and green chilli, squid with coriander, and slices of red snapper fried in a spiced semolina crust. The crab curry is a house specialty, made with mud crabs from Kannoor simmered in a spicy gravy, ethereal lingering flavours that dissolve on my tongue. It is a standout.

One a recent visit, I drove an hour out of the city to Shreya's Retreat, which took me into a totally different realm. A stylish, exclusive, calm oasis with bungalow-style tents set in expansive gardens – away from the everyday hum drum and daily routine. It's designed as a luxurious escape that pampers the body and soul. I came for a restorative stay, to practise yoga, be mindful, eat healthily and recalibrate the body and mind through ayurvedic practices. I left feeling rejuvenated.

COORG
The 'Scotland of India'

There are rural areas of Karnataka worth getting off the beaten track and exploring. One is Coorg (Kodagu), a little-known region in the Western Ghats. This district is considered one of India's most beautiful areas, with panoramic views, idyllic countryside and a refreshingly cool climate that is a welcome change after the steamy humidity of the coast. These attributes, along with its mountain setting, mean that Coorg is often referred to as the 'Scotland of India'.

Heading west out of Bangalore, we pass through Mysore, renowned for its yoga retreats, sandalwood and incense, stopping to visit the Mysore Palace which looks like an opulent wedding cake or something out of a fairytale. We dip into Devaraja Market, soaking up its atmosphere and sampling various locally made pickles at the pickle shops. Whenever we drive along roads less travelled in India, we make it a habit to stop at a roadside stall in some small village for a glass of hot tea from a chai-wallah. Blink and you will miss these humble, open-fronted shacks, which are often cobbled together from wooden slats or corrugated-iron sheets. And no sooner are we out of Mysore than the Jesus Tea Stall catches our eye – we simply have to stop at a place with a name like that! Within minutes we are sitting on plastic chairs sipping steaming-hot cups of chai and watching village life go on around us. Next door is a room that turns out to be the local kindergarten, and on the footpath, a guy is getting a haircut and a shave with a dodgy-looking antique cut-throat razor – an open-air barber's shop. *Only in India* comes to define the myriad experiences I witness every time I visit.

Our journey continues through an undulating landscape of verdant hills and fertile agricultural land. We drive past fields where red berries from coffee plants are laid out on mats, drying in the sun. This land of coffee plantations, lush forests and rice paddies has customs that set it apart from its neighbours. The Coorgis or Kodavas are a warrior tribe, Kshatriyas by caste, and have contributed much to the military might of India since Independence. Tall, strong and fair, they are thought to be descended from people of Kurdistan and Kashmir. Coorgi women have the right to inheritance and ownership of land tenure, unlike many of their Indian sisters.

The small villages in these parts are picturesque, and tourism is starting out, with some plantation owners establishing small eco-lodges that welcome travellers, mostly from within India. We stay at Chikkana Halli Estate (formerly Orange County Resort), near Siddapur, by the Cauvery (Kaveri) River, a wilderness retreat that oozes rustic charm. The resort is part of the expansive Chikkanahalli Estate, one of the oldest coffee plantations in India. Walking around the working plantation, which is bordered by a towering bamboo forest, we listen to birdsong as our trekking guide diligently points out the various spice plants. We appreciate the majesty and beauty of the place and realise we have come across something quite special.

Coffee is the main cash crop around these parts, and we wander through row upon row of leafy bushes. No pesticides or chemicals are used here, and it's refreshing to experience such environmental awareness. Other crops include cardamom, black pepper and sugar cane, and freshly pressed sugarcane juice is served for breakfast. The resort grows its own vegetables in gardens planted along the banks of the river. Avocado and jackfruit trees are dotted across the property, and are laden with fruit. Full of the pride that comes from cooking with the finest and freshest produce, the chefs set up a makeshift kitchen in one of the courtyard gardens under a frangipani tree and cook several Coorgi recipes for us to taste.

The Coorgis hunt and fish as they have always done and are known to enjoy a dish of partridge pie – a hangover from colonial times – just as much as some of their own delicacies, such as the wonderful stew of young bamboo shoots and jungle mushrooms eaten with otty, a flat rice bread.

MADHUR JAFFREY, *A TASTE OF INDIA*

HAMPI

Venturing north from Bangalore, we drive six hours to Hampi, the largest archaeological temple site in the world, UNESCO world-heritage listed and one of India's most sacred Hindu historic temple sites. The landscape looks like something straight out of the Flintstone's Bedrock with gigantic granite boulders perched precariously over the undulating terrain, magnificent and majestic all at once. It is clear that it was once an incredibly prosperous grand city, apparently the second most important medieval city in the world in the early sixteenth century.

Each day our expert guide, Viru, takes us to different parts of these ruins on either side of the river, filling our heads with ancient history, recounting how this site reflects a highly evolved, multi-religious and multi-ethnic society. We walk to the royal compound with its perfectly intact geometric stepwell, the Lotus Palace, the Queen's Bath, the elephant stables, the bazaars, the stone chariot, the massive Ganesh monument carved from a single boulder, and the Shiva and Vishnu temples of the bygone kingdom of Vijayanagar. We climb Matanga Hill to watch the sunset one evening, enjoying an expansive bird's-eye view across the whole area as the full moon was rising – the scale and grandeur of the site was breathtaking. Dotted amongst the ruins are tracts of banana plantations giving the appearance of oases in the desert.

From our modern palace compound on the outskirts of town, we drive through local villages each morning, giving us the opportunity to take in the pace and rituals of daily life, to stop and chat. Women walking along the side of the road carrying large water urns on their heads or doing the daily laundry down on the riverbank, kids walking to school in their pressed uniforms, men manoeuvring loads on bullock carts, and monks performing a blessing ceremony. We are swept along in the kaleidoscope of colour and movement.

Dinner each night at our hotel, Kamalapura Palace, is a revelation of distinctive flavours and untried dishes of the region. I got hooked on *bale hoovu palya*, shredded banana blossom cooked with coconut, curry leaves, spices and mustard; *royala sukka*, prawns spiced with black pepper; and *gongura masmam*, a spicy lamb curry cooked in a gravy of gongura leaves, green chilli and tamarind. Sweetened *malpuas* (pikelets) made with millet flour and served with *rabdi* (milk reduced to a cream) are so dangerously good it's impossible to stop at one, even after a decadent thali with its multitude of dishes.

As we leave to head off on other adventures, I am reminded of the sheer diversity that every region in India has to offer. It's like peeling back layers and always finding something new.

Pumpkin Curry

SERVES 8

This is a heavenly vegetable dish that is simple to make and typical of home-style cooking I tasted at the Green Hotel in Mysore. With its vibrant colour, it is perfect for winter.

2 small dried red chillies, broken into pieces
1 teaspoon coriander seeds
1 teaspoon cumin seeds
2 tablespoons ghee
3 tablespoons toor dal, washed
2 teaspoons brown mustard seeds
20 curry leaves
½ teaspoon fenugreek seeds
3 cloves garlic, minced
1 small green chilli, minced
2 teaspoons minced ginger
1 teaspoon ground turmeric
600 g pumpkin, skin and seeds removed, cut into 3 cm cubes
300 ml coconut milk
35 g grated fresh coconut
2 teaspoons salt
1 tablespoon lemon juice
2 tablespoons chopped coriander leaves

Dry-roast the dried chillies, coriander seeds and cumin seeds separately over a gentle heat until fragrant. Cool, then grind together to a powder.

Heat the ghee in a wide, heavy-based saucepan and fry the toor dal and mustard seeds over a high heat until the seeds pop. Add the curry leaves, fenugreek, garlic, green chilli, ginger and turmeric and fry for 2 minutes until fragrant. Add the pumpkin, coconut milk, grated coconut, salt and roasted spices and bring gently to a boil. Simmer for about 15 minutes until the pumpkin is soft but still holding its shape.

Add the lemon juice and coriander, then taste and adjust the seasoning if necessary. Serve with steamed rice or Paratha (see page 351).

Rice Chapatis ›
Akki Ooty

MAKE 12

A typical and versatile bread of Karnataka, rice chapatis are served from breakfast right through to dinner. The dough is flattened in a hand press that has two round metal plates joined together at the handle, similar to a jaffle iron.

100 g cooked rice
50 g rice flour
2 tablespoons salt
¼ teaspoon ground cardamom
vegetable oil, for brushing

Using your hands, work the cooked rice into a thick paste. Knead the flour, salt and cardamom into the rice and work until thick. Roll into small balls about the size of a golf ball. Line a chapati press with plastic film and press the rice balls in it one at a time to flatten (or press flat with a rolling pin).

Heat a non-stick frying pan over a medium heat and brush with oil. Cook the chapatis one at a time and flip them over when they start to bubble. Each one will take about 2 minutes to cook and should remain pale in colour, not brown. Serve warm with Coorgi Pork Curry (see page 283).

Coconut Sesame Chutney ›
Kodagu Paji

MAKES 1 CUP (250 ml)

In the Coorg district, this chutney is eaten for breakfast with Rice Chapatis (see left).

200 g grated fresh coconut
150 ml Tamarind Liquid (see page 379)
50 g small green chillies, chopped
50 g jaggery, shaved
1 teaspoon salt
2 teaspoons white sesame seeds
2 tablespoons ghee
1 teaspoon brown mustard seeds
10 curry leaves

Combine the coconut, tamarind liquid, chilli, jaggery, salt and seseame seeds. Mix in a blender with 2 teaspoons water until smooth, then spoon into a serving bowl.

Heat the ghee in a frying pan and fry the mustard seeds and curry leaves over a high heat until the seeds pop. Spoon over the chutney and serve.

Leafy Greens with Onion & Coconut
Padpe Upkari
SERVES 4

A flavoursome vegetable dish typical of Karnataka that I first tasted at the Dakshin Restaurant in Chennai (see page 199), and then again at the Raintree in Coorg.

250 g silverbeet leaves
250 g pumpkin leaves
2 teaspoons vegetable oil
½ teaspoon brown mustard seeds
1 teaspoon urad dal
½ teaspoon cumin seeds
2 small dried red chillies, broken into pieces
1 white onion, finely diced
2 small green chillies, finely sliced
salt
35 g shredded fresh coconut

Roughly chop the silverbeet and pumpkin leaves, then wash and drain them.

Heat the oil in a frying pan and fry the mustard seeds, urad dal, cumin seeds and dried chilli over a medium heat until the seeds start to crackle. Add the onion and green chilli and cook until softened and translucent. Add the chopped greens and cook for about 5 minutes until any moisture has evaporated.

Remove from the heat and season with salt to taste. Stir through the coconut to serve.

Curry-leaf Chicken ›
SERVES 4

For me, this is one of the enduring tastes of Bangalore. I never imagined I would come across something so completely delicious served unadorned on a small plate as a pub snack – this recipe comes from the Windsor Pub.

1.2 kg chicken thigh fillets,
    cut into 4 cm chunks
4 tablespoons Cashew Paste (see page 375)
2 large dried red chillies
1 teaspoon salt
2 tablespoons shredded curry leaves
2 tablespoons Fried Curry Leaves
    (see page 377)

MARINADE
1 teaspoon chilli powder
1 large dried red chilli, broken into
    small pieces
1 teaspoon freshly ground black pepper
1 teaspoon ground turmeric
1 teaspoon garam masala
1 tablespoon Ginger Garlic Paste
    (see page 377)
3 tomatoes, chopped
150 g thick plain yoghurt

To make the marinade, combine all the ingredients. Add the chicken and mix to coat, then set aside to marinate for 10 minutes.

Tip the chicken and its marinade into a large frying pan and bring to a simmer. Cook gently for 10 minutes. It should not be too wet – the marinade should have reduced and coated the chicken. Stir in the cashew paste, chillies, salt and shredded curry leaves. Cook for another few minutes. Remove from the heat and sprinkle over the fried curry leaves to serve.

‹Coorgi Pork Curry
Pandy Curry
SERVES 4

This is one of the recipes prepared for us at Chikkana Halli Estate, a country resort in the Coorgi mountains. You can make this curry up to two days ahead and reheat it when required. Add the ginger and fresh coriander at the last minute, as you are about to serve.

500 g pork belly, cut into 3 cm chunks
200 g finely diced onion
1 teaspoon chilli powder
1 teaspoon roasted ground coriander
2 teaspoons ground turmeric
1 tablespoon Ginger Garlic Paste
  (see page 377)
3 small green chillies, split in half
  lengthways
2 teaspoons salt
2 tablespoons vegetable oil
2 pieces dried kokum or 2 tablespoons thick
  Tamarind Liquid (see page 379)
1 tablespoon thin julienne strips ginger
2 tablespoons chopped coriander leaves

COORGI DRY MASALA
100 g coriander seeds
50 g cumin seeds
50 g black peppercorns
1 teaspoon ground cinnamon
½ teaspoon cloves
¼ teaspoon ground cardamom
¼ teaspoon small dried red chillies
¼ teaspoon white poppy seeds
¼ teaspoon brown mustard seeds
¼ teaspoon fenugreek seeds
100 g rice

To make the Coorgi dry masala, dry-roast the coriander seeds in a frying pan over a low heat until dark brown (the colour of ground coffee). Dry-roast the remaining ingredients separately and allow to cool. Mix with the dark-roasted coriander and grind together to make a fine powder. Store in an airtight container.

Put the pork in a bowl and add the onion, chilli powder, ground coriander, turmeric, ginger garlic paste, green chillies, salt and 2 tablespoons Coorgi dry masala. Mix to coat the pork. Leave to marinate for 2 hours.

Heat the oil in a large saucepan and add the pork and its marinade. Fry over a high heat for 15 minutes, stirring constantly, until the meat starts to brown. Add 1 cup (250 ml) water, the kokum or tamarind liquid, and 2 tablespoons Coorgi dry masala and stir until the meat is well coated. Reduce the heat and simmer for 20 minutes, uncovered, until the meat is tender. Scatter over the ginger and fresh coriander to serve.

‹Moong Dal Pancakes with Chilli Ginger Chutney
Pesar Attu
SERVES 4

These breakfast pancakes were served at our hotel in Bangalore. They are truly delicious, with a savoury spiciness that wakes your palate first thing in the morning.

300 g moong dal flour
1 tablespoon rice flour
1 teaspoon minced ginger
1 teaspoon minced small green chilli
1 teaspoon salt
3 tablespoons melted ghee

CHILLI GINGER CHUTNEY
10 small dried red chillies, coarsely ground
2 teaspoons minced ginger
1 tablespoon Tamarind Liquid (see page 379)
1 teaspoon shaved jaggery
salt to taste

To make the chutney, use a mortar and pestle or small blender to grind all the ingredients to a fine paste.

Blend the dal and rice flours, ginger, green chilli and salt together, adding 300 ml water to make a thin batter.

Heat a large frying pan and, when it is hot, spread spoonfuls of the batter very thinly over the surface using the back of a ladle or large spoon. Sprinkle a little melted ghee over the top, then flip the pancakes over and cook until crisp on both sides. Remove and keep warm while you continue with the rest of the batter.

Serve the pancakes hot with the chutney.

Coorgi Vegetable Samosas
Karjikai
MAKES 15

Here is an appetising afternoon snack
that was served with pre-dinner drinks
at Chikkana Halli Estate in Siddapur.

225 g plain flour
1 teaspoon salt
3 tablespoons ghee
vegetable oil, for deep-frying

VEGETABLE FILLING
2 tablespoons vegetable oil
½ teaspoon cumin seeds
1 tablespoon chopped curry leaves
1 teaspoon minced garlic
2 teaspoons minced ginger
1 small green chilli, minced
½ teaspoon ground coriander
½ teaspoon chilli powder
½ teaspoon ground turmeric
1 teaspoon salt
150 g potato, parboiled and diced
150 g sweet potato, parboiled and diced
125 g shelled green peas

Sift the flour and salt into a bowl. Add ghee and
100 ml water. Mix until smooth, then knead the
dough on a floured surface for 5 minutes until
it becomes pliable and shiny. Wrap in plastic film
and refrigerate for 1 hour.

Meanwhile, make the vegetable filling. Heat the oil
in a frying pan and fry the cumin seeds and curry
leaves over a medium heat until the seeds pop.
Add the garlic, ginger and green chilli and fry for
a minute until fragrant. Stir in the ground spices
and salt, then add the potato, sweet potato and peas.
Toss to combine so the vegetables are coated with
the spices. Reduce the heat to low and cook for
5–6 minutes until the vegetables are soft. Taste
and adjust the seasoning if required. Remove from
the heat and allow the filling to cool completely.

Divide the dough into 15 pieces and shape each
piece into a ball. Roll out each ball on a floured
surface into a flat round, about 10 cm in diameter.
Spoon some vegetable filling into the centre of
each round. Brush the edges with a little water to
moisten, then fold the dough over to make a half-
moon shape. Press the edges together to seal.

Heat the oil in a kadhai or wok to 180°C. To test
the temperature of the oil, sprinkle in some flour –
if the flour sizzles, it is ready. Deep-fry the pastries
a few at a time for 4 minutes, then turn over and
fry for another 2 minutes until golden and crisp.
Drain on paper towel and serve hot.

Pappadam Masala ›
MAKES 8

A perfect quick-and-easy snack we were
served at Bangalore's Windsor Pub. And
it's clever, too! This is a variation on masala
pappads (made with crisp lentil wafers) from
the state of Maharashtra, where they feature
on the snack repertoire in Mumbai bars just
as in Bangalore.

3 tablespoons diced tomato
2 tablespoons diced white onion
2 teaspoons minced green chilli
1 tablespoon chopped mint leaves
1 teaspoon ground cumin
½ teaspoon salt
vegetable oil, for deep-frying
8 large black-pepper pappadams
   (preferably Patak's)

Mix the tomato, onion, chilli and mint in a bowl
and season with the cumin and salt.

Heat the oil to 180°C. To test the temperature of the
oil, sprinkle in some flour – if the flour sizzles, it
is ready. Fry the pappadams until crisp. Drain on
paper towel.

Spoon a little tomato mix onto each pappadam to
lightly cover the surface. Stack on a plate and serve.

Spinach Roti

MAKES 20

We were served this savoury flatbread at Halli Mane Rural Restaurant in Bangalore and it went perfectly with our spicy kebabs. I watched as the chef cooked several roti at a time on a large, flat plate that sat over hot coals, giving them a slightly smoky characteristic. The trick is to add just the right amount of ghee when you cook – too little and the bread will burn and be too dry; too much and the roti will be greasy.

200 g small spinach leaves,
    stalks removed
250 g plain flour
250 g wholemeal flour
2 teaspoons salt
2 teaspoons ghee
extra melted ghee, for frying

Blanch the spinach in boiling water for 20 seconds, then remove it from the pan and run cold water over it to stop further cooking. Drain and press to extract as much excess moisture as possible. Finely chop the spinach, then squeeze again to remove any further moisture from the leaves.

Sift the flours and salt into a large bowl. Rub in the ghee, then add the spinach and mix with your hands. Add 1 cup (250 ml) tepid water and mix until a dough forms. Knead the dough on a floured surface for 5 minutes to stretch the glutens, then cover with a cloth and leave to rest for an hour.

Divide the dough into 20 pieces and roll each piece into a ball. Roll out each ball on a floured surface to make a thin flat round, about 1 mm thick. Heat a tawa or flat frying pan and drizzle in a little melted ghee. Cook the rotis one at a time for about 1 minute until they start to brown, then turn them over to cook the other side. Stack the cooked rotis and cover them with a cloth to keep warm.

Black Pepper Prawns ›

SERVES 4

We were served a sumptuous thali dinner at Tuluva, one of the restaurants at Kamalapura Palace in Hampi. Showcasing the flavours and authentic dishes of northern Karnataka, this was a dish to swoon over, so the kitchen generously shared the recipe with me.

35 g shredded fresh coconut
1 tablespoon vegetable oil
3 small cloves garlic, crushed
1 teaspoon brown mustard seeds
20 curry leaves
1 brown onion, finely diced
2 small green chillies
1 tablespoon minced ginger
2 tomatoes, chopped
2 teaspoons freshly ground black pepper
¼ teaspoon ground turmeric
2 teaspoons ground coriander
1 teaspoon ground cumin
1 teaspoon salt
12 jumbo king prawns, peeled and deveined,
    tails intact
1 teaspoon lime juice
1 tablespoon shredded coriander leaves

Preheat the oven to 160°C. Spread out the coconut on a baking gray and roast in the oven until lightly golden. Grind to make a paste and set aside.

Heat the oil in a deep frying pan and fry the garlic, mustard seeds and curry leaves until fragrant. Add the onion and cook until softened, about 2 minutes. Stir in the green chilli and ginger and cook for 1 minute, then add the chopped tomatoes and cook for 5 minutes until softened.

Add the ground spices and salt and mix well. Add the prawns and stir in 2½ tablespoons water, then cover and cook over a medium heat for 3-4 minutes until the prawns are just cooked and the sauce has thickened. Stir in the roasted coconut paste.

Sprinkle the lime juice and shredded coriander over the top and serve.

Masala Prawns, Lemon & Pine Nut Rice Pilaf

SERVES 6

Elegant, astutely spiced dishes like this feature on the menu at Karavelli Restaurant, Bangalore's outstanding seafood restaurant. Its menu is a celebration of the coastal bounty. I have used chicken stock instead of water to give the rice added flavour and lustre, but this is optional.

1 teaspoon ground chilli
1 teaspoon ground turmeric
4 cloves garlic, minced
1 teaspoon salt
12 large raw tiger prawns,
    peeled and deveined, tails intact
2 tablespoons ghee
4 golden shallots, minced
1 tablespoon curry leaves
2 tomatoes, peeled and chopped
1 teaspoon finely grated lemongrass
    (use a microplane)
1 teaspoon ground coriander
½ teaspoon ground cumin
1 tablespoon lemon juice

PILAF
350 g basmati rice
50 g ghee
1 tablespoon brown mustard seeds
12 curry leaves
2 teaspoons nigella seeds
4 cloves garlic, minced
1 large red chilli, minced
½ teaspoon ground cardamom
1 teaspoon finely grated lemon zest
3 cups (750 ml) White chicken Stock
    (or water), hot
2 tablespoons lemon juice
3 teaspoons salt
4 tablespoons roasted pine nuts
2 tablespoons shredded mint leaves

Make a start on the pilaf by soaking the rice in a large bowl of cold water for 30 minutes.

Preheat the oven to 150°C.

Meanwhile, to prepare the prawns, mix the ground chilli, turmeric, garlic and salt in a shallow bowl, add the prawns and set aside for 15 minutes.

Drain the rice and set aside.

Heat the ghee in a wide-based ovenproof pan and fry the mustard seeds until they start to pop. Add the curry leaves and nigella seeds and fry for another 20 seconds. Stir in the garlic and chilli, then add the cardamom and lemon zest and fry for a few seconds longer. Add the rice and stir to coat with the spices.

Pour in the hot chicken stock, then cover the pan and transfer to the oven. Bake for 20 minutes until the rice is tender and all the liquid has been absorbed. Remove from the oven and stir in the lemon juice, salt, pine nuts and mint. Taste and adjust the seasoning if necessary.

While the pilaf is cooking, heat the ghee in a frying pan and fry the shallots over a medium heat until softened. Add the curry leaves and fry for another 2 minutes. Add the tomato, lemongrass, ground coriander and cumin and cook until the liquid has evaporated and the mixture appears quite dry. Add the prawns and marinade and cook, tossing, until the prawns change colour. Stir in the lemon juice, then taste and adjust the seasoning if necessary.

To serve, spoon the rice pilaf onto plates and arrange the prawns on top.

Fried Dal Patties

Mysore Bonda

SERVES 4–6

These fried balls of spiced dal are crunchy on the outside and creamy-soft on the inside – an excellent example of the way humble ingredients can be transformed into delicious things. They can also be served with a yoghurt sauce – just stir some ground cumin, chilli, nigella, salt and pepper into thick plain yoghurt and add the hot bonda balls.

2 tablespoons thick plain yoghurt
1 teaspoon bicarbonate of soda
150 g urad dal flour
1 teaspoon ground cumin
1 teaspoon salt
½ teaspoon freshly ground black pepper
2 small green chillies, minced
2 tablespoons shredded coriander leaves
vegetable oil, for deep-frying

Whisk the yoghurt and bicarbonate of soda in a bowl with ½ cup (125 ml) water until combined. Add the flour, cumin, salt, pepper, chilli and coriander and stir for several minutes to combine thoroughly. The mixture should be firm but not too stiff.

Heat the oil in a kadhai or wok to 180°C. To test the temperature of the oil, sprinkle in some flour – if the flour sizzles, it is ready. Drop small spoonfuls of the batter into the hot oil and cook for 2 minutes until brown, flipping over to cook both sides. Drain on paper towel and serve hot with Coconut Chutney (see page 208).

Egg Curry with Potatoes

SERVES 4

This curry recipe from north Karnataka was given to me by chef Arvind in Hampi. It's perfect Sunday-night comfort food when you're lying low at home, and want to cook something easy that will get the tastebuds firing.

4 tablespoons vegetable oil
1 onion, finely diced
4 cloves garlic, minced
2 tablespoons minced ginger
1 tablespoon curry leaves
4 small green chillies, minced
250 g potatoes, peeled and
    cut into 2 cm chunks
1 teaspoon salt
6 hard-boiled eggs, shelled
    and halved lengthways
2 teaspoons lemon juice

COCONUT MASALA
4 small dried red chillies
½ teaspoon black peppercorns
2 teaspoons coriander seeds
½ teaspoon cumin seeds
seeds from 2 green cardamom pods
2 cm piece cinnamon stick,
    broken into pieces
4 cloves
½ teaspoon ground turmeric
35 g grated fresh coconut

To make the coconut masala, dry-roast the chillies, peppercorns, coriander and cumin seeds, cardamom seeds, cinnamon and cloves together for a couple of minutes until fragrant. Cool, then grind to a fine powder. Mix with the turmeric and coconut and grind in a blender.

Heat the oil in a large saucepan and fry the onion, garlic, ginger, curry leaves and chilli until softened. Add the coconut masala and cook for a few minutes until it is starting to colour. Add the potato, tossing to coat with the aromatics, and just enough water to cover. Simmer over a medium heat for about 15 minutes until the potato is soft.

Add the salt, then taste and adjust the seasoning if necessary. Add the eggs. Reduce the heat and cook for a couple of minutes until the eggs are heated through. Add the lemon juice and serve hot.

Bamboo-shoot Curry

SERVES 4

Following sound environmental and sustainable practice, all the ingredients for this dish are grown in the grounds of the Chikkana Halli Estate resort in Coorg – it was originally devised to utilise the tender shoots from the massive stands of bamboo forests that border the coffee plantation.

100 ml vegetable oil
1 teaspoon brown mustard seeds
2 small dried red chillies
100 g finely diced onion
3 small green chillies, chopped
100 g seeded chopped tomatoes
1 teaspoon Coorgi Dry Masala (see page 283)
150 ml Tamarind Liquid (see page 279)
2 teaspoons salt
400 g fresh bamboo shoots, sliced
1 tablespoon chopped coriander leaves
2 tablespoons Fried Curry Leaves
   (see page 377)

GREEN PASTE
7 curry leaves
35 g grated fresh coconut
1 teaspoon ground cumin
1 teaspoon ground fennel
1 teaspoon minced ginger
4 small green chillies, chopped
2 cloves garlic

To make the green paste, blend all the ingredients in a food processor to a smooth paste.

Heat the oil in a frying pan or wok. Add the mustard seeds and dried chillies and fry over a high heat until the seeds pop and splutter. Add the onion and green chilli and fry until golden, then add the tomato and cook for a few minutes. Stir in 3 tablespoons green paste and the Coorgi dry masala. Cook until fragrant and the oil separates on the surface, about 6–8 minutes. Add the tamarind liquid and salt and bring back to simmering point. Stir in the bamboo shoots and simmer for 5 minutes.

Remove from the heat and sprinkle over the fresh coriander and fried curry leaves. Serve with steamed basmati rice.

Semolina Pudding

SERVES 4

A popular dessert in the south, not dissimilar in texture to barfi (see page 87), this humble pudding has appeared at quite a few dinners during my travels. It can be decorated with edible silver leaf if you so desire, giving it a festive appearance.

2 tablespoons ghee
1 tablespoon raw cashews, chopped
1 tablespoon pistachio slivers
2 tablespoons seedless raisins or sultanas
2 tablespoons milk
a few saffron threads
80 g unsalted butter
250 g fine semolina
200 g caster sugar
¼ teaspoon ground cardamom
2 tablespoons shredded fresh coconut,
   lightly toasted

Heat the ghee in a frying pan and fry the cashews, pistachios and raisins or sultanas over a medium heat until the nuts are golden. Remove from the pan and drain on paper towel.

Heat the milk to simmering point and add the saffron. Allow to infuse for 5 minutes, then remove from the heat and cool.

Heat the butter in a large frying pan and fry the semolina for 10 minutes, stirring occasionally, until golden brown. Gradually pour in 300 ml hot water, stirring constantly to avoid lumps forming. Add the sugar, cardamom and saffron milk and cook over a low heat for 6–8 minutes to thoroughly combine. Stir through the shredded coconut, nuts and raisins or sultanas. The mixture should be firm but not too dry.

Pour into a lightly buttered shallow dish or tin to a thickness of about 3 cm. Spread and press the mixture to make it even, then refrigerate for 1 hour until set.

Turn the semolina pudding out onto a flat board and cut into your desired shapes – squares, diamonds or triangles. Serve cold.

Stir-fried Banana Blossom
Bale Hoova Palya
SERVES 4

Light in texture and easy to prepare, this is a staple vegetable dish of Karnataka that we chose from the menu at Kamalapura Palace in Hampi. It's an ideal accompaniment to spicy kebabs or simply served with steamed rice and rasam.

1 banana blossom
3 tablespoons buttermilk
2 tablespoons vegetable oil
½ teaspoon brown mustard seeds
1 teaspoon chana dal
¼ teaspoon asafoetida
3 sprigs curry leaves
2 small green chillies, finely sliced
3 tablespoons shredded fresh coconut
½ teaspoon salt
1 tablespoon lemon juice
3 tablespoons chopped coriander leaves

Remove the leaves from the banana flower until you reach the white heart in the centre, then cut crossways into thin julienne slices and soak in the buttermilk for 15 minutes.

Tip the blossom slices and buttermilk into a saucepan, cover and simmer over a gentle heat for 6–8 minutes until softened.

Heat a small frying pan, add the oil and fry the mustard seeds until they start to splutter. Add the chana dal, asafoetida, curry leaves and green chilli and fry for a few minutes until golden.

Stir in the cooked banana blossom, then add the shredded coconut and salt and simmer for another 2 minutes.

Remove from the heat and stir through the lemon juice and coriander leaves.

Millet Pancakes & Cream ›
Malpua Rabdi
SERVES 4

A typical dessert of Bangalore, this was on the menu at Tuluva Restaurant in Hampi, where the kitchen made them with red millet flour instead of the usual wheat flour to excellent effect. Instead of making rabdi, which is sweetened milk cooked until it has reduced to cream consistency, I serve the little pancakes with rich pure cream for a decadent flourish.

150 g millet flour
1 tablespoon caster sugar
1 teaspoon baking powder
½ teaspoon ground cardamom
1 teaspoon ground fennel
½ teaspoon salt
180 ml evaporated milk
3 tablespoons melted ghee
1 cup (250 ml) Sugar Syrup (see page 379), flavoured with ¼ teaspoon ground cardamom
2 tablespoons rich pure cream

Mix the flour, sugar, baking powder, spices and salt in a bowl. Stir in the evaporated milk to make a thick batter – aim for the same consistency as a pancake batter.

Heat the ghee in a non-stick frying pan over a medium heat and drop spoonfuls of batter into the pan, a few at a time. Make them the same size as a pikelet (about 5 cm in diameter).

Cook for 2 minutes, then flip over and cook the other side for 1 minute. Remove the pancakes from the pan and set aside. Repeat until all the batter is used.

Heat the cardamom sugar syrup in a clean saucepan over a low heat. When warm, add the pancakes and leave to soak for 2 minutes. Turn off the heat, remove the pancakes and serve warm, topped with rich cream.

Cardamom Caramel Creams

SERVES 4

A variation of the classic creme caramel, this dessert was served at Koshy's in Bangalore, a stalwart of the city where the menu is a blend of popular Indian and British colonial dishes. I like to serve the creams with pears or apricots poached in a light vanilla syrup.

500 g caster sugar
2 cups (500 ml) cream
2 cups (500 ml) full-cream milk
½ teaspoon ground cardamom
2 eggs
8 egg yolks

Preheat the oven to 140°C.

Put 300 g of the caster sugar in a heavy-based saucepan and add 1 tablespoon water. Cook over a high heat until the sugar is a golden caramel colour. Do not stir. Working quickly, pour the hot caramel into four dariole moulds or ramekins. Fill one mould at a time, swirling the caramel to coat the inside of the mould, then tip the caramel into the next mould and so on, until all the moulds are coated. Put the moulds in a baking dish.

Heat the cream, milk and cardamom to simmering point in a saucepan. Whisk the eggs and yolks with the remaining sugar in a bowl until just combined (don't aerate too much). Pour in the hot cream mixture and whisk lightly until just combined. Fill the caramel-coated moulds with the custard mix.

Pour boiling water into the baking dish to come halfway up the sides of the moulds. Cook the caramel creams in the oven for 1 hour or until just set. Remove from the oven and leave to cool in the water bath, then refrigerate for 4 hours until cold.

To serve, dip the base of each mould in hot water to loosen the caramel, then run a small knife around the edges and turn out onto a plate.

Coorgi Vermicelli Dessert ›
Semian Payasa

SERVES 4

This is a relative of a Keralan payasam that features on the dinner menu at Chikkana Halli Estate in Coorg. Local friend Sarita also served it with morning tea when I visited her in Bangalore. It's pure comfort food.

200 g rice vermicelli
150 ml full-cream milk
50 g white sugar
pinch of saffron threads
¼ teaspoon ground cardamom
1 teaspoon pistachio slivers
1 teaspoon roasted cashews
2 teaspoons sultanas
50 g ghee, melted

Bring 1 cup (250 ml) water to a boil in a saucepan and add the vermicelli – it should be just covered with the water. Boil until the vermicelli is half-cooked, about 4–5 minutes. Add the milk and stir continuously for a few minutes or until the vermicelli is soft. Stir in the sugar until it has dissolved, then stir through the remaining ingredients. Serve warm.

HYDERABAD

Nizams, Palaces, Chillies

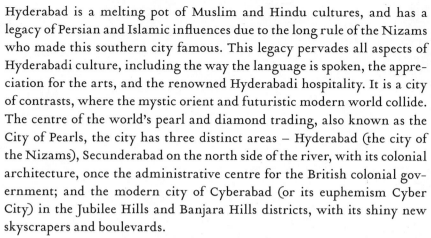

Hyderabad is a melting pot of Muslim and Hindu cultures, and has a legacy of Persian and Islamic influences due to the long rule of the Nizams who made this southern city famous. This legacy pervades all aspects of Hyderabadi culture, including the way the language is spoken, the appreciation for the arts, and the renowned Hyderabadi hospitality. It is a city of contrasts, where the mystic orient and futuristic modern world collide. The centre of the world's pearl and diamond trading, also known as the City of Pearls, the city has three distinct areas – Hyderabad (the city of the Nizams), Secunderabad on the north side of the river, with its colonial architecture, once the administrative centre for the British colonial government; and the modern city of Cyberabad (or its euphemism Cyber City) in the Jubilee Hills and Banjara Hills districts, with its shiny new skyscrapers and boulevards.

I will never forget my first visit to this former royal city when I was whisked from the airport by Rolls Royce to Falaknuma, a breathtaking royal palace perched on a hill with 360° city views. Made entirely of marble, it is the former home of the 7th Nizam of Hyderabad, the world's richest man at the time of India's independence. It has been beautifully restored to its former glory after an extensive and very expensive renovation by the Taj Hotels group. Anyone fortunate enough to be travelling on a generous budget can stay here and get a sense of what it must have felt like to be pampered in royal style. Nothing prepared me for the extravagance and sheer opulence – it took luxury to a whole new level. I splurged and stayed in one of the lavish royal suites with discreet personal butler service and acute attention to detail. It was one of the most enduring Indian experiences imaginable. In 2013 I was invited to present a 'Feast on Literature' dinner hosted by the Australian High Commission in the decadent, bejewelled Durbar Hall. With the benefit of previous visits, I knew the scale of opulence and the resources I had to work with. Needless to say, it was a memorable over-the-top affair.

HYDERÁBÁDI FOOD

Home to some of the hottest chillies in India, outside of Assam and Nagaland, with the hottest considered to be the *gingur*, euphemistically called the bomb chilli (or bum stinger), it is used to make the fiery, tangy fish curry called *chapu pulusu*. Small amounts of the curry are mixed into steamed rice to temper the heat. Typical Andhra (Hindu) cooking is deliciously spicy and hot, known for its gutsy robust flavours, while Hyderabadi cuisine, the food of the Muslim Nizams, is richer and less spiced, heavily influenced by the royal culture. Its most famous preparation *kacchi biryani* (lamb in a yoghurt marinade and rice layered in a wide pan and cooked over a slow fire) is one dish that has come to define the city.

My friend Jonty Rajagopalan gave up her successful career as an international marketing guru and founded her travel company *Detours India* to introduce visitors to the veritable buffet of offerings centred around

her native city with customised and personalised guided adventures. Spending a few days with her on a serious food reconnaissance gave me a direct conduit to the city. Biryani is savoured in all parts of India and forms an integral part of Indian cuisine. The Nizam's kitchen boasted 49 varieties, including biryani made from fish, quail, shrimp, deer and hare. Biryani is the culinary symbol of the city. On Jonty's Biryani tour, I discovered hidden gems of the city that would have been impossible to find without her expert guidance. Winding our way through many of the city's biryani hubs, we explored this rice dish in all its variations. We visited a couple of keen home cooks, who each make biryani from family recipes handed down through the generations. At her home, Begum Mumtaz Khan showed us how to make a soothing white chicken biryani, delicate and gently spiced, the chicken cooked in an onion and cashew paste with cream and yoghurt, unlike anything I had tasted. From an aristocratic family of Khansamas (royal cooks) that dates back to the days of the Qtub Shahi dynasty, Begum Mumtaz Khan was well known for her cooking skills and is credited with having popularised the Hyderabadi cuisine. She was an authority on the preparation of typical Muslim fare of the region and revived some almost forgotten recipes. She passed away in 2017 so I feel blessed to have spent time with her at her kitchen bench, gaining from her vast knowledge.

My early morning ritual in this city is a visit to Govind's Dosa street cart near Charminar, joining the queue for one of his sublime butter dosas. The dosa batter is spread onto a hotplate, spread with a wicked amount of butter then a spicy chilli and tomato paste, fried until crisp underneath and rolled up with one end tucked into paper, ready for eating. For me, it's a breakfast that defines the city. For another flavour hit, we head around the corner to a shop that makes the best creamy lassi in town.

We venture around Hussain Sagar, the large man-made lake that separates the two cities, across to Secunderbad to visit Pradama's Sweets, Hots and Pickles, a wonderful food shop that sells traditional Telangana spices and masala pastes to the local market and ships overseas to those expats homesick for its flavours. We stop at bakeries and sweet shops for a sneaky sweet treat, tasting as we go, and have coffee and snacks at one of the many Irani cafes in town. It's a heady whirlwind of activity which I absolutely adore. I find the best way to get to know a city is through its food, my stomach and curiosity leading the way.

Then it's over to the newer city, to the Banjara and Jubilee Hills districts where I find the best Andhra food. There are many restaurants to choose from and I zero in on my three favourites – Southern Spice, Simply South and Southern Mirchi, where the food is authentic and fiery, setting my tastebuds on fire.

Late one night Jonty takes me to a samosa factory – an overstatement for a place that is no more than a shed in a dimly lit back lane, where two men sit cross-legged on the floor making thousands of samosas, deftly folding the strips of pastry around the minced lamb and potato filling to form perfect little triangular parcels. These are collected by street vendors

who take them to cook at their street carts, or stack them onto large brass trays that perch on top of their heads as they weave their way amongst the cars in the congested traffic. I have to admire the ingenious productivity of India, where many hands make things happen.

To spend time with Jonty exploring the city's diverse food cultures is one of life's great joys, her enthusiasm infectious and her knowledge extraordinary.

ROYAL ARCHITECTURE

Hyderabad is a heady place with a lot to digest, literally and metaphorically. When we're not eating we spend our time exploring the architecture of the city's finest buildings. In the old town, there's Chowmohalla, the eye-poppingly opulent palace where the Nizam kings lived and ruled. The surrounding lawns are beautifully maintained and our tiffin tins packed with goodies enable us to have an impromptu lunch al fresco.

Nearby, the Nizam's Museum houses the world's largest wardrobe, amongst other fascinating artifacts. Apparently, nothing was worn twice! We climb the Charminar with its four towering minarets to the top floor and look across to the Mecca Masjid, the city's largest mosque. Back on the street, we head across the road to the Laad Bazaar, where it's frenetically busy – one street is filled with a row of shops whose walls are lined with dazzling colourful bangles. Of course, there are also *ittars* (essential oils), *soorma* (kohl), *mehendi* (henna) and spices on display. It's positively psychedelic. Only in India.

We drive about 45 minutes from our palace hotel to the once-impregnable Golconda Fort. Built at the time of the Qutab Shahi rulers, it is one of the most spectacular and significant fortress complexes in India, with a citadel built on a granite hill and surrounded by crenulated ramparts constructed out of large masonry blocks. This thirteenth century fort was built by the Kakatiya rulers as a mud fort and was expanded by subsequent dynasties into a massive granite fort. It remained the capital of the Qutab Shahi dynasty until the late sixteenth century when the capital was moved to Hyderabad to mark the beginning of Nizam rule. Nearby are the Qutab Shahi tombs, arguably the world's largest royal necropolis. The Indo-Saracen architecture is simply beautiful in detail and symmetry.

We also visit the Paigah tombs, which reflect the aesthetic tastes of one of the greatest noble families of Hyderabad, who even in death wanted to lie in grandeur. They left a remarkable architectural heritage for posterity. Heading back to the hotel, we stop to visit the Salarjung Museum, the envy of global collectors. This treasure house of antiques has an amazing display of art, the largest collection in the world owned by a single person.

Hyderabad is a city unlike any other, with its distinctive cuisines, opulent royal architecture, futuristic modernism and technological industries. So many influences have shaped the character of this city, making it a fascinating place to explore. I taste it in every bite.

Hyderabadi Lamb Biryani
Kacchi Gosht Ki Biryani
SERVES 4

One of the most perfect and delicious biryanis imaginable, this is the epitome of the royal cooking of the Nizams, as prepared by chef Ashfer at Hyderabad's Falaknuma Palace.

80 g Ginger Garlic Paste (see page 377)
100 g Green Papaya Paste (see page 378)
30 g Kashmiri chilli powder
½ teaspoon ground cardamom
2 teaspoons salt
500 g boneless lamb shank,
    cut into 4 cm chunks
500 g boneless lamb leg,
    cut into 3 cm chunks
2 teaspoons garam masala
4 small green chillies, finely sliced
500 g thick plain yoghurt, plus extra to serve
small handful of chopped mint leaves
large handful of chopped coriander leaves
200 g Deep-fried Onion Slices (see page 377)
1 teaspoon green cardamom pods, cracked
1 teaspoon black cumin seeds
1 teaspoon cloves
2 cm piece cinnamon stick
½ teaspoon saffron threads
150 g ghee
Gram Salt (see page 378), to taste
800 g basmati rice
1 tablespoon rosewater

Mix the ginger garlic paste, papaya paste, chilli powder, cardamom and salt in a large non-reactive bowl. Add the lamb chunks, rubbing the paste into the meat, then cover and leave to marinate in the refrigerator for 4 hours.

In another bowl, combine the garam masala, green chilli and yoghurt with half the chopped herbs and fried onion slices, reserving the rest for garnish. Add this yoghurt mixture to the marinated meat and stir thoroughly to combine.

Bring 4 litres water to the boil in a stockpot or large saucepan, then add the whole spices, saffron, 100 g of the ghee and gram salt to taste. Pour in the rice and cook over a medium heat for about 8 minutes until half-cooked. Strain the rice, then spread out on a large tray and leave to dry for 30 minutes.

Put half the lamb and its yoghurt marinade in a large wide-based pan and cover with half the rice. Repeat with the remaining lamb and rice, then cover with a tight-fitting lid, sealing the edges with a rope of dough (see page 366) or rolled foil and cook over a low–medium heat for 1 hour.

Remove from the heat and set aside to rest for 30 minutes before removing the lid – the residual heat will complete the cooking to perfection. Uncover and drizzle the rosewater and remaining melted ghee over the rice. Sprinkle with the remaining herbs and fried onion slices, then spoon the rice and meat onto serving plates. Serve with extra yoghurt.

Lemon Rice
SERVES 6

This is a delicious rice dish from Jonty's everyday home-cooking repertoire, one she often cooks for her guests.

1 tablespoon vegetable oil
½ teaspoon brown mustard seeds
1 teaspoon roasted chana dal
12 curry leaves
2 tablespoons raw peanuts
1 teaspoon minced ginger
2 green chillies, finely chopped
¼ teaspoon ground turmeric
330 g cooked rice (day-old cooked
    and cooled rice works best)
2 tablespoons lemon juice
1 teaspoon salt, or to taste
2 tablespoons chopped coriander leaves

Heat the oil in a frying pan and add the mustard seeds and chana dal. Once they start to splutter, add the curry leaves, peanuts, ginger and green chilli.

Add the turmeric, then immediately add the rice and stir to combine.

Cook over a medium heat for a few minutes until warmed through, then add lemon juice and salt and toss to combine. Garnish with the fresh coriander.

‹Andhra Fish Curry
Chapu Pulusu
SERVES 4

A fiery, tangy fish curry from Andhra Pradesh, also popular on menus in Bangalore and the south. This recipe comes from chef Praveen at Dakshin Restaurant in Chennai, as a homage to his Andhra birthplace. In Hyderabad, an equally excellent version can be found at Simply South Restaurant. The recipe calls for seer fish, which is common in India; I use kingfish, mulloway, Spanish mackerel or bonito in its place.

600 g seer fillet, cut into 3 cm cubes
2 tablespoons chopped coriander leaves
1 tablespoon Fried Curry Leaves
   (see page 377)

PULUSU GRAVY
120 ml vegetable oil
2 teaspoons brown mustard seeds
2 teaspoons fenugreek seeds
1 teaspoon cumin seeds
2 teaspoons channa dal
2 white onions, finely diced
2 tablespoons curry leaves
4 small green chillies, split in half
   lengthways
2 tablespoons Ginger Garlic Paste
   (see page 377)
300 ml tomato puree
2 tablespoons tamarind pulp
½ teaspoon ground turmeric
2 tablespoons chilli powder
4 tablespoons ground coriander
2 teaspoons salt

To make the pulusu gravy, heat the oil in a frying pan and fry the mustard, fenugreek and cumin seeds and channa dal over a medium heat until the seeds start to pop. Add the onion and stir to combine. Fry until the onion becomes translucent, then stir in the curry leaves, split chillies and ginger garlic paste, along with 2 tablespoons water. Fry for 2 minutes, then add the tomato puree, tamarind pulp and 2 cups (500 ml) water. Bring to a boil and cook over a high heat for 3 minutes. Add the ground spices and salt, then reduce the heat and simmer for 15–20 minutes or until the gravy thickens. The oil should separate and be visible on top. Taste and adjust the seasoning if necessary.

Add the fish to the gravy and simmer until cooked, about 3–4 minutes. Garnish with the fresh coriander and fried curry leaves to serve.

Curry Leaf Chutney
Karuveppilai Chutney
MAKES 200 ML

This fresh chutney is full of the vibrant flavours of the south and really packs a punch. Just one of the spicy chutneys served at Southern Mirchi, I had it as a condiment with spicy fried quail, like a double dose of heat. It adds a boost to fried snacks and curd rice or is served as a condiment to dry curries and any flatbread. I love it with appams (see page 240).

3 tablespoons coconut oil
2 cups (tightly packed) fresh curry leaves,
   washed & patted dry
4 tablespoons channa dal
4 tablespoons urad dal
2 teaspoons minced ginger
3 tablespoons hot chilli powder
1 teaspoon ground cumin
2 teaspoons ground coriander
1 tablespoon white sesame seeds,
   lightly roasted
1 tablespoon shredded coconut
1 tablespoon ground almonds
1 teaspoon salt
1 tablespoon tamarind puree

Heat the coconut oil in a frying pan and gently fry the curry leaves until crisp, about 30 seconds. Remove from the oil with a slotted spoon and drain on paper towel. Reserve the oil for another use.

Dry-roast the channa and urad dal in a non-stick frying pan for a few minutes until lightly roasted. Allow to cool completely.

Place all the ingredients in a food processor and blend to form a coarse paste. Keep in an airtight container in the refrigerator for up to one week.

Shikampuri Kebabs

SERVES 4

A Hyderabadi specialty, invented by the Khansama chefs in the royal kitchens of the Nizam and directly influenced by the Mughal cooking of the north. Having tasted these melt-in-the-mouth kebabs at Firdaus Restaurant at the Taj Krishna Hotel, I asked chef Nitin Mathur for the recipe and he kindly shared it with me. Traditionally, the kebabs are cooked on a hot stone plate over coals that give off a gentle smoky flavour.

20 g channa dal
1½ tablespoons vegetable oil
1 cinnamon stick
3 green cardamom pods, cracked
1 black cardamom pod, cracked
1 teaspoon black cumin seeds
1 bay leaf
2 green chillies, split in half lengthways
200 g boneless mutton (or lamb), finely sliced
½ teaspoon ground turmeric
1½ teaspoons garam masala
2 teaspoons ground coriander
1 teaspoon chilli powder
2 teaspoons salt
1 brown onion, finely diced
2 cups (500 ml) meat stock
    (made with lamb or mutton bones)
1 large egg
1½ tablespoons melted ghee

STUFFING
20 g curd (drained yoghurt)
1 tablespoon finely diced brown onion
1 teaspoon chopped mint leaves
¼ teaspoon garam masala
½ teaspoon salt

Soak the channa dal in warm water for 2–3 hours.

Heat the oil in a frying pan and fry the cinnamon, cardamom pods, black cumin seeds and bay leaf over a medium heat for 40 seconds until fragrant. Add the green chillis and mutton and cook for a few minutes. Add the ground spices and salt, stirring to coat the meat.

Add the onion and cook for few minutes until softened, then pour in the stock and cook until the meat is tender and starts to shred. Stir in the dal and cook until the dal is soft and all the liquid has been absorbed. The mixture should be quite dry. Allow to cool, then place in a food processor with the egg and blend until smooth.

Mix together all the stuffing ingredients in a bowl. Form the meat mixture into four evenly sized balls and hollow the centre with your thumb. Add one -quarter of the stuffing to each ball, then roll the ball in your hands to conceal the stuffing. Flatten each kebab into a patty with rounded edges.

Heat the ghee in a non-stick frying pan and fry the kebabs for 4 minutes. Flip them over and fry for another 3–4 minutes until brown on both sides and cooked through. Serve hot with mint chutney and lime wedges.

Cauliflower 65 ›
Ghobi 65
SERVES 6

Here, cauliflower is cooked with the famous spice blend of the region, a mix that is widely available in packets at food stores. At Southern Mirchi restaurant, they offer this vegetable version as well as the popular version with chicken, made in the same way, and served with Curry Leaf Chutney (see page 307) or mango pickle.

1 tablespoon cornflour
2 tablespoons plain flour
2 large eggs, beaten
1 tablespoon lime juice
2 tablespoons Ginger Garlic Paste
    (see page 377)
4 small green chillies, minced
1 tablespoon chilli powder
½ teaspoon freshly ground black pepper
2 teaspoons salt
1 cauliflower, cut into bite-sized florets
vegetable oil, for deep-frying
2 tablespoons Fried Curry Leaves
    (see page 377)

In a bowl, mix the flours, beaten egg, lime juice, ginger garlic paste, green chilli, chilli powder, pepper and salt, stirring to combine. Add just enough water to make a thick paste, then add the cauliflower florets and stir until evenly coated with the paste. Set aside for 30 minutes to marinate.

Heat the oil in a wok or deep saucepan to 180°C. To test the temperature of the oil, sprinkle in some flour – if the flour sizzles, it is ready. Add the florets in batches, swirling them around in the oil so they don't stick together. Fry for 4 minutes or until crisp and golden. Drain on a paper towel. Garnish with fried curry leaves to serve.

White Chicken Biryani

SERVES 6

Another rice preparation rooted in the history of the Persians and Afghans that found its way into the Nizam's royal court. This is how Mumtaz Khan prepared it when I had dinner at her home. It is usually served on auspicious and special occasions.

700 g chicken thigh fillets,
    cut into 5 cm chunks
300 g basmati rice, rinsed
    and soaked in cold water for 1 hour
6 green cardamom pods
1 cinnamon stick
1 teaspoon cumin seeds
½ teaspoon ajwain seeds
1 tablespoon Ginger Garlic Paste (see
    page 377)
1 cup (250 ml) full-cream milk
1 teaspoon salt
¼ teaspoon ground cardamom
3 tablespoons melted ghee
3 tablespoons thick cream
½ onion, finely sliced and deep-fried until
    crisp

YOGHURT MARINADE
8 cloves
8 green cardamom pods, cracked
1 cinnamon stick
½ teaspoon freshly ground black pepper
2 tablespoons Ginger Garlic Paste
    (see page 377)
5 small green chillies, finely chopped
2 tablespoons cashew paste
    (see page 375)
1 tablespoon lime juice
1 teaspoon salt
280 curd (drained yoghurt), stirred
2 tablespoons thick cream
2 tablespoons melted ghee

To make the marinade, mix together all the ingredients in a large bowl. Add the chicken and stir to combine, then leave to marinate for 1 hour at room temperature.

Preheat the oven to 180°C.

Rinse the rice and drain.

Pour 2 cups (500 ml) water into a large saucepan and add the cardamom, cinnamon, and cumin and ajwain seeds. Stir in the ginger garlic paste and bring to a boil. Add the milk and salt and bring back to the boil. Stir in the rice, then reduce the heat and cover the pot. Cook for 8 minutes until rice is two-thirds cooked and most of the liquid has been absorbed.

Remove the pan from the heat and strain the rice, reserving any excess liquid.

While the rice is cooking, heat a wide-based deep ovenproof pan over a medium heat and add the chicken chunks with the marinade – the chicken should fit snugly in a single layer. By the time the rice is ready, the chicken should be simmering in the pan.

Turn the chicken chunks over, then spoon the par-cooked rice over the chicken, sprinkling with a little of the reserved cooking liquid as you go, just enough to moisten without making the rice wet.

Mix the ground cardamom, ghee and cream and sprinkle over the rice.

Cover the pan and transfer the oven, then bake for 15 minutes until the chicken and rice are cooked. Remove from the oven and leave the pan covered for another 10 minutes – do not lift the lid at this point as the steam completes the final cooking.

To serve, use a spoon to gently mix the chicken into the rice, working from the edges into the centre, just so some of the chicken is visible in the rice.

Garnish with fried onions and serve hot.

Prawns in Tomato Coconut Gravy ›

Royala Eguru

SERVES 4

A coastal Andhra preparation – Royala means prawn and Eguru means reduction of gravy. This prawn delicacy is popular in households throughout Andhra Pradesh and Telengana.

> 800 g raw jumbo king prawns, peeled and deveined, tails intact
> 1 tablespoon Ginger Garlic Paste (see page 377)
> ½ teaspoon ground turmeric
> 2 teaspoons chilli powder
> 1 tablespoon lemon juice
> salt
>
> MASALA PASTE
> 2 tablespoons shredded fresh coconut
> 1 tablespoon white poppy seeds
> 3 tablespoons vegetable oil
> 4 cloves
> 4 green cardamom pods, cracked
> 1 cinnamon stick
> 2 brown onions, finely diced
> 1 tablespoon Ginger Garlic Paste (see page 377)
> 200 g chopped tomatoes
> 1 tablespoon ground coriander
> 1 tablespoon chilli powder
> 20 curry leaves
> 3 small green chillies, finely sliced
> 1 teaspoon salt
> 1 tablespoon lemon juice

Make a slight incision down the length of each prawn tail on the top side, but don't butterfly it open too much. In a bowl, mix the ginger garlic paste, turmeric, chilli powder, lemon juice and salt. Add this spice mix to the prawns and turn to coat well. Set aside.

To make the masala paste, blend the shredded coconut and poppy seeds together in a food processor to make a coarse paste.

Heat the oil in heavy-based frying pan, add the cloves, cardamom and cinnamon stick and fry until it begins to crackle. Stir in the onion and cook until golden brown.

Add the ginger garlic paste and cook until fragrant, about 4 minutes. Add the chopped tomatoes and cook until softened, about 10 minutes. Stir in the ground coriander and chilli powder, along with the coconut and poppy seed paste.

Cook the masala until the oil leaves the sides of the pan, about 5-6 minutes. Add the curry leaves and green chilli and cook, stirring, for 1 minute.

Add the prawns and their marinade to the pan and cook for 5-6 minutes until prawns are just cooked through. Season with salt and lemon juice to serve.

Almond Halwa

Badam Halwa

SERVES 10

Throughout India any auspicious occasion traditionally demands a sweet dish, and this halwa is a favourite across the south. A simple yet rich dessert that demands time during cooking (to continuously stir the pot) – it's a real labour of love. This version is from chef Challu's restaurant Simply South.

> 2 cups (500 ml) full-cream milk
> 500 g whole blanched almonds
> pinch of saffron threads
> 500 g ghee
> 450 g caster sugar
> 2 tablespoons flaked almonds, lightly roasted

Bring milk to the boil in a medium saucepan, then take it off the heat and add the blanched almonds. Leave to soak for 20 minutes, then strain, reserving the milk.

Place the almonds and ½ cup (125 ml) hot milk in a food processor and blend to make a coarse paste, adding a little extra milk if necessary.

Mix together the saffron and 2½ tablespoons hot milk in a bowl. Set aside to steep.

Heat the ghee in a heavy-based frypan. When sizzling, add the almond paste and stir continuously over a very low heat for 45 minutes, being careful not to let it catch on the bottom. During this time, the almond paste will absorb the ghee. Once it is cooked well, it will start releasing the ghee to the surface and looking a little oily.

When this happens, add the sugar and keep stirring continuously for another 15-20 minutes. Finally, stir in the saffron milk until evenly absorbed.

Serve hot in small bowls, garnished with roasted almond flakes.

GOA
Beaches, Vindaloo & Cashews

Sossegade – take it easy - adopt the local motto and you'll be charmed by Goan food, architecture, history and pure vibrancy. Goa holds the honour of being the country's smallest state, joining India more than a decade after independence. Sandwiched between Karnataka to the south and Maharashtra to the north, it is a sun-kissed place where the temperatures and humidity soar during summer.

Regarded as something of a hippie nirvana with the arrival of the 'drop out' culture in the late 1960s, for many Goa still conjures up images of all-night parties, the ravers having taken over where the hippies left off. But there is so much more to this tiny state than sea and sand, hippies and hedonists. More recently, Goa has become more hip than hippie, with well-heeled middle-class Indians frequenting the rash of flashy new resorts, restaurants and design stores, looking determinedly cool as they cruise by on their motorbikes. In places, the coastline has been subject to overdevelopment, and it takes an astute eye and trusted local knowledge to duck and weave around this. A word of warning: peak season is not the ideal time to visit if you are hoping for an ounce of tranquillity. Choice of location plays a vital role.

THE PORTUGUESE INFLUENCE

Goa's history has ensured that its persona, a rich amalgam of Portuguese colonial and traditional Hindu influences, is unlike any other in India, and this alone makes it a fascinating place to explore. When the Portuguese arrived in the late fifteenth century, they christened Goa the 'Pearl of the Orient' and stayed for almost 500 years. The colonists ruled by suppression and cruelty (the inquisition in Goa is considered the dirtiest and most repressive of all) and, during their reign, the Portuguese conquistadors destroyed every Hindu temple. Despite India gaining independence from the British in 1947, Goa wasn't handed over to the Indian government until 1961, when Nehru sent in the Indian army and the Portuguese surrendered to the sheer force of numbers.

The Portuguese left an indelible impression on the people and the landscape. Today, Goa is 60 per cent Hindu and 35 per cent Catholic. Goans still take a siesta every afternoon, and many are Catholic with distinctive family names; garden Hindu shrines stand cheek-by-jowl with crucifixes; and pork features heavily on the menu. Palm groves and rice paddies vie for space with imposing colonial mansions and beautiful houses, a few converted into stylish boutique hotels for the discerning traveller. We also have the Portuguese to thank for introducing chilli and vinegar to India – the chilli in particular having had the most profound effect on Indian cuisine.

North Goa bore the brunt of the hippie invasion of the late 1960s. Stretching from Fort Aguada, just outside the capital city of Panaji (Panjim), to Fort Tiracol, at the state's northernmost tip, the coastline suffers from the huge number of tankers that ply the waters offshore,

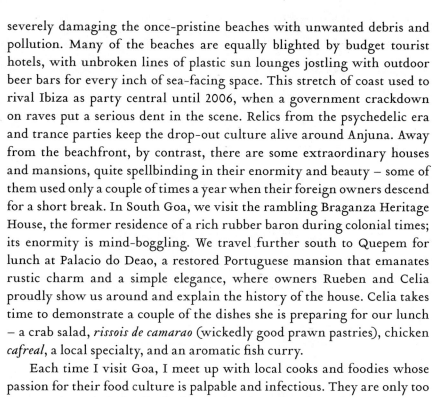

severely damaging the once-pristine beaches with unwanted debris and pollution. Many of the beaches are equally blighted by budget tourist hotels, with unbroken lines of plastic sun lounges jostling with outdoor beer bars for every inch of sea-facing space. This stretch of coast used to rival Ibiza as party central until 2006, when a government crackdown on raves put a serious dent in the scene. Relics from the psychedelic era and trance parties keep the drop-out culture alive around Anjuna. Away from the beachfront, by contrast, there are some extraordinary houses and mansions, quite spellbinding in their enormity and beauty – some of them used only a couple of times a year when their foreign owners descend for a short break. In South Goa, we visit the rambling Braganza Heritage House, the former residence of a rich rubber baron during colonial times; its enormity is mind-boggling. We travel further south to Quepem for lunch at Palacio do Deao, a restored Portuguese mansion that emanates rustic charm and a simple elegance, where owners Rueben and Celia proudly show us around and explain the history of the house. Celia takes time to demonstrate a couple of the dishes she is preparing for our lunch – a crab salad, *rissois de camarao* (wickedly good prawn pastries), chicken *cafreal*, a local specialty, and an aromatic fish curry.

Each time I visit Goa, I meet up with local cooks and foodies whose passion for their food culture is palpable and infectious. They are only too eager to share their family food secrets with me. Generous hospitality goes with the territory. Rui, one of those local cooks, won me over when he said, 'Indian food is not spicy, it is full of spices.' According to his gospel, the holy trinity in Goa is rice, coconut and fish. Other times, I wander through the vibrant Mapusa produce market north of Goa with local guide Jonas leading the way, checking out the wonderful displays of spicy *chorico* (pork sausage), spices, fish (fresh and dried), vegetables, fruit and meat. It's a delightful smorgasbord for the senses. We stop at a local cafe to taste *chorico pulao* – rice cooked with the local sausage and garlic, rich in its porky spiciness. After the market, we head north to Calungate Beach for a swim, then lunch at my favourite beach shack – Pousada by the Sea. Stylish and chic, owner Neville Proenca is one of Goa's most charming hosts and his kitchen serves utterly delicious food perfectly suited to its ambience. We feast on fresh salads, the ultimate prawn balchao and perfectly grilled fish. For dessert, I always order their ethereal Allebelle, a coconut ice-cream pancake that sum up the flavours of beachcomber Goa.

Goa is an ancient crossroads and its history has ensured that its personality, a rich amalgam of Portuguese and Indian influences, is unlike any other in India. This alone makes it a vital place to explore, with its multi-religious, multilingual blend of modern and ancient that has come together to craft such a fascinating place.

South Goa is dominated by large international brand hotels and beach cottages of varying standards which have taken up prime position along the coastal strip from Colva to Benaulim, and in the more fashionable stretch between Varca and Cavelossim. Some people choose to transfer directly to their resort on arrival and never stray from the compound.

A shame really, as this means they miss out on experiencing the languid pace and colonial ambience of Panaji. The city is like an Indian-Iberian melting pot, with baroque flourishes mixed in with Hindi Krishna design and faded Portuguese vernacular. It's fascinating to wander aimlessly along the narrow cobblestoned streets of the Fountainhas district (Latin Quarter) early in the morning when everything feels and looks so fresh.

HEADING INLAND
A ghost town and a spice plantation

Keen to get away from the tourist throngs that occupy the beaches and discover the Hindu aspect of Goa, we head into the hills inland from Panaji. Our final destination is a spice plantation in the Ponda district, home to some of the most important Hindu sites in the state, which survived because the region largely escaped Portuguese control. On the way, we stop at Old Goa, the original capital of the Portuguese colony but now a ghost town. Once a thriving walled city of 250,000-odd people, the population was ravaged by cholera and malaria epidemics in the seventeenth century, and the place was virtually deserted by 1775. Little remains of the fabric of the town, save for a handful of grand edifices. The Basilica of Bom (baby) Jesus, with its intricately carved woodwork, gold-covered pillars and impressive altar, houses the remains of St Francis Xavier. This Spanish priest from the Basque region founded the Jesuit order, making this a revered pilgrimage site for Catholics. Across the road, Se Cathedral is the largest Dominican cathedral in Asia, and the hilltop lookout nearby gives the most brilliant view of the area along the river towards the coast.

Continuing southeast through the hills, we arrive at the Tropical Spice Plantation, where we have been invited as guests of the Satakr family. It is one of the few plantations that allows visitors, and we walk through the gardens of spice trees to meet three generations of the family – grandparents, their four sons and their wives and a gaggle of kids all sharing the big house at the back of the plantation. The food for our lunch is lovingly prepared by two of the wives, Anita and Sarita. Their saris swish about as they grind the masala pastes in a massive stone mortar and pestle and stir the pots, cooking up a storm of a dozen or so dishes in pots set over an open fire. Their hospitality and generosity are humbling. It's a swelteringly hot and humid day at the start of the monsoon season – but, despite the stifling heat, this has become one of my many cherished memories of India. It is such a joy to experience the other side of Goa, to begin to understand the many faces this tiny state reveals to the world, and to be wrapped in its charm.

Portuguese-style Fish Stew
Fish Guisado
SERVES 4

This is easy to prepare and a favourite for family Sunday lunch at Oscar's mum's place in Panaji.

salt
6 fillets of any fleshy fish
   (preferably kingfish or large pomfret)
2 tablespoons vegetable oil
2 onions, sliced
2 tomatoes, sliced
1 teaspoon Ginger Garlic Paste (see page 377)
½ teaspoon ground turmeric
3 cloves
1 cm piece cinnamon stick
pinch of freshly ground black pepper
2 red capsicums (peppers), sliced
3 tablespoons extra virgin olive oil
white wine vinegar (optional)

Salt the fish lightly and set aside.

Heat the vegetable oil in a shallow frying pan and fry the onion over a medium heat until translucent. Add the tomato, ginger garlic paste, turmeric, cloves and cinnamon and fry well. Pour in 2 cups (500ml) water and cook over a low heat until the mixture thickens a bit.

Add the fish and pepper, then cover and cook until the fish is almost done, about 8 minutes. Add the capsicum and drizzle with the olive oil. Cook for another 4–5 minutes until the capsicum has softened. Taste and add a little extra salt and a dash of vinegar, if required.

Green Mango Curry ›
Uddamethi
SERVES 8

Choose mangoes that are slightly ripened for this dish. They should still feel firm but the fruit should be vaguely yellow, meaning it won't be too sour. This was served to us for lunch at the Tropical Spice Plantation.

2 tablespoons vegetable oil
1 teaspoon brown mustard seeds
pinch of asafoetida
20 curry leaves
300 g small green mangoes, peeled
   and chopped into large chunks
2 tablespoons shaved jaggery
2 teaspoons salt

SPICED COCONUT PASTE
12 small dried red chillies
1 tablespoon urad dal
2 teaspoons fenugreek seeds
1 tablespoon rice
2 tablespoons coriander seeds
2 teaspoons cumin seeds
1 teaspoon ground turmeric
2 teaspoons white poppy seeds
175 g grated fresh coconut

To make the coconut paste, pound the ingredients together with 100 ml water using a mortar and pestle, or whiz in a blender until smooth.

Heat the oil in a frying pan and fry the mustard seeds over a medium heat until they splutter, then add the asafoetida and curry leaves and cook for a minute until the curry leaves are crisp. Add the mango and its juices and cook for 5 minutes until it starts to boil. Add the coconut paste, jaggery and 100 ml water and bring back to a boil. Reduce the heat, then add the salt and simmer for 5 minutes. Serve with steamed rice.

Eggs with Coconut & Tamarind

Egg Xec-xec

SERVES 4

This spicy egg dish can be cooked at any time of the day. It's great comfort food, Goan-style, and perfect for the family table.

140 g grated fresh coconut
1 teaspoon cumin seeds
1 teaspoon coriander seeds
4 cloves garlic
½ teaspoon ground turmeric
3 green chillies
2 tablespoons thick Tamarind Liquid
   (see page 379)
1 tablespoon vegetable oil
2 onions, finely diced
2 tomatoes, diced
handful of tiny (harbour or school)
   prawns, peeled and deveined
1 teaspoon salt
6 eggs

Line a large glass bowl with a double layer of muslin.

Put the coconut, cumin and coriander seeds, garlic, turmeric, chillies, tamarind liquid and 2 cups (500 ml) water in a food processor and blend until smooth. Pour into the muslin-lined bowl. Gather up the muslin and tie around the mixture to secure. Squeeze by hand to extract as much liquid as possible, then discard the solids left in the muslin. Allow the liquid to settle for 20 minutes – the thicker cream will rise to the surface and the thinner milk will settle on the bottom. Carefully spoon the cream into another bowl so you have a bowl of thick coconut cream and a bowl of thin coconut milk.

Heat the oil in a frying pan and fry the onion over a medium heat until translucent. Add the tomato and prawns and fry for 5 minutes. Pour in the reserved thin coconut milk and add the salt. Cook over a low heat until the mixture begins to boil, then break the eggs gently into the pan. Cover and cook over a low heat until the eggs are almost done, about 3 minutes, then pour in the reserved thick coconut milk. Cook for another 5 minutes and serve immediately.

Green Masala Clams ›

SERVES 4

You can use mussels or pipis in place of the clams with equal success. Goan green masala tastes different from its counterpart in southern India – less sour and richer with the addition of coconut, and excellent with these bivalves.

500 g small clams, washed
100 ml vegetable oil
200 g red shallots, peeled
   and quartered lengthways
2 teaspoons salt

GREEN MASALA PASTE
70 g grated fresh coconut
3 teaspoons ground coriander
1 tablespoon ground cumin
½ teaspoon freshly ground black pepper
½ teaspoon ground turmeric
10 small green chillies
2 teaspoons chopped ginger
4 cloves garlic
2 tablespoons chopped coriander leaves

Put the clams and 100 ml water in a frying pan over a high heat. Cover and heat for 1–2 minutes, just until the clams open (discard any that don't open). Take the pan off the heat and remove one half-shell from each clam. Strain and reserve the cooking liquid.

To make the green masala paste, grind the coconut, ground spices, chillies, ginger, garlic and fresh coriander to a smooth paste.

Heat the oil in a frying pan and fry the shallot over a high heat until golden brown, stirring occasionally so it cooks evenly. Add the masala paste and cook over a gentle heat for 5 minutes. Add the clams on their half-shells and the salt and stir until the clams are thoroughly coated with the sauce. Let the clams simmer in the sauce for 2 minutes, just enough to warm through. Serve with steamed rice.

‹ Stuffed Squid

SERVES 4

A popular dish I have tasted at a few beach-front cafes whose menus specialise in seafood. This one is from a fish shack on Agonda Beach.

250 g baby squid (each about 8 cm in length)
2 tablespoons vegetable oil
1 tablespoon Red Masala Paste
  (see page 329)
2 tablespoons tomato puree
2 teaspoons shaved jaggery

TOMATO STUFFING
2 tablespoons vegetable oil
100 g red shallots, finely diced
100 g tomatoes, finely diced
2 small green chillies, minced
2 teaspoons minced ginger
4 cloves garlic, minced
½ teaspoon chilli powder
½ teaspoon ground turmeric
2 teaspoons lime juice
1 teaspoon salt

Remove the tentacles from the squid and finely dice the tentacles. Remove and discard the innards from the squid tubes and wash the tubes thoroughly.

To make the tomato stuffing, heat the oil in a frying pan and fry the shallot until softened. Add the tomato, green chilli, ginger and garlic and fry for 10 minutes over a high heat until the tomato softens and the paste becomes golden brown. Add the chilli powder and turmeric, then stir in the diced tentacles, lime juice and salt. Remove from the heat.

Blanch the squid tubes in boiling water for 10 seconds, then remove from the pan and plunge into iced water to prevent further cooking. Drain. Fill each tube with tomato stuffing and secure the opening with a toothpick.

Heat the oil in a frying pan and shallow-fry the stuffed squid over a medium heat, turning them with a spoon for even cooking. Add the red masala paste, tomato puree and jaggery and shake the pan gently to combine and to coat the squid. Cook for 2 minutes until heated through and the squid is tender. Serve with a tomato onion salsa.

Lobster Curry

SERVES 4

I watched over his shoulder and took notes as Rui cooked this for dinner at his beachside kitchen, using lobsters caught off the coast that morning. Prawns can just as easily be used instead of lobster, if preferred.

70 g grated fresh coconut
1 tablespoon chopped ginger
2 teaspoons ground turmeric
50 g coriander seeds, roasted and ground
1 teaspoon ground cumin
10 small dried red chillies
2½ tablespoons vegetable oil
1 onion, finely diced
1 cup (250 ml) Tamarind Liquid (see page 379)
500 g raw lobster meat, cut into large chunks
3 small green chillies,
  split in half lengthways
2 teaspoons salt

Grind the coconut, ginger, turmeric, coriander seeds, cumin and dried chillies with 2 tablespoons water to make a fine paste.

Heat the oil in a frying pan and fry the onion for 5–6 minutes over a medium heat until brown. Add the coconut paste and tamarind liquid and bring to a boil. Reduce the heat and simmer for 10 minutes until fragrant. If the sauce thickens, add a little extra water.

Stir in the lobster, green chillies and salt and simmer for 5 minutes until the lobster is just cooked. Taste and adjust the seasoning if necessary. Serve with steamed rice.

Pickled Prawn Relish
Balchao
MAKES 1½ CUPS (375 ml)

I collected this recipe from a local cook in South Goa on my first visit. It makes a versatile accompaniment, but I especially love it stirred into a simple rice pilaf or steamed rice. Delicious.

    1 teaspoon salt
    ½ teaspoon ground turmeric
    ½ teaspoon chilli powder
    2 teaspoons lime juice
    750 g small (harbour or school) prawns,
       peeled and deveined
    200 ml vegetable oil
    2 small white onions, finely diced
    2 tablespoons curry leaves
    2 tablespoons Ginger Garlic Paste
       (see page 377)
    2 small green chillies, finely sliced
    5 tablespoons Red Masala Paste
       (see page 329)

Mix the salt, turmeric, chilli powder and lime juice and rub into the prawns. Put the prawns in a colander and stand it over a bowl to catch any excess liquid. Leave to marinate for 30 minutes.

Heat the oil in a frying pan and fry the onion over a high heat until lightly coloured. Add the curry leaves and when they become crisp (about 1 minute), add the ginger garlic paste and green chilli and cook for 5 minutes. Add the prawns and stir to combine. Cook for a few minutes, then add the masala paste and cook for another 10 minutes or until the liquid has evaporated. Store in an airtight container in the refrigerator for up to 1 week.

Fried Breadfruit ›
SERVES 10

This recipe comes from the Tropical Spice Plantation, in the Ponda district. These fritters are utterly delightful and decidedly simple to make when you have a fresh breadfruit to use – an unexpected pleasure from this fruit and great to accompany drinks.

    ½ small unripe breadfruit, peeled and
       cut into thin wedges
    2 teaspoons salt
    2 teaspoons ground turmeric
    2 teaspoons chilli powder
    160 g semolina
    4 tablespoons vegetable oil

Put the breadfruit in a colander and sprinkle over the salt. Leave for a few minutes to draw out any excess liquid. Drain and pat dry with paper towel.

Mix the turmeric and chilli powder with just enough water to make a thick paste. Rub the spice paste over the breadfruit, then lightly coat with semolina.

Heat the oil in a frying pan and fry the breadfruit over a high heat for 4 minutes, then flip over and fry the other side for 3 minutes or until golden. Remove from the pan with a slotted spoon and drain on paper towel.

Chicken Xacuti

SERVES 4

This is one of Goa's most recognised chicken dishes, rich with aromatic spices and coconut. I was given this recipe by Judy Cardoza when she hosted a private cooking class in her home in the Panaji suburb of Miramar, making good use of her masala dabba (spice box) as she talked and cooked up a feast.

2 onions, sliced and fried until crisp
400 g shredded fresh coconut
3 tablespoons vegetable oil
3 tablespoons chopped red shallot
1 teaspoon ground turmeric
500 g chicken thigh fillets,
    cut into 4 cm chunks
2 teaspoons salt
2 teaspoons lime juice
3 tablespoons chopped coriander leaves

DRY MASALA MIX
3 mace blades
1 teaspoon white poppy seeds
1 teaspoon chilli powder
1 teaspoon ground turmeric
½ teaspoon grated nutmeg
3 cloves
1 teaspoon black peppercorns
4 small dried red chillies
2 teaspoons coriander seeds
1 teaspoon broken cinnamon stick
½ teaspoon fenugreek seeds
2 teaspoons salt

GREEN MASALA PASTE
2 green chillies, chopped
10 curry leaves
3 cloves garlic, peeled
2 teaspoons chopped ginger
3 tablespoons chopped coriander leaves
2 teaspoons lime juice

To make the dry masala mix, dry-roast all the ingredients, except the fenugreek seeds and salt, together over a low heat until fragrant. Cool, then grind to a fine powder with the fenugreek seeds and salt. Store in an airtight container and use as required.

To make the green masala paste, blend all the ingredients in a food processor to make a fine paste. Store in an airtight container in the refrigerator and use as required.

Place the fried onion and shredded coconut in a blender with enough water to make a paste and blend until smooth.

Heat the oil in a frying pan and fry the shallot over a high heat until starting to colour. Add the turmeric and 3 tablespoons of the green masala paste and stir for a minute. Add the chicken and stir to coat with the masala. Reduce the heat and simmer for 5 minutes (if cooking the chicken on the bone, increase the cooking time to 10 minutes). Add the onion and coconut paste and stir until simmering, then add the salt and 2 teaspoons of the dry masala mix and cook over a gentle heat for 10 minutes or until the chicken is tender.

Stir in the lime juice, then remove from the heat and sprinkle with the fresh coriander to serve.

Red Masala Paste

Rechead Masala

MAKES 2 CUPS (500 ml)

This red masala paste is used for vindaloos and curries and can also be used to pickle tiny prawns. It's a staple in any Goan kitchen.

150 g small dried red chillies
1 teaspoon cumin seeds
1 teaspoon cloves
1 teaspoon black peppercorns
1 teaspoon ground cinnamon
2 small red onions, chopped
10 small cloves garlic
1 tablespoon minced ginger
200 ml Tamarind Liquid (see page 379)
2 cups (500 ml) white vinegar
150 ml lime juice, strained
1 tablespoon white sugar
2 teaspoons salt

Grind the whole spices together to make a fine powder. Blend with the remaining ingredients in a food processor to make a fine paste.

Recipes from Maria d'Cunha

Oscar, who has been my guide on several India trips, comes from Goa. His mother, Maria d'Cunha, lives in Raia in South Goa, an area relatively untouched by tourism and with a strong Portuguese influence. She passed these recipes (some of Oscar's favourites) on to me as a reminder of the authentic flavours of Goa.

Prawn Balchao

SERVES 8

I collected this recipe from chef Kevin at Neville Proenca's chic beach shack Pousada by the Sea at Calangute Beach, where it's served as part of a Goan-style meze plate – perfect for its relaxed beachside ambience. It makes a versatile accompaniment, but I especially love it stirred into steamed rice or tossed through noodles. Delicious and addictive.

3 tablespoons vegetable oil
3 cloves garlic, finely sliced
2 tablespoons curry leaves
2 small red onions, finely sliced
2 tablespoons dried shrimp, ground to a floss
1 kg raw small prawns, peeled and deveined
1 teaspoon salt

RED MASALA PASTE
100 g long red chillies, chopped
2 teaspoons ground cinnamon
2 teaspoons ground cloves
2 teaspoons freshly ground black pepper
10 g minced garlic
10 g minced ginger
1 teaspoon ground turmeric
1 teaspoon ground cumin
2 cups (500 ml) fermented (toddy-based)
   coconut vinegar

To make the masala paste, grind all the ingredients together to make fine paste.

Heat 2 tablespoons of oil in a frying pan and cook the garlic over a medium heat for 20 seconds. Add the curry leaves and cook for 20 seconds, then add the onion and fry until golden. Stir in 100 g of the prepared red masala paste and the dried shrimp powder and cook until it binds together, about 20 minutes. Remove from the heat and cool. Pour the sauce into an airtight container and refrigerate for 1 week to allow the flavours to develop.

Add 1 tablespoon of oil to a frying pan. When hot, toss prawns for a minute or so until they start to change colour. Add the sauce and a little water (just enough to loosen the mix) and cook for another 3–4 minutes. Remove from the heat, season with salt and set aside. Serve at room temperature.

‹ Banana-flower Dal
Bondi Bhaji
SERVES 8

The variations of dal preparations in India are astounding but not surprising, given dal is a vegetarian staple for the majority of the population. Another recipe from Anita and Sarita at the Tropical Spice Plantation, this dal has a mild tropical flavour and uses the abundance of the garden.

> 1 teaspoon lime juice
> 3 teaspoons salt
> 200 g shredded banana flower
> 200 g moong dal, coarsely ground
> 70 g grated fresh coconut
> 1 tablespoon shaved jaggery

Add the lime juice and 2 teaspoons of the salt to a large bowl of water. This is to soak the banana flowers in to prevent discolouration. Add them as soon as they are shredded and leave them in the acidulated water until you are ready to cook.

Pour 3 cups (750 ml) water into a large saucepan and bring to boiling point. Add the moong dal and cook for 5 minutes, then drain the banana flower and add to the dal. Simmer for 15 minutes until the water has been absorbed and the mixture has thickened. Add the coconut, jaggery and remaining salt and stir over a medium heat for another 5 minutes until combined. Taste and adjust the seasoning if necessary before serving.

Goanese Duck Vindaloo
SERVES 6

Collected from an old Portuguese home cook in South Goa many years ago, this has become my staple vindaloo recipe. A similar version was served to us at Ahilya by the Sea on a recent visit, as part of a Goan thali dinner cooked by local chef Sarita.

> 8 small dried red chillies, broken into pieces
> ½ cup (125 ml) white vinegar
> 4 cloves garlic
> 2 teaspoons minced ginger
> 2 teaspoons ground cumin
> 2 teaspoons ground coriander
> ½ teaspoon ground cinnamon
> 6 duck marylands (leg and thigh portions), cut into leg and thigh joints
> 2½ tablespoons vegetable oil
> 2 teaspoons salt
> 2 teaspoons white sugar
> 2 tablespoons chopped coriander leaves

Soak the broken chillies in the vinegar for 20 minutes. Blend the chillies and vinegar with the garlic, ginger and ground spices to make a fine paste. Rub the spice paste liberally over the duck until well coated. Cover and marinate for 2 hours in the refrigerator.

Heat the oil in a large cast-iron casserole. Remove the duck from its marinade, reserving the marinade, and fry in a single layer over a high heat until browned on both sides. Drain off any fat, then add the salt, sugar, reserved marinade and 1 cup (250 ml) water to the pan. Cover with a tight-fitting lid. Reduce the heat to low and simmer for 1 hour or until the duck is tender.

Skim off any excess fat and transfer the duck to a serving dish. Stir the fresh coriander through the sauce and pour over the duck to serve.

Oyster & Potato Pie

SERVES 4

This reminds me of a seafood version of shepherd's pie. I have altered the recipe that was given to me by Maria, as we would usually cook Australian oysters for a shorter time.

 2 tablespoons vegetable oil
 2 small white onions, diced
 2 tomatoes, diced
 1 teaspoon Ginger Garlic Paste (see page 377)
 ½ teaspoon saffron threads
 ½ teaspoon freshly ground black pepper
 1 red capsicum (pepper), cut into julienne strips
 2 tablespoons olive oil
 1 tablespoon coconut vinegar
 30 large (Pacific) oysters
 salt

 MASHED POTATO
 4 potatoes, peeled and cut into cubes
 20 g butter
 1 tablespoon olive oil
 salt

Preheat the oven to 170°C. Lightly oil a baking dish.

To make the mashed potato, cook the potato in boiling water until soft, about 15 minutes, then drain. Mash the potato with the butter, olive oil and salt to taste. Set aside and keep warm.

Heat the vegetable oil in a frying pan and fry the onion over a medium heat until softened and transparent. Add the tomato and cook for about 5 minutes until softened. Add the ginger garlic paste and cook for a few minutes until fragrant, stirring occasionally. Stir in the saffron and pepper, then add the capsicum, olive oil and vinegar and cook for a few minutes until the liquid has evaporated. Remove from the heat and add the oysters and salt to taste, stirring to combine.

Transfer the oyster mixture to the baking dish and spread so it covers the base. Evenly spread the mashed potato on top. Bake for 15 minutes or until the potato is golden. Serve immediately.

Chorico Sausage & Dal

SERVES 4

The Portuguese influence is obvious in this recipe, which uses the familiar chorico spicy pork sausage (Spanish chorizo) to flavour the lentils.

 grated flesh of 1 coconut
 2 tablespoons vegetable oil
 2 onions, finely diced
 2 tomatoes, chopped
 1 teaspoon Garlic Paste (see page 377)
 250 g masoor dal, soaked for 1 hour, then drained
 2 chorico sausages, diced
 salt

Whiz the coconut and 300 ml water in a food processor, then strain. Set aside the thick coconut milk. Put the coconut back into the food processor and add 2 cups (500 ml) water. Whiz, then strain. Set aside the thin coconut milk.

Heat the oil in a frying pan, then add the onion and fry over a medium heat until translucent. Add the tomato and garlic paste and fry until softened, about 10 minutes. Add the reserved thin coconut milk and bring to a boil. Add the dal and cook over a low heat for about 10 minutes. Add the chorico and reserved thick coconut milk and cook gently for another 10 minutes or so until the sauce has reduced and thickened slightly. Season with salt to taste and serve hot.

Goan Pork Kebabs
Pork Espetada
SERVES 6

Kebab-style barbecued pork is so simple to prepare. I remember this from years ago when I was staying in South Goa and we went for drinks and snacks at Zeebop by the Sea beach bar. It was cooked over hot coals on a barbecue set up on the sand, which seemed to make it taste even more delicious. I like to serve a couple of different spicy pickles and roti or rumali (handkerchief bread) as accompaniments, using the bread to wrap around the meat.

5 dried red chillies
15 black peppercorns
4 cloves
1 teaspoon cumin seeds, roasted
1 teaspoon ground turmeric
1 teaspoon ground cinnamon
100 ml vinegar
2½ tablespoons vegetable oil
10 cloves garlic
2 teaspoons minced ginger
3 small green chillies, minced
handful of chopped coriander leaves
1 kg pork shoulder, cut into 3 cm cubes

Finely grind the dried chillies and whole spices together, then combine with the ground spices.

Blend the vinegar, oil, garlic, ginger, green chilli and coriander leaves to make a smooth paste. Stir the spice mix into the vinegar masala and add the pork, stirring to coat thoroughly. Marinate for 4–5 hours.

Thread the pork onto skewers and cook over hot coals or on a barbecue for 8–10 minutes until tender, turning every few minutes to ensure even cooking.

Bebinca ›
SERVES 8

This rich layer cake is a typical dessert and unique to Goa. The best restaurant version I have tasted was at Konkan Cafe, and this version, cooked to perfection for us by Jonas' mother on a recent visit to Goa.

250 g caster sugar
450 ml coconut milk
4 egg yolks
seeds from 2 vanilla beans,
    split in half lengthways
300 g plain flour
½ teaspoon grated nutmeg
¼ teaspoon ground cardamom
125 g ghee, melted

Preheat the oven to 175°C.

Combine the sugar and coconut milk in a large bowl and stir until dissolved. Beat the egg yolks and vanilla seeds until pale and creamy, then fold into the coconut-milk mixture and mix thoroughly. Sift the flour, nutmeg and cardamom together, then add to the coconut milk mix, whisking constantly until it forms a smooth batter.

Lightly grease a 20 cm round or square cake tin with melted ghee and pour in a ladle of batter, just enough to make a 1 cm thick layer, swirling the tin to cover the base.

Bake for 12 minutes or until the top is dark brown, so it caramelises before adding the next layer – this is what gives the cake its distinctive dark layers once sliced.

Take the cake out of oven and brush with more melted ghee. Add another ladleful of batter to make a second 1 cm thick layer and bake again until it sets, about 8 minutes. Repeat these layers until you have used all the batter and have multiple layers that are cake-like in consistency.

Allow the cake to cool in the tin, then turn it upside-down onto a plate. Cut the cake into thin slices to serve.

MUMBAI
Bollywood, Bazaars & Billionaires

The capital of Maharashtra state and one of my favourite launching points when visiting India, Mumbai is a city that thrills, horrifies, seduces, questions and delivers in equal measure. (Although the city's name was officially changed to Mumbai in 1995, most still refer to it as Bombay, and the two names seem to be used interchangeably.) Jam-packed and unnerving, with a population so dense it feels hard to breathe at times, the pace is frenetic, and the air crackles with electricity. For all that, it's a city to be savoured, not endured, and people either love it or hate it. Some find it too confronting; a gentler introduction to the country can be had in Kerala or Delhi. But for me, Mumbai and Kolkata are like my bookends to India; I love them both for different reasons and I love everything that sits between them.

[Mumbai] is a city of mind-bending extremes, where $8 martinis coexist with eight million slum dwellers. It is the city of Asia's oldest stock exchange, the world's most prolific film industry and some of the priciest apartments on earth. It is also a city hopelessly two-named.

ANAND GIRIDHARADAS
INTERNATIONAL HERALD TRIBUNE, 1 MARCH 2005

Mumbai evolved as a seething port capital spread across seven islands. The modern city is a large, sprawling and massively overcrowded metropolis where squalor on the streets is juxtaposed with overt displays of corporate wealth in the phallic office towers of Nariman Point and the bastions of business in downtown Churchgate. At the other extreme are the city's sprawling slums, coined Slumbai, and so memorably portrayed in the Oscar-winning movie Slumdog Millionaire. The city is home to more than 2000 slums.

I vividly remember flying into the old airport in the late 1970s and early 1980s and seeing slums surrounding the runways on all sides; the runways were sometimes even used as cricket pitches in between landings and take-offs! The city is India's economic powerhouse, rich with educational opportunities amid the thriving, mad and glamorous world of Bollywood. It exudes optimism and enthusiasm. After all, these are what lure the endless procession of eager hopefuls from across the country in search of opportunity and a better life. Everyone, whether local or a visitor, wants a piece of Mumbai's fame and fortune. If you have ever seen a Bollywood movie, then you can only begin to imagine the drama of everyday life here. Operatic and exaggerated as it may seem, it underpins the essence of India. It is sensory overload.

Mumbai is mesmerising: an exciting, exhilarating, edgy urban jungle; a kaleidoscope of riotous colour and energy that can't help but leave a lasting impression; and a melting pot of cultures where you can't help but feel alive. I find it impossible not to be inspired and moved by the people, the architecture and, of course, the food.

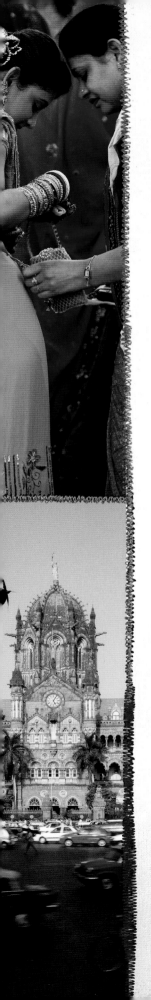

A DAY IN THE LIFE OF THE CITY

My favourite base in Mumbai is the opulent Taj Mahal Palace Hotel in Colaba, which resembles a multi-tiered wedding cake and overlooks the grandiose Gate of India on the shores of the Arabian Sea. From this central location, it is easy to access the sights of the city. Up at the crack of dawn, I head to Sassoon Docks with local friend Anjali where we witness the catch of the day being unloaded by the Koli fishermen as many of the city's cooks and chefs queue to get their orders filled; be mindful that it's action-packed and an assault on the senses – it takes nerves. Heading back into the heart of the action, we stop for breakfast at Yadzani Irani Café for a *brun maska* (soft bread roll with butter and jam) and Irani chai. We buy a freshly baked apple pie to take with us for an afternoon treat. We walk past splendid colonial buildings stained with pollution, marvelling at the neo-Gothic architecture of the High Court, the Prince of Wales Museum and Victoria Terminus.

An ideal place to see Mumbai's enormous array of fresh produce is the Crawford Market, a short walk north of the terminus. It's like stepping into an Aladdin's cave piled high with all things edible. Vying for attention are mangoes, displayed and packed in boxes of straw to prevent bruising; polished apples; ripe strawberries from Mahabeleshwar, a hill station in Maharashtra; and enormous bunches of green herbs. Coolies hang around the main entrance and clamour to be hired as carriers. Shoppers can engage them to carry any purchases in large round baskets, woven from reeds, that the coolies balance on their heads.

At lunchtime, I often make for one of the local cafes in the Churchgate or Marine Lines area, where it is mandatory to order a thali. The protocol is to start from the left and work your way around the plate, mixing little bits with the mound of rice in the centre each time and using your right hand to scoop the food like a spoon – and then turn to see hundreds of eyes fixed on you to see if you are doing it like a local.

One way of escaping the frenzy for a time is to take a ferry to Elephanta Island to visit the fourth-century cave temple, a shrine dedicated to Shiva, and admire the magnificent stone carvings. From the water, you see a different aspect of Mumbai: beyond the buzzing charter boats, private vessels and public ferries that congregate around the dock at the Gateway to India, calmer vistas of Art Deco mansions are revealed.

To immerse yourself in India's more recent history, visit Mani Bhavan, where Mahatma Gandhi stayed from 1917 to 1934, and the focus of his political activities during that time. Situated on a quiet leafy street in Gamdevi, the modest house is like a shrine, and Gandhi's presence is palpable thanks to the chronological display of his photographs and words. Afterwards, I like to zip around the corner for a snack or a sandwich at By the Way, a cafe run by the Seva Sadan Society for the empowerment of underprivileged girls and women. This place also operates as an orphanage, a school and a centre for vocational training. It feels good to be able to support such a worthy cause, to nourish while being nourished.

Around sunset, there's no better way to get a sense of the city than hanging with the locals on Chowpatty Beach and joining the queue at the Great Pani Puri Seller, one of the many food carts on the beach. The scene is remarkably different from Australian beach culture, as everyone is totally covered: it's a riot of colour, with the saris and scarves, kurtas and kaftans of family groups and friends who meet and share chai, snacks and gossip. But no one swims! As the evening wears on, kick back over a cocktail at one of the modern bars that face the beach along Marine Drive. (The rooftop Dome bar at the InterContinental has the best views.) Look across the bay to the Hanging Gardens and Malabar Hill, which has some of the most expensive real estate in the world – it's magical at night with the lights stretched out like a perfect pearl necklace.

THE FOOD OF MUMBAI

Several distinct cooking styles make up the food of Mumbai. The city's original inhabitants were fisherfolk called kolis, whose goddess, Mumbadevi, gave the city its name. Their Koliwada food features vegetable dishes and fiery-hot curries with lots of gravy. The Konkan food of the west coast is rich in its diversity, from the meat and fish dishes of the Bombay Catholics to the Anglo-Indians, whose diet included beef and pork, to the Maharashtrian Hindus, whose cuisine emphasises fish and prawns. The Bori Muslims, who brought their traditions with them from neighbouring Gujarat, use more meat in their cooking, which features mild kormas, wet gravy dishes, kebabs and mildly spiced biryanis.

The Parsi community (Zoroastrians who arrived in India many centuries ago, fleeing religious persecution in Persia) also has a strong presence in Mumbai. Noted for its richness and sophistication, their food is different again from the Mughal cooking of the Arabs who settled in northern India. Parsi food adds yet another layer to the complex Indian tapestry of tastes, with its unique mix of spices, dried fruit, nuts, eggs, chutney and coconut. Dishes may be punctuated by sauces that are sharp and rich simultaneously, with a liberal use of pomegranate, tamarind and lime; many are also influenced by the Gujarati love of sweet and sour. Cream and eggs feature strongly – and for celebratory days, puff pastries filled with sweet cream (*malai na khaja*) are an essential treat. Parsis like to eat . . . and keep eating. They have a near-obsession with food and are masters of improvisation, easily accommodating the arrival of unexpected guests.

A typical Parsi wedding feast is an opulent display of extravagance. We were fortunate enough to attend a wedding recently in Mumbai and the Parsi feast did not disappoint. Starting with a wedding pickle (*lagan achar*) and crisp, crunchy potato wafers, it moved on to a ghee-soaked roti, an egg dish (*akoori*), fish in banana leaves (*patra ni machni*), chicken or mutton with spiced apricots and straw potatoes, a baked savoury custard with nuts, white cheese (*pani nu paneer*), mutton pulao and *dhan sakh dal*, with kulfi ice-cream as the grand finale.

And of course, this being India, food is incorporated into every stage of life. *Goud Bharai* (or *Auti Bhavna* in the Marathi language) is a traditional Maharashtrian ceremony for a seven-months-pregnant expectant mother and her baby. It is primarily a celebration for women, and the mother is decorated with jewellery, clothes and flowers. Those attending the ritual pray that both she and her baby will be in good health and that the mother will have an easy delivery and the baby will have a good life. Family and friends bring gifts for the mother and shower blessings on the unborn baby. Food is served, with sweets featuring significantly in the offering. A rupee coin is hidden in one sweet and a small ring in another; the mother has to choose a sweet, and the one she opens supposedly predicts the sex of the baby – the rupee for a boy and the ring for a girl. Mythology is omnipresent in every aspect of life, even to this day.

STREET FOOD, TIFFIN & CHAI WALLAHS

Part of the charm of visiting India is hitting the streets and sampling tiffin snacks, or watching the chai wallahs work at a furious pace. And Mumbai's eating scene is among the most vibrant in the country – its street food, in particular, is brilliant and a cuisine unto itself. Nothing beats munching on delicious *bhel puri*, a snack of potato and onions dressed with tamarind with crispy puffed rice flakes scattered over the top – it's incredibly addictive. Equally enticing are *pani puri* – small puri puffs with spicy chickpeas spooned into the hollow and dressed with tamarind, cumin water and mint. They make the best snack imaginable and I found that the best ones are served at Elco, a puri centre in Bandra West to the north of the city. It's one of my favourite places to eat chat snacks in Mumbai. I also love the piquancy of *papri chat* – broken puris mixed with steamed potato chunks and tossed with chat masala spice mix – whose distinctive sour taste comes from *amchur* (dried mango powder). Other show-stoppers include crisp *bhajia* – vegetable fritters fried in a gram-flour and turmeric batter; *kanji vada* – deep-fried savoury doughnuts spiced with chilli; and *sukha bhel* – dried, crispy bhel morsels wrapped in newspaper cones for a snack on the run. Vegetable samosas and the luscious sweet threads of syrupy orange jalebi complete the picture.

The tiffin or dabba wallahs are an urban marvel, a Mumbai institution delivering lunch each day to hundreds of thousands of workers in handy dabbas – round, three-tiered metal containers. After the workers set off for the office, the food for each worker's lunch (typically vegetable curry, dal, pickles, rice and chapatis) is cooked in their home kitchens and then delivered to their workplace in time for lunch, like clockwork. Streaming in from the suburbs on mid-morning trains, the wallahs start arriving at Churchgate station around 11.20 a.m. and have dispatched their wares by 11.45, loading them onto long wooden planks strategically balanced on their heads. With their unique coding system and streamlined

efficiency, the tiffin wallahs oil the wheels of commerce each and every day by ensuring that workers get their personalised, freshly cooked lunch delivered right to their desk.

Highly visible on Mumbai's streets, chai wallahs act as a mobile tea service, serving glasses of milky tea from a central point that are then carried by boys on trays or in little baskets to shop owners, passers-by, people waiting at train stations and anyone else who wants one – and all for a pittance. Chai is the drink of the masses, transcending caste, creed and class.

Kebab vendors join the throng in the evenings and set up makeshift kitchens in many lanes across town. In a laneway behind the Taj Mahal Palace Hotel, the ever popular Bademiya has been in business for many decades with its time-worn, open-faced caravan, pumping out all manner of kebabs, grilled meats and roti rolls to meet demand. It's like entering a movie set – action-packed and fascinating just to stand in the midst of the pulsating energy, absorbing and observing. People queue for one of the much sought-after pavement tables, picnic in their car, or co-opt a motorbike's petrol tank as an impromptu table.

In the caravan, a man standing over a floured bench rolls rumali bread at a furious pace, using an upturned wok sitting over a gas ring to cook the bread. He stretches and flips the dough in the air, making it tissue-thin, and is fearless of the heat, using his fingers to flick the bread onto the pan and then over to cook the other side – an extraordinary sight. I figure each sheet of bread takes 15 seconds. The kebabs, meanwhile, are threaded onto thick metal skewers and cooked over hot coals in a long rectangular box. When they are ready, they are wrapped in bread to make roti kebab. Everything we order tastes delicious, and the place pumps until the wee hours of the morning, sating many an appetite.

A TASTE OF VILLAGE LIFE

Eager for a counterpoint to the city, we take a 90-minute ferry ride south to Alibarg, a close getaway for affluent locals. On the wharf, we grab a bag of spicy samosas sprinkled liberally with a fiery-hot chat masala to sustain us for the one-hour drive further south through lush countryside to my friend Jamshyd's beach house at Nandgaon, a small coastal village, where we are to stay for a few days. Surrounded by a massive grove of coconut palms, the house is a tropical paradise, with louvred walls and fold-back doors that catch every breeze. There is the soothing sound of water lapping over the rocks at the front of the yard, and a white sandy beach that contracts and expands with the ebb and flow of the tide. As the sun goes down each day, families appear and stroll on the sand; bullock carts glide by; village girls walk along with enormous bundles resting precariously on top of their heads, making it look ever so easy; and boys play cricket with makeshift wickets and bats.

Our days slip into an easy rhythm. After an early-morning swim or walk along the beach, we breakfast on new-season Alphonso mangoes with psychedelic-orange flesh (a speciality of Maharashtra), dark-red juicy figs and pomegranate juice, luxuriating in such simple pleasures. Another breakfast treat is the soft white bread rolls called *pao*, which we purchase from the village shop soon after they are baked. We have them with butter and a drizzle of Himalayan nectar honey, which oozes through the dough and fills all the tiny holes, like a crumpet – I christen them honey buns!

Each morning, fishing boats haul in a bounty of seafood at the nearby village of Nurud, and the choice between mussels, clams, lobsters, prawns, sea salmon, seer fish and pomfret determines what's for dinner each day. We buy watermelons to make fresh juice and limes to squeeze into our sunset gin-and-tonics. As we wander through the village, industriousness surrounds us: some of the village girls and women are out doing their washing at the communal well, while others sweep out their houses; and kids are getting ready for school. Nandgaon is a Muslim village and the midday call to prayer from the nearby mosque is the signal to the house cooks – Mousie, Seema and Usha – to start preparing lunch.

Late one afternoon, when the tide has gone out, the beach is suddenly transformed into a seething mass of people who have come from all around for the monthly carnival. They watch and bet on bullock-drawn cart races from one end of the beach to the other, willing their preferred bullock team to win. It's a loud spectacle, with much yelling, whistling and honking, in stark contrast to the tranquillity and solitude of every other day here. Nandgaon is one of the loveliest, most unspoiled villages I have come across in my travels around India.

All too soon we return to Mumbai, retracing our steps by road and water. But everywhere I look, there's incredible beauty in the chaos, and I find myself as enthralled as ever by the splendours that India has to offer. India is a land of paradoxes, contradictions and contrasts, highs and lows, beauty and despair, joy and sadness, wealth and poverty – and Mumbai has all of these in unequal measure.

Hindus believe in the theory of rebirth and reincarnation. Were it possible to be reborn with the memory and vision of past lives and past journeys intact – a capacity that is indeed granted to some fortunate 'seers', according to both Hindu and Buddhist legends – I, too, would be a believer. For after this odyssey, I know that one lifetime, one memory, is not enough to eat, know, and absorb India.

CHITRITA BANERJI, *EATING INDIA*

One Hundred Almond Curry
Sao Badaam

SERVES 8

When a lamb or goat (or sometimes a chicken) is sacrificed for a family feast or to mark a significant occasion, it calls for an extravagant preparation like this. The sacrifice is a way of saying thank you for helping, when the community has banded together for a common cause. Money is not exchanged; rather, a feast is offered, making everyone happy – except perhaps the lamb or chicken. This Parsi speciality, known as 'one hundred almond curry' is another dish I have cooked with Jamshyd when staying at his house.

2 kg suckling lamb leg on the bone, cut into large chunks
1 tablespoon black peppercorns
6 slices ginger
2 bay leaves
1 teaspoon salt
3 litres White Chicken Stock (see page 380)
240 g blanched almonds
1 onion, finely sliced
2 tablespoons Ginger Garlic Paste (see page 377)
12 dried Kashmiri chillies, broken into small pieces
2 teaspoons cumin seeds
1 tablespoon coriander seeds
2 tablespoons white poppy seeds
3 tablespoons ghee
300 ml coconut milk
75 ml Tamarind Liquid (see page 379)
3 tomatoes, quartered, seeded and sliced lengthways

Put the lamb, peppercorns, ginger, bay leaves and salt in a large, heavy-based saucepan and pour in the stock. Bring to boiling point over a medium heat, then reduce the heat and simmer for 1 hour or until the meat is very tender.

Remove the lamb from the reduced stock and set aside. Strain the stock, discarding the solids.

Blend the almonds with the onion, ginger garlic paste, chilli and cumin, coriander and poppy seeds to make a fine paste. Heat the ghee in a large pan and fry the almond spice paste over a low heat for a few minutes until it starts to colour. Add the coconut milk, tamarind liquid and 2 cups (500 ml) of the strained stock, stirring to combine. Simmer for 10–15 minutes until the gravy has reduced slightly and thickened. Taste and adjust the seasoning if necessary – a little extra salt may be required.

Add the lamb and tomato to the gravy and stir until well coated. Simmer for 10 minutes. Serve hot with steamed rice or Roti (see page 103).

Jamshyd's Chicken Dhan Sakh

SERVES 8

This famous feast dish is perhaps the most well-known of all Parsi dishes and essential to any Parsi wedding banquet. Traditionally made with lamb, it's just as rich, complex and spicy when made with chicken. There are several parts to the preparation, so give yourself plenty of time; extra hands are very helpful, too. I assisted Jamshyd in his home kitchen prepare this for dinner one evening.

3 tablespoons ghee
2 onions, finely sliced
2 cm piece cinnamon stick
2 cloves
3 black cardamom pods, cracked
2 star anise
2 tablespoons Ginger Garlic Paste
  (see page 377)
3 tomatoes, quartered, seeded and diced
2 tablespoons curry leaves
6 green onions, finely sliced
3 tablespoons shredded coriander leaves
1 tablespoon shredded mint leaves
100 ml Tamarind Liquid (see page 379)
1 tablespoon shaved jaggery
3 tablespoons lime juice
2 teaspoons salt

KACHUMBER

2 small red onions, finely diced
1 small cucumber, seeded and finely diced
2 tomatoes, seeded and finely diced
2 tablespoons chopped coriander leaves
1 small green chilli, minced
½ teaspoon salt
½ teaspoon Chat Masala (see page 376)

DHAN SAKH MASALA

2 teaspoons chilli powder
1 tablespoon coriander seeds, roasted
2 teaspoons cumin seeds, roasted
1 bay leaf
1 teaspoon ground turmeric
1 teaspoon fennel seeds
2 teaspoons brown mustard seeds
1½ teaspoons fenugreek seeds
2 teaspoons freshly ground black pepper
1 teaspoon ground cinnamon
1 tablespoon salt
1 teaspoon ground mace
½ teaspoon asafoetida
3 cloves

DAL MIXTURE

200 g toor dal
100 g moong dal
100 g masoor dal
200 g channa dal
2 tablespoons urad dal
1 × 1 kg chicken, cut into
  5 cm chunks (with bone)
2 teaspoons ground turmeric
1 teaspoon chilli powder
1 tablespoon ground cumin
2 tablespoons ground coriander
1 tablespoon salt
2 tablespoons minced ginger
3 cloves garlic, chopped
2 potatoes, peeled and chopped
8 tomatoes, chopped
4 small green chillies, finely sliced
2 tablespoons chopped coriander leaves
1 tablespoon chopped mint leaves
150 g pumpkin, diced
3 small zucchini (courgettes),
  chopped into chunks
1 small eggplant (aubergine),
  chopped into chunks
1 bunch mustard greens, cut into
  2 cm lengths

RICE

400 g basmati rice
2 tablespoons ghee
2 white onions, finely sliced
2 cm piece cinnamon stick
6 cloves
seeds from 3 black cardamom pods
2 teaspoons salt

To make the kachumber, combine all the ingredients. Set aside.

To make the dhan sakh masala, grind all the ingredients to a fine powder. Store in an airtight container and use as required.

To make the dal mixture, wash each of the dals separately and drain. Mix the washed dal with the chicken, spices, salt and 2 tablespoons dhan sakh masala, stirring until thoroughly combined. Tip into a large saucepan, then add the remaining dal mixture ingredients with enough water to cover. Bring to a boil, then reduce the heat, cover and simmer for 50 minutes, stirring occasionally, until the chicken is very tender. Remove the chicken pieces from the saucepan and set aside. Blend the cooked dal-and-vegetable mixture using a stick blender, then pass it through a sieve to make it as smooth as possible.

For the rice, wash the rice and soak it in cold water for 25 minutes. Drain. Heat the ghee in a large frying pan and fry the onion and spices until brown. Add the rice and stir to coat with the spices and ghee. Fry for 2 minutes. Add 1 litre boiling water, or enough to cover the rice by 2 cm. Cover and simmer for 20 minutes or until the water

has been absorbed and little holes appear in the surface of the rice, and the rice is tender. Add the salt, stirring to combine. Keep warm until ready to serve.

While the rice is cooking, heat the ghee in a large frying pan and fry the onion and whole spices over a medium heat until the onion starts to brown. Add the ginger garlic paste and 2 tablespoons dhan sakh masala and stir to combine. Add 1 tablespoon water to prevent the spices from burning and cook for a couple of minutes. Add the tomato and cook for 1 minute until softened, then stir through the curry leaves, green onion, coriander and mint.

Pour the smooth dal vegetable puree into a large, clean saucepan. Add the chicken and stir through the spiced onion mix. Simmer for 10 minutes until heated through.

Heat the tamarind liquid and jaggery in a small pan until the jaggery has dissolved. Remove from the heat and add the lime juice and salt. Stir this into the dal mixture, then taste and adjust the seasoning if necessary. Serve with the rice and kachumber.

Bhel Puri

SERVES 6

This is one of Mumbai's best-known and best-loved street snacks. There are quite a few steps in the production (many hands help!), so it's no wonder everyone heads to the streets to buy them. The puffed rice and sev can be found at Indian grocers.

20 g puffed rice
10 g sev
2 red shallots, minced
6 thin slices green mango, cut into fine matchsticks
2 tablespoons chopped coriander leaves
2 tablespoons diced tomato
3 teaspoons lime juice
½ teaspoon Chat Masala (see page 376)
250 g potatoes, boiled and finely diced
salt, to taste
chilli powder, to taste

PURIS
300 g plain flour
100 g semolina
½ teaspoon salt
vegetable oil, for frying

TAMARIND CHUTNEY
200 ml Tamarind Liquid (see page 379)
75 g jaggery, shaved
1 tablespoon minced ginger
2 teaspoons ground fennel
1 teaspoon Chat Masala (see page 376)
½ teaspoon chilli powder
1 teaspoon ground cumin
1 teaspoon black salt, crushed

CORIANDER MINT SAUCE
50 g coriander leaves
50 g mint leaves
2 small cloves garlic
2 small green chillies
2 red shallots
1 tablespoon lime juice
1 teaspoon white sugar
1 teaspoon salt

To make the puris, combine the flour, semolina and salt in a bowl. Add ½ cup (125 ml) water and knead to make a firm dough. Wrap the dough in plastic film and refrigerate for 1 hour. Divide the dough into three pieces and roll out each piece on a floured surface to 2 mm thick. Using a 4 cm pastry cutter, cut the pastry into rounds and prick all over with a fork. Heat the oil in a kadhai or wok to 180°C. To test the temperature of the oil, sprinkle in some flour – if the flour sizzles, it is ready. Fry the puris in small batches until golden and crisp. Drain on paper towel.

To make the tamarind chutney, heat the tamarind liquid, jaggery, ginger and fennel in a saucepan over a low heat, stirring, until it simmers and the sugar has dissolved. Add the remaining ingredients and simmer for 5 minutes until thickened. Remove from the heat and cool.

To make the coriander mint sauce, use a stick blender to blend all the ingredients to a smooth paste. Keep refrigerated until required.

Using your fingers, combine the puffed rice, sev, shallot, mango, fresh coriander, tomato, lime juice and chat masala in a bowl. Season the potatoes wtih salt and chilli powder to taste, then add to the bowl. Mix in enough tamarind chutney and coriander mint sauce to season and moisten the mixture. Lightly crush the fried puris and combine them with the bhel mixture, adding a little extra tamarind chutney and coriander mint sauce as required. Spoon into small bowls to serve.

Parsi Scrambled Eggs with Potato & Pine Nuts
Bharuchi
SERVES 4

Parsis are big on eggs as they symbolise fertility and life, and eggs feature in many dishes. They play an important role in Parsi feasts and rituals, especially weddings. My friend Jamshyd oversaw the production of this grand egg dish one morning for breakfast at his beach house. We certainly needed a long walk afterwards. It's rich, rich, rich!

125 g ghee
250 g potatoes, peeled and cut into thin matchsticks
3 small red onions, finely diced
1 teaspoon minced ginger
4 cloves garlic, minced
3 small green chillies, minced
2 teaspoons salt
8 eggs, beaten
2 tablespoons pine nuts, lightly roasted
1 tablespoon sultanas
1 tablespoon chopped coriander leaves

Heat the ghee in a frying pan and fry the potato straws over a high heat until golden and crisp. Remove from the pan with a slotted spoon and drain on paper towel. Set aside.

Add the onion to the pan and fry over a medium heat until it starts to colour. Stir through the ginger and garlic and cook for a minute until fragrant. Add the chilli and salt, then pour in the eggs and cook over a gentle heat, stirring occasionally, until just starting to set.

Combine the fried potato, pine nuts, sultanas and fresh coriander and gently stir into the eggs until combined. By now the eggs should be just set. Serve with Roti (see page 103) or Chapati (see page 85).

Vegetable Pakoras
MAKES 30

Pakoras are one of my favourite street-food snacks in Mumbai. Their crunchy texture makes them ideal palate teasers. Equally delicious and just as popular are prawn pakoras (made with the same batter), usually found in restaurants rather than on street carts.

75 g finely diced potato
75 g finely diced pumpkin
75 g finely diced eggplant (aubergine)
1 red onion, finely diced
2 silverbeet leaves, finely shredded
vegetable oil, for deep-frying

PAKORA BATTER
100 g chickpea (gram) flour
35 g plain flour
1 teaspoon baking powder
2 teaspoons salt
1 teaspoon garam masala
½ teaspoon chilli powder
½ teaspoon ground turmeric
1 teaspoon Ginger Garlic Paste (see page 377)
1 tablespoon vegetable oil

To make the pakora batter, combine the flours, baking powder, salt and spices. Add ¾ cup (180 ml) water, ginger garlic paste and oil and blend to make a smooth batter. Cover and refrigerate for 2 hours.

Make sure the potato, pumpkin, eggplant and onion have been cut to uniform small dice, then combine. Check the batter – if it is too thick, add a little water. Add the mixed vegetables and silverbeet to the batter and stir until thoroughly coated.

Heat the oil in a kadhai or wok to 180°C. To test the temperature of the oil, sprinkle in some flour – if the flour sizzles, it is ready. Drop in small spoonfuls of the batter, a few at a time, and fry until golden and crisp, flipping over after a minute to cook evenly on both sides. Remove from the oil with a slotted spoon and drain on paper towel.

Serve with hot mango or lime chutney.

Tomato & Spinach Baked Eggs
Tamatar Paredu
SERVES 4

Paredu means 'egg on top' and is a Parsi signature dish that can be made with any vegetable or meat. This is another of the breakfast recipes prepared for us at the beach house by Seema, the house cook. It was served with fresh white bread rolls that were more like small buns, lightly toasted and spread with a little butter, of course!

1 tablespoon vegetable oil
2 red onions, finely sliced
2 teaspoons ground cumin
3 cloves garlic, minced
2 small green chillies, minced
1 teaspoon salt
2 teaspoons sugar
1 tablespoon malt vinegar
5 large ripe tomatoes, peeled and chopped
3 tablespoons chopped coriander leaves
225 g chopped blanched spinach
4 eggs

Preheat the oven to 180°C.

Heat the oil in a frying pan and fry the onion and cumin over a high heat until the onion is translucent and starting to brown. Add the garlic, chilli, salt, sugar, vinegar and tomato and simmer for 5 minutes until the tomato is mushy. Add the fresh coriander and spinach and cook for another minute until the spinach has heated through.

Pour the mixture into a baking dish and smooth the surface. Using a spoon, make four depressions and crack an egg into each one. Bake for 4–5 minutes until the eggs are set. Serve immediately.

Kachumber Relish

This relish is a staple fresh condiment served with fish, dal or fried pastries in India —an Indian-style salsa.

2 tomatoes, peeled, seeded and diced
3 tablespoons diced cucumber
1 red onion, finely diced
1 small green chilli, minced
2 tablespoons shredded coriander leaves
1 teaspoon salt
½ teaspoon Kashmiri chilli powder
2 tablespoons lime juice

Combine all the ingredients in a bowl and use on the same day.

Paratha
MAKES 12

A staple of the Indian table, this flatbread is easy to make and an ideal accompaniment to many different dishes of the Konkan Coast.

500 g plain flour
1 egg
pinch of bicarbonate of soda
1 teaspoon white sugar
1 teaspoon salt
1½ tablespoons milk
2 teaspoons oil
melted ghee

Sift the flour into a bowl, add the egg, bicarbonate of soda, sugar, salt and milk and mix to make a firm dough. Roll the dough into a ball and rub it with oil. Cover with a damp cloth and leave to rest for 30 minutes.

Divide the dough into 12 small balls. Roll out each ball four times on a floured surface, folding and flattening each time and brushing each layer with ghee, to form four layers.

Heat a tawa pan and drizzle in a little ghee. Cook the parathas one at a time, drizzling in a little more ghee before cooking each one. Stack on a plate and cover with a cloth to keep warm while you cook the rest.

Moong Dal with Coconut

SERVES 6

A favourite dish from Jamshyd's mother, Nurgaz, that gives comfort with every spoonful. She suggests sprinkling some crunchy sev or ghatai puri over the cooked dal for a wonderful textural contrast. Reading through Nurgaz's recipes in an heirloom notebook of family treasures gave me a special insight into the care and love bound up in food, and how taste memories are cherished.

400 g moong beans
salt
4 tablespoons grated fresh coconut
4 cloves garlic, minced
½ teaspoon cumin seeds
½ teaspoon ground turmeric
½ teaspoon chilli powder
2 tablespoons vegetable oil
2 tablespoons garam masala
1 tablespoon lemon juice
2 tablespoons chopped coriander leaves
2 green onions, finely sliced

Soak the moong beans in cold water overnight, then drain. Keep the moong beans in a damp cloth until they start to sprout, about 2–3 days.

Put the sprouted moong beans in a saucepan with twice their volume of water. Add 2 teaspoons salt and cook for 30 minutes until softened, then drain.

Return the sprouted beans to the pan, cover with boiling water and simmer for another 30 minutes or until tender, then drain.

Using a mortar and pestle or a blender, grind the coconut, garlic, cumin seeds, turmeric and chilli powder to make a fine masala paste. Heat the oil in a frying pan and fry the masala paste for a few minutes over a medium heat until it is starting to colour. Add the cooked dal and stir until coated, then add the garam masala and salt to taste. Cook for a few minutes, then turn off the heat and stir through the lemon juice and fresh coriander. Sprinkle the green onions over to serve.

Sev Puri ›

SERVES 6

This rivals bhel puri as my favourite snack. You can buy ready-made puris and sev from an Indian food store. I have to thank Robin, one of my local guides in Mumbai, for procuring this recipe from one of his friends.

500 g flat sev puri or small jeera puri
100 g coarsely chopped potato
100 g finely diced onion
100 g finely diced tomato
100 g sev
2 tablespoons chopped coriander leaves
1 tablespoon finely diced green mango
1 tablespoon Chat Masala (see page 376)

SWEET CHUTNEY
100 g tamarind pulp
4 dates, pitted and chopped
50 g jaggery, shaved

HOT CHUTNEY
½ bunch coriander
4 sprigs mint
4–5 small green chillies
4 small cloves garlic, peeled
½ teaspoon cumin seeds
salt, to taste

RED-HOT CHUTNEY
4–5 red Kashmiri chillies
1 teaspoon coriander seeds
4 cloves garlic, peeled
salt, to taste

To make the sweet chutney, boil the tamarind pulp, dates and jaggery in a little water for 5 minutes. Press through a sieve and discard the solids. The chutney should be smooth and of medium consistency – not too thick or thin.

To make the hot chutney, blend all the ingredients together with a little water.

To make the red-hot chutney, blend all the ingredients together with a little water.

Arrange the puris on a flat plate in a single layer without overlapping. Spoon a little potato onto each puri, then some onion and tomato. Pour over all three chutneys to your preferred taste. Sprinkle liberally with sev to cover the puris. Garnish with the fresh coriander and mango and a sprinkle of chat masala.

Spinach Dal
Palak Masur
SERVES 4

This recipe is from Jamshyd's friend Radha. We had this dal for dinner at Jamshyd's beach house in Nandgaon, where it made a great accompaniment to a fiery red chicken curry.

100 g masoor (brown lentils)
1 bunch spinach, finely chopped
1 small onion, finely diced
3 tablespoons Tamarind Liquid (see page 379)
2 teaspoons salt
1 teaspoon chilli powder
1 teaspoon ground turmeric
1 tablespoon Deep-fried Garlic Slices
  (see page 377)

MASALA PASTE
1 tablespoon vegetable oil
4 cloves
4 black peppercorns
½ teaspoon white poppy seeds
4 cloves garlic, minced
2 teaspoons minced ginger
1 tablespoon channa dal
2 onions, finely sliced
70 g grated fresh coconut

Soak the lentils in cold water overnight, then drain. Keep the lentils in a damp cloth until they start to sprout, about 2–3 days.

Put the sprouted lentils in a large saucepan with the spinach and onion and enough water to cover. Cook for 15 minutes.

To make the masala paste, heat the oil in a large frying pan and add all the ingredients except the coconut. Fry over a high heat until the onion is softened and translucent. Add the coconut and fry until the mixture is lightly browned. Allow to cool, then grind to a fine paste.

Stir the masala paste, tamarind liquid, salt, chilli powder and turmeric into the lentil and spinach mixture. Bring to simmering point, then cook for 3–4 minutes for the flavours to infuse. Taste and adjust the seasoning if necessary.

Sprinkle the fried garlic slices over the top to serve.

Maharashtrian Dal
Masur Usal
SERVES 6

This dal is generally served with fish or meat curry, steamed rice and Kachumber Relish (see page 351).

400 g masoor (brown lentils)
2 tablespoons vegetable oil
5 cloves garlic, minced
2 teaspoons minced ginger
2 small green chillies, minced
1 small red onion, finely diced
1 teaspoon ground turmeric
2 teaspoons salt
35 g grated fresh coconut
2 tablespoons chopped coriander leaves

Soak the lentils in 1 litre cold water overnight, then drain, reserving the soaking liquid (store in the fridge until needed). Keep the lentils in a damp cloth until they start to sprout, about 2–3 days.

Heat the oil in a frying pan and fry the garlic, ginger, chilli and onion over a high heat until the onion has softened and is starting to colour. Stir in the sprouted lentils and add the reserved soaking liquid, then bring to a boil and cook for about 20 minutes until the lentils are soft and the liquid has been absorbed.

Add the turmeric, salt and coconut, stirring to combine. Cook for a few minutes for the flavours to develop. Turn off the heat, then stir through the fresh coriander and serve.

Spiced Cluster Beans with Yoghurt

SERVES 4

This vegetable is a local variety and features in Gujarati thalis. It is hard to replicate, but you can use sliced green beans, snake beans or flat roman beans.

3 tablespoons vegetable oil
1 bay leaf
½ teaspoon cumin seeds
5 dried red chillies, broken into small pieces
pinch of asafoetida
½ teaspoon mustard powder
250 g cluster beans, cut into 3 cm lengths
1 teaspoon salt
3 tablespoons thick plain yoghurt, whisked
1 teaspoon chilli powder
½ teaspoon ground turmeric
1 tablespoon garam masala
½ teaspoon amchur
1 teaspoon ground coriander
½ teaspoon white sugar
2–3 pieces dried mango, soaked to soften
2 tablespoons chopped coriander leaves

Heat the oil in a frying pan and fry the bay leaf, cumin seeds, broken chillies, asafoetida and mustard powder over a medium heat until fragrant, stirring continuously. Add the beans and salt and toss the pan to coat with the spices. Add the yoghurt, stirring to combine.

Combine the ground spices and sugar in a bowl with enough water to make a paste. Stir the spice paste into the beans and add the mango. Cook over a gentle heat until the mixture is quite dry, about 8–10 minutes. Garnish with the fresh coriander.

Trishna's Spinach & Fresh Cheese

Trishna's Saag Paneer

SERVES 4

I have eaten saag paneer in many places in India and in many Indian restaurants around the world, but Trishna in Mumbai triumphs with the best version. While it's not the prettiest of dishes, it is a perfect blend of soft, luscious textures. If you can't find freshly made paneer or don't fancy making it yourself, you could substitute a firm ricotta (or cubes of silken tofu, though this is less authentic).

leaves from 300 g spinach
2 tablespoons ghee
2 red shallots, finely diced
3 teaspoons Ginger Garlic Paste
   (see page 377)
2 tomatoes, finely diced
1 teaspoon garam masala
½ teaspoon cumin seeds,
   roasted and ground
½ teaspoon coriander seeds,
   roasted and ground
¼ teaspoon fenugreek seeds, roasted
1 teaspoon salt
250 g Paneer (see page 154),
   cut into 1 cm cubes

Blanch the spinach leaves in boiling water for 30 seconds, then strain and refresh in iced water to prevent further cooking. Strain again, squeezing out any excess water. Finely chop the blanched spinach and set aside.

Heat the ghee in a frying pan and fry the shallot and ginger garlic paste over a high heat until softened and starting to colour. Add the tomato and spices and bring to simmering point. Add the spinach and stir to combine. Cook until all the liquid has evaporated, about 5 minutes. Season with the salt, then gently fold through the paneer, taking care that the cheese doesn't break down or become mushy. Remove from the heat and serve hot.

Crab Pepper Fry

SERVES 4

Mahesh Lunch Home is one of my favourite
seafood restaurants in Mumbai and their
speciality is crab, whether it's cooked in the
tandoor, tossed with garlic pepper butter or
like this, with its seductive combination of
flavours and textures.

1 × 1 kg mud crab
salt, to taste
¼ teaspoon ground turmeric
75 g ghee
1 teaspoon brown mustard seeds
1 tablespoon curry leaves
10 red shallots, finely sliced
2 cloves garlic, finely sliced
3¼ tablespoons fish stock
1 tablespoon freshly ground black pepper
25 g unsalted butter
1 tablespoon chopped coriander leaves
2½ tablespoons lime juice
2 tablespoons rice flour mixed with enough
    cold water to make a thick paste (optional)

Wash and clean the crab, then cut it into eight
pieces, discarding the top shell. Combine the salt
and turmeric and rub into the crab. Set aside.

In a heavy-based pan, melt the ghee and fry the
mustard seeds and curry leaves over a medium
heat until the seeds crackle. Add the shallot and
garlic and fry until light brown and aromatic.
Add the marinated crab pieces, stock and pepper
and simmer for 4–5 minutes until the crab is cooked.

Finish with the butter, fresh coriander and lime
juice, thickening the pan juices with the rice-flour
paste if necessary.

Konkan Masala Clams

SERVES 4

We ate this dish – a different take to the
Goan version (see page 322) – at Mumbai's
Trishna Restaurant, where it was cooked
to perfection with clear and defined flavours.
You could also use small mussels, pipis or
surf clams.

1 kg clams, washed
3 tablespoons vegetable oil

GREEN MASALA PASTE
1 tablespoon minced ginger
4 cloves garlic, chopped
70 g grated fresh coconut
1 teaspoon chilli powder
15 curry leaves
2 teaspoons mild curry powder
10 red shallots, chopped
1 teaspoon salt

Tip the clams into a large frying pan and add
100 ml water. Cover and heat for 1–2 minutes over
a high heat, just until the clams open. Take off the
heat and remove and discard one half-shell from
each clam. Discard any clams that have not opened.
Strain and reserve the cooking liquid.

To make the masala paste, grind all the ingredients
in a blender to make a paste.

Heat the oil in a frying pan and fry the masala
paste for a few minutes over a medium heat until
fragrant, then add the clams and the reserved
cooking liquid. Toss to coat the clams with the
paste, then cover and simmer for 3 minutes until
heated through. Serve immediately.

Fried Bombay Duck

SERVES 5

This lizardfish, also known as bumla or bombil, swims in Konkan waters. The fish has a translucent appearance and a strong aroma that dissipates on cooking. We had this simple dish for lunch one day, served with a delicious sweet red pumpkin chutney. Bombay duck is not generally available outside India, but you can cook garfish in the same way.

10 whole Bombay duck, boned
1 teaspoon salt
5 small green chillies
1 clove garlic, finely sliced
1 tablespoon cornflour
2 tablespoons rice flour
vegetable oil, for deep-frying

Wash the fish and dry with paper towel to remove any excess moisture. Rub the salt over the fish. Make a paste with the green chillies and garlic and rub the paste over the fish.

Mix the cornflour with half the rice flour and enough water to make a thin batter. Dust the fish with the remaining rice flour.

Heat the oil in a kadhai, wok or deep-fryer to 180°C. To test the temperature of the oil, sprinkle in some flour – if the flour sizzles, it is ready. Coat the fish with the batter and slide into the hot oil a few at a time. Fry for 4 minutes until crisp and golden. Drain on paper towel and serve.

Dry-fried Malvani Prawns
Taleli Sungte

SERVES 4

A typical seafood dish cooked in villages and towns along the Malvani coastline, where tiny prawns are prevalent.

1 tablespoon lime juice
2 teaspoons ground turmeric
1 teaspoon salt
12 raw king prawns, peeled and deveined
2 tablespoons vegetable oil
4 tablespoons rice flour
lime wedges, for serving
1 tablespoon finely sliced green onion
1 small green chilli, finely sliced

TALELI MASALA
300 g Goan chillies
200 g Kashmiri chillies
2 cloves garlic
200 ml thick Tamarind Liquid (see page 379)
100 g cumin seeds, roasted and ground
100 g rice flour

Combine the lime juice, turmeric and salt in a bowl, add the prawns and toss to coat. Leave to marinate for 30 minutes.

To make the taleli masala, blend all the ingredients to make a smooth paste.

Add the masala to the prawns and leave to marinate for another 30 minutes.

Heat the oil in a kadhai or wok. Dust the prawns with the rice flour and fry over a high heat until crisp and golden, about 3 minutes. Drain on paper towel. Arrange the prawns on a plate with lime wedges and sprinkle over the green onion and chilli to serve.

Chicken & Eggs Roasted with Banana Leaves

Popti

SERVES 4

A family recipe from Sarika, one of my Mumbai guides, popti is specific to the Alibarg and Elephanta Island region. It's a simple one-pot number cooked with hot coals to impart a lovely smoky flavour to the food; the leaves act as insulation during the cooking process. I have read of a Parsi dish called oomberiu (itself a take on the Gujarati oondhyu) that uses a similar technique, layering papri beans, assorted vegetables, mango and banana leaves in an eathernware pot.

4 banana leaves, cut into strips
3 teaspoons salt
2 red onions, sliced into thick rings
4 potatoes, peeled and quartered
2 teaspoons chilli powder
4 eggs
4 chicken thigh fillets, cut in half
3 large pieces hot charcoal

Line the base of a handi or round earthenware pot with some of the banana-leaf strips and sprinkle with half the salt. Layer the onion and potato over the top, sprinkling chilli powder liberally between the layers. Add a little more salt, then nestle the eggs (still in their shells) and chicken on top and sprinkle with the remaining salt. Make a well in the centre and cover with a strip of banana leaf, then sit the hot charcoal on top. Fill the pot with the remaining banana-leaf strips.

Stand the pot on a charcoal fire or over a medium heat on the stovetop. Cook for 45 minutes.

Remove the pot from the heat and let stand for 10 minutes. During this time, the ingredients in the pot will continue to roast and absorb some of the smoky flavour imparted by the hot charcoal.

Remove the leaves from the pot and discard the charcoal. Transfer the food to a serving dish and serve hot – remind your guests to shell the eggs before eating!

Fried Cauliflower & Okra ›

Phool Gobi Bhindi Bejule

SERVES 4

Serve this vegetable dish with steamed rice and Appam (see page 240) for a wonderful light lunch. It's a treat for the senses.

1 tablespoon ground turmeric
2 teaspoons Red Masala Paste (see page 329)
2 teaspoons salt
1 tablespoon rice flour
800 g small okra
400 g cauliflower florets
vegetable oil, for deep-frying
1 teaspoon brown mustard seeds
5 small green chillies, sliced
2 onions, finely diced
100 g thick plain yoghurt
2 tablespoons curry leaves

Combine the turmeric, masala paste, salt and rice flour. Add enough water to make a thin batter and toss the okra and cauliflower through until coated.

Heat the oil in a kadhai or wok to 180°C. To test the temperature of the oil, sprinkle in some flour – if the flour sizzles, it is ready. Deep-fry the vegetables in small batches for 2 minutes until crisp and golden. Drain on paper towel.

Heat 100 ml vegetable oil in a frying pan and fry the mustard seeds and chilli over a medium heat until the seeds pop. Add the onion and cook, stirring, until translucent. Add the yoghurt and fried vegetables. Check the seasoning and adjust if necessary.

Stir through the curry leaves to serve.

‹ Stuffed Eggplants
Bharleli Vanghi
SERVES 4

Another winning way with eggplants from Konkan Cafe in Mumbai.

2 onions, finely diced
1 teaspoon chilli powder
1 teaspoon salt
2 tablespoons shaved jaggery
½ cup (125 ml) thick Tamarind Liquid
    (see page 379)
2 teaspoons ground roasted peanuts
500 g small round eggplants (aubergines)
100 ml vegetable oil
½ teaspoon ground turmeric

COCONUT ONION PASTE
2 tablespoons vegetable oil
1 onion, finely sliced
70 g grated fresh coconut,
    lightly toasted

GARLIC PEPPER PASTE
1 tablespoon vegetable oil
5 cloves garlic
5 black peppercorns
1 cm piece cinnamon stick
3 cloves
2 teaspoons coriander seeds
1 teaspoon anise seeds

To make the coconut onion paste, heat the oil and fry the onion over a high heat until translucent. Add the coconut and fry until browned. Cool, then grind to a smooth paste.

To make the garlic pepper paste, heat the oil and fry the remaining ingredients together over a medium heat for 3–4 minutes until fragrant. Cool, then grind until smooth.

Mix the diced onion with both pastes, then add the chilli powder, salt, jaggery and tamarind liquid. Mix well, then stir through the ground peanuts.

Wash and dry the eggplants. Slit each eggplant once through and then again to make four separate equal parts, leaving the eggplants intact near the stem. Soak each split eggplant in a bowl of salted water for 10 minutes. Dry with paper towel, then stuff each eggplant with the spiced onion mixture and set aside.

Heat the oil in a large frying pan. Add the turmeric and stir. Arrange the eggplants evenly in the pan in a single layer, stems facing up. Add 100 ml water, then cover and cook the eggplants over a medium heat for 25–30 minutes, turning them halfway through, until tender. Add more water if the pan dries out too much, but all the liquid should have been absorbed by the end of the cooking. Serve hot.

Mashed Eggplant
Baigan Bharta
SERVES 4

Along with a plethora of other dishes, this typical Maharashtrian preparation is served as a condiment for lunch at Gypsy Corner, a typical vegetarian restaurant in north Mumbai. The readily available large purple eggplant is fine for this, but if you can get a silky eggplant (with the mauve and white striped skin), it is better as it has very few seeds, tastes less bitter and has a smoother texture.

2 teaspoons vegetable oil
1 × 300 g eggplant (aubergine)
1 large onion, finely diced
3 small green chillies, minced
2 tablespoons chopped coriander leaves
3 tablespoons grated fresh coconut
140 g curd (drained yoghurt)
salt, to taste

Rub the oil over the skin of the eggplant and cook it over a direct flame or coals until the skin is blistered and black, about 10 minutes. When it is cool enough to handle, remove the charred skin using your fingers. Roughly mash the flesh and combine with the remaining ingredients. Serve.

Pomfret with Turmeric Leaves

Haldi Panatahli Papplet

SERVES 4

This was one of my favourite dishes on the menu at Ankur seafood restaurant in the Fort district. The masala paste and the gravy can be made ahead of time and refrigerated, which makes the final cooking much quicker and more straightforward. If pomfret is not available, you could use kingfish, mulloway or bonito.

½ teaspoon ground turmeric
½ teaspoon salt
1 tablespoon lime juice
4 × 125 g pomfret fillets
4 turmeric leaves or banana leaves

GREEN MASALA
½ bunch coriander, chopped
3 small green chillies, chopped
1 clove garlic, sliced
1 tablespoon thick Tamarind Liquid
  (see page 379)
1 teaspoon ground turmeric
½ teaspoon salt
1 tablespoon vegetable oil
1 onion, finely diced
2 tomatoes, diced

COCONUT GRAVY
2 tablespoons vegetable oil
4 long dried red chillies, broken into pieces
1 teaspoon coriander seeds
2 tablespoons grated fresh coconut,
  lightly roasted
1 teaspoon cumin seeds
½ teaspoon black peppercorns
½ teaspoon white poppy seeds
½ teaspoon brown mustard seeds
2 teaspoons curry leaves
1 tablespoon chopped mint leaves
2 tablespoons thick Tamarind Liquid
  (see page 379)

Combine the turmeric, salt and lime juice and rub over the fish fillets. Set aside.

To make the green masala, blend the coriander, chilli, garlic, tamarind liquid, turmeric and salt to make a smooth paste.

Heat the oil in a frying pan and fry the onion over a medium heat until translucent. Add the tomato and cook for 5 minutes until it starts to break down. Add the masala paste and cook over a low heat until the flavours develop and the mixture no longer tastes raw, about 25 minutes. Remove from the heat and allow to cool to room temperature.

Rub the green masala over the fish as its second marinade, then wrap each fillet in a turmeric or banana leaf, resting it on the join to secure.

To make the coconut gravy, heat half the oil in a frying pan and fry the chilli, coriander seeds, coconut, cumin, peppercorns and poppy seeds over a medium heat for a few minutes until fragrant. Cool, then blend to a smooth paste. Heat the remaining oil and fry the mustard seeds and curry leaves over a medium heat until the seeds pop. Stir in the mint and the coconut paste, then add the tamarind liquid and simmer for 2 minutes. Taste and adjust the seasoning if necessary.

Lay the fish parcels in a single layer on a plate in a large steamer. Cover and steam for 6–8 minutes, depending on the thickness of the fish. Unwrap and slide each fillet onto a plate. Spoon the hot coconut gravy over to serve.

‹ Prawns Koliwada

SERVES 4

This dish is named for a specific fishing area in central Mumbai waters where the Sikhs, renowned as enterprising restaurateurs and genial hosts, have their off-the-pavement restaurants. It was the Sikhs who popularised the Koliwada cooking style, named after the local Koli fishing communities, in which spices are mixed with butter and used for frying seafood.

1 tablespoon Ginger Garlic Paste
   (see page 377)
½ teaspoon chilli powder
½ teaspoon ground turmeric
pinch of asafoetida
1 teaspoon salt
2 tablespoons cornflour
500 g harbour or school prawns,
   peeled and deveined
vegetable oil, for deep-frying

MINT CHUTNEY
100 g mint leaves
75 g coriander leaves
2 tablespoons lemon juice
1 small green chilli, minced
2 teaspoons minced ginger
5 tablespoons thick plain yoghurt
2 red shallots, finely diced
2 teaspoons Chat Masala (see page 376)
½ teaspoon salt
pinch of chilli powder

To make the mint chutney, blend the mint, coriander, lemon juice, chilli and ginger to make a smooth paste. Stir in the yoghurt, shallot, chat masala, salt and chilli powder. Refrigerate until ready to serve.

Combine the ginger garlic paste, ground spices, salt and cornflour in a bowl with just enough water to make a paste. Add the prawns and toss until well coated.

Heat the oil in a wok or kadhai. Add the prawns and deep fry for 3 minutes until just cooked. The spice coating should become slightly crisp. Serve with the mint chutney and Paratha (see page 351).

Tomato Mutton

SERVES 6

A Maharashtrian Hindu recipe handed down to Jamshyd by Radha, a family friend. At our request, the house cook prepared it one night for dinner at the beach house after we had purchased some fresh goat meat from the village butcher.

2 tablespoons vegetable oil
2 bay leaves
4 cloves
4 green cardamom pods, cracked
500 g red onions, finely sliced
8 cloves garlic, minced
2 teaspoons minced ginger
500 g mutton or goat, diced
2 teaspoons salt
2 tablespoons chopped coriander leaves

TOMATO GRAVY
2 tablespoons vegetable oil
4 cloves
1 green cardamom pod, cracked
500 g ripe tomatoes, quartered

To make the tomato gravy, heat the oil and fry the cloves and cardamom over a medium heat for a minute until fragrant. Add the tomato and cook over a low heat, covered, for 30 minutes until the tomato has broken down and the mixture is thick and sauce-like. Pass it through a strainer and discard the seeds. Set aside.

Heat the oil in a large frying pan and fry the bay leaves, cloves and cardamom over a medium heat until fragrant, about 1 minute. Add the onion and cook for a few minutes until starting to soften, then add the garlic and ginger. Cook over a low heat, covered, for 10 minutes. When the onion turns pale pink, add the mutton or goat and stir to combine. Cover and cook for 10 minutes.

Add the tomato gravy and the salt, then cover and simmer for 40 minutes until the mutton is cooked and tender. Check the seasoning and adjust if necessary. Stir through the fresh coriander to serve.

Abdul's Lamb Biryani

The recipe for this Bori Muslim biryani was given to Jamshyd several years ago by his old mate Abdul, and Jamshyd in turn shared it with me. It is cooked in the dum style and is drier in texture, with more subtle spicing than a Mappila or Mughal biryani, and the garam masala blend is different. But like any biryani, it's perfect for a family feast. In Mumbai, I head to one of the local modest cafes in Bhuleshwar, the Bori Muslim enclave, when I want to eat this.

10 dried red chillies, seeded
2 tablespoons minced ginger
10 cloves garlic
3 tablespoons vegetable oil
3 onions, finely diced
4 ripe tomatoes, chopped
1 tablespoon cumin seeds
1 kg lamb shoulder, diced
3 small green chillies, minced
5 small potatoes, peeled and quartered
280 g curd (drained yoghurt)
1 tablespoon coriander seeds
2 teaspoons garam masala
3 green cardamom pods, cracked
1 cm piece cinnamon stick
7 cloves
750 g basmati rice
1 teaspoon freshly ground black pepper
1 bay leaf
225 g plain flour
2 tablespoons melted ghee
2 tablespoons chopped mint leaves
1 tablespoon chopped coriander leaves
6 small red onions, finely sliced
   and fried until crisp

Soak the dried chillies in hot water for 30 minutes, then drain and grind. Grind the ginger and garlic together to make a fine paste.

Heat the oil in a large, heavy-based saucepan and fry the onion over a high heat until softened, then add the tomato and cook for 10 minutes. Add the cumin seeds and cook for 5 minutes until fragrant. Stir in the ground chilli, ginger garlic paste and the lamb. Add enough water to cover the meat, then cover and cook over a low heat for 1 hour until the meat is tender.

Add the green chilli, potato and curd and stir to combine. Stir in the coriander seeds, garam masala, cardamom, cinnamon and four of the cloves.

Put the rice in a separate saucepan with enough water to just cover it. Add the pepper, bay leaf and remaining cloves. Cover and cook over a medium heat until the rice is half-cooked and the water has been absorbed, about 12 minutes.

To make the dough to seal the pot, mix the flour and ¾ cup (180 ml) water in a bowl to a workable dough. If it is too dry, add a little extra flour; if too wet, add a little extra water.

Spread the ghee over the base of a flameproof baking dish with a lid. Spoon in one-third of the rice. Mix the mint and coriander into the meat mixture with two-thirds of the fried onions. Add half the meat mixture to the dish, spreading it evenly over the rice. Add half the remaining rice, then the remaining meat mixture. Spread over the remaining rice. Cover the rice with a damp cloth (this retains moisture and humidity during the final cooking), then put on the lid. Roll out the dough on a lightly floured surface and shape into a sausage that is long enough to wrap around the top edge of the dish. Wrap the dough around the join and press firmly to seal the dish completely.

Cook over a very low heat for 45 minutes. During this time the rice will cook completely and the spicy meat flavours will infuse the rice.

Sprinkle over the remaining fried onions and serve.

Mousie's Prawn Kebabs

SERVES 4

A Nandgaon beach-house treat prepared by Mousie, the senior house cook, as a late-afternoon snack while we sat under the swaying coconut palms, glasses of wine in hand, and watched the sun set over the sea.

2 slices white bread, crusts removed
1 green onion, chopped
1 teaspoon minced ginger
1 small clove garlic, minced
2 small green chillies, minced
½ teaspoon ground cumin
1 kg small (harbour or school) prawns, peeled and deveined
1 tablespoon salt
3 tablespoons chopped coriander leaves
1 tablespoon lime juice
fine dry breadcrumbs, to coat
100 ml vegetable oil

Soak the bread in water to soften, then drain and squeeze out any excess liquid.

Grind the onion, ginger, garlic, chilli and cumin until smooth.

Wash the prawns and roughly chop. Mix with the ginger paste, salt, fresh coriander, lime juice and soaked bread. Roll the mixture into small balls and coat with the breadcrumbs.

Heat the oil in a frying pan and fry the kebabs over a high heat until golden, about 3–4 minutes. Drain on paper towel and serve.

Meat & Potatoes

Ras Chawal

SERVES 4

A treasured family recipe that Jamshyd gave me from his mother's personal notebook. According to her notes, the dish is reputed to have therapeutic healing qualities and is customarily cooked for someone who is convalescing.

250 g potatoes, peeled
3 tablespoons vegetable oil
1 onion, finely diced
1 tablespoon chopped ginger
6–8 cloves garlic
500 g mutton, lamb or chicken, diced
2 teaspoons cumin seeds, lightly ground
4 cloves
2 cm piece cinnamon stick
2 long dried red chillies, seeded and lightly crushed
2 small tomatoes, chopped
2 teaspoons salt

Cut the potatoes into cubes the same size as the meat.

Heat the oil in a large saucepan and fry the onion over a medium heat until translucent. Blend the ginger and garlic to make a smooth paste, then add to the onion and cook for a few minutes until the onion has softened and is starting to colour. Add the meat, spices and chillies and stir to coat. Cook for a few minutes until the meat is browned.

Add the potato and fry for a few minutes until it starts to brown. (It is important for the flavour that the meat and potato are browned at this stage of the cooking.) Add the tomato and cook for 5 minutes, then add enough water to cover. Add the salt and cook over a low heat for 40 minutes or until the meat is tender.

Taste and adjust the seasoning if necessary. Serve hot with steamed rice.

Masala Chicken with Apricots & Fried Potato Straws

Sali jerdaloo Ma Gosht Murghi

SERVES 4

A well-known Parsi dish that I have tasted at various Irani restaurants in Mumbai. This home-cooked version comes from Jamshyd's repertoire, and it's even better. Its sweet, sour and savoury flavours make it a great lunchtime dish served with chapatis. According to many Indian cooks I have spoken to, the secret to a good curry (gravy), lies in the slicing and frying of the onion and spices to make a good base.

1 teaspoon ground turmeric
2 teaspoons chilli powder
¼ teaspoon ground cardamom
2 teaspoons ground cumin
2 tablespoons vegetable oil
4 chicken marylands (leg and thigh portions), cut into leg and thigh joints
80 g ghee
3 onions, finely sliced
2 bay leaves
2 cm piece cinnamon stick
seeds from 1 black cardamom pod
1 teaspoon cumin seeds
2 dried red chillies
5 cloves
1 tablespoon Ginger Garlic Paste (see page 377)
3 small green chillies, finely sliced
2 tomatoes, finely diced
1 cup (250 ml) White Chicken Stock (see page 380) or water
2 teaspoons salt
600 g dried apricots, rinsed
3 tablespoons malt vinegar
1 tablespoon white sugar

FRIED POTATO STRAWS
250 g ghee
500 g potatoes, peeled and cut into thin matchsticks, then rinsed and soaked in iced water

To make the fried potato straws, drain and dry the potato matchsticks. Heat the ghee in a frying pan and fry the potato over a high heat until golden and crisp. Remove from the pan with a slotted spoon and drain on paper towel. Set aside.

Mix the ground spices with the vegetable oil and rub into the chicken until coated. Leave to marinate for 30 minutes.

Heat the ghee in a large saucepan and fry the onion, bay leaves and whole spices over a high heat until the onion is starting to brown. Add ½ cup (125 ml) water and simmer until the onion is mushy and soft and the water has evaporated, about 15 minutes. Add the ginger garlic paste and green chilli, stirring to combine. Cook for 1 minute, then add the spiced chicken and fry on both sides until brown, about 8 minutes. Add the tomato, stock or water and salt, stirring to combine. Bring to a boil, then reduce the heat to low, cover and simmer for 15 minutes.

Add the apricots, vinegar and sugar and stir to combine. Simmer for 20 minutes or until the chicken is tender. The sauce should be reduced and thick by this stage. Taste and adjust the seasoning if required.

Transfer to a serving dish or plates and cover with the fried potato straws. Serve with Roti (see page 103) or Chapati (see page 85) and a cooling raita.

Spinach in Buttermilk

SERVES 4

This simple and delicious way to prepare spinach is a typical Hindu vegetarian dish to serve with dal and steamed rice. I also like to make it with silverbeet or rainbow chard, as the leaves have a lovely texture.

leaves from 1 bunch spinach, chopped
300 ml buttermilk
2 tablespoons chickpea (gram) flour
2 tablespoons vegetable oil
4–5 cloves garlic, finely chopped
3 small green chillies, minced
1 tablespoon cumin seeds

Heat a large saucepan, then add the spinach and 1 tablespoon water. Cover and cook over a medium heat for 2 minutes until the spinach is wilted and soft. Combine the buttermilk and flour to make a paste, then stir into the spinach until combined.

Heat the oil in a frying pan and fry the garlic, chilli and cumin seeds over a medium heat until the seeds pop. Pour the garlic mixture over the spinach and stir to combine. Serve.

Fried Chicken Kasaijor

SERVES 4

From the menu at Konkan Cafe in Mumbai, this is one of the best fried-chicken dishes imaginable. Forget those lacklustre fast-food imitations – this is what I call finger-licking-good chicken! Try it and see for yourself.

4 tablespoons Taleli Masala (see page 357)
2½ tablespoons lime juice
100 g Ginger Garlic Paste (see page 377)
800 g chicken breast fillets, cut into
    long thin strips
200 g rice flour
1 teaspoon ground turmeric
1 teaspoon salt
vegetable oil, for frying
1 teaspoon brown mustard seeds
2 tablespoons curry leaves
8 small green chillies, sliced
500 g thick plain yoghurt
1 teaspoon freshly ground black pepper

Combine the taleli masala, lime juice and ginger garlic paste in a bowl. Add the chicken and mix to coat. Leave to marinate for 30 minutes.

Combine the rice flour, turmeric and salt and add enough water to make a thick batter. Add the marinated chicken and toss to coat.

Heat 150 ml oil in a kadhai or deep-fryer to 180°C. To test the temperature of the oil, sprinkle in some flour – if the flour sizzles, it is ready. Deep-fry the chicken in small batches for 4 minutes until golden. Remove from the oil using a slotted spoon and drain on paper towel.

Heat 2 teaspoons oil and fry the mustard seeds, curry leaves and chilli over a medium heat until the seeds start to pop. Remove from the heat, then stir in the yoghurt and pepper. Toss the chicken through the yoghurt and serve.

Parsi Prawn Kebabs

We were served these as a starter to our dhan sakh feast while we listened to Jamshyd reminisce about his Parsi heritage and its rich food traditions. Richness in every mouthful, and the ideal precursor to what was to follow.

500 g small raw prawns,
    peeled and deveined
3 tablespoons Deep-fried Onion Slices
    (see page 377)
3 small green chillies, minced
2 tablespoons minced garlic
1 teaspoon ground turmeric
1 teaspoon chilli powder
1 tablespoon Dhan Sakh Masala
    (see page 346)
½ teaspoon ground cumin
½ teaspoon ground coriander
1 tablespoon lime juice
1 teaspoon salt
1 egg, beaten
120 ml vegetable oil
lime wedges, to serve

Coarsely chop the prawns. Combine thoroughly in a bowl with the remaining ingredients, except the oil and lime wedges. Roll the prawn mixture into small balls and flatten slightly.

Heat the oil in a frying pan and shallow-fry the prawn kebabs in batches over a high heat for 2 minutes. Turn over the kebabs and fry the other side for 1–2 minutes until golden. Remove from the pan with a slotted spoon and drain on paper towel.

Serve hot with lime wedges.

Sweet Coconut Dumplings
Modak
MAKES 20

My guide Sarika explained how she made these Maharashtrian steamed dessert dumplings. They are prepared as an offering to celebrate the start of the Ganesh festival (Ganesha Chaturthi) every September, an important and auspicious date of the Hindu calendar. Sometimes dried fruit (such as peaches, apricots and raisins) are added to the filling.

½ teaspoon salt
150 g rice flour
melted ghee

COCONUT FILLING
140 g shredded fresh coconut
½ cup (125 ml) full-cream milk
200 g shaved jaggery
2 tablespoons unsalted pistachios, chopped
2 tablespoons unsalted cashews, chopped
pinch of ground cardamom

To make the coconut filling, combine the coconut, milk and jaggery in a saucepan and cook over a low heat for 4–5 minutes, stirring continuously to prevent burning. Stir in the pistachios and cashews and cook for another minute. Add the cardamom, remove from the heat and allow to cool.

Bring 1 cup (250 ml) water and the salt to boiling point in a saucepan. Whisk in the rice flour and 1 teaspoon melted ghee until the mixture is smooth and all lumps have disappeared. Reduce the heat to low and cover the pan. Cook for 10 minutes, then remove the lid and stir for a few minutes until the dough is glossy.

Tip the dough onto your workbench. Moisten your hands with a little melted ghee and knead the dough until it is dry (but not too dry) and not sticky. Form into a ball, then roll into a cylinder shape. Cut into 20 pieces. Press each piece to flatten into a cup shape with a hollow in the centre.

Lightly oil a baking tray. Put 1 teaspoon coconut filling into each dough cup, then fold the dough over to make a peak at the top and press the edges to seal. Pinch together so the dumpling resembles a head of garlic. Stand the prepared dumplings on the baking tray. Steam the dumplings in batches over simmering water until cooked.

Serve drizzled with melted ghee.

Mango Lassi
SERVES 2

We had this drink as a sundowner each afternoon at the Nandgaon beach house, celebrating the start of the Alphonso mango season. Lassi is cooling and refreshing and aids digestion. Make sure it's served icy cold.

2 ripe mangoes, peeled and diced
thick plain yoghurt
½ teaspoon Chat Masala (see page 376)

Make sure the mango and yoghurt are both very cold. Blend the mango with an equal amount of yoghurt and a little ice until smooth.

Pour into tall glasses, sprinkle with the chat masala and serve immediately.

Sweet Flatbread
Puran Poli
MAKES 20

This sweetmeat is a Maharashtrian favourite, made for the Diwali festival celebrations. The recipe was given to me by Sarika, one of my city guides.

300 g plain flour
vegetable oil
melted ghee, to serve

CHANNA JAGGERY PASTE
400 g channa dal, soaked for 4 hours
400 g shaved jaggery (or to taste)
1 teaspoon ground cardamom
¼ teaspoon ground saffron threads
¼ teaspoon grated nutmeg

To make the channa jaggery paste, cook the dal in boiling water until soft. Drain well (the dal needs to be absolutely dry) and return to the pan. Add the jaggery and cook over a medium heat until it has completely dissolved, stirring so it doesn't burn. Mash into a soft paste. Add the cardamom, saffron and nutmeg and mix well. Form into 20 balls of equal size and set aside.

Mix the flour, turmeric, 3 tablespoons oil and ¾ cup (180 ml) water to make a very soft, sticky dough. Knead well, using extra oil as necessary, until smooth. Divide into 20 equal portions.

Grease the palms of your hands with a little oil, then take one portion of dough and flatten it into a disc the size of your palm. Place a ball of channa jaggery paste in the centre, then fold in the disc from all sides to cover the paste completely. Repeat with the remaining dough and paste.

On a sheet of plastic film or a well-floured board, gently roll out each poli to a 15 cm disc that is 2 cm thick. This can get tricky as the paste will try to slide out, so sprinkle lightly with flour as you roll.

Heat a grill plate or tawa pan to hot. Cook each poli on both sides until golden, about 2–3 minutes each side. Do not use oil or ghee.

To serve, smear both sides with melted ghee. Serve warm with extra ghee or a bowl of milk.

Jalebi ›
MAKES 30

One of India's most recognised sweet treats, jalebi can be found all over the country. Some versions are better than others. The ones made for us at Konkan Cafe in Mumbai were the best I have ever tasted – not too sickly sweet and without the iridescent fake orange colour used by some cooks.

½ teaspoon saffron threads
300 g plain flour
1½ tablespoons fine semolina or rice flour
¼ teaspoon baking powder
2 tablespoons curd (drained yogurt)
660 g caster sugar
½ teaspoon ground cardamom
1½ tablespoons rosewater
ghee or vegetable oil, for frying

Gently dry-roast the saffron threads in a small frying pan. Cool, then grind to a powder.

Combine the plain flour, semolina or rice flour, baking powder, curd and 180 ml warm water in a bowl (preferably a ceramic bowl). Whisk well, then add 120 ml warm water and ⅛ teaspoon of the saffron powder and whisk until smooth. Set aside for about 2 hours to ferment.

To make the syrup, dissolve the sugar in 800 ml water over a high heat. Simmer for 5 minutes, then add the cardamom and remaining saffron. Cook for 2 minutes, then add the rosewater and turn off the heat.

When you are ready to cook the jalebi, whisk the batter thoroughly. Heat the oil in a kadhai or wok to 160°C. To test the temperature of the oil, sprinkle in some flour – if the flour sizzles, it is ready. Pour in the batter in a steady stream (or through a coconut shell with a hole) to form coils. Make a few at a time. Deep-fry for 2–3 minutes until golden and crisp all over, but not brown. Remove with a slotted spoon and drain on paper towel, then immerse in the syrup for at least 4–5 minutes so the jalebi soak it up. Remove from the syrup and serve hot.

INGREDIENTS & EQUIPMENT

Agar Agar

Used to make jellies and milk-based sweets, this flavourless setting gel is made from seaweed extract and is sold as flakes or powder. Suitable for vegetarian food, it creates a more brittle, firmer texture than gelatine.

Ajwain

These tiny seeds are related to cumin, caraway, parsley and dill. They have a similar fragrance to cumin, but with a more intense and assertive flavour that resembles thyme with liquorice overtones. Used whole to flavour breads, lentils and pulses, ajwain is popular in North Indian cooking, particularly with root vegetables and fried snacks. Available from Indian food stores.

Amchur

Made from dried green (under-ripe) mangoes, this tangy powder is used as a souring agent and flavouring that gives balance and provides acidity without adding moisture. It is used extensively in Indian pickles and vegetable dishes. Added to hot oil at the beginning of the cooking process, amchur powder gives a deep taste; when added at the end of cooking, a more subtle flavour results. Available from Indian food stores.

Anise Seeds

These oval seeds (also known as aniseed) come from a herb closely related to cumin and fennel and have a bittersweet flavour with a hint of liquorice. The seeds are used whole in soups, stews and curries and are ground for use in cakes, biscuits and sweets. Available from gourmet food stores and specialist spice suppliers.

Asafoetida

Made from the resinous sap of a large fennel-like plant, asafoetida is sold in either powdered form or as a resin that is ground as required. It has a characteristic pungent, sulphuric smell and an unappealing taste when raw, but when cooked it counter-balances acidity and combats flatulence. Available from Indian food stores.

Bamboo Shoots

There are many bamboo forests in the mountains of India and, like the coconut, the plant has many valuable uses. The shoots are a common vegetable across Asia: the smaller winter shoots are best to use, and they must be cooked; they have a pleasing, crunchy texture and a mild taste. Look for fresh bamboo shoots in Asian grocers and markets.

Banana Flowers

These reddish-purple bud-like flowers have a mildly bitter taste that's refreshing in salads and other light dishes. To prepare them, peel away the outer leaves and shake out the bitter stamens. Shred the pale inner leaves, plunging them into cold acidulated water straight away to prevent blackening.

Basil Seeds

The tiny black seeds from the lemon basil plant are used primarily in Asian sweet drinks and desserts. They have an oily, slightly pungent flavour, and are usually soaked in water for 15 minutes before use, during which time they develop a gelatinous coating. Available from Asian food stores.

Bitter Gourd

With its distinctive bright green wrinkled skin, this vegetable is one of India's most ancient and is considered a delicacy. Bitter gourd (also known as bitter melon) aids digestion, and certainly no Bengali or Punjabi meal would be complete without its appearance on the table. A brief blanching in salted water removes some of the bitterness, and the flavour mellows further with cooking.

Black Cardamom

Sometimes referred to as 'greater' or 'brown' cardamom in Indian texts, this has a larger pod, coarser seeds and a more antiseptic, harsher flavour than green cardamom. Used only in savoury cooking, the seeds act as a tenderiser in meat marinades when lightly crushed and are also used in some garam masala mixes and to flavour rice biryanis. They are available from Indian food stores and specialist spice suppliers.

Black Cumin Seeds

Grown in North India's high mountains and sometimes called royal cumin, these seeds (*shahi jeera*) are slightly smaller and finer, with a dark-brown to black colour and a sweeter flavour than regular cumin. They are used specifically in the cooking of Kashmir, Iran and Pakistan. Available from Indian food stores and specialist spice suppliers.

Black Salt

Used in North Indian cooking, particularly in street snacks, drinks and salads, black salt (*kala namak*) has a mild but interesting flavour and smells more pungent than it tastes. Volcanic in origin, it is mined in quarries on the fertile plains of central India. Sometimes sold as rock salt, the amber to dark-brown crystals become a smoky grey when ground. Available in crystal or powder form at Indian food stores.

Black Sesame Seeds

The flavour of black sesame seeds is slightly stronger and earthier than that of the more common white ones. Used raw or lightly roasted in cooking, they are an important ingredient in deity worship in Hindu temples and in Ayurvedic medicine. Available from Asian grocers.

Black Urad Lentils

see Urad Lentils

Boondi

A popular fried Indian snack made with chickpea (gram) flour and cashews, and usually seasoned with fenugreek or cardamom. The dough is rolled into small balls, which are fried in oil. They can then be added to a raita for texture, or soaked in a sugar syrup (sometimes flavoured with rosewater) to make sweet boondi laddu. Boondi are readily available in packets at Indian grocers.

Buttermilk

Traditionally a by-product of churning butter, buttermilk is made commercially by adding cultures to milk. In Indian cooking, it is used to add a tangy note to sauces and curries; in some regions of India, buttermilk is another name for lassi (a yoghurt-based drink).

Cardamom

see Black Cardamom; Green Cardamom

Cashew Paste

This is made by blending raw cashews with an equal volume of water in a food processor to make a thick, smooth paste, and is used for thickening curries and gravies.

Cassia Bark

Cassia bark (*dalchini*) comes from a camphor laurel native to Assam in north-eastern India and to Burma. It is used in a similar fashion to cinnamon, and is often confusingly referred to as Chinese cinnamon. Much harder and coarser than cinnamon, however, cassia has a more pronounced pungency and an intriguing flavour. If a recipe calls for ground cassia, it is best to buy a small quantity already ground, as the tough bark will damage domestic spice grinders.

Channa Dal

One of the most popular of Indian dals, this is made from split black chickpeas (*kala channa*) and is available from Indian grocers. Yellow split peas can be used instead, but will need longer cooking.

Chat Masala

Chat is an Indian term for appetisers or small morsels eaten as a snack, so it follows that this spice mix is used to flavour fried pastries and various potato dishes, as well as tomato-based preparations. Its raw spiciness and tart flavour mean it is best suited to fruit or vegetables – it works wonders when added to cooked root vegetables, accentuating their rich, earthy flavour.

    1 teaspoon black peppercorns
    1 teaspoon cumin seeds
    ½ teaspoon ajwain seeds
    3 cubeb peppercorns
    1–2 teaspoon dried
        pomegranate seeds
    seeds from 3 green cardamom pods
    1 teaspoon ground black salt
    1 teaspoon amchur
    1 teaspoon ground ginger
    ¼ teaspoon asafoetida
    1 teaspoon chilli powder

Grind the whole spices to a fine powder, then stir in remaining spices. Store in a sealed jar. Makes 2½ tablespoons.

Chickpea (Gram) Flour

Known as besan or gram flour in India, this finely milled flour is made from roasted channa dal and is pale yellow in colour. It is used to make pakoras, bhaji and sweets, and to thicken gravies and sauces. Available at Indian and health-food stores.

Chilli

Chilli varieties are specific to regions throughout the country and there are innumerable types, shapes, sizes, flavours and levels of heat.

Kashmiri chillies are among the most widely used. They are an intensely coloured, deep-red chilli with a soft pungency and mild flavour.

Goan chillies tend to be quite small and round, with a spicy, hot flavour – and they are usually cooked when green.

Degi chillies are red, finger-length chillies with a fat body (not unlike a jalapeno) and a mild flavour; they are often stuffed with a masala paste before being roasted or fried.

Chilli Paste

This is made by grinding red chillies to a fine paste, which is then usually cooked in a little oil for 20 minutes to soften its sharp flavour. The heat level is determined by the type of chillies used.

Chilli Powder

This is simply sun-dried chillies ground to a fine powder, with the flavour profile being determined by the type of chilli used. One of the most widely used in Indian cuisine is Kashmiri chilli powder – made from the highly regarded long red Kashmiri chilli, this has a gentle, rounded heat with a sweet note. Chilli powder made with smaller chillies tends to have a higher heat level, so taste before you cook and add according to your own palate.

Cluster Beans

Also known as guar beans, these grow in clusters (hence the name); while the pods are eaten, the leaves and stems are used to feed cattle. Originally from Africa, they were introduced to India by Arab traders, and are now used in Gujarati and Konkan cooking. They are not generally available outside India, but green beans, snake beans or flat roman beans can be substituted.

Coconut

The fresh fruit of the coconut palm has diverse uses. The firm white flesh of the mature brown-shelled coconut can be sliced, shredded or grated and used fresh. Conveniently, shredded or desiccated coconut is also dried and sold in packets, and is widely available. Young coconut is the immature fruit, with a softer green husk and gelatinous flesh inside that is easy to spoon out. The coconut water or juice that is found inside coconuts is one of nature's healthiest drinks.

To shred fresh coconut, crack the coconut in half with a cleaver over a bowl to catch the water (this can be drunk or added to salad dressings or sauces for flavour), then use a zester to shred the firm coconut flesh. It is best used fresh, but will keep for 2 days refrigerated.

To grate fresh coconut, crack the coconut in the same way, then grate the flesh using a coconut grater (a contraption that can be fitted onto a benchtop with a hand-cranked spindle), turning the coconut around as you go, so the flesh is grated evenly. Alternatively, run a zester across the flesh of each coconut half or prise chunks of the flesh from the shell and grate each piece using a box grater, avoiding the brown skin.

Coconut Milk & Coconut Cream

To make coconut milk, put grated coconut flesh with an equal volume of hot water in a food processor and blend for a minute. Usually a coconut will yield about 2 cups (500 ml) coconut milk and 1 cup (250 ml) coconut cream. Line a sieve with a double layer of muslin cloth and place over a bowl. Tip the blended coconut into the muslin and twist the top to secure. Squeeze the muslin to extract as much coconut milk as possible. Discard the solids and use the milk the same day, otherwise it will sour.

To make coconut cream, first extract coconut milk (see above) then leave it to rest for 1 hour. The thicker cream will rise to the surface, and can be scooped off carefully with a spoon or ladle.

Prepared coconut cream and milk are available in cans and tetra packs; having been pasteurised for a longer shelf life, these have a different flavour to the fresh product but still make acceptable substitutes.

Coconut Oil

Pressed from coconut flesh, this oil is a traditional cooking medium in southern India, although some cooks are now forsaking it in favour of olive or sunflower oils. With a high smoking point, it is very heat stable and keeps well, even in tropical climates. Look for virgin coconut oil in health-food shops and Indian grocers.

Coconut Vinegar

Sourced from the sap of the coconut tree, this fragrant vinegar has low acidity and a cloudy white appearance. You'll find it at Asian food stores.

Coriander Seeds

The sweet, woody aroma and clean, orange-like flavour of coriander seeds (*dhaniya*) complement many foods and, when used with other spices, never mask their presence. If roasted ground coriander is called for, it is best to roast and grind the seeds as required, as this gives maximum flavour. Roasting intensifies the flavour: dry-roast the seeds in a heavy-based pan or skillet over a low heat until their colour darkens slightly and they become brittle. The cooled roasted seeds are then ground before being added to gravies, or used to flavour vegetables or sweets. Coriander seeds are widely available.

Cubeb Pepper

Slightly larger than a peppercorn and with a distinctive tail, the dried, dark-brown, unripe fruit of the cubeb pepper plant (*kebab chini*) has a warm, aromatic and bitter taste that is probably closer to allspice than pepper, although it is used in a similar way to pepper. Available from specialist spice suppliers.

Cumin Seeds

These small ridged, golden-brown seeds (*jeera puri*) are a staple of the Indian spice cupboard. They have a distinctive aroma and an assertive, slightly bittersweet, warm and earthy flavour. As with so many spices, dry-roasting the seeds enhances their flavour. It is best to buy the seeds whole and grind them when required, as they lose their flavour quickly when ground. Cumin seeds are widely available.

Curd (Drained Yoghurt)

Indian yoghurt – *dahi* – is thick and creamy due to its high butterfat content. In order to more closely approximate the yoghurt used in most Indian recipes, excess moisture needs to be removed to produce curd. To do this, place thick plain yoghurt (I use buffalo-milk yoghurt for its rich flavour) in a sieve lined with a double layer of muslin, then set it over a bowl in the refrigerator and leave to drain overnight. The curd will keep for several days in the fridge.

Curry Leaves

Used across India in many different dishes, curry leaves (*meetha neem*) are fragrant with a distinct spicy aroma and flavour. They are often tempered in hot oil or ghee to release their flavour or deep-fried in hot oil for 20 seconds until crisp and used as a garnish. Curry leaves are available fresh from Indian food stores and some greengrocers. The dried leaves have no flavour, so don't bother using them.
See also Fried Curry Leaves

Curry Powder

Generally referred to as masala in India, the spice blends commonly called curry powder in the West vary according to region and who makes them, but are usually composed of spices that are readily available locally. The best flavour results from the whole spices being ground on a stone slab with a stone pestle and used immediately. If buying ready-made curry powder, find a reliable spice merchant, buy it in small quantities and use it promptly.

- 1 tablespoon cumin seeds
- 2 tablespoons coriander seeds
- 1 tablespoon brown mustard seeds
- 1 teaspoon fenugreek seeds
- 1 teaspoon urad dal
- 4 small dried chillies
- 15 curry leaves
- ½ teaspoon black peppercorns
- 1 tablespoon ground turmeric

Dry-roast the cumin, coriander, mustard and fenugreek seeds with the urad dal in a cast-iron pan over low heat for 2–3 minutes until fragrant, being careful not to burn them. Allow to cool, then grind to a powder using a pestle and mortar or spice grinder.

Dal

see Channa Dal; Masoor Dal; Moong Dal; Toor Dal; Urad Dal

Deep-fried Garlic Slices

To make this garnish, finely slice garlic cloves, then deep-fry in medium–hot (170°C) oil in small batches until brown and crisp. Drain on paper towel and store in an airtight container.

Deep-fried Onion Slices

To make these, finely slice onions, then deep-fry in medium–hot (170°C) oil in small batches until brown and crisp. Drain on paper towel and store in an airtight container.

Degi Chilli

see under Chilli

Dried Mango Powder

see Amchur

Drumstick Vegetable

This long, thin, ridged green vegetable specific to India is well named: the long 'drumsticks' hang from the branches of a tall tree. An essential ingredient in the vegetarian cooking of South India and a favourite across the country, the drumstick vegetable has a woody skin, and it is best to remove the fibrous outer layer after cooking, leaving the soft, fleshy centre. Drumstick vegetable is in very limited supply outside India; green beans can be used in its place, but will need less cooking.

Fennel Seeds

The warm, sweet and intense liquorice flavour of fennel seeds mellows with dry-roasting. An essential element in many Indian spice mixes and pastes, pickles and chutneys, fennel seeds are widely available.

Fenugreek Seeds

These small, smooth, hard seeds are brownish-yellow, with a pronounced aroma not dissimilar to curry or celery, and a lingering bitter and astringent flavour. Used in Indian masala pastes, sambars and condiments, the seeds are often dry-roasted or tempered in oil, or softened in vinegar before being added to other spices to make a masala or curry. They are also used extensively in pickling solutions.
See also Kasoori Methi (Dried Fenugreek Leaf) Powder

Flour

Different grades of wheat flour are used in Indian cooking, as they are in Western cooking. Atta is a finely ground wholemeal flour used for chapatis and other breads, while maida is a refined white flour (similar to our plain flour) used for cakes and pastries. Fine-textured (gluten-free) rice flour is commonly used in the cooking of South India, for making breads, idlis, batters and desserts.
See also Chickpea (Gram) Flour; Moong Dal Flour; Urad Dal Flour

Fried Curry Leaves

To make this garnish, heat some vegetable oil to 170°C and fry fresh curry leaves in small batches for 20 seconds until their colour darkens. Remove from the oil with a slotted spoon and drain on paper towel. Store in an airtight container.

Fried Onion Paste

When this is called for, fry onions in a little oil until soft and golden, then allow to cool slightly before blending into a paste – you'll need about 1 large onion to make 2 tablespoons fried onion paste.

Garlic Paste

This is simply garlic blended with water. For each tablespoon of garlic paste required, roughly chop 2–3 garlic cloves, then blitz in a blender or small food processor, adding enough water to make a smooth paste.

Ghee

One of the essential cooking mediums of India, ghee is made by heating butter until all the moisture and milk solids have evaporated, leaving a pure, clean-tasting, clarified oil that is ideal for cooking as it has a much higher burning point than butter. It also adds great flavour, and is used for anything from vegetables, fish and meat to flatbreads, dal and sweets.

Ginger Garlic Paste

This paste is used in many Indian recipes. The amounts given below make approximately 4 tablespoons but the quantities can be increased as required.

- 10 large garlic cloves, roughly chopped
- 8–10 cm piece ginger, roughly chopped (you need 3 tablespoons chopped ginger)

Blend the chopped garlic and ginger with a little water in a food processor or pound with a mortar and pestle until you have a smooth paste.

Ginger Paste

This is ginger blended with water. For each tablespoon of ginger paste required, roughly chop a 4 cm piece of ginger, then blitz in a blender or small food processor, adding enough water to make a smooth paste.

Goan Chilli
see under Chilli

Gram Salt
To make this seasoning, dry-roast 1 tablespoon toor dal and 1 tablespoon urad dal until nutty and aromatic. When cool, use a spice grinder or mortar and pestle to grind them together with 1 tablespoon salt to a fine powder. Store in an airtight container.

Green Cardamom
The small green pods of the cardamom plant contain fragrant, sticky black seeds which, when crushed, release a strong camphor-like aroma. The seeds taste sweet and have a cooling effect on the body. Once ground, cardamom quickly loses its essential oils and flavour, so always purchase plump green pods that are closed, look fresh and are even in colour (they fade to khaki as they age), then remove and grind the seeds as you require them. Green cardamom pods are available from Indian food stores, specialist spice suppliers and most supermarkets.

Green Papaya Paste
To make this, peel and remove seeds from green papaya and chop the flesh, then puree in a blender with a little water to make a smooth paste.

Jaggery
This dark, unrefined Indian palm sugar is soft enough to shave with a knife and has a caramel flavour. Available from Asian grocers and some supermarkets.

Kadhai
This Indian cooking vessel is a bowl-shaped pan similar to a Chinese wok (which makes an ideal substitute), with a rounded bottom and two handles. Made from brass or tin, kadhais vary in size from small to extra-large and industrial strength. Available from Indian food stores and some Asian supermarkets.

Kashmiri Chilli
see under Chilli

Kashmiri Chilli Powder
see under Chilli Powder

Kasoori Methi (Dried Fenugreek Leaf) Powder
The leaves of the fenugreek plant are used fresh as a vegetable in Indian cooking and dried as a flavouring. The fresh leaves are not widely available outside Asia, but the dried and powdered form known as kasoori methi is sold in packets at Indian food stores and specialist spice suppliers.

Khoa
Also called *mawa*, this forms the basis of a wide variety of Indian sweets. It is produced by slowly reducing milk in a cast-iron pan, stirring to prevent caramelisation, until it becomes milk solids that can be shaped into balls or small pats. To approximate it, simmer condensed milk until further reduced and thickened; in some recipes, a firm ricotta can be substituted.

Kokum
Kokum is the dried rind of the purple-fleshed fruit from the kokum tree, which is native to India. A souring agent, it is most widely used in the cuisines of Gujarat, Maharashtra and Kerala. It needs to be rinsed, sliced and soaked in cold water before use. Available from Indian food stores and specialist spice suppliers.

Lentils
see Masoor Dal; Toor Dal; Urad Lentils

Lotus Root
The whole plant is used in Indian cooking – from the leaves to the root, seeds and stalks. Kashmiri lotus roots tend to be smaller and can be fried or braised with mushrooms or meat. Fresh lotus root is available at Asian grocers when it's in season (from late summer to late winter). Peel off the outer skin before slicing the root into discs.

Mace
Mace is the aril or seed-covering that encases nutmeg – it looks like a red lacy glove, but the colour fades to a dusty orange–yellow when dried. Mace has a perfumed, sweet scent and a clean, bitter flavour that is completely different from that of nutmeg. Mace is best purchased as whole arils (often referred to as blades) and ground as required for use in spice pastes and desserts. Look for mace blades in Indian or gourmet food stores.

Masoor Dal
From the cool climate of northern India, masoor or brown lentils are usually sold split (masoor dal) to reveal their reddish-orange centres. With a nutty, fresh taste and a soft texture, they do not need to be soaked before cooking, and so are quick and easy to prepare. They are often used with coconut and tomato-based gravies, and in the making of kebabs. Whole brown lentils are sometimes sprouted and used to make a more robust dal.

Melon Seeds
Only white melon seeds are used in Indian cooking. With a nutty, sweet flavour, they are roasted for snacks, sprinkled on top of halwa, or mixed with jaggery and nuts to make a sweet confection. Available from Indian food stores.

Mogro Mushrooms
This type of black mushroom is specific to India, but can be substituted with shiitake or small field mushrooms.

Moong Beans
Prolific across India, moong (mung) beans are small green beans with a chewy texture and musky aroma. They are easy to cook, as they don't need to be soaked beforehand.

Moong Dal
This is moong beans that have been split, revealing their creamy yellow insides. They make a light and very quick-cooking dal.

Moong Dal Flour
A fine flour stone-ground from moong beans and used to make savoury pancakes. Available from Indian food stores.

Moong Sprouts
Similar to regular bean sprouts, but with more texture and flavour, these are great for salads. They are available from health-food stores and some greengrocers – or you can make your own by soaking moong (mung) beans in water overnight, draining them and then keeping them in a damp cloth for about 2–3 days until they start to sprout.

Mustard Oil
This is used extensively as a cooking medium and flavouring in the regional cooking of eastern and northern India, where the mustard plant grows prolifically. It has a pungent, distinctive flavour and a deep golden colour, and is usually brought to smoking point in the pan before aromatics or spices are added, as this softens the flavour of the oil and makes it easier to digest. It should be kept refrigerated and used quickly, as it has a short shelf life. Available from health-food shops and Indian grocers.

Mustard Seeds
Pungent, hot and aromatic, with an acrid taste, mustard seeds are commonly used in Indian food as a flavouring and to thicken sauces. Yellow and brown mustard seeds are used, and both are widely available.

Neem Leaves

The edible leaves of this iconic Indian tree have a bitter flavour and are used as a seasoning for vegetables. The fresh leaves are not available outside India, but sometimes you can find dried neem leaves in powdered form at Indian grocers.

Nigella Seeds

These tiny, pungent, black seeds are nutty in flavour with a hint of pepper and poppy seed. In Indian cooking, they are added to spice pastes and blends, breads, salads and rice pilafs. Available from Indian and Asian food stores and specialist spice suppliers.

Onion Paste

To make this, chop white or brown onions and puree with a little water in a food processor or blender to make a fine paste. Onion paste needs to be cooked immediately, to prevent discolouration – it is usually fried in a little oil or ghee. *See also* Fried Onion Paste

Paneer (Fresh Cheese)

An unripened fresh cheese, paneer is ubiquitous in India. Easy to make (see page 154), it is a staple of the vegetarian diet and a valuable source of protein. It has a similar consistency to firm ricotta, but its lower water content makes it more stable for cooking.

Pistachios

Introduced into India by the Mughals, these pinkish-green nuts have become a key ingredient of many Indian sweets and pastries. For most sweets, the nuts are shelled and then ground using a small food processor or a mortar and pestle.

Pomegranate Seeds

This ancient fruit grows in the drier climates of India. The fresh seeds are combined with yoghurt to make raita, or added to sweets and desserts. To extract seeds from the fresh fruit, break it in half and squeeze until the seeds pop out – discard the white pith, which tastes extremely bitter. The dried seeds (*anardhana*) come from wild pomegranates that grow in the foothills of Kashmir and have a distinctly sour flavour; they are used in kachoris and stuffed parathas.

Poppy Seeds

see White Poppy Seeds

Puffed Rice

see under Rice

Rice

Polished rice is the correct term for what we know as white rice – the outer bran layer has been removed through milling and polishing the grains. This means it has less fibre and fewer minerals and nutrients, but is quicker to cook and easier to digest. White long-grain rice is the most widely consumed rice in India, with the fine, elongated grains of basmati rice being the most prized.

Puffed rice is made from grains that have been dried to remove all moisture, then cooked until they puff and become translucent with a fragile texture. It is used primarily for its crisp texture, and is an essential ingredient in bhel puri mix, roadside snacks and sweets. Available from health food stores, supermarkets and Indian grocers.

Himalayan red rice (patni) is a village rice of the mountains, and is used extensively across the Himalayan region. A long-grain unmilled rice, it is robust in texture with a rich nutty flavour. Available at Indian and Asian grocers and organic food stores.

Screwpine (Pandan) Essence

This fragrant extract of the pandan leaf is used to flavour rice and milk desserts – its concentrated flavour means that a few drops are all that is required.

Sesame Oil

Also known as gingelly oil or til oil in India, this is a versatile cooking medium that is also highly esteemed in Ayurvedic medicine. Look for pale-coloured, cold-pressed sesame oil – not the darker version produced from roasted sesame seeds, which is too strongly flavoured.

Sev

These crisp-fried vermicelli are made from chickpea (gram) flour. A popular snack food across India, they can be purchased in packets from Indian grocers.

Sev Puri

These crisp sev are broken into small pieces and used as to add texture to the stuffing and garnishing of bhel puri snacks.

Silver Leaf

Lucknow is home to the craft of varq (silver) smiths, who make silver leaf by pressing silver between sheets of paper and leather covers then beating it repeatedly until it is tissue thin and extremely fragile. Used as an embellishment for sweet and savoury dishes, it has no flavour or aroma. Edible silver leaf can be purchased from Indian grocers or speciality shops that stock dessert products.

Spinach Puree

To make this, blanch spinach leaves in boiling water for 30 seconds, drain and chop then puree in a blender or food processor.

Sugar Syrup

To make approximately 2 cups (500 ml) sugar syrup, bring 350 g caster sugar and 350 ml water to the boil in a saucepan and simmer for a few minutes until all the sugar crystals have dissolved. Cool and keep refrigerated until ready to use.

Tamarind Liquid

The most refined way to use tamarind is to make tamarind liquid, extracting maximum flavour without the coarse, fibrous texture of the pulp. Simmer 1 part tamarind pulp to 3 parts water for 30 minutes or so, then pass the pulp and water through a coarse-meshed or conical sieve. Discard fibre and seeds. If the tamarind liquid seems too thick or paste-like, stir in a little extra water. Refrigerate for up to 1 month.

Tamarind Pulp

Used as a souring agent, dried tamarind pulp is widely available in packets from Asian grocers and some supermarkets.

Tawa

This cast-iron griddle pan with a wooden handle is used for making flatbreads (chapati, paratha and roti) and for dry-roasting spices. Available from Indian grocers.

Thali

This term applies both to the food and the vessel on which it is served – a circular metal tray that is used as a plate. At large gatherings or in villages, disposable, eco-friendly banana leaves are used for serving thali. The small bowls that sit on the thali – katoris – are filled with different preparations, a mound of rice is placed in the centre, and pickles and condiments are spooned directly onto the thali.

Timur (Sichuan Pepper)

Sichuan pepper is used in the mountain cooking of northern India, due to its close proximity to China. Technically it is not a pepper at all but rather the berries from the prickly ash tree, which is native to the Sichuan province of western China. After picking, the reddish-brown berries are dried and the small bitter black seeds removed. To maximise its earthy flavour and tongue-tingling sensation, dry-roast Sichuan pepper before grinding. Available from Asian food stores and specialist spice suppliers.

Tomato Puree

This is a puree of ripe tomatoes that is strained to remove skin and seeds and cooked for 15–20 minutes in a little oil. Widely available in small tins, it has a milder, sweeter flavour than tomato paste, which is thicker and more concentrated. If you can only find regular tomato paste, I suggest you use half the amount.

Toor Dal

These small, soft, pale-yellow lentils are quick to cook and easy to digest, with a pleasant nutty flavour. They are often oiled to extend their shelf life, especially for export – in which case, they need to be soaked in warm water for 20 minutes, then rinsed before cooking.

Turmeric

This rhizome grows underground (like ginger and galangal), and is one of the main spices used in Indian cooking, where it adds both colour and flavour. It also plays an important role in Brahmin and Buddhist ceremonies. Fresh turmeric is available from Asian food shops, and needs to be peeled before use. Dried and powdered turmeric is widely available. The long green leaves of the turmeric plant are used for wrapping food when roasting or grilling over hot coals. They are not generally available outside Asia, but banana leaves or foil can be used instead.

Turmeric Water

To make this, place 2 tablespoons minced turmeric and 2 tablespoons water in a food processor and blend for a minute or two, then press through a fine-meshed sieve to extract as much turmeric water as possible.

Urad Dal

Urad dal is sold with the black skin still attached (for a more subtle flavour than the whole lentils) or skinned to produce a creamy white dal that cooks more quickly and has a softer texture. Skinned urad dal is used extensively in South Indian cooking to make dosa, idli and appam, and to add a nutty flavour to oil during tempering.

Urad Dal Flour

This stoneground flour made from urad dal is used to make dosa, idli and appam. Available from Indian food stores.

Urad Lentils

Also known as black gram or sabut urad, whole urad lentils are black with a strong musky flavour and a slightly gelatinous texture when cooked. They are popular all over India, from the breakfast tables of Tamil Nadu to the Punjabi dinner table.

Water Spinach

This green leafy vegetable with hollow stems is popular throughout south-east Asia and in parts of India. To prepare it, chop the leaves and stems into lengths – it requires minimal cooking and, like spinach, its volume reduces dramatically when cooked. Small spinach leaves make a good substitute.

White Chicken Stock

    1 chicken carcass
    1 x 1.5 kg free-range
        or organic chicken
    6 slices fresh ginger
    handful of green onion tops
    2 teaspoons white peppercorns,
        cracked

Wash the chicken carcass and chicken in cold water to remove any blood. Put all the ingredients in a stockpot and cover with cold water. Bring to a boil over gentle heat and simmer slowly for 2 hours, skimming frequently to remove any scum that rises to the surface. Remove the solids carefully, stripping the meat from the chicken for another use; discard all the other solids. Strain the stock through a fine-mesh sieve, then allow to cool completely. Remove any fat that rises to the surface, then transfer to airtight containers and refrigerate for up to 5 days or freeze for up to 2 months.

White Poppy Seeds

Three varieties of poppy seeds are available – the grey European version, the brown seeds from Turkey and the white seeds (kus kus) of the Indian plant. In Indian cooking, the tiny white seeds are sprinkled whole over bread, or may be ground together with other spices to thicken sauces and add a nutty flavour. They are also used for desserts and in making halwa. White poppy seeds are available from India food stores and specialist spice suppliers.

White Pumpkin

This Indian pumpkin species has white flesh and a more watery consistency than the Western varieties, with a texture more like marrow, so if you are substituting a firmer pumpkin in a recipe, you may need to slightly increase the cooking time to allow the vegetable to cook.

White Squash

This summer vegetable has pale-green skin and white flesh; zucchini can be used in its place.

DIRECTORY

For a detailed comprehensive list of recommendations of where to stay and eat throughout India, refer to my book – *A Personal Guide to India & Bhutan* (published 2015, Lantern Books). To purchase a copy, see my website christinemanfield.com

KOLKATA

Accommodation

GLENBURN PENTHOUSE

glenburnpenthouse.com
A luxury boutique hotel on the top 3 floors of Kanak Building in central Kolkata with expansive views to Victoria Memorial and the Maidan. An intimate and elegant haven with rooftop pool and deck, the 9 suites are furnished with discerning taste and contemporary sensibility and the food is classic home-style cooking.

TAJ BENGAL

taj.tajhotels.com
Opposite the Zoo in Alipore and 10 minutes from the city centre, this hotel offers excellent service. For total pampering, request one of the larger rooms or suites on the club floors. Home to Sonargaon restaurant serving authentic Bengali food, refined and perfectly executed. Don't miss the mutton kakori kebabs or the signature star anise chicken kebabs cooked in the tandoor.

RAJBARI BAWALI

therajbari.com
A former noble mansion lovingly restored to its former glory to create a classical lakeside palace replete with Italianate architecture, its graceful colonnades surrounded by farmlands. An hour's drive from Kolkata city centre, offering a glimpse of rich noble traditions amidst rural village life. The rooms are spacious, the gardens create an idyllic landscape, and the thali menu interprets authentic Bengali dishes, carefully crafted by chef Mrinalinee.

Eating

KEWPIE'S KITCHEN
2 Elgin Lane (off Heysham Road)
T: 2475 9880

kewpieskitchen.com
Rakhi Dasgupta opened this restaurant in her renovated house in 1998. Her mother wrote the definitive *Calcutta Cookbook*, and Rakhi is spreading her mother's gospel through her own cooking and classes at Kewpie's. The restaurant features typical Bengali specialities, and it's best to let the staff create a menu for you – engage with them, but make sure to try the panch phoran (Bengali 5 spice) prawns, Kewpie's tomato chutney, their mustard kasundi, *shorshe chingri* - mustard prawns and the spiced poppy seed chicken if they are on the menu.

BHOJOHORI MANNA
23A Priyanath Mullick Road (and other branches across the city)
T: (033) 2454 5922
Serving authentic food, this a lunchtime favourite with locals. The jumbo prawns in spicy gravy (*jumbo chingri malaikari*) are sensational, as is the fried bhekti fish and the *chhanar dalna* (cottage-cheese curry) and *shukto*, a vegetable staple of Bengali cuisine is a perennial favourite.

NIZAM'S
24 Hogg St, New Market
Join the queues at this city institution, the birthplace of the kathi kebab roll with chicken and egg and my favourite item on their menu. Nothing to write home about in terms of ambience, it pays to engage and enjoy the buzzy atmosphere while you watch the kitchen action as they pump out vast numbers of this popular snack to a never-ending queue of locals.

DARJEELING

Accommodation

GLENBURN ESTATE

glenburnteaestate.com
A working tea estate about a 90 minute drive from the centre of Darjeeling, the hillside plantation has 2 elegant, colonial style bungalow houses – Burra and Water Lily, each with 4 generously proportioned en-suite bedrooms offering warm hospitality. There are exceptional views of the Darjeeling Valley and Kanchenjunga mountain range when the clouds behave

- October and November considered the best time to visit. The home-cooked food makes the experience even more magical, with much of the produce coming from its kitchen garden, with a different menu each night. There's plenty to see and do during your stay, so make sure you include either a picnic lunch down by the Runjeet river at Glenburn Camp, in front of Glenburn Lodge (a log cabin) or hike down to Rung Dung river with its sandy beach, rock pools and clear mountain water. A visit to the tea factory to get some excellent tuition on the art of tea and a tea tasting with Parveez Hussain, the estate manager is mandatory.

Eating

PENANG
Laden La Road (opposite the post office)
The Nepalese thali and momos (steamed dumplings) at this modest local café are the reasons to visit.

GLENARYS
The Mall, Darjeeling
This two-storey place in the centre of the pedestrian mall serves pastries and cakes downstairs with its air of faded glory, Art Deco touches, an abundance of paper doilies in the tea house. Upstairs is more restaurant style, with Indian and local dishes on the menu, try the soup with momo dumplings. The decor is quaint and old-world charm, a little time-worn and tatty around the edges.

HIMALAYAS

Accommodation

SHAKTI HIMALAYA

shaktihimalaya.com
Shakti Himalaya invites its guests to *"share the rejuvenating effects of remote surroundings – to provide privileged access to places far removed from the noise and clutter of the modern world, where space, peace and epic landscapes provoke the imagination and nourish the soul."* Much about Shakti is intangible. It's their intention to provide you with the space to go, discover and fill in your own story. Their purpose is to take you on an adventure – softly – and help you to create memories that last forever. This is responsible tourism with a sharp focus on eco-tourism; sustainable conservation tied with a strong sense of community. For the most immersive and

pampered mountain experience, none compare to the Shakti experience and the food is spectacular.

360° LETI LODGE, KUMAON
This is an idyllic Himalayan retreat, far from the madding crowd, where contemporary design meets authentic tradition. With only 4 spacious pavilions, it offers exclusivity and privacy and where the food cooked by house chef Yeshi is truly sublime. Situated on a stunning mountain spur close to where Nepal, Tibet and India meet and with mind-blowing views of the Nanda Devi Range, this luxury lodge is one of a kind. Getting there is all part of the journey, a unique experience.

KUMAON VILLAGE HOUSES
Jwalabanj, Deora, Kana

SIKKIM VILLAGE HOUSES
Hatti Dunga, Hee and Radhu Khandu

LADAKH VILLAGE HOUSES
Stok, Nimoo, Likhir, Taru and River House

Village walks are at the heart of any Shakti experience, enabling you to enjoy the villages and rural life in remote mountain regions. Accompanied by local porters and guides, you step out of the modern world, walking between villages that are remote, and staying in sensitively renovated traditional village houses and having the most delicious food. These are among my most cherished memories of my travels in India.

VIVANTA BY TAJ DAL VIEW
Srinagar, Kashmir
vivantabytaj.com
A spectacular location set high on Kralsangri Hill with commanding views of Dal Lake and the surrounding mountains, this contemporary design hotel offers an international standard of luxury woven into the essence of Kashmiri traditions. The deluxe rooms are the way to go - expansive, warm as toast in winter – watch the snow falling over the lake and mountains from your cosy interior, then take advantage of the infinity pool, private outdoor terraces and balconies during summer.

SUKOON HOUSEBOAT
Dal Lake, Srinagar, Kashmir
sukoonkashmir.com
The most luxurious houseboat on the lake and the first eco-stylish one, a labour of love for A.B.Chapri Retreats who have meticulously restored this 5 en-suite bedroom floating residence into an essential place to stay when in Srinagar. Sukoon is moored in an enviable position on Dal

Lake and a quick shikara (water taxi) ride across from Ghat Number 19A. With its hand carved wooden interiors and inviting rooftop deck, you are afforded breathtaking vistas of the snow-capped mountains and unhurried serenity of the lake, preferably with glass of wine in hand – sunrise and sunset are particularly spectacular.

THE COTTAGE NIGEEN
Srinagar, Kashmir
thecottagenigeen.com
A family home transformed into a charmimg guesthouse with 4 en suite rooms for guests to stay and get a first-hand experience of the hospitality that Kashmir is famous for. Passionate about her home state, Shakila Riyas is an engaging host whose home cooking is second to none - refined, distinctive and outstanding.

DELHI

Accommodation

THE IMPERIAL
Janpath, Connaught Place
theimperialindia.com
This grand colonial hotel is the epitome of chic and beats everything else in town, hands down, for glamorous art-deco style, class and attention to detail. Impeccable (if a little formal) service adds to its credentials. It's a joy to just walk around the expansive hallways, lounge in any of the bars or restaurants (1911, overlooking the garden, is a treat), swim in the garden pool at sunset or just stay room-bound for a day and be pampered by room service. It has generous-sized rooms and suites and a very indulgent breakfast buffet.

OBEROI GURGAON
oberoihotelscom/hotels-in-gurgaon
Located close to the airport in Delhi's fast-growing business precinct, this urban oasis is a welcome addition to the hotel scene in Gurgaon. Ultra-modern and stylish with spacious rooms that focus on creature comforts with excellent service. Their Asian restaurant threesixtyone is without doubt the best Asian food in the city and worth a visit even if you're not staying in-house. Kitchen stations are scattered throughout the space, each one specialising in a different cooking medium – teppanyaki, sushi bar, Chinese dim sum, a wok station and tandoor. Amaranta is their other fine dining restaurant serving excellent food with a menu dedicated to India's coastal cuisine.

Eating

INDIAN ACCENT
Lodhi Hotel
indianaccent.com
India's most noted chef Manish Mehrotra leads the vanguard for the most inventive, contemporary Indian food in Delhi. His menu at this sophisticated restaurant is a roll call of refined tastes and highlights include the potato chat, *phulka* (puffed wheat bread) stuffed with lamb curry and topped with a crisp potato disk, the *meetha achaar* Chilean spare rib (pork) with sun dried mango and toasted nigella seeds is memorable and not to be missed is the basa fish steamed with spices and flavoured with green mango juice and cumin. The move from the Manor Hotel to the Lodhi in late 2017 has only enhanced the experience, it's elegance personified. For a taste discovery of familiar flavours with a new theatrical twist, this is the place to be.

KAINOOSH
122-124 DLF (Emporio) Promenade Vanast Kunj
T: 9560175544
Chef owner Marut Sikka was brave enough to establish one of the city's first free standing restaurants with a menu of clear authentic Indian flavours presented in a contemporary style - small plates for sharing, in stylish surroundings. The bespoke thali is the perfect way to experience the excellent talents of this Indian chef.

KARIM'S
16 Gali Kebabian, Gate 1, Jama Masjid
Walk down Matya Mahal (just off Kasturba Hospital Marg, behind the mosque) to reach this Muslim canteen that has fed the workers and locals of Old Delhi for ages. Karim's is something of a landmark. It's a little oasis hidden off a laneway lined with many other food shops. The outdoor kitchen has men sitting cross-legged behind huge handis (cooking pots) dispensing various curries, including an intriguing brain curry, and a long grill with glowing hot coals churning out delicious kebabs.

JAI HIND PARATHA BHAWAN
36 Gali Parathe Wali, Chandni Chowk, Old Delhi
discovering the hidden gems in Old Delhi is a quintessential experience. The most heavenly stuffed parathas are to be found at this family run business, something of an institution in the old city. Expect a queue.

SWAGATH
14 Defence Colony Market (near Lodi Gardens)
T: 2433 0930
Features Mangalorian seafood and chicken dishes. The chicken or prawn gassi (cooked in spiced coconut milk) should not be missed, and the parathas and appams are a must have.

AGRA

Accommodation

AMARVILAS
Taj East Gate End, Taj Nagri Scheme
amarvilas.com
The definitive place to stay to be up close and personal to that mighty, white marble palace. All rooms face the Taj Mahal and the elaborate gardens reflect the opulent Mughal legacy. Esphahan is the hotel's fine dining restaurant serving the most interesting food in Agra with a menu of Mughlai specialties, cooked with care and attention to detail and possessing exquisite flavours.

Eating

PESHAWARI
ITC Mughal Hotel, Fatehabad Road
Tel: 0562 2331701
The menu features kebabs, breads and favourites from the north-west Punjabi region. The butter rich dal and the flaky parathas are not to be missed.

CHIMMAN LAL PURI WALA
Chimman Lal Chauraha (near the mosque)
For a taste of Agra's street food, come to this small hole-in-the-wall to sample their delicious puris – an essential snack to have at any time.

LUCKNOW

Accommodation

VIVANTA BY TAJ GOMTI NAGAR
vivanta.tajhotels.com
The swimming pool is set in lovely gardens at the back of the hotel, a private oasis away from the frenetic bustle of the city and a room overlooking the pool is the best choice. Home to Oudhyana restaurant, a grand dining room with the classic Awadhi cooking of the Mughals with elaborate biryanis and kebabs.

Eating

TUNDAY KEBABS
Aminabad, centre of town, near Akbari Gate, Chowk area
Considered the best kebab shop, this is a landmark in the city. There's history here – the *Tunda ke Kebab* is the highly regarded speciality of the city. The uniqueness of this kebab is the masala that seasons and flavours the meat, a zealously guarded secret prepared by the women in the family. Also try the kakori and the silky soft shami kebabs.

CHOTE NAWAB
Sagar Hotel, 14a Jopling Road, near Butler Place
T: 522 2206 644
A firm favourite with a solid local following, its name means 'Little King'. Order the eggplant curry, chicken kebabs and roomali roti. There are some delicious Persian style dishes on the menu too.

AMRITSAR

Accommodation

TAJ SWARNA HOTEL
taj.tajhotels.com
With enviable proximity to the Golden Temple and a welcome addition to the city, this hotel reflects the best of Punjab's history, art and culture oozing traditional yet modern elegance, the lobby a popular meeting place for guests and locals alike, adding to the social fabric of the place. It's an easy walk to the bazaars and nearby sights, some of the city's best street food vendors are only moments away. I like the rooms on the higher floors that afford views across the city and make good use of the swimming pool after a day wandering the streets.

Eating

CRYSTAL RESTAURANT
Crystal Chowk
T: 91 183 222 5555
A typical family hangout, this air-conditioned restaurant (a blessing when it's hot) is upstairs from the more informal street side cafe. Well patronised by locals, I follow their lead and order the tandoori platter to start – lots of different meats, fish and paneer cooked in the tandoor and served with *podina* (mint chutney). Then continue with several dishes to share (it helps to go with several friends), the sensational *murgh peshwari*, mutton rogan josh, fish tawa frontier, *dal makhani*, *jeera* (cumin) rice and a few different breads like onion kulcha, butter naan and missi roti. Typical of the Punjab, it's all about feasting and having a good time.

BHARAWAN DA DHABA
Circular Rd, Town Hall
T: 0183 253 2575
This is usually my first pit stop when I visit Amritsar, a bustling family owned business that is always packed with locals, though the wait is never long for a table. Order the *bhatura* (puffed wheat bread) with *chole* (chickpea dal), *paneer burjie* (perhaps my favourite paneer dish in India), *ajwain paratha*, *palak paneer* and *jeera aloo* – all dishes come with a wonderful tangy lemon pickle. Don't pass on their delicious yoghurt lassi either.

KULCHA LAND
Distt. Shopping Centre, Ranjit Ave (opp MK hotel)
T: 5050552
Samarjit Singh is perhaps one of the best kulcha wallahs in town, come for breakfast – the cooked-to-order flat breads are mouthwatering and one is never enough! Kulcha is a crisp flaky roti, stuffed usually with potato and cooked in the tandoori and seasoned with ghee. Order the *masala* (spicy) kulcha or the *paneer* (cheese) kulcha – served with *chole* (chickpeas) and fresh mint chutney. They also make a great chai.

VARANASI

Accommodation

BRIJRAMA PALACE
brijrama.com
A restored sandstone haveli with an imposing riverfront presence at Darbanga Ghat. Opt for one of the suites with spectacular views of the river if your budget allows, as the regular rooms are more pedestrian. Lavish architecture, antiques and artworks speak of the palace's royal history and every effort is made to make you feel like royalty. Dinner on the rooftop terrace is a magical experience with local musicians providing terrific atmosphere.

GANGES VIEW HOTEL
hotelgangesview.com
River facing hotel, the ancestral house of owner Shashank, considered the cultural hub of the city with its prime location at Asi Ghat (near the Benares University). Style is modest and homely, request a room that looks directly over the river – breakfast on the terrace is a perfect way to start the day. Food is home style and pure

vegetarian Satvik traditions are practiced. The houseboys are terrific and helpful. A gem for the budget conscious traveller.

NADESAR PALACE
Nadesar Palace Grounds, Cantonment
Tel: 0542 2503 001
taj.tajhotels.com

situated by the Varuna River, a tributary of the Ganges and a 40 minute drive from the old city, this exclusive property is the former summer palace of the Maharaja, set in 28 acres of beautifully landscaped gardens. Live the pampered royal life of yesteryear and indulge in one of their thali feasts for dinner on the garden terrace. A lovely serene place to retreat to after the frenetic action of life on the river.

Eating

KASHI CHAT BHANDAR
D 37/49 Godowlia
Tel: 0542 2412116

Owned by the Keshari brothers, this open fronted street café serves some of the best chat snacks in Varanasi. Opens 3-10pm daily so make it an early evening pit stop on your way down to the river. The Golgappa, Aloo Tikka and Tomato Chat were my favourites.

VARUNA RESTAURANT
Taj Gateway Hotel, Nadesar Palace Grounds, Cantonment
Tel: 0542 2503001

This is a grand dining option with a menu of authentic Varanasi and Mughlai classics. Must-haves are the *makai ki seekh* (corn kebabs), aubergine cooked on the tawa, *baigan ka bhatha* (smoked eggplant with tomato and chilli, *murg sirka pyaz* (chicken roasted in tandoor then simmered in a spicy tomato onion gravy and the *dal dhuaan* (green dal cooked in clay pot with spices).

RAJASTHAN

Accommodation

RAMBAGH PALACE
Bhawani Singh Road, Jaipur
taj.tajhotels.com

The royal palace hotel for total pampering, the ultimate extravagance in central Jaipur. The suites and rooms are sumptuous, and lunch or a well-deserved gin and tonic on the verandah terrace overlooking the gardens is an indulgent necessity. Home to the opulent Suvarna Mahal Restaurant with its menu of regional specialities and royal cuisine offered in this grand palatial dining room, with attentive and helpful service and a terrific wine list.

RAJMAHAL PALACE
sujanluxury.com/raj-mahal

A former private royal palace lovingly restored and extravagantly decorated with flamboyant flourish to contemporary standards, this city oasis is an intimate compound surrounded by lush gardens that embodies its rich heritage. A great place to stay if you fancy a little over the top living with an exacting attention to detail.

SHAHPURA BAGH
Shahpura, district Bilwara
shahpurabagh.com

Four hours south of Jaipur, this magnificent family property set in a 40 acre wooded estate with wonderful lakeside views, owned and managed by the Singh family who are fabulous hosts, offers a sense of timelessness, one of my favourite Rajasthani home stays. Once the summer residence of the Rajadhiraj of Shahpura, the house has been beautifully restored and furnished with a wonderful mix of antique and contemporary pieces. With only 7 suites and 2 rooms, guests are welcomed and treated as family. There are two residences – Nahar Nivas (where family also live) has 1 suite and 2 rooms and Umaid Nivas has 6 suites – and this building is the pick. The surrounding wetlands are terrific for bird watching and fishing. With sustainability in mind, the houses are solar-powered and a farm and village visit in an open air jeep is essential to experience the daily rituals of rural life where agricultural is the mainstay. A bevy of family aunties help supervise the kitchens where delicious home-cooked Rajasthani cuisine is produced from the local gardens and cooked on open wood and charcoal fire stoves or in terracotta pots. Sundowners are served in the garden by the pool each evening and a welcome gin and tonic is poured on arrival.

JAWAI LEOPARD CAMP
Bisalpur (near Perwa village), District Pali
sujanluxury.com

Tented luxury beyond compare – lavish yet contemporary in design, the detail is just perfect, the beds amongst the most comfortable I have ever slept on. Each of the 10 tented pavilions has a private outdoor deck looking out to the bush, guaranteeing privacy and exclusivity, the service is unobtrusive – things magically happen when your back is turned. If you want to keep it really private, you can arrange for breakfast in the bush, a picnic lunch by the lake or a candlelit dinner in one of the granite outcrops. The organic kitchen garden provides the salad greens, herbs and some vegetables, the *surmai* fish comes from the lake and other produce is sourced locally. The food has a sharp focus on healthy lighter options, usually salads and fish for lunch and a typical Rajasthani thali for dinner, often seated around the campfire. There is an obvious and strong commitment to community and eco-friendly tourism, treading lightly to leave no footprint. Leopards roam the craggy granite hills, the countryside is simply divine, the leopards - elusive yet ever present. There is much wildlife to observe - birds, marsh crocodiles and flamingoes. You will also spot the nomadic Rabari herdsmen with their distinctive red turbans, take the chance to stroll along with one of them and his herd of goats or take a brisk 2 hour walk to the lake and back.

RAAS JODPHUR
raasjodphur.com

A beautiful contemporary property in Jodhpur, this boutique hotel (developed from an old haveli) is an oasis of calm with the most stunning location and packed with glamorous understated style in the heart of the old walled city. The entrance is breath-taking and the luxury rooms have unparalleled views of the fort. Dinner on the terrace of their Darikhana restaurant is impossibly romantic with views of the illuminated Mehrangarh Fort. Make this a compulsory visit.

UMAID BHAWAN
Jodhpur
taj.tajhotels.com

One of the grandest and largest palaces in Rajasthan, an impressive building that defines Jodphur from its position on the outskirts of the city. The royal suites are mind-boggling in their extravagance and chic style. One of its wings remains the private residence of the Maharaja of Jodhpur, and the rest has been converted into a luxury hotel, capturing a finely tuned sense of space, proportion and opulence. Sundowners on the expansive terrace overlooking the garden is a quintessential experience.

MIHIR GARH
Rohet, District Pali
mihirgarh.com

The luxurious purpose-built fort (its name means fort of the sun) and glamorous sister property to nearby Rohet Garh, with nine beautifully appointed spacious suites (some with private plunge pools), this is the ideal place to just be, with spectacular, expansive views of the Thar desert. It's a short 15 min drive further on from Rohet and has a wonderfully relaxed yet exclusive ambience, like staying in a private mansion or chateau, the food prepared to the same exacting standard as Rohet Garh under the watchful eye of matriarch Rashmi Singh. Aside from giving in to the gentle pace of life, you can take a jeep safari through the nearby Bishnoi tribal villages, check out the wildlife, indulge in a royal picnic under a typical Rajasthani open-sided tent set up under a large tree near a small lake, or arrange a private candlelit dinner in the sand dunes. For the more energetic, they offer serious horse-riding safaris, boasting the best stable of Marwari horses in India from their tented campsite - Wilderness Camp, a stone's throw away, within sight of the fort with 8 pavilion tents.

CHHATRA SAGAR
Nimaj
chhatrasagar.com
A luxury tented campsite owned and managed by the Singh family, overlooking a lake, two hours from Jodhpur or six hours from Jaipur. Bird watching, village walks and rural safaris are part of the experience and the food makes it even more memorable. It's the exceptional cooking by the women of the house that makes it an essential pilgrimage for me.

SERAI TENTED CAMPSITE
Bherwa, Chandan, Jaisalmer
sujanluxury.com
Thirty minutes' drive from the fort city, luxury tents offer a stylish and sophisticated glamping experience. A pleasant 4 hour drive west of Jodhpur on a good road across the stony Thar Desert, close to the Pakistan border and thirty minutes drive from the medieval fort city of Jaisalmer. The campsite is set on an expansive private estate amongst the indigenous desert scrub and offers a stylish and sophisticated camping experience. Its magical location gives a sense of solitude and calm and it's an ideal base for exploring the desert and this far flung city. Sunset drinks on the sand dunes is a treasured moment etched into my memory. The food is deliciously authentic and rustic, perfect for its surrounds. Stick with the Rajasthani thali that includes vegetable dishes made with indigenous produce, like sangri desert beans, ripe tomatoes stewed with spices, tiny eggplant braised in a masala gravy and a yellow dal cooked with Indian spinach leaves.

RAWLA NARLAI
Narlai, near Ranakpur
narlai.com
For the ultimate Rajasthani experience, this place is a hidden gem, a little off the beaten track but worth the effort. A former royal hunting lodge of the Maharajah converted into a boutique hotel, its recent makeover

makes it even more stunning - the focus is on the total experience. The food is authentic Rajasthani and the service is considered and attentive. A candlelit dinner in the nearby stepwell leaves me spellbound every time.

LAKE PALACE
Udaipur
taj.tajhotels.com
The iconic hotel of Rajasthan floats magically in the middle of Lake Pichola and is impossibly romantic and decadent. The rooms and suites have water views. Dinner at Neel Kamal Restaurant is a feast of Rajasthani and Mughlai specialties from their menu, the tandoori quail is assiduously spiced and meltingly tender, and the crisp okra sticks are not to be missed. A private candlelit dinner on the rooftop completes the experience.

RAAS DEVI GARH
Delwara village, near Udaipur
raasdevigarh.com
A fabulously decadent hilltop fort restored with contemporary, elegant minimalist style, near the village of Delwara, 40 minutes' drive from Udaipur. Pinch yourself when you arrive and are sprinkled with red rose petals as you walk through the enormous elephant gate. The service is attentive and pampering, and the property has blossomed since the Raas group have taken ownership, ensuring that everything is on point.

Eating

LAXMI MISTHAN BHANDAR (LMB)
100 Johari Bazaar, Jaipur
T: 256 5844
In the main street surrounded by market shops, this place has been operating for more than 300 years. The Rajasthani vegetarian thali is the way to go here – start with a plate of *dahi bada* (lentil balls in spiced yoghurt) if you're hungry.

NANDA LAL ALOO TIKKA
outside 147 Johari Bazaar, Jaipur
A street cart offering very delicious potato snacks that is a great place to stop for an early-evening snack after shopping in the bazaar. The fried potato balls in masala gravy are wickedly good.

SHRI MISHRILAL HOTEL LASSI SHOP
Jodhpur
Right by the Clock Tower at the entrance on right side as you enter facing the bazaar, this modest shop has been here since 1927. I have tasted lassi all over India and this

place remains a firm favourite, one of the best you will find anywhere. Be indulgent and go for the one with extra cream on top, it's utterly delicious. They also serve fried snacks and sweets but it's the lassi menu that has everyone coming back for more.

GUJARAT

Accommodation

HOUSE OF M.G.
(the House of Mangaldas Girdhardas)
opposite Sidi Saiyad Jali (mosque), Lal Darwaja, Ahmedabad
houseofmg.com
A former private mansion converted into a boutique heritage hotel, family owned and in high demand for a quintessential Ahmedabad experience. Ideally situated in the heart of the old town, this place captures the spirit of the city. The grand deluxe rooms are generously proportioned, avoid the rooms at the front as the traffic is incessant and noisy. You just have to love a place whose breakfast menu offers '*a healthful gratification*' – with an array of egg dishes, dosas, uppams and upma (steamed vegetables seasoned with tempered spices and green chilli). Dinner at Agashiye, the seductive rooftop terrace restaurant, celebrates the art of the Gujarati thali with a seasonal and perfectly balanced menu that changes daily. Standouts are the smoked *brinjal* (eggplant) and the *kadhi*, a yoghurt gravy (made with very fresh yoghurt so it isn't sour) thickened with chickpea flour and flavoured with cumin, ginger, mustard seed and a dash of sugar – served in a small bowl, it was impossible to stop eating. A Gujarati thali is about the balance of flavours – sweet, salty and sour. They offer a bowl of fresh jaggery if you wish to add a dash of sweetness to anything. A typically Gujarati habit – where food is sweeter than other parts of India. The salted *chhas* (buttermilk drink) made the perfect digestive.

Eating

ANAND DAL WADA
Ashram Road, Usmanpura (next to Gujarat Vityapith College)
This street vendor does a roaring trade with nearby students and workers, dishing out plates of crisp *dal wada* (fried lentil balls), sold by the 100 gram weight for a mere 20 rupees. Sprinkled with *amchur* (dried mango powder) and served with slices of raw red onion and half a lime to squeeze over, it makes an ideal snack any time of the day.

SWATI SNACKS
Sera, Law Garden, Panchavati Road, Ellisbridge
T: 2640 5900

A Gujarati benchmark with all the well-known vegetarian favourites on the menu, from snacks to more substantial dishes. An inviting casual atmosphere and friendly service, locals flock to this place for lunch and dinner every day. For starters, try *pani puri* (puris in spicy pepper water) or *dahi sev puri* (with yoghurt) and the *chola methi dhokla* (made with chopped methi leaves and flour, steamed and drizzled with tempered mustard seeds and shredded coconut) are light as a feather, the best I have tasted anywhere. Other highlights from the menu are *mung khichdi* or any one of their roti breads. Whatever you do, make sure you order the *panki chatri* – savoury rice pancakes flavoured with turmeric and steamed in banana leaves, served with mint chutney and green chillies – they are sublime.

TAMIL NADU

Accommodation

TAJ COROMANDEL
37 Mahatma Ghandi Road, Nungambakkam, Chennai
T: +91 44 6600 2827
taj.tajhotels.com

Offering luxury in an ideal central location of the business district, its more recent makeover has added glamour and style. Service is first rate. This was my first ever experience in India, where I was invited as guest chef in the mid-nineties. It's fine dining restaurant Southern Spice serves delicious food with authentic flavours and generous spiciness. Don't miss the appams or idlis, made to order or the tamarind lentil rasam and the deep fried soft-shell crabs dusted with semolina.

PALAIS DE MAHE
cghearth.com/palaisdemahe

A stylish boutique hotel in the coastal town of Pondicherry that oozes colonial character and charm. Centrally located and close to the sea front which makes it easy to wander the surrounding streets of the historic French quarter. Relaxing by the central courtyard pool is a treat and dinner at its rooftop grill restaurant *Mahe de Malabar* is an intriguing fusion of French Tamil seafood favourites.

BANGALA
thebangala.com

A family run home-stay with elegant charm, this is a simply furnished bungalow house with family heirlooms in the heart of the Chettinad region, with delicious home-style regional food overseen by its owner, Mrs Meena Meyappan. To get there you need to fly south from Chennai to Trichy and drive 80 km (2 hours) along dusty roads, but well worth the visit.

VISALAM
cghearth.com

Close to the palace in Kanadukathan village, this is a cute-as-a-button 15-room boutique hotel in a renovated Chettiar mansion with lavish attention to detail. It has a swimming pool – a bonus when it's hot – and the outstanding food - organic produce from the hotel's gardens, is the pride of the region.

Eating

SARAVANA BHAVAN
228 NSK Salai, Vadapalani, Chennai
T: 2480 2577
saravanabhavan.com

There are over 20 branches of this vegetarian tiffin restaurant in the city and more further afield. It's fast, reliable, authentic and always packed with locals – beats Macca's any day! An essential breakfast experience – idli, vada and masala dosa. The lunch thali is a real treat also.

DAKSHIN RESTAURANT
ITC Park Sheraton Hotel, 132 TTK Road, Ra Puram
T: +91 44 24994101
itcwelcomegroup.in

Offering perhaps the finest South Indian food of any restaurant in southern India, scholarly chef Praveen Anand weaves culinary magic with traditional recipes from India's four southern states. The menu features classic dishes from Tamil Nadu, Karnataka, Andhra Pradesh and Kerala, and it is wise to follow the staff's expert advice when deciding what to order.

KANCHI KUDIL
53A Sangeetha Vidwan Nayanar Pillai Street, Kanchipuram,
indiamart.com/kanchikudil

A renovated, heritage ancestral property in the temple town of Kanchipuram that offers a glimpse into the agricultural life of yesteryear. The gracious hosts offer two set menus for lunch, by arrangement. This is uncomplicated, honest rural cooking and well worth the drive from Chennai for a day visit.

KARNATAKA

Accommodation

TAJ WEST END HOTEL
Racecourse Road (opp Turf Club), Bengaluru
taj.tajhotels.com

A stately grand and elegant hotel with ideal central location for sight seeing – the place to stay to feel pampered but do request a room with windows. Its beautiful colonial buildings are set in massive, lush established gardens opposite the Polo Club and racecourse. It's home to Masala Klub with a menu featuring contemporary Indian cuisine. Ask for an outdoor table on the terrace under the tamarind tree.

GREEN HOTEL
Chittaranjan Palace, Mysore

greenhotelindia.com

A former palace built for the Mysore princesses, this modest oasis in the city's centre prides itself on its sustainable and eco-friendly practices with a fabulous garden for relaxing, generous sized rooms and terrific home-style food.

TAJ MADIKERI RESORT

COORG
taj.tajhotels.com

These beautifully designed villas and cottages built into the hillside of a large rainforest showcase typical Kodagu architecture that gives a sense of place. With a mix of adventure sports, relaxation and a pampering spa centre on offer, it ticks all the boxes when travelling to this less travelled region. I opt for the wellness menu at Dew restaurant using produce from their garden with lots of herbs and plant life on the plate.

CHIKKANA HALLI ESTATE
Siddapur, Coorg
evolveback.com

Formerly the Orange County Resort before being recently rebranded to embody the company's philosophy of 'spirit of the land', this family resort is located 2 hours from Mysore by the Cauvery River in the heart of the Coorg region, renowned for its coffee plantations and often referred to as the Scotland of India. Its thatched roofed, plantation cottages are set among 120 hectares of spice and coffee plantations, bordered by a massive bamboo forest. The occasional elephant can be spotted if you're lucky during an afternoon walk with a guide. There are many different outdoor activities like boating, fishing, bird watching and bushwalking on offer and the kitchen prepares typical local dishes with organic produce from their garden.

SHREYAS RETREAT
Santoshima Farm, Gollahalli Gate, Nelamangala

shreyasretreat.com

An hour's drive from downtown on the outskirts of Bengaluru, this is my go-to place to relax and detox when in India. Taking up residence in one of the well-appointed tented cottages in the expansive gardens of this luxury ashram is like entering a private oasis and nothing beats the personalised attention from their ayurvedic doctors, their naturopathy remedies, the switched-on chefs or the sublime rejuvenating treatments at the wellness spa centre. A retreat that focuses on the practices of Ayurveda, yoga, spiritual healing and meditation, you can engage in as much or as little as you fancy, but food is at its core. The vegetarian food is pitch perfect with produce from their extensive kitchen garden cooked with care and minimal intervention, the raw salads a welcome escape from the usual local fare, the focus very much on holistic health and wellbeing. I leave feeling most virtuous.

EVOLVE BACK KAMALAPURA PALACE
Hampi

evolveback.com

Finally, Hampi has luxury accommodation close to this revered religious and historical archaeological site in northern Karnataka. A palace hotel built to reflect the Vijayanagara architecture of the monuments and temples of Hampi's UNESCO heritage site, you can opt for complete privacy in one of their ornate villas or a spacious suite on the first floor overlooking the swimming pool and gardens. A delightful place to retreat after a day exploring the sites and nearby villages. Dinner at Bahmani restaurant is an extravagant affair and I found the best option was to let the chefs create a tasting menu of local dishes drawing inspiration from their royal heritage - the *royala sukka* (prawns simmered in a green chilli, ginger and black pepper sauce) left a lasting impression.

Eating

KARAVELLI
Gateway Hotel, 66 Residency Cross Rd, Ashok Nagar, Bengaluru
T: 6660 4545

Set in a lush garden behind the hotel, this restaurant serves the very best seafood in Bangalore, the menu showcasing coastal cuisine of the south west. Every dish is expertly spiced and the chilli crab curry is knockout.

WINDSOR PUB
7 Kodava Samaja Building, 1st Main Road Vasanthnagar, Bengaluru
T: 2225 8847

A modest suburban pub serving terrific food - the curry leaf chicken is to die for, the spicy prawn curry is heaven and the masala pappads are the best snacks imaginable to have with a cold Kingfisher beer.

HALLI MANE RURAL RESTAURANT
14, 3rd Cross, Sampige Rd, Mallesvaram, Bengaluru
T: 41279754

A bustling place (Village House) and one of the city's favourites with some of the best local vegetarian food served from this frenetic open kitchen. Order the *chow chow bhath* (*khara* and *kesari bhath* served together), curd *vada* or lentil *vada* for breakfast, or *ragi roi*, little balls of finger millet (a Karnataka cereal) served with sambar or vegetable korma. Don't miss the sweets – the creamy *baasundi*, syrupy *jalebi* and *holige* (coconut crepe) are my favourites.

MAVALLI TIFFIN ROOM
Lalbarg Fort Rd (at front gate of the Botanical Gardens), Bengaluru

A local favourite canteen constantly bustling - that is great for breakfast – masala dosas, idlis and vadas with chutney and dal or for their renowned thalis at lunch.

MYLARI
79 Nazarbad Road, Mysore
T: 9448698710

This is a great no-frills vegetarian place for authentic Mysore masala dosa and idlis.

ANDHRA PRADESH

Accommodation

FALAKNUMA PALACE
Hyderabad

taj.tajhotels.com

A breathtaking royal palace perched on a hill with 360° city views, made entirely of marble, the former home to the 6th Nizam of Hyderabad. Nothing can prepare you for the sheer extravagance and opulence of this extraordinary property, taking luxury to a whole new level. Splurge and stay in one of the royal suites with discreet butler service and attention to detail. An early morning walk in the palace gardens and high tea in the Jade Room are a must when staying. The table in the Dining Hall seats 101 guests, each with a personal butler, a

private dinner here is an extravagant affair. A more intimate option is a sumptuous banquet at Adaa, the restaurant that features royal Hyderabadi cuisine and the fragrant *kacchi* (lamb) biryani is pure heaven.

TAJ KRISHNA HOTEL
Banjara Hills

taj.tajhotels.com

In a city with many luxury hotels to choose from, this stalwart is a favourite, centrally located in the heart of the scenic Banjara Hills district with close proximity to restaurants and shopping, a little oasis in this fast-paced city where the service is first rate and attentive. I like the Taj Club rooms for their extra little extravagances. The signature restaurant Firdaus is a showcase of Nizami opulence and I always make time to explore the menu of royal Hyderabadi specialties, choosing a few of their kebab preparations, fragrant white chicken korma and *nalli gosht* (lamb shanks in spiced yoghurt).

Eating

SIMPLY SOUTH RESTAURANT
Jubilee Hills
T: 9100717999

Chef Challu's menu at his popular fine dining restaurant takes your tastebuds on an adventure with the clever blending of robust and spicy flavours channelling the regional classics of India's south. My favourites include quails in a fiery chilli and pepper gravy, prawns in spiced tomato sauce, masala mushrooms and the coconut payasam dessert.

SOUTHERN SPICE
8-2-350/3/2, Road No 3, Banjara Hills
T: 40 2335 3802

Some of the best and most authentic Andhra cooking in the city, don't miss their fiery Anellwan Meriyal Kodi (pepper chicken), a perfect accompaniment to either the Kheema Pulao, a minced lamb biryani or the vegetarian thali.

GOVIND'S DOSA
Mutti Ka Shaed, near Charminar

One of the city's favourite street vendors, he starts in the early morning and packs up when his dosa batter runs out, usually by 12.30pm, so it's best to go for breakfast and indulge in a sublime butter dosa and make sure you also try his idlis, *tava idli* with chilli, and the best vadas imaginable.

KERALA

Accommodation

MALABAR HOUSE
268 Parade Road, Fort Kochi
malabarhouse.com

This feels like a large family beach house, its relaxed ambience makes it an ideal base when visiting Kochi, full of style and charm and excellent service. It's also within walking distance of the many historical sights of the area. The house restaurant Malabar Junction in the courtyard honours the flavours of Kerala, the seafood tasting menu is my preferred choice for dinner and its wine bar serves Indian wines by the glass, cocktails, delicious fruit smoothies and a fine espresso.

KALARI KOVILAKOM
kalarikovilakom.com

Ayurvedic retreat with treatments, yoga and meditation. The accommodation is as grand as you can get at a health retreat, the service and care immaculate. Minimum stay is 2 weeks, so come prepared to give yourself over and emerge feeling rejuvenated and brand new.

SHALIMAR SPICE GARDEN
Murikkady, Thekaddy
amritara.co.in

Surrounded by spice plantations and close to Periyar Wildlife Reserve, private bungalow-style cottages are set in beautiful landscaped gardens that create an idyllic sanctuary of calm and natural beauty. The swimming pool is a welcome treat, as it is nearly always hot enough for an afternoon swim. Early morning walks through cardamom and pepper plantations are a must.

PHILIP KUTTY'S FARM
Pallivathukal, Vechoor, Kottayam
T: +91 4829 276529
philipkuttysfarm.com

A family-owned boutique farmstay on a small island to the north east of Alleppey, accessed by *vallum* (canoe), offers an insight into waterside farm life with sustainable eco-friendly practices. A hideaway retreat of separate waterfront villas, be sure to arrange a cooking class with Mummy (Aniamma Philip) and her daughter in law, Anu - the most gracious hosts. Their heavenly home cooking makes the visit even more perfect. A treasured experience.

LAKES & LAGOONS
Alleppey
lakeslagoons.com

Luxury small rice barges converted to houseboats that come with engaging local cooks and unobtrusive service. An idyllic escape, a wonderful way to observe the languid pace of life on the waterways.

NEELESHWAR HERMITAGE
Kasaragod, North Kerala
neeleshwarhermitage.com

At the northern end of Kerala and a 2 hour drive south of Mangalore airport, this delightful beachfront property of 12 private cottages with garden courtyards, thatched roofs, a yoga pavilion and terrific home cooking is the perfect place to kick back, unwind and make the most of the unspoilt beach setting.

Eating

FORT HOUSE
Fort House Hotel, 2/6A Calvathy Road, Fort Kochi
T: 484 2217103

The restaurant of this modest colonial hotel is outdoors on a waterfront pier, an ideal candlelit dinner setting, specialising in Keralan seafood. Don't miss the Keralan coconut pancake with honey.

GINGER HOUSE
Jew Town, Mattancherry, Kochi
T: 96458 35129

A casual riverfront restaurant set amidst a showroom of antique furniture and artefacts. Naturally, ginger plays a starring role on the menu whether you choose a ginger lime soda or ginger tea, to grilled ginger prawns or fish with appams or ginger ice cream.

50 MILE DIET
Spice Village, Thekkady
cghearth.com

Sustainable eco-tourism at its best - all produce is organic and sourced within a 50 mile radius at this outdoor garden restaurant. Try the green pepper quail, masala grilled rabbit and the ranger wood mutton. A brilliant new initiative delivered with enthusiasm and care.

NIMMY PAUL
nimmypaul.com

For an authentic home-style experience, lunch or dinner comes with a cooking class in Nimmy and Paul's seafront home in Fort Kochi, with two bedrooms for a homestay visit. Nimmy is gracious, knowledgeable and in step with how to draw keen cooks into understanding and appreciating the nuances and myriad flavours of the Syrian Christian cooking of Kerala.

GOA

Accommodation

AHILYA BY THE SEA
ahilyabythesea.com

This boutique, family-style guesthouse has just nine rooms, a hideaway retreat in Dolphin Bay overlooking Coco Beach that offers privacy and serenity. The lush tropical gardens have been tastefully landscaped and have two beautiful swimming pools. The food is elegant home style and a local woman chef comes each week to cook a sublime Goan thali feast for dinner.

POUSADA TAUMA
Porbavaddo, Calangute, Bardez
T: +91 832 2279061
pousada-tauma.com

A gorgeous, eco-friendly, small boutique hotel in North Goa, with modest rooms and villas, some with private terraces set amid beautifully manicured gardens and a heavenly swimming pool. Run by Neville Proenca, the delightful hands-on owner, the place has been designed to use minimal resources and features traditional architecture. It offers a lovely respite from the frenzy of nearby tourist resorts and its restaurant, Copper Bowl, serves elegant European food and superlative Goan specialities.

ELSEWHERE
North Goa
aseascape.com

Simple luxury and a pure Goan experience. Situated on a coastal strip separated from the mainland by a saltwater creek, this property is prized for its remote and private location, away from the crowds. There are four houses and three tents facing the beach or the creek. Closed during the monsoon season.

VIVENDA DOS PALHAÇOS
vivendagoa.com

A 100-year-old Hindu–Portuguese house converted into a seven-room guest house in a quiet village near Majorda, Goa's longest beach. Contemporary and stylish and lovingly restored, this is a slice of heaven amidst the big brand international hotels that occupy much of the beach frontage along south Goa. I like the front rooms in the Portuguese section of the house. There's also a fab swimming pool in the garden. Ideally, go with a group of friends and book out the whole place, your own private hideaway.

Eating

BOMRA'S
247 Fort Aguada Road, Candolim
(near Fort Aguada Hotel)
T: +91 9822106236
bomras.com
A fab and funky newcomer to the Goan dining scene, owner/chef Bomra Jap is Burmese, his excellent food is essentially Burmese with SE Asian influences, a triumph with locals and those in the know, with pure and spicy flavours. I particularly loved the spicy tuna larb, the squid and spicy papaya salad, the crispy pork with pomelo and pomegranate and the sweet tamarind duck curry. He draws on his rich heritage and the close connection India and Burma have shared for aeons. This is beachside outdoor dining at its best – Goa has arrived!

MUM'S KITCHEN
854 Martins Building, DB Street,
Miramar Beach, Panaji
mumskitchengoa.com
The menu is compiled by the 'Mothers of Goa' and has an emphasis on heritage recipes and home cooking. The crab xec-xec alone is worth a visit. Kismur – a relish of dried prawn coconut and red chillies is an essential condiment when you have fish curry rice.

RITZ CLASSIC
1st Floor, Wagle Vision, 18th June Road, Panjim
T: 664 4796
This is a local institution and always packed, so it's essential to book ahead. Come for the fish curry rice – a must for lunch – complete in itself and my go-to dish on the menu. The Goan fish curry, grilled pomfret or a butter garlic crab are also very good. The décor is classic fifties, just like its name and the service is old school, efficient and friendly.

MUMBAI

Accommodation

TAJ MAHAL PALACE HOTEL
taj.tajhotels.com
The luxury flagship of the Taj hotel group, the grand imperial style of this hotel is matched by its exemplary service in either the heritage wing or the more modern tower wing. It is my home away from home when I'm in Mumbai, with glamour and style by the bucket load and the social hub of the city. It presides over the Gateway of India and the waterfront, and its central location is convenient for exploring the sights of south Mumbai.

Eating

SOAM
Ground floor, Sadguru Sadan, Grant Road (opposite Babulnath Temple), Girgaum (near Kemps Corner)
T: 2369 8080
The food on their Gujarati vegetarian menu is sensational. Don't miss the chat: bhel puri, sev puri, pani puri and dahi puri are a must, then try a few farsan (snacks). The sweet and salty lassi (yoghurt drink) is heaven. The decor is modern and chic, there are no bookings, so be prepared to queue as this is one of Mumbai's most popular lunch places.

SWATI SNACKS
248 Karai Estate, Taredo
Grand Road Station (opposite Bhatia Hospital)
T: 6660 8405
Serves Gujarati staples and Bombay snacks and some of the best street food in Mumbai, a perennial favourite with locals. Try channa chur (western-style Bombay mix), pani puri (puris in spicy pepper water) or a Mumbai speciality, bhel puri (small crisp puris stuffed with spiced vegetables). No reservations are taken, but queues move quickly (or you can order takeaway). Waiting is part of the experience and allows you to get in among the locals; it's like an informal social club on the footpath. They have more recently opened another branch in Colaba.

TRISHNA
7 Sai Baba Marg, Kala Ghoda
T: 2270 1623
The most notable seafood restaurant in the city, a favourite for the city's sophisticated movers and shakers. Reservations are essential and make sure you request a table in the front (main) dining room, order the prawns koliwada, butter pepper garlic crab and the green masala pomfret, all signature classics of the restaurant.

BOMBAY CANTEEN
Unit-1, Process House, S.B. Road,
Kamala Mills, Lower Parel
T: 022 49666666
The cool hipster crowd and local office workers flock to this modern café bar where the kitchen produces delicious food that is innovative, fresh and modern drawing inspiration from age-old classics like bel puri and a clever take on a vada pao sandwich in the chhota (snack) menu to more substantial items from the bada section, think various curries and rice dishes, while the bar is well known for its clever cocktails.

SHREE THAKKER BHOJANALAY
1st Floor, 31 Dadiseth Agiary Marg, off Kalbadevi Rd, Bhuleshwar
T: 2201 1232 or 2206 9916
The ideal approach is to walk through the laneways and congested streets of the wholesale cloth market, jewellery market and past the kitchen utensil market to arrive at this hidden gem. The vegetarian lunch thali is considered the best in town, the menu items change regularly but you can expect corn dhokla, aloo rasawala, a vegetable pulao and more. The variety of flatbreads they serve is second to none and they love it when you ask for seconds. The room is modest with the ambience of an informal workers canteen. The staff are friendly and welcoming. One of the city's essential food experiences.

MASALA LIBRARY
Ground floor, First International Finance Centre, G Block, Bandra Kurla Complex (BKC), Bandra
T: 6642 4142
This modern, glamorous restaurant attests to the city's thirst for serious fine dining, showcasing contemporary Indian food using modern culinary techniques at its most promising. Situated in the new BKC business hub in north Mumbai, this is a destination restaurant where it pays to put your faith in the chef's tasting menu, the bite sized appetizer snacks have the most thrilling bursts of flavour and texture. The inside-out vada pav is a clever interpretation of the staple street snack, curry leaf and pepper prawns with curd rice and banana chips is delicious and the tiny lamb cutlet glazed with maple syrup, tamarind and kokum is inspired. A sister restaurant opened in Delhi in 2016 adding to the city's fine dining experiences.

ACKNOWLEDGEMENTS

My frequent travels to India since the mid-1990s have been life-changing adventures. I have met some amazing people, had extraordinary experiences, been humbled and challenged on all fronts and found myself always eager to return for more to this most intriguing country.

Travels that have somehow turned into pilgrimages and given life to this book would not have been possible without the unfailing support of Jamshyd Sethna and Lucy Davison at Banyan Tours, and Shakti Himalaya, a team who have provided me with expert advice and excellent ground support.

Jennifer Wilkinson of Epicurious Travel for arranging and sharing some of our group adventures, thank you for your adventurous spirit and stimulating companionship; Julie McIntosh of Classic Safari Company who initiated my Spice Tours to India back in 1999, thanks for your trust and support; to Husna-Tara Prakash at Glenburn Tea Estate and Seema Mohanchandran at the Taj Hotels group, thank you for your unfailing practical support, generous hospitality, enduring friendship and the open welcome to keep returning.

My travelling buddies Jewels and Anson have shared some of these adventures with me, making the experiences even more special and rewarding. A journey shared is a richer experience and these journeys would never have been as much fun without your fabulous company, undying enthusiasm and valuable insights – thank you for the great teamwork. Anson Smart, your stunning visual imagery lives on in your photos, your eye has brought India to life on these pages, you have captured its very essence. Julie Gibbs, my wise and wonderful publisher, you embraced this journey from the start. It was such a pleasure to introduce you to India and watch you fall under its magical spell. Your faith and utter devotion to this book and its rebirth has made me strive to do the best work possible.

I would like to acknowledge the incredible teamwork that brought this book to fruition. Designer Daniel New for your exacting attention to detail; Katrina O'Brien of Illustrated Publishing, your expert editing has breathed new life into this book; Rachel Carter for your meticulous proofread; Daniel Ruffino at Simon & Schuster, thanks for your faith and support.

Thanks to a couple of India-devotee friends, Brian Tunks of Bison Home for supplying some of your beautiful ceramics for food photography; Joan Bowers for generously sharing some of your exquisite Indian fabrics, and to Amber Dunsford for your capable assistance with the final food preparations.

I would like to make special mention of a few women who have opened their homes, kitchens and hearts to me. My food heroes and some of the best home cooks of India: Nimmy Paul and Faiza Moosa in Kerala; Anu and Anaissa Philip at Philip Kutty's Farm in the Kerala backwaters; Vasundhara and Shrinidri Singh at Chhatra Sagar; and Rashmi Singh at Rohet Garh, the stars of Rajasthan. A special thanks to Yeshi Lama, a gentle soul who inhabits the Shakti kitchens across the Himalaya and cooks like an angel. Your food brings balance and harmony to mountain life; you are a joy to share a kitchen with. To the countless home cooks and chefs who have cooked for me and shared some of your culinary secrets and treasured family heirloom recipes so generously. Your collective voices have given resonance, depth and clarity to this story. Mother India – it is a writer's gift to be embraced by all within your borders.

The most essential element has been the loving support and influence of my partner in life, Margie Harris. My most favourite travelling companion, she shares my big dreams and curiosity for the world and is the first to encourage me to get out there and explore. You have been part of the journey every step of the way. Thank you for always being there for me, for showing me how to bring perspective and an intuitive sensitivity to my work.